Library of
Davidson College

From Ploughshare to Ballotbox

Derek W. Urwin

From Ploughshare to Ballotbox

The Politics of Agrarian
Defence in Europe

Universitetsforlaget
Oslo - Bergen - Tromsø

© UNIVERSITETSFORLAGET 1980
ISBN 82-00-05394-6

Distribution offices:

NORWAY
Universitetsforlaget
Postboks 2977 Tøyen
Oslo 6

UNITED KINGDOM
Global Book Resources Ltd.
37, Queen Street
Henley-on-Thames
Oxon RG9 1AJ

UNITED STATES and CANADA
Columbia University Press
136 South Broadway
Irvington-on-Hudson
New York 10533

Published with a grant from
The Norwegian Research Council
for Science and the Humanities

Cover design: Per Syversen

Printed in Norway by
Nye Intertrykk A.s., Lommedalen

Omnium rerum, ex quibus aliquid acquisitur, nihil est agricultura melius, nihil uberius, nihil dulcius, nihil homine libero dignius.

       Cicero

Give a man the secure possession of a bleak rock and he will turn it into a garden: give him a nine years' lease of a garden and he will convert it into a desert.

       Arthur Young

Not by the law of force, but by the law of labour, has any man right to the possession of land.

       John Ruskin

TABLE OF CONTENTS

	page
Preface	9
Introduction: On Agriculture and Politics	11
1. Towards Capitalism and Industrialization	23
2. The Impact of Industrialization and the Crystallization of the State	51
3. The Agrarian Response: Mobilization, Association, Representation	87
4. Agrarian Political Participation	111
5. Agrarian Political Behaviour	131
6. The Formation of Agrarian Parties	159
7. The Social Cohesion and Support of Agrarian Parties	209
8. The Behaviour of Agrarian Parties	233
Conclusion: Agrarian Political Movements	253
Notes	275
Bibliography	326
Index	353

Preface

This study would not have been possible without the assistance
of many people and institutions. As the research progressed I
was forced to examine the main highways and little known lanes
of several academic disciplines. This would have been impossible
without the invaluable assistance received from the Andersonian
Library of the University of Strathclyde, the Universitets-
bibliotek of the University of Bergen, and especially from the
vast reservoir of literature contained in the Sterling Library
of Yale University. I would like to thank the Ford Foundation
for the visiting Research Fellowship which enabled me to visit
New Haven in 1969-70. I am also grateful to the Norwegian
Research Council for Science and the Humanities for that
financial assistance which enabled me to assemble the material
and to attend various international conferences where I received
valuable comments and criticisms of earlier versions of the
manuscript. The study may also be regarded as a contribution
to the cross-national analysis of social structure, party
systems and voting behaviour being undertaken by a working
party of the Committee on Political Sociology of both the
International Political Science Association and the International
Sociological Association: to many colleagues on the working
party and the wider Committee I wish to offer my appreciation
of the stimulating environment they have created over the years.

Space precludes mentioning all those who have been my
mentors. It must suffice to state that I have benefited from
all those students of politics, many of whom are referred to in
the bibliography, who have offered in print their thoughts and
conclusions on European and agrarian society, history and

politics. In particular, I wish to express gratitude to the
following for their critical comments on earlier versions of
the manuscript and/or for refreshing discussions on the
theoretical and empirical problems involved: Frank Aarebrot,
Hugh Berrington, David Cameron, John Coakley, James Cornford,
Keith Hill, Stein Kuhnle, Arend Lijphart, Val Lorwin, Thomas
Mackie, Sten Sparre Nilson, Malcolm Punnett, Lars Svåsand,
Charles L. Taylor, Henry Valen, John Whyte. Above all, I would
like to express my indebtedness to Richard Rose for suggesting
the profitability of such a study, and to Juan Linz and
Stein Rokkan, all of whom provided many enlightening discussions
not only on agrarian politics, but also on the theoretical and
empirical problems of comparative political sociology. I would
also like to acknowledge the assistance of the secretarial
staff of the Institute of Sociology and Political Studies at
the University of Bergen, who have laboured over the many
versions of the manuscript. Finally, I am deeply indebted to
my wife for enduring over a period of several years what must
have appeared as the idiosyncratic obsession of a life-long
urban dweller for things rural.

In a work of this nature the main criteria of presentation
must be selection and condensation. I have therefore selected
for discussion those phenomena which seem to me to be of most
value for an understanding of European agrarian politics. By
drawing upon the experiences of numerous countries, I may have
done justice to none. Hopefully, however, the comparative interdisciplinary orientation of the study does indicate the
integrated approach which social science must adopt.

Introduction: On Agriculture and Politics

Is the study of agrarian society and politics in Europe a profitable exercise? An affirmative answer might begin by pointing to the overwhelmingly agricultural nature of human society until fairly recently. Anyone who is interested in the general problems of political mobilization rapidly appreciates the importance of agriculture as an economic activity in which significant numbers of people have been employed. For most of the world's history most people have not resided in urban areas: moreover, many "urban" areas of several centuries ago would by today's standards be probably classified as semi-rural. Most people have tended to live <u>on</u> the land or <u>from</u> the land. Even today, the median place of residence in the world may well be something like a large village, and until recently this would have been the median residence also in Europe. Britain, the first country to become industrial and urban, did so conclusively only during the nineteenth century. Many European societies remained rural and agricultural for a considerably longer period of time. As late as the interwar decades significant numbers of Europeans were engaged in agriculture. When we find one-third or more of a country's population dependent upon agriculture, it means in essence that agricultural considerations are politically just as potentially important as industrial concerns.

Almost as a parenthesis it might be useful first to say something about what we mean by Europe, since defining Europe for purposes of analysis is not as simple as might be imagined. Etymological connotations are usually of less value than the specific context in which the word is used: "Europe is a term of convenience, rather than a precise social science concept".[1]

Since Europe does not possess unambiguous borders either in terms of physical geography or culture, the definition employed here remains essentially one of convenience. The chosen universe simply includes all those territories, from Iceland to Russia west of the Urals and from Scandinavia to the Mediterranean, which geographically have been ascribed to the European land mass and its insular outliers. Within these territorial confines Europe can be regarded as a culture area rather than a continent, bearing the "visible imprint" of a single broad cultural heritage.[2] Europe would seem to be a good laboratory in which to study the relationships between agriculture and politics, for the various regions of the continent, notwithstanding markedly different rates of political and economic development, have experienced broadly similar historical trends and have been exposed to common stimuli. But while the similarity of European experiences is such that the area may be treated as a whole for research purposes, internal differentiation, especially between states, has been and still is an outstanding characteristic of European political life. However, as Richard Rose has observed, "to note that each country has a unique history is not to say that its problems and alternatives for choice are unique, but that the sum total of past events is never exactly and entirely reproduced elsewhere".[3] Similarly, the problems may have been common to all states: the way of and the degree of success in resolving these problems have not.

    Stated generally, the objective of this study is to explore the interconnections between agrarian structure, socio-economic change and political activity. More particularly, the focus is upon the emergence of agrarian political organizations (or their absence) in the decades between the late nineteenth century and the Second World War, and upon how far their emergence was influenced by internal agricultural structures, by the experiences of industrialization, urbanization and political democratization, and by changes in the state landscape of the continent.[4] In this sense the study specifically attempts to test and expand upon the hypotheses advanced by Lipset and Rokkan in their seminal study of the historical preconditions of social cleavages and party divisions in Western Europe.[5] Within their terms of reference these authors are concerned with explaining the generation of urban-rural conflicts and the formation of political parties for agrarian defence. Their brief analysis begins with historical patterns of estate representation and, drawing upon examples from Scandinavia, England and Germany, concludes that distinctly agrarian parties have emerged only in non-Catholic Europe where strong cultural oppositions deepened and embittered the strictly economic conflicts in the commodity market. One criticism of this model is its restriction to Western Europe. Other areas of the continent have undergone broadly similar historical experiences, yet their later political development seems at first glance to cast some doubts upon these authors' conclusions, including their list of conditions for the emergence of parties for agrarian defence.[6]

The traditional starting point for many studies of agrarian structure has been to take up the challenge presented by the stereotypes of the peasant and the commercial farmer. In recent years social scientists, recognising that rural societies predominate in most areas of the globe and that since they are a major component of many states their political role may not be insignificant, have turned the study of peasantry into "one of the growth points of interdisciplinary comparative research".[7] Yet this growth industry still appears to lack a consistent and uncontested definition or set of related definitions. Because its unfulfilled quest is littered with casualties, this more traditional conceptual approach is a highly perilous undertaking: from a European perspective it is also perhaps rather profitless, for reasons that will be indicated later.

Let us begin instead with the idea of agrarian structure. In its broadest sense this notion refers to a set of relationships and institutions that help to determine the operation of land as a source of production. Such a general definition goes beyond a simple reference to patterns of land tenure and utilization to embrace also wider aspects of human relationships that may affect land occupation and its use: authority profiles and relations, hierarchy and status structures, legal rights and obligations, economic practices and liabilities. To suggest that broad attributes can exist across a wide variety of historical and ecological backdrops is not to argue for total homogeneity everywhere - least of all political homogeneity. After all, it is merely banal to state that some form of abstract analytical construct is helpful for an appreciation of tangible realities. At any rate, most commentators seem to agree that political problems and conflicts may be generated by at least two broad elements of agrarian structure: the impact of the market economy, and the nature of land ownership.

In its widest form the market can affect the individual farm unit in a variety of ways, as well as engendering potential disputes between different styles of agricultural production, between producers of different agricultural commodities, or between agrarian and urban interests over the cost and distribution of food. It is the market which in one form or another has served, at the crudest level, as the basic factor differentiating peasants from farmers. However, to move on to use the notion of the market in a delineation of general social categories in a broad analytical-historical scheme is perhaps self-defeating, not least in the European context. The transformation from peasant to farmer in Europe was a complex and lengthy process that extended over several centuries and passed through several phases, with the social artefacts of various phases frequently existing side by side in the same locality at the same point in time. Moreover, it seems clear that Europe has possessed simultaneously a "market" and a "domestic subsistence" economic orientation throughout most of recorded history. In his magisterial review of agricultural developments in Western Europe, Slicher van Bath suggests that a system of "direct agricultural consumption", that is of partial self-sufficiency with surpluses being offered to non-agricultural populations in a system of barter exchange, essentially ended in the mid-twelfth century. Since then, Western Europe has been characterized by "indirect agricultural consumption", where market relationships are dominant, or at least where the impact of the market is pervasive.[8] It might be wiser therefore to ignore the questions of who and what is a peasant and/or farmer: at a minimum it should be sufficient simply to identify the <u>kinds</u> of structure that existed in actual situations. In this way market relationships can be clearly linked to patterns of land ownership. Proprietary liens to land constitute the basic feature of agrarian differentiation. Landownership rights and patterns tend to be handed down through the generations: they are almost invariably a consequence of historical, most specifically political, circumstances which had little to do with agriculture. The persistence of particular property landscapes may indeed take little account of other socio-economic changes: rather, aspects of agricultural organization and production are often simply accommodated to the prevailing mode of land ownership.

Together, the distribution of land ownership and the organization and economic objectives of the individual farm enterprise encapsulate the essence of the agricultural world. They have been incorporated into a variety of taxonomies of agrarian structures. With the possible exception of studies on Latin America, such classificatory schemes have rarely been employed in a systematic cross-national examination of the relationship between agrarian structure and political activity.[9] Perhaps the most comprehensive and imaginative scheme is that of Jeffrey Paige, who has attempted first to construct a typology of structures based upon a juxtaposition between agricultural export sectors and relationships between cultivators and non-cultivators, and then to marry it to a typology of social movements.[10] This empirical analysis is based upon data from 70 countries and 135 export sectors. From this Paige builds a fourfold typology of social and political movements:

1. reformist commodity movements directed against the capitalist control and direction of markets;
2. reformist labour movements, most frequently arising out of "industrialized" plantation systems;
3. agrarian revolt against commercial haciendas;
4. revolution - socio-economically radical in the case of estates with sharecropping labour forces, and territorially radical (nationalist) where there is migratory labour.

Paige's forceful analysis is only marginally based upon European data, and while it could perhaps be applied to the continent's experiences, the reservations that it would necessarily entail could well defeat the purpose of the whole exercise. For the long history of the market involvement of European agriculture and, even more so, the political and legal origins of proprietary rights to land have produced in Europe a bewildering variety of mosaics that are not easily amenable to rigorous compression and classification. Juan Linz has summarized the problem admirably in his excellent review of the voting behaviour of European agricultural groups: "The fact that many patterns of rural property rights, and consequently of social structure, are the result of political power relations rather than of more or less impersonal economic processes makes for a much greater variety from country to country, and even within one country, than in urban society, which is shaped much more by economic changes resulting from industrialization and technology".[11]

The relative complexity of the European experience can perhaps be deduced from comparing the wealth of information collected and analyzed by European economic historians with the work of social scientists who have been concerned with the politics of agriculture in the "Third World". Yet to seek to construct an analytical framework which is simultaneously restrictive and highly specific might simply be beyond the capacity of available resources. Consequently, it may prove best to avoid the issue by adopting a strategy which sets out only to plot the broad contours of the sociopolitical map within fairly flexible parameters. The most parsimonious path is that followed by Juan Linz, who has argued that a viable analysis can still be pursued when the complexities of possible typologies of land ownership and economic objectives are reduced to a handful of categories of agricultural enterprises.[12] Linz's rural stratification scheme may perhaps be further subsumed under seven broad types of farming operations that combine land tenure patterns and market orientations:

1. owners of large agricultural enterprises;
2. owners of capitalist agricultural enterprises;
3. owners of farmer-capitalist agricultural enterprises;
4. tenants of farmer-capitalist agricultural enterprises;
5. owners of domestic consumptive ("subsistence peasant") enterprises;
6. tenants of domestic consumptive ("subsistence peasant") enterprises;
7. hired labourers.

This minimum listing, it should be reiterated, is composed only

of abstractions. It is intended primarily as an embarkation
point for a more detailed empirical analysis. Nevertheless,
some of the major stereotypes of agrarian society should be
discernible. The first two categories identify the larger
estate and its proprietor, and perhaps also the ancient figure
of the landlord. The next two categories correspond to the
notions of commercial agriculture and the commercial farmer (the
"agricultural businessman"), while the following pair suggest
the world of the traditional peasant. Hired labourers, in a
sense, constitute a residual category: their situation will vary
considerably with their terms of employment and the nature of
their employer. The same, indeed, may be said of the whole
field of owner-tenant relationships. Overall, this classification
of enterprises embraces the three constants of the agrarian
world: the question of <u>land ownership</u>, the <u>size</u> of enterprise,
and the role of the <u>market</u>.

A social or political movement is a multi-faceted phenomenon.
It would be beyond the scope of this study to embrace all
aspects of agrarian political movements throughout the centuries.
Instead, the bulk of the succeeding chapters, with due regard
for historical antecedents and heritages, will focus upon the
decades between approximately the mid-nineteenth century and
1940. The justification for this parameter are several:

1. Rapid and increased industrialization affected the status of
   agriculture as a mode of production and a generator of wealth.
   Agriculture went into decline as a sector of employment at
   the same time as technological innovation revolutionarized
   cultivation, offered a potentially much higher level of
   productivity, and intensified market operations as well as
   extending their geographical scope.
2. Political mobilization and democratization occurred on a much
   greater scale, and facilitated the entry, on a regularized
   basis, of large numbers of people (including cultivators)
   into the constitutional framework of political activity. New
   and different opportunities for political participation
   introduced new and different demands upon the mobilization
   and organization of political expression.
3. A technological revolution, especially in communications and
   transportation, increased the ease with which governments

could attempt to regulate and direct the daily life of their citizens, at the same time as states came to claim intervention in socio-economic affairs as a duty, as well as a right.
4. The political contours of Europe underwent a radical transformation, especially in 1918. The redrawing of the political map of Europe inevitably had a far-reaching effect upon government-subject relations.

The beginning of the Second World War is a convenient date with which to close the period. In the first instance, the various inheritances from the past had coalesced to such an extent that political oppositions had been frozen by the 1920s into a mould that persisted through future decades.[13] Second, the consequences of World War II produced in Eastern Europe a series of Communist regimes in which governmental policy and control contributed towards a very different kind of agrarian structure: they certainly reduced drastically the number of strategic and organizational options available to agrarian populations. References will be made to the post-1945 period only when it is felt that some exposition will illuminate or further clarify important questions or problems raised in the mainstream narrative.

A more or less comprehensive picture of agrarian political movements should be a mix of several ingredients: conditions of formation, structure, composition, behaviour, and external relationships. The various elements can be assembled under four broad investigatory areas, which together form the analytical focus of the following chapters.

To take up the problem of agrarian political movements is in the first instance to focus upon the conditions which metaphorically give birth to such movements. Can different forms of political expression be identified with specific forms of agrarian structure or with relationships with the wider society? In addition, the question ought to be raised whether different kinds of stimuli contribute towards different kinds of movements, even given comparable agrarian structure.

A second concern is with the nature of agrarian movements. Their character can be assessed in terms of both their objectives and the means employed to achieve these aims. The structure and content of agrarian demands, the extent to which these are incorporated into a coherent programme or even elevated into an ideology, the <u>modus</u> <u>vivendi</u> of operation, all can be audited according to their clarity, intensity and extensiveness. <u>Clarity</u> refers to the coherence of expression, ranging from the amorphous through to a high degree of instrumental calculation. <u>Intensity</u> has a double meaning. It may allude to the degree of commitment in pursuing, and the depth of feeling about, chosen aims: alternatively, it may be used to point to the extent to which the objectives and activities of agrarian movements involve or imply a radical societal restructuring. By contrast, <u>extensiveness</u> refers to the range of their subject matter. Do, for example, agrarian movements propound only one objective, or many? Alternatively, do they pursue only one strategic option, or several? In addition, movement and organization are not necessarily synonymous. Consequently, therefore, it is of interest to look at the degree and kind of organization that appeared, and the conditions under which such a coordination of agrarian political activity was consolidated or failed to develop.

Agrarian movements are macro-phenomena in so far as they are composed of an aggregate of individuals. Hence, a further topic for exploration raises the question of the composition of agrarian movements, at both the elite and mass levels. Two more specific points need to be noted about leadership recruitment and mass support. Are agrarian political movements built by cultivators themselves, or are they forged or subverted by external elites for essentially non-agricultural objectives? In addition, this aspect of participation and support can be considered within the wider perspective of the political choice of agrarian groups. It is merely inconsequential to point out that all agrarian groups within a country do not throw their weight unreservedly behind a single agrarian movement, or even behind agrarian movements of various hues. More generally, therefore, the questions of the extent to which mobilization is restricted to agrarian structures or of which groups constitute the core of agrarian movements must be complemented by looking at how the political prejudices and behaviour of agrarian groups fit within the whole spectrum of available political choice. Cultivators may be mobilized by or subsumed within a gamut of political movements that may not be directly or seriously concerned with agricultural problems.

Agrarian groups and movements do not exist in isolation. A final arena of exploration would incorporate the nexus of relationships with society at large. Do agrarian movements have "natural" allies or opponents, or not? Questions of coalition strategy entail an examination of the involvement of non-agricultural groups with agrarian movements, and the form that this involvement takes.

The analysis that follows will take up these issues. The simple outline of agricultural enterprise as an amalgam of land tenure and economic objective offers a convenient and flexible means of broaching and harmonizing the multiple strands in the political story of European agriculture. The first chapter presents a broad overview of the various themes prior to the industrialization of the continent. Chapter 2 discusses the socio-economic and political changes that occurred during and after the nineteenth century, while Chapter 3 analyses the various agrarian responses to changes and pressures. The political behaviour of agrarian groups - more specifically their participation and partisan choice within the electoral context - is the theme of the following two chapters. Finally, Chapters 6-8 take up what is perhaps the supreme political expression, the agrarian political party, and consider this manifestation of political concern and involvement in the light of conditions conducive to formation and survival, the nature of mass support, and the style of political activity. In conclusion, it might be valuable to draw attention to the limitations of the analysis. There is no attempt to construct a theoretical edifice. Nor, strictly speaking, is the study a systematic empirical analysis of cross-national variations. The methodological orientation of subsequent chapters is relatively non-rigorous. The approach is essentially eclectic in that the design incorporates the insights and strategies of several academic disciplines. Such a multi-disciplinary approach was deemed advisable because both the societies and groups examined, and the dynamics of change involved did not seem to possess clearly differentiated and autonomous boundaries to a degree which would merit the retention of conventional disciplinary purity. Moreover, the empirical basis is unsatisfactory. Much of the information is impressionistic and qualitative, while the origin and value of some of the quantitative data employed are open to criticism. While these comments draw attention to the considerable limitations surrounding the analysis, the inadequacies ought not constitute an insurmountable barrier against an exploratory study and broad synthesizing overview of the political behaviour of agrarian groups in Europe.

CHAPTER 1   Towards Capitalism and Industrialization

Since patterns of landownership and styles of farming differ quite considerably from country to country, some historical overview would seem to be useful in order to plot changes in the agrarian economy and the relationship of cultivators with other social groups. Without history there can be only an incomplete understanding of the political mobilization of cultivators under the movement towards universal suffrage, urban-rural divisions, non-agricultural dimensions of social differentiation, and the political behaviour of agrarian groups in the period of mass politics. The historical development of European agriculture and its various political expressions are the themes of the next three chapters.

The problem as always is one of cut-off points. Where to begin, and where to end? The selection of historical periods is a game that often seems to be without a referee, and one where the final whistle has yet to be blown. The period selected here, not entirely arbitrarily, ranges approximately from the feudal structures of medieval times to about the first half of the nineteenth century. For the beginning, for instance, Slicher van Bath dates the twelfth century as the decisive break with the primacy of direct agricultural consumption.[1] Thereafter a domestic orientation had to cope with a market only sometimes buoyant but always present and increasing in intensity. Around the same time, the frontiers of Europe were consolidated agriculturally, culturally and politically. It was an era of large-scale colonization, with massive reclamation of waste land and settlement of virgin territory.[2] Despite later invasions, political expansion, especially reconquest on the southern and eastern rims, and the territorial organization of the feudal units produced internal boundaries and external parameters to the texture of life that are discernible in later centuries. Perhaps the most obvious marker indicating the close of the period is Britain's embrace of the Industrial Revolution. Around 1800 there was a definitive consolidation of national markets, closely followed by a heightened visibility of states, an increase in the tempo of their activities, a massive growth in the numbers of non-agricultural populations, and the introduction of possibilities for mass political participation on a regular, institutionalized basis.

These centuries were, as any historian knows, far from being static, normatively consistent, or structurally homogeneous over time. On the contrary, Europe experienced over these centuries numerous and significant economic, scientific and technological innovations. In particular, Immanuel Wallerstein has pointed to the sixteenth century as a great watershed heralding the beginning of a capitalist world economy, in which the interplay of market mechanisms and state activities generated a new form of surplus appropriation based upon more efficient and expansionary modes of production.[3] Nevertheless, for the purposes of this study the economic and political situation of European agriculture before and after the advent of democratization and massive industrialization seems to be sufficiently distinctive for the earlier centuries to be treated collectively. Until at least the beginning of the nineteenth century, Europe was agricultural and rural. Cultivators comprised the vast majority of the population nearly everywhere. They formed the lowest stratum of a hierarchical society into which they were more or less integrated because of their subjection to demands and sanctions imposed by individuals, such as a monarch or local lord, outside their own social stratum. The rural scene was dominated by the landlord, deriving the major part of his income from money rent and for services received for the use of land to which he had legal title, and having a prior claim upon the earnings of his tenants, irrespective of whether or not he shared in the risks of production. Landlords were frequently also the state's administrative and judicial representative or official. A landlord may have <u>owned</u> the land, but the state or ruler claimed to <u>govern</u> it. Where communications, transport and central resources were imperfect, the simplest solution for the European state system was to permit whoever lived in the local mansion or castle to govern the local territory in the name of the state as well as to own it. Ownership did not necessarily distinguish between control of law and control of men: the lord of the manor was often expected to direct the locality as he considered appropriate. The characteristics of this social and political structure may be reviewed under three general headings: methods and purposes of agriculture, social groups and patterns of land tenure, and the peasantry.

1. Methods and Purposes of Agriculture

Agricultural production had a dual orientation in nearly every region of Europe. Its more immediate objective was to provide sufficient produce for all those in the locality. But there was also involvement in a wider market economy, most particularly in areas near urban centres. The commercial production of crops was especially prominent in Central Europe, along and around the trade belt of cities which had emerged in the Middle Ages from the Baltic to Northern Italy.[4] With relatively large populations by the standards of the period, these urban centres relied almost exclusively upon the importation of food. They were the economic nodes of the feudal system, for while the landlords on the desmesnes could acquire an agricultural surplus, as long as the bulk of the surplus was in kind it was of little value unless it could be exchanged in a market. Commercial involvement, however, existed almost everywhere. For example, very rural regions in Eastern Europe such as Poland and the Ukraine were already heavily engaged by the fifteenth century in the export of grain to urban areas further west. But even in those regions which were, comparatively speaking, more urbanized and which possessed a more well-defined market economy, most large estates and peasant holdings produced primarily for themselves and the local market: little surplus produce was deliberately planned. Moreover, farm production was still diversified, with little concentration upon a single cash crop. For example, Northern Italy was noted between the fifteenth and seventeenth centuries for the strength of its cities and the quality of its urban civilization. Yet the region was predominantly rural. Farms were oriented towards some commercial production, but they were very small and production was on a poor scale.[5]

One of the more significant innovatory developments was the emergence of the wool trade in Flanders and its spread across the Channel to East Anglia and other parts of England. The development of the wool trade is important in that it involved a switch away from a more labour intensive horticulture to a livestock production which not only entailed less labour, but also generated associated agriculturally-derived industries. More and more, the English textile industry came to be located in rural areas. From the fourteenth century onwards, the importance of commerce increased markedly in the English countryside: people began to consider land in economic and commercial terms. In this sense, the later Tudor dynasty's attempt to transform the traditional social structure through, for instance, the enclosure movement was not a particularly revolutionary process, but rather a confirmation of a trend already apparent for about two centuries.[6] The total configuration of these developments in England and their consequences did not occur or did not sustain their momentum in any other region of Europe.

Agricultural methods followed relatively well-defined patterns, in which land reclamation schemes and techniques to increase production played a secondary role. This is not surprising, since the primary motivation of cultivation was not perhaps the maximizing of production: an important aim was the preservation of the traditional rural social structure. While it is true that, at least compared with other areas of the globe, a fairly robust agricultural economy with considerable technical innovation had established itself in Europe even during the early Middle Ages, many agricultural techniques militated against the maximization of production or economic profit. The number of technical improvements that automatically and immediately stimulated organizational changes was very limited.[7] Moreover, a law of diminishing returns came into operation with further attempts to bring more and more marginal land under cultivation. The yield of traditional European crops did not increase significantly or permanently between the late fifteenth and the late eighteenth centuries. More intensive methods had been developed in England and Northern France, but tended to be confined to large estates: even here they were comparatively rare. The major innovative breakthrough in England did not occur until the eighteenth century, when the increased use of fertilizers, new crops, and new methods of crop rotation revolutionarized agricultural production. But the enclosure movement was by then nearing completion, the country was already characterized by large, economically viable farm units, and agriculture was accepted as a commercial enterprise.[8] One further technical point inhibited the development of a greater level of commercial agriculture in Europe before the Industrial Revolution. The low level of mechanization and the almost total reliance upon human labour imposed severe limits upon the amount of land an individual or family could cultivate. These restrictions upon the output of horticultural farming without a reasonable degree of mechanization simply emphasize the significance of livestock farming wherever it occurred.[9]

2. Social Groups and Patterns of Land Tenure

Relationships among the various social classes and status groups were extremely complex: moreover, cross-regional and cross-national variations in these relationships were also very great. Any assumption of some kind of "natural evolution" of European society from feudalism and its disintegration through monarchical absolutism and bourgeois revolution to modern democracy is of course both misleading and oversimplified. The general histories of European societies may follow this development, but we should not overlook the richness of variation in both the "original" societies and the manner of social and economic developments. These variations affect later political developments.[10] By the fifteenth century there was little similarity between the English copyholder or tenant farmer, occupying property under the common law, and the French métayeur or Italian mezzadro shareholding under the indulgence of the local lord or superior:

the sharecropper may have had personal and legal freedom in theory, but he was still more obliged to accept feudal dues and services. Equally, few of the low status groups in Western Europe were similar to the Prussian or Polish lassit working in the lord's estates under an even more repressive serfdom. And even within these countries and categories variations could be immense.

One major factor affecting these cross-regional variations was the structure of landownership and occupations. Speaking very generally, there consisted three kinds of landownership: all had different consequences for the peasantry. Under patrimonial or "feudal" ownership, control of the land rested with a rural elite which inherited property because of membership in kinship groups or lineages. The structure of patrimonialism was hierarchical, with the implication that higher status orders possessed the right of tribute in the shape of goods or services from lower orders. The hierarchy could be rather extended, as in the clan structure of the Scottish Highlands, but the peasant was always at its base. Second, prebendal ownership was not heritable: instead, possession of land was awarded to bureaucratic officials who exacted tribute in their capacity as servants of the state. Ownership in this case is a grant of income, and was more typically associated with strongly centralized bureaucratic states, such as the Byzantine Empire and its Ottoman successor. These two forms of landownership are characteristically justified by a ceremonial framework: because they are presented in the form of a reciprocal contract, the ceremonial offers a kind of ritual compensation to the lower orders for their depressed condition. Finally, mercantile ownership exists where land is regarded as the private property of the landowner to be bought or sold as he desires, and to be employed to produce economic profit for the owner in the form of surplus production if owner-occupied, or as rent if farmed by tenants. This last kind of ownership is regarded as the most "modern", since land is treated more as an impersonal economic object rather than primarily a base of social prestige and status or political power: hence, it is more characteristically associated with commercial farming and a market economy.[11]

These categorizations are no more than ideal types, and are

certainly not mutually exclusive. All could be found existing side by side almost everywhere in Europe.[12] But their combination helped to determine the structure of rural society, the pattern of land occupation and tenure, and the size of holdings in any one region. Moreover, conflicts between different patrimonial and feudal structures also affected patterns of land tenure.[13] Simplification almost inevitably introduces distortion, but perhaps the truth will not be violated unduly by the assumption of two very broad patterns of land occupation. While both could be found existing side by side in most parts of Europe, there was overall a fairly distinct geographical differentiation. Peasant smallholdings generally predominated in Northern and Western Europe. While it is true that in most cases the peasant did not own his land outright, it often forming part of a large estate, one important point was the greater freedom of action of the peasant. While he was expected to offer the landlord some labour duties or services on the domain land, he was more free to concentrate on his own enterprise and plan his own agricultural output. Quite often, the peasant smallholding concentrated on domestic production while the domain land was used for commercial crops. Moreover, he was in several instances free to leave his land and locality, or even to buy or sell land.

In Northern Italy, for example, Piedmont was divided into several large estates. However, single estates were comparatively small, and were divided almost everywhere into numerous smallholdings worked by peasants under the risk-minimizing métayage system. Despite limitations on the freedom of action of the peasantry, Piedmont was characteristically a region of peasant smallholdings dominated by typical peasant commitments.[14] The extreme instance was Scandinavia, or rather Norway and Sweden, where peasant owner-occupation was a widespread form of land tenure. As early as the late Middle Ages one-half of the land in Sweden was owned by peasant smallholders. Norway was even more extreme: traditional landholding patterns, along with the devastation of the Black Death, produced at an early date a nation of peasant smallholders with almost no native aristocracy.[15] In addition, many of these smallholding regions, such as parts of Northern France and Western Germany, were characterized by strip cultivation and land held in common, emphasizing the nuclear role of the village as a peasant community, the need for some forms of cooperation in determining the time-table of day to day activities, as well as the likelihood that localized disaster would be suffered by all families in the neighbourhood. The importance of the village is perhaps best symbolized by the Russian word *mir* (meaning "world" or "peace"). To a considerable extent each village was an autonomous community: certainly, they were not linked directly with each other, but to an outside urban centre of exchange and control.[16]

By contrast, Eastern Europe, Southern Italy and large areas of the Iberian peninsula were characterized by large manorial estates. In Eastern Europe the juridical basis of aristocratic landownership was of recent origin, and consequently the pattern of land occupation was much more simple.[17] In Prussia over 60 per cent of the land was contained in large estates, and inevitably the manor lord possessed feudal rights and privileges over the rest: he also enjoyed exclusive access to legal protection from national rulers and in the national courts.[18] In addition, in several regions of Eastern Europe the aristocracy was the only social group allowed to own land: for example, this was the case in East Prussia until 1808. Moreover, these regions were typified by an increasing limitation in the freedom of action of the peasantry and the reduction or elimination of any patrimonial rights they may once have possessed. For instance, Salomon's excellent study of New Castile illustrates the fundamental conflict between various types of property, especially that between communal peasant property and aristocratic and ecclesiastical property, and the complex way in which a basically feudal or patrimonial pattern of land occupation was transformed into a "seigneurial" pattern, with previously independent smallholders becoming tenants or even farm labourers.[19] Similarly, in Southern Italy the aristocracy and the Catholic Church became almost the sole landowners by the close of the eighteenth century: it was estimated that the Church controlled as much as 80 per cent of all arable land in some provinces. Over the centuries the patrimonial rights of the large landowners expanded to incorporate absolute ownership of nominally free peasant smallholdings, as well as common and

<u>demesne</u> lands: the so-called "personal rights" of the landowner were also greatly increased.[20] The major distinctions between this kind of situation and that which was present throughout much of Western Europe were based not only upon the size of holding or degree of involvement in the market economy, but also upon the freedom of action of the peasant. The peasantry may have enjoyed absolute ownership of land in few areas of Europe, but under manorial ownership the number of landless peasants was far greater, the security of a peasant's tenure rested on far more precarious foundations, and restrictions upon his activity were much greater.

The "traditional" manorial system, however, did not apply to that part of Europe incorporated into the Ottoman Empire. European Turkey never experienced feudalism in the western sense. The Balkan regions were ruled essentially by a military hierarchy assisted by tax-collectors from the central bureaucracy: the Turkish presence was usually inconspicuous, being limited primarily to military forces at strategic centres. The peasantry emerged early as occupiers of land, since there was no native aristocracy or rural elite. But Balkan peasants were subjected to the land tenure relations and vassalage systems of the Ottoman Empire. They essentially achieved independence only after the waning of Turkish suzerainty, especially after the Congress of Berlin in 1878. The tax burden imposed by the Ottomans was not particularly onerous. However, the system of collecting taxes was lax and inefficient. Officials tended not to exercise their functions for long periods only suddenly to demand (under central pressure) immediate payment of all taxes owed. If the peasant was unable to pay, everything he owned was liable to expropriation. Life under the Ottomans may have been uncertain and oppressive, but in some ways the peasants experienced less exploitation and perhaps had greater freedom of action than under a manorial system.[21]

Although analogies can be drawn with other estate areas of Europe, English developments represented perhaps a major exception to these patterns. In England radical changes in land tenure in the seventeenth and eighteenth centuries were the culmination of the increasing commercialization and productivity of agriculture. Beginning with the commutations of the late

Middle Ages and following on from the enclosures of the sixteenth century, the later enclosure movement, at its peak between about 1760 and 1820, expanded rapidly the amount of arable land (about one-half) that had already been wrested from traditional open field techniques. Moreover, this final enclosure phase carried the force of parliamentary law: the earlier phases had been essentially private enterprises. Overall, these changes invoked an increasing crystallization of capitalist power in English agriculture. More and more, land and labour were both utilised in a rational economic manner. Tenant farmers paid monetary rent, while large estates employed hired labour without the complications of feudal rights and obligations. This pattern of large farm units was markedly different from the manorial system prevalent in Eastern Europe.[22] Table 1.1 offers a tentative summary of this discussion with a crude classification of European regions according to the dominant forms of land occupation and styles of farming about 1800.

Table 1.1: A Tentative Classification of European Regions According to Dominant Forms of Land Occupation and Style of Farming, about 1800

Commercial, Mercantile Estates and Farms	Peasant Smallholding (not necessarily peasant ownership)	Mixed Peasant Smallholding and Manorial	Manorial
England	Ulster	Denmark	South Spain
Scotland	Norway	Ireland	South Portugal
	Sweden	France	South Italy
	Netherlands	North Spain	Prussia
	Belgium	North Portugal	Rumania
	West Germany (especially Bavaria, Baden, Württemberg, Dithmarschen)	Austrian Alpine Provinces	Poland
			Russia
			Austria-Hungary (excluding the Alpine Provinces)
	Switzerland		
	North Italy		
	Serbia		
	Bulgaria		

3. The Peasantry

Almost everywhere, the peasantry, living in highly traditional closed communities, was oriented primarily to the domestic economy. The peasant formed the bottom rung of the national or local status hierarchy, in societies which retained more than the trappings of feudalism, as defined in terms of formal rights and obligations cast in a ceremonial framework that possessed moral and religious, as well as social, economic and political sanctions. The peasant was guided and controlled from above in all aspects of his social behaviour. The role of the market was undoubtedly important in the agricultural economy. However, its significance was perhaps secondary to a domestic and labour commitment and a subservient position in an enclosed local social status order. Barrington Moore has aptly summarized this point as follows:

It is true that the market played an important part in the medieval agrarian economy... Yet, in contrast to later times the lord together with his peasants to a great extent constituted a self-sufficing community able to supply a large part of their needs from local resources and with local skills.[23]

The variations may have been innumerable, but this was the basic structure of rural society throughout most areas of the continent. The rights (and obligations) of the peasant existed only because of the particular structure of his fealty relationship with his local <u>seigneur</u>. The latter claimed and was accepted as having jurisdiction over the entire community because of this fealty relationship. Political involvement by the peasantry might entail one of two things: either they could rebel against the authority of the local lord, or they could support the lord's political ambitions, for example through conscription in a military venture to assert his jurisdiction in other communities and over other communities of peasants. Moreover, there tended to be a basic distrust, or even fear, of all social groups and individuals - urban dwellers, itinerant traders, and representatives of the central authority - from outside the community.

There were obviously exceptions to these generalizations. The Swedish peasantry, for example, succeeded in retaining a relatively high level of political awareness. However, this was probably due to a more independent status and their institutionalization within a curial system which survived despite an increase in aristocratic landownership in the seventeenth century. They were regarded by Swedish monarchs as an important counterweight to the influence of the aristocracy: even throughout the so-called Freedom Era of parliamentary political conflict between the Hats and the Caps during the eighteenth century, the peasantry retained marked monarchist sympathies.[24] However, such instances elsewhere were comparatively rare. The only accepted outside force or institution was the church. But the church was not seen by the peasantry as an institution linking the peasants' daily life with some metaphysical system of theology. It was more specifically identified as a community church reinforcing traditional community values: in most instances the local priest or clergyman came from the district or was himself from a peasant family.[25] The most interesting example of religion being closely identified with the economic, social and political values of enclosed communities occurred in the Vendée during the French Revolution. The Catholic clergy played a prominent and respected role in the life of the isolated Vendée villages. The Revolution came to be seen not simply as an attack upon the Catholic Church, but also as a direct threat to the entire social fabric: the Vendée became counter-revolutionary.[26]

Apart from the few exceptions like the Swedish peasants, the political awareness of the peasantry, when it became manifest, was largely confined to the local arena and the activities of the local lord. Political structures were essentially parochial. The lord exercised all powers of local government and possessed direct responsibility in all government action. Moreover, he was often in charge of central government functions in the locality: in Prussia, for example, the local lords were not only landowners, but also judges, administrators, prosecutors, and police officials. The Swedish nobility's local dominance of the peasantry was perhaps due more to their function as regulatory and tax agents of the political centre than to patrimonialism within the local community. The peasant tended not to be interested in wider issues such as representation and central government reform, except where they impinged upon his local orientation and commitments. The aims of the peasantry were quite simple. They desired to strengthen their relative economic independence vis-à-vis encroachments, especially by large landowners. This could entail a struggle for greater personal freedom from patrimonial obligations and for greater security of tenure. Peasants were also concerned with maintaining the autonomy and culture of their own locality: thus they often proved hostile to centralizing efforts by both bureaucracies and religions backed by the state apparatus. Their loyalties to local cultures and domestic commitments found a common cause in resisting attempts by either the central bureaucracy or patrimonial lords to increase their tax burden.[27]

Three avenues of activity were available to the peasantry. They could appeal to the local landowners and patrimonial elites for protection or redress of grievances; they could attempt to remedy their grievances by direct action and rebellion against either the state or the local lord; or they could foster the establishment of enduring and well-organized political movements. While all three avenues were utilized by European peasants, the uprising was the most frequent after the erosion of a feudal structure and before the beginnings of mass political mobilization under suffrage expansion. Peasant rebellions, in fact, have been endemic in European history. The list is too numerous to present in any detail, but from at least the sixteenth century onwards, peasant uprisings became almost annual events in European history. The objectives of the peasantry remained fairly constant throughout. If they were landless, they tended to seek land reform and some security of tenure: if they possessed land they saw their livelihood threatened by the encroachment of large estates. Thus, in England the main peasant uprisings of the sixteenth century were directed against the enclosure movements. Peasant unrest blossomed throughout the seventeenth century in France, as population growth increased pressures upon large owners, small owner-occupiers, and métayage peasants. The successful combination of high returns and low cultivation costs typical of a share-cropping system eroded rapidly under the triple assault of increasing state demands, endemic disease, and persistent poor harvests.[28] Demands were made not only for an easing of burdens, but also for more land.

Richer peasants tended to join the large landowners in resisting the appropriation of common lands for redistributive purposes. However, in a recent comparative study Roland Mousnier objects to this broad interpretation and stresses more specifically that unrest sprang directly from the increasing penetration of the central bureaucracy into rural areas: the imposition of new and more substantial taxation went hand in hand with a reduction of traditional local privileges and autonomy.[29]

These interpretations are not necessarily incompatible: rather they are complementary. The important point is simply the heightened political and economic pressures upon the countryside. A "quantum jump" in military technology in the fifteenth century had multiplied the cost of war, and in so doing had helped to undermine the future political viability of city states and medieval baronies. The emergence of strong territorial centres paralleled the birth of the capitalist world economy. Where productivity was constant, then the appetite for a larger surplus could be satisfied only by increasing the labour burdens of the peasantry or by reducing its real income.[30] More directly perhaps, administrative centralization and the development of commerce challenged the social prestige, political influence and economic well-being of the rural elites. In turn, these tended to introduce policies that worsened the lot of the peasantry and, in the absence of alternative channels, drove them towards direct action. This seems to have been the case of the decline in the manorial system in England which led to the peasant revolt of 1381. The lower nobility in the West German provinces underwent similar experiences in the early sixteenth century. Their attempts to preserve their economic and political strength by increasing the economic burden of the peasantry was a major cause of the numerous uprisings which coalesced into the <u>Bauernkrieg</u> of 1525 and related chiliastic movements such as the <u>Bundschuh</u> of the Upper Rhine.[31]

From the time of the great peasant revolts of the fourteenth century, unrest and violence became a normal part of agrarian life. Peasant uprisings did not occur all the time, nor did they appear everywhere simultaneously. The immediate causes were almost always localized grievances. A bad harvest, famine, drought, unemployment, the imposition of new taxes or obligations, the siphoning of more produce away from the locality - any one was liable to spur the peasantry into action. The relatively non-integrated nature of society, the parochial character of political structures, the relative weakness of central protection or forces, the absence of adequate transportation and communications, and the isolation of most rural communities all tended to inhibit local outbursts from turning into general revolutions. Further barriers were created by the peasantry's distrust of outsiders and of organized activity, and also by their own agricultural commitments: generally, this kind of anomic political activity could not be permitted to disrupt the seasonal routine of agrarian life. There was no clear sense of purpose, action or political awareness beyond the improvement of local conditions.[32] Because he was in theory and practice the arbiter of local conditions, the lord was the immediate target of peasant aims. Moreover, in most instances the whittling away of local autonomy by the central state bureaucracy had not produced a completely polarized society where everyone was fixed in a rigid social order in which peasants had been reduced to the worst levels of serfdom. Only where the latter was the case did central penetration perhaps provoke the peasantry into a genuine revolutionary situation, as in seventeenth century Russia.[33] Peasant uprisings were an expression of economic rather than political grievances, and frequently the lord rather than the state was seen as the giver of remedies. Indeed, in many instances the peasants continued to emphasize their loyalty to the king even while engaged in revolutionary activity.

What counted was the relative deterioration of the peasants' condition. Where this involved the replacement of strong centralized rule by greater autonomy for rural elites, the objective of the peasantry was often to demand a return to centralized rule.[34] If the masses attained their objectives and achieved rectification of their grievances, they lapsed back into an apolitical stance. Economic satisfaction superimposed upon their local orientation turned them full circle from revolution to support for the status quo. Political uprisings by other elements of society were often unable to generate anything more than minimal rural support.[35]

However, on occasions peasant uprisings did turn into

revolutions aimed at a fundamental political transformation of society. Again, the immediate cause was a deterioration in economic conditions. But the catalyst which brought several localities together in a general uprising tended to be religion. It was a pietistic view of religion which made the masses susceptible to millenarian religious teachings that transformed local quarrels into national and even cross-national revolutions.[36] Religion, moreover, not only provided a cross-local tie and an absolute call to action, but also tended to represent the total community as perceived by those who lived in it. Religious foundations for peasant revolts existed in medieval Europe, such as the English revolt of 1381, although during this period millenarianism was much more of an urban phenomenon. However, they became much more visible with the Reformation: the Hussite wars of the fifteenth century and the German <u>Bauernkrieg</u> a few decades later are outstanding examples. But, as Cohn strongly argues, it should be remembered that although revolutionary millenarian groups always tend to emerge in the midst of great upheavals, they rarely have had much in common with the mass uprisings they seek to exploit, a particularly apt point with regard to agriculture.[37]

The Elbe has always been an agrarian and cultural frontier, and a comparison of East and West Germany at the time of the <u>Bauernkrieg</u> is instructive in illustrating the economic origins of agrarian unrest. The peasant rebellion in the west ranged from Westphalia through the Rhineland and South-West Germany to Switzerland and the Alpine provinces of Austria. These regions were characterized by both scattered peasant smallholdings with either freehold possession or reasonable security of tenure, and a fairly extensive diffusion of landownership, judicial authority, and liege lordships. The peasant reaction was against the attempts of the local elites to strengthen their own political and economic position through the imposition of new obligations upon the peasantry. The uprisings were relatively successful because of the political and military weakness of both central and local authorities: the peasants were fighting to retain an established communal way of life that incorporated a satisfactory market involvement, especially in wine production.[38] The new religious ideas of the Reformation offered them a moral and metaphysical justification for their struggle. By contrast, the peasantry in Prussia enjoyed little freedom. The few rights that existed were of fairly recent origin and had been granted by the state to encourage the immigration of labour from other areas. Similarly, most village communities were "artificial": their charters of rights were of recent origin and had been conferred by the state rather than being rooted in tradition and strengthened by previous successful struggles against encroachment. Agricultural methods had lagged behind those of Western Europe. The aristocracy were gradually entering the capitalist economy by producing grain for the western urban centres. They wanted more men to grow grain: the simplest way to achieve increased production was through the utilization of regimented labour. The more depressed level of the peasantry, a labour shortage, the stronger position of both the state and the local lord, all helped to impose discipline and restrictions upon the peasantry and to prevent a general peasant uprising. The only outbreak of unrest in 1525 similar to the Bauernkrieg came from the freehold peasants of the Königsberg region.[39]

In addition, participation in direct action was rarely limited to peasants. While the peasantry supplied the overwhelming majority of participants, the leadership of and initiative for both localized unrest and general uprisings almost always came from outside the rural masses. Within the rural world, it was the local lord demanding military support from his peasants, or the richer cultivator, fearing for his economic credibility, who were more prone to spark off agricultural ferment. The coincidence of chiliastic revolution with direct peasant action does not mean that the latter caused the former. Rather, the new religious prophets attempted to manipulate peasant unrest in order to obtain a mass support for the propagation of millenarian ideas that for centuries had been part of the Christian tradition. It was precisely those cultivators who saw a threat to their economic position who responded most readily to direct action. A threat to security of tenure, the vagaries of a capitalist market, the forced extractions and export of a surplus from areas enjoying high productivity, all could provide the fuel for insurrection. It only remained for someone to ignite the explosive mixture.[40]

4. Regional Variations

The failure of the Bauernkrieg to spread eastwards to Prussia indicates the existence of marked regional differences in the situation of the peasantry, due partly to the greater retention of feudal and manorial practices in areas of large estates. By the sixteenth century and the advent of a capitalist economy, feudal restrictions upon agriculture had been eliminated or greatly reduced throughout most of Western Europe. While tax burdens and feudally-derived obligations remained, the peasantry was generally legally free. The spread of individual proprietors and secure tenants spearheaded the consolidation of the farmer-capitalist enterprise and a consequent emphasis upon monetary resources. Legal freedom implied a potential labour mobility either from locality to locality, or to urban centres. In most countries in North-West Europe, personal liberty, private property and labour mobility prevailed more and more over feudal or patrimonial ties. The advance of capitalism also affected the peasantry indirectly through the reaction of the rural elites to the market and their desire for greater monetary assets.

In his fascinating analysis of the historical preconditions of pluralist democracy or authoritarian rule in modern states, Barrington Moore suggests that "the ways in which the landed upper classes and the peasants reacted to the challenge of commercial agriculture were decisive factors in determining the political outcome."[41] Moore argues that two major responses in Western Europe were the liberation of the peasantry from all obligations and their removal from the land, and the retention of the peasantry who "shared" their produce with the local seigneur. His two case studies are England and France. In England the landed nobility became heavily involved in commercial agriculture. While perhaps it was more the lesser gentry who were the vanguard of agrarian capitalism, they headed a transformation in which great numbers of people participated, most notably the wealthier peasants (the new yeoman class) and urban commercial groups. The French path involved a seigneurial reaction with commercial habits penetrating French agriculture essentially by "feudal" practices. The landed nobility took up agrarian capitalism through the peasantry. The latter, in de facto occupation of the land, survived as producers. The nobility preferred to serve as "middlemen", extracting a share of the yield from the peasantry before selling it in the market.

Drawing upon Prussian and Russian developments, Moore suggests that a third European response was through a "manorial reaction" that re-emphasized serfdom and a labour-repressive agriculture.[42] Land in the east was in abundance, but labour was not. Increased production and capitalist profit were achieved through the imposition of restrictions upon, and proscription of freedom of action of a hitherto relatively free peasantry. The manorial reaction differed qualitatively from classic feudalism: production was designed for a capitalist rather than a local economy. Moreover, serfdom was imposed with the consent and cooperation of powerful state authorities: medieval feudalism by contrast, had arisen on the basis of weak central authority. Up to the sixteenth century Prussia consisted of several scattered territories held together only loosely by the Hohenzollern dynasty in Brandenburg. Under the influence of the Hanseatic league the towns had been relatively prosperous and the peasants relatively free. But with the dissolution of the Teutonic Order in 1525, the decay of the Hansa, and later devastation by war, there was little opposition to the encroachment of a Hohenzollern-aristocracy coalition on the autonomy of both the towns and the peasantry. Serfdom was consolidated by the middle of the seventeenth century.[43] In Russia political circumstances perhaps provided the first motive for the imposition of serfdom, affording a means of operating estates in order to support tsarist officials who had been granted land. For several decades the Russian peasants escaped the severe depressed conditions of their Prussian counterparts, partly perhaps because of the strength of the traditional local community.[44] But for a while, according to Wallerstein, Russia remained apart from Europe's new capitalist economy: the binding of the peasantry to full serfdom by 1649 was a consequence of agrarian capitalism.[45] To sum up, then, the sixteenth century saw a major parting of the ways between east and west. Western Europe was to be the centre of the new capitalist order: within its framework farmer-capitalist enterprises were becoming an important economic sector at the same time as enclosures brought more arable land into production as the source of an expanding livestock husbandry. Eastern Europe was to remain at the economic periphery. The victory of the large estate operating with a shackled labour force was to turn the area into a major granary of the west.

Servile conditions, however, frequently remained even after "feudal" or "manorial" restrictions were legally abolished. Serfdom was ended in Denmark in 1702, but the peasantry was still obliged to stay in the same area, usually on the same estate, as long as they were eligible for militia service. True liberation came about only towards the end of the century when opinion swung to the belief that all these restrictions inhibited economic development and prosperity.

Prussian peasants were legally entitled to rid themselves of feudal obligations after 1807, but they had to give at least one-third of their property to the landlord as compensation. In fact, a true redistribution of land did not affect much more than three per cent of all peasant land. One estimate suggests that in the Prussian provinces east of the Elbe (East and West Prussia, Brandenburg, Pomerania, Silesia), while 45,000 farmers became independent between 1811 and 1848, no less than 100,000 smallholdings disappeared, with about two-thirds having to be offered as compensation while the remainder were purchased by large estate owners. The most unfortunate victims were those who failed to acquire any claims to land, while still losing whatever share in communally held property they had previously possessed. About one-third of the total agricultural area was in fact transferred from smallholders to large estate owners and some compensation payments still remained outstanding at the outbreak of the First World War. The consequence was that these provinces continued to be dominated by large estates up to the Second World War.[46]

The Balt aristocracy in the Baltic provinces of Russia ended serfdom between 1816 and 1819 without yielding up any of their de facto control. For the next century, less than one per cent of the population controlled 60 per cent of the land in Estonia, while 75 per cent of the population of North Livonia and 55 per cent of the Estonian population were landless. Likewise, under two per cent of the Latvian population owned over one-half of the province, while 60 per cent of the agricultural population owned no land at all. Virtually all the large estates in the provinces were owned by the alien German Balts.[47] Serfdom was officially abolished in Hungary in 1848, not because of the democratic revolutions that swept across Europe in that year, but rather because the Magyar nobility sought to mobilize the peasantry behind their efforts to wrest more autonomy from the Hapsburgs and to gain greater control over other nationalities within their own territories. No benefits were accorded to the peasantry: indeed, more efficient central penetration and police control depressed them further. When emancipation came in Russia, the peasant secured little of the rich farming land. Compensation repayments and the retention of the village as a legal collective entity meant in practice that the peasant remained tied to the land.[48] By contrast, Austrian emancipation was on the whole favourable towards the peasant - certainly when compared to Prussia or Russia. The peasant gained personal economic freedom and in most regions the right to dispose of land immediately.[49] However, in Austrian Galicia, for example, the way in which serfdom was ended combined with the population increase of the nineteenth century to produce a greatly fragmented structure of holdings: indeed, much later legislation was concerned with restricting the peasants' rights to sell or to fragment their holdings. But overall emancipation from serfdom remained largely a paper freedom throughout most areas of large estates. It might have implied that the peasant was free to leave his locality for another estate or the towns if he so desired, but this was of little value if his economic condition remained unchanged. Above all, a variety of legal and illegal pressures by landlords and central governments inhibited potential mobility. In his survey of Eastern European agriculture before 1914, David Mitrany suggests that "the bulk of the large estates were tilled for the benefit of absentee owners by the peasants, generally with the latter's animals and plough, and often also with their seed".[50] The result: an ubiquitous and large poverty-stricken labour force.

It was perhaps this condition of the manorial reaction that largely fuelled the endemic series of peasant riots in these areas. For example, several hundred sporadic and isolated risings occurred in Russia alone in the 1790s: between 1826 and

1861 Russia experienced 1,186 major peasant uprisings.[51] Actual hardships and specific events were not always necessary preconditions of disorder: throughout the eighteenth and nineteenth centuries even rumours of new central directives, land redistribution or emancipation were often sufficient to spark off unrest. But in no instance did a peasant revolt, no matter what its objectives, succeed in areas of large estates. The ending of serfdom invariably was brought about by rural and urban elites for their own political and economic strategies, without specific peasant action being involved. Indeed, the reverse was often true: the major consequences of peasant revolt were military defeat, the imposition of further punitive restrictions, and greater social and economic depression. The case of Hungary is instructive in this respect. In 1514 the Archbishop of Esztergom summoned the peasantry to wage a crusade against the "infidel" Turks. The positive peasant response was rapidly turned against the Magyar nobility who had wanted the peasants to stay on the land. In the ensuing struggle the peasants were easily defeated. The net result was that the peasantry had to forfeit most of its traditional and patrimonial rights: for the next three centuries this harsh policy was pursued without respite by Magyar governments and nobles. The agrarian landscape of Eastern Europe continued, at least to the middle of the nineteenth century, to be characterized by large estates polarized between a rural elite and a large mass of dwarf peasants and landless labourers. The only successful peasant uprising in Eastern Europe occurred in Serbia under the leadership of the merchant, Kara-George, between 1804 and 1806. However, this had been a traditional smallholding region, and the revolt was against attempts by the Ottomans, tempted by the prospects of selling more grain to western markets, to introduce quasi-feudal arrangements for the first time. While subjugation succeeded in several parts of the Balkans, it failed in Serbia, and to a lesser extent in Greece, where there was no native aristocracy.[52]

A similar tableau appeared in Western Europe whenever the peasantry attempted to overturn the fundamental power structure of society. In many instances, traditional rights and privileges, and forms of relationships institutionalized in earlier centuries were weakened or destroyed. The peasants of Dithmarschen were subordinated by the aristocracy of Denmark and Holstein, while the peasant communities in many Swiss cantons were defeated by the larger landowners and urban elites in the peasant war of 1652-1653. In Scandinavia the contagion of capitalist agriculture had contributed by the seventeenth century to a persistent decrease in the proportion of land possessed by a freeholding peasantry.[53] However, these reversals occurred primarily in areas where feudal practices had earlier been established only incompletely or not at all. The Alpine valleys, the Dithmarschen fens of Schleswig, and much of Scandinavia were isolated and relatively poor regions where penetration by central elites in earlier centuries had been limited. In effect, a levelling process operated throughout much of Western Europe. In some places the peasants were forced to relinquish some freedoms, yet escaped the servility that appeared in the east. Elsewhere, the rural elite rejected serfdom as unprofitable while still preserving large scale enterprises that were suitable for commercial agriculture.

It would be dangerous to push this east-west schism too far, but there is no doubt that such a dimension existed. Several interrelated factors went into the marked differences in agrarian structures. First, the rural elites in most of Western Europe never achieved the complete social and political dominance that emerged in the east. Their pre-eminence was challenged by the monarchs who, as in Sweden, often attempted to use the peasantry as a counter-balance to aristocratic influence. Again, western regions mostly avoided the stark consequences of an unmitigating alliance between crown and landed nobility of the kind forged in Prussia. Urban populations were already significantly stronger throughout most of Western Europe: particularly in the Netherlands and Switzerland the influence of the rural elite was in constant decline after the fifteenth century.[54] Moreover, Western nobilities seemed to be more amenable and flexible in their attitudes towards the peasantry and agricultural economics. By the sixteenth century, extensive cultivation was common in the west. More and more the nobility was less interested in the numerical size of the peasantry as such than in the productive capacity of both the land and the cultivator. They more readily encouraged new agricultural techniques and more wholeheartedly embraced agrarian capitalism. The form that the latter took in Western Europe seems, directly or indirectly, to have strengthened a spirit of independence among the mass of rural society.

Marked differences also existed within agrarian society. In Western Europe there were more significant gradations within the peasantry in terms of wealth, productive capacity, tenure, and size of farms. Under the manorial system in Eastern Europe there was an almost unrelieved peasant uniformity. Wealthier peasants were more independent, more easily mobilized for political action, and could more easily resist attempted subjugation. Moreover, Western peasants tended to be more literate and could more readily see the consequences of social and economic relationships upon their own situation. The principle of education for low status groups appeared in Western Europe during the period of enlightened absolutism. In Denmark elementary schools with adequate staffs were established on the royal domains by Frederick IV as early as 1721. Although these schools collapsed because of aristocratic hostility, a similar and successful system was imposed upon the whole country after 1787 by Frederick VI. Similar developments occurred in other western states.[55] Again, community life in Western Europe was far more developed than in Eastern Europe where many villages were of recent origin and artificial. Western peasants possessed a strong orientation to the local community: they were accustomed to and encouraged cooperative endeavours. Perhaps the only eastern parallels were the collective mir and zadruga. Throughout his excellent analysis of the Bauernkrieg Franz stresses the importance of the community life of South and West Germany as compared to the more isolated peasantry of the North and East. Similarly, it has been claimed that the successful struggle of the Friesian peasants against feudal and manorial encroachments was due in no small measure to their experience of cooperative efforts such as building dikes.[56]

What generalizations, then, can be deduced from this cursory bird's-eye glance at European agricultural history-without committing too great an injustice against the complexity of the past? Two major factors, perhaps, stand out as explanations of these regional variations, which in their turn affected future developments: the penetration of the market, and the nature of urban-rural relationships. Wallerstein's emphasis upon the sixteenth century as the great watershed points to the prime mover of capitalism, for it is important to remember that the east had repeated the Western trend away from feudal labour obligations.[57] The course of historical events made Western Europe the centre of the new economy: the east would be on the periphery. Intense commercial agriculture had appeared around the market towns of Flanders in the late Middle Ages, with an emphasis upon both industrial crops such as flax, and livestock husbandry: it was this agricultural pattern that consolidated itself in England. Overall, the great social changes in much of Western Europe after the fifteenth century entailed the breakdown of the more rigid institutionalized patterns of feudal structures into more fluid relationships. In particular, relationships and attitudes towards the land revolved more and more around the "pure" marketable values of both labour and property. By contrast, decomposition was halted in Eastern Europe with the introduction of a "new feudalism".

One essential ingredient in the challenge of capitalism was the strength of cities and the urban-rural balance. The penetration of the market throughout the size range of agricultural enterprises appears to be closely related to the central belt of trade-route cities from North Italy to the Baltic outlined in Stein Rokkan's geopolitical map of Europe.[58] In other words, what counted was not only variations in the structure of the primary economy, but also the balance and nature of the integration between the rural and urban economies. Cities and towns, totally dependent upon the import of food, sought to build up the most stringent control over this most vital of commodities.[59] Especially after the beginnings of capitalism, the strong empires and states that carved out their territory to the west of the city belt saw the continued growth of a large non-agricultural population. Cities in the eastern empires remained totally ineffective: the penetration of agrarian capitalism moulded these states into granaries for the west. Urban groups in the imperial states of Prussia and Russia were as severely depressed as the peasantry, and were excluded from political influence by a rural elite that was hostile to and contemptuous of city life: moreover, ethnic groups distinct from those of the countryside figured prominently in the commercial life of the eastern towns.[60] Furthermore, urban middle class groups frequently sought rural support in their attempts to acquire political rights: agrarian society could be a crucial element in the urban middle class involvement in politics. Obviously the possibility and potential of such an urban-rural alliance were limited in Eastern Europe where cities did not exist or were very weak. With the growth of industrialization, the question of the integration of rural and urban groups became critically important in the next phases of economic and political change.[61]

5. Dimensions of variation within Europe

Perhaps we may summarize a rather diffuse discussion of agrarian structures and the ascendancy of capitalism in the countryside by pointing to four broad dimensions important in the generation of variations in the situation of agrarian populations: the concentration of landholding and the relative subservience or independence of the peasantry <u>vis-à-vis</u> the rural aristocracy; the degree of involvement of agrarian populations and their placement within a capitalist market; the strength of cities and the nature of urban-rural relationships; and the nature and strength of political centres and the success of efforts at state-building. The effect of these four dimensions upon the various regions of Europe can be summarized fairly crudely in a tabulation of their interactions (Table 1.2). Several points emerge from this regional classification. First, it emphasizes that considerable importance attaches to the belt of trade cities in Central Europe and communications networks running from the areas of the old Hanseatic League southwards to Northern Italy. The presence of these cities inhibited attempts to establish effective conquest centres. Here, peasant occupation of land and peasant liberties survived to a much greater extent than elsewhere. Moreover, the presence of the cities entailed a higher market involvement.

volatile politics of the central and eastern regions of the continent in the early twentieth century.

One further element entered the horizon of the agrarian population: the urban groups in the growing cities. In nearly every country cultivators still formed the majority of the population: as late as 1870 Britain was the only state where agriculture did not constitute the economic basis for a majority of the population. Even by 1900 agriculture remained the largest economic sector throughout most of Europe (see Table 2.1).

Table 2.1: Proportion of National Populations dependent upon Agriculture, about 1900

Country	Percentage	Country	Percentage
Bulgaria	82	Greece	46
Rumania	79	Ireland	45
Spain	72	Norway	44
Finland	71	France	43
Portugal	65	Germany	40
Austria	62	Netherlands	34
Italy	59	Switzerland	31
Sweden	55	Belgium	25
Hungary	55	Britain	12
Denmark	46		

No data: Albania, Czechoslovakia, Estonia, Iceland, Latvia, Lithuania, Luxembourg, Poland, Yugoslavia.

Note to Table 2.1: The data refer to the national territories as defined after 1918, with the exception of Germany where the figure refers to the Second Reich, and Ireland where the figure refers to the whole island before partition.

Sources: National Statistical Yearbooks (these are not listed separately here or in subsequent tables, since there are so many); D. Warriner, The Economics of Peasant Farming (London, 1964), p. 47; N. Spulber, "Changes in the Economic Structures of the Balkans 1860-1960", in Jelavich and Jelavich, The Balkans in Transition p. 367.

The further penetration of central authority and the development of education had helped the peasantry to develop political awareness and a stronger desire for political participation. Demands for suffrage extension often accompanied the growth in nationalist sentiment. Urban groups, more aware of the pressures and limited opportunities under alien rule, sought to utilize both aspirations for their own ends to such an extent that they provided the driving force and leadership of rural mobilization in the late nineteenth century and later.[33] The lack of an indigenous agrarian leadership is not altogether surprising in view of the traditional structure of rural society and its orientation. Experience in local affairs did not lead inevitably to a sense or an understanding of the nature of politics. Where they had contributed to the solution of problems, the peasantry had been concerned less with policy than with administrative details. Moreover, they mainly submitted proposals and ideas to the authorities above them - landlord, church or administrator - and expected in this way to be protected from adopting mistaken suggestions: village government was limited to parochial and often non-political affairs.[34]

To take one example, political activity in Norway remained limited for several decades after the 1814 Constitution had given the vote to freehold peasants and to those who had leased a farm for at least five years. However, few of these were involved in a money economy: the boundaries of their vision were still essentially parochial. The impact of the democratic suffrage was not felt until rising prices and crop failures fed into the first wave of mobilization in the 1830s: this, however, was a wave of protest against state taxation in general and the role of local administrators in particular, and though it resulted in the institution of communal self-government in 1837, in its epidemic and ad hoc nature it was quite similar to the peasant protests and "wars" of the past. The decisive mobilizing thrust did not come until the 1860s and 1870s. The appearance of the "Friends of the Peasant" movement in 1865 marked the beginnings of rural political organization. With a national network of provincial branches, a substantial membership, and its own press this movement was able to be both active and effective in the processes of communal and national representation. It, too, appealed most strongly to those who still stood at the margins of agrarian capitalism, especially in the south and west. It was this organization which, by gradually amalgamating with urban liberals, provided the rural wing of the Norwegian <u>Venstre</u> party. The problem of adjustment seems to have been less in one country where peasants had traditionally enjoyed political rights and participation. The persistence of peasant estate representation in Sweden eased considerably the assimilation of the better-off cultivators into the political community, as well as stimulating the early appearance of a political movement for agrarian defence, the <u>Lantmannaparti</u>.[35]

The entry of the rural masses into the political community itself brought them closer to urban society and made it easier for urban politicians to mobilize the peasantry in a struggle either for national independence or over domestic political issues. The extension of political and citizen rights to the rural masses led eventually to the equalization of individuals within a standardized system of electoral decision-making: this development was a significant aspect of the overall process of political mobilization within a state territory. Furthermore, political mobilization ensured a steady increase in the number of individuals who were linked directly to the central urban authorities.[36] However, irrespective of whether urban groups sought to mobilize the rural masses behind a political party or fraction, or behind the banner of national independence, the political and nationalist ends remained secondary for the cultivator. His attention remained firmly focused on the land. The political support of proprietors was dependent upon promises to alleviate economic conditions and guarantees of continued viability. Where a majority of peasants were landless - the case of many nationalist struggles in Central and Eastern Europe - their support was dependent upon the promise and subsequent enforcement of land redistribution.

The case of Latvia is extremely instructive. The fall of Tsarism in 1917 was the catalyst which enabled Latvian independence to become a serious possibility for the first time: previously, the maximum hope had been for a large degree of autonomy. Urban politicians took the lead in summoning deputies from the communal administrations to Riga in order to establish a parliamentary assembly. However, the new urban leaders assumed that their opposition to the Balt aristocracy and Russian officials was sufficient to secure the support of the landless Latvian peasantry. Consequently the landless classes were excluded from these discussions. The nationalists ignored peasant land-hunger and the fact that the Latvian units in the imperial Russian army were almost exclusively recruited from the peasantry. Moreover, the declaration of independence made on December 11, 1917, specifically requested German assistance in peace negotiations with Russia: the peasants saw this request as confirmation of their fears that the supremacy of the Balt Germans would be maintained. Hence, in Latvia the peasants were at first <u>opposed</u> to independence. The Latvian battalions were the only regiments of the old Tsarist army to join the Red Army with all units intact: before Latvia was overrun in 1918 by German forces, soviets had been established without Russian assistance.[37]

5. Land Reform

The redistribution of land was the most prominent agricultural outcome of the political upheavals of World War I and its aftermath. A radical expropriation of property and large estates occurred in all the successor states except Poland, Hungary and Austria: the former two had always been characterized by the highest level of aristocratic landownership in Europe. But while it is true that in these two countries the survival of large estates ensured a continued prominent political influence for the traditional rural elites, it is misleading to depict them solely in terms of large landlords and landless labourers, as is often the case in the literature. While the survival of a landed nobility is a marked contrast to the neighbouring states, small peasant farms did predominate in several regions, especially in Western Galicia and in Hungary west of the Danube. The new Austrian republic also preserved intact the remaining large estates and forests, thus disappointing many peasants who had supported republicanism in the belief that a redistribution of estates would follow.[38]

Decisions by political leaders in the successor states to

initiate land reform were not adopted simply from altruistic motives. The peasantry's commitments and aspirations had been sharpened by nationalist sentiment and, in several instances, utilized by nationalist leaders. However, land reform was probably granted less as a payment for past support. There is sufficient evidence to suggest that the driving motive was fear and anticipation of future peasant revolutions. The national elites were not disposed towards land reform because of western influence and the penetration of western culture, but rather because of traditional peasant commitments and the size of the rural population. In certain instances the possible consequence of the Russian Revolution and the plans of the short-lived Bela Kun regime in Hungary to collectivize rather than to redistribute land may have been contributory factors. However, the collectivist implications of Bolshevism were anathema to those peasant communities, such as the Rumanians, who were aware of them. Moreover, elites were beginning to realize that the retention of large estates was not the only available means of securing social and political influence: David Mitrany has said that in most of the new nations of Eastern Europe "the ruling landed classes hastened to give up the land so as to retain power".[39]

Norms were established for a desired minimum farm size, but these could be as low as five hectares, as in Bulgaria, Rumania and Yugoslavia. The result was in general the creation of a mass of owner-occupied peasant holdings, mostly too small to be economically viable.[40] In Finland, where in 1910 only 33 per cent of the agricultural population were owner-occupiers, the 1918 land reform enabled over 90,000 tenants and cottars to become landowners: in the following two decades the crofter class virtually became extinct and the number of farmers rose.[41] The fledgling Baltic states carried through stringent reforms. Latvia was transformed instantaneously into a region of small and medium-sized farms, over 90 per cent of which were owner-operated. About 65 per cent of the farms were 20 hectares or less, and only seven percent were more than 50 hectares: the latter, however, still covered about one-quarter of all arable land. Similarly, 87 percent of Estonian farms were owner-occupied: nearly all the redistributed land (86 percent) was expropriated from the Balt lords. Of 133,500 farm units, 81,000 were under 20 hectares, and only 6,500 above 50 hectares.[42] A limited land reform was proposed in Poland in 1925, but its implementation was postponed, primarily for political reasons, and never initiated before World War II. But it would not have altered radically the existing situation: 96 per cent of all farms were under 20 hectares, and only one per cent were more than 50. However, the former occupied only 47 per cent of farm land, and the latter 50 per cent.[43] The range in size of most enterprises was limited throughout Eastern Europe. Even an already egalitarian Bulgaria abolished its larger farms in 1921: 45 per cent of peasant holdings were less than four hectares.[44] Legislation was frequently passed restricting the amount of land that an individual could own: the 1919 reform law in Rumania, for example, made it illegal for one man to own more than 140 hectares of arable land, or more than 250 hectares in all.[45] The land reforms constituted a social, political and economic revolution: Mitrany asserts that they

did not merely redistribute property, they abolished the class of large landholders altogether; while protecting the peasants in their new freeholds, they set a low limit to the amount of land anyone might own in the future. The change in the division of the land also brought with it considerable changes in the use of the land, as the eastern peasants preferred a system of mixed farming for their own subsistence to raising staple crops for marketing. All that implied at the same time a political revolution: land being the chief sources of wealth and power in the eastern countries the loss of one shook the hold of the upper class on the other, and opened the way for organized peasant influence.[46]

Mitrany's conclusion about the increased political influence of the peasants may be unduly optimistic, as we shall see later. Here it will suffice to point out that although giant estates dominated perhaps only in Hungary after 1918, the political influence of vested interests survived elsewhere, even for instance in Czechoslovakia and Rumania where a substantial area of land belonged to large-scale holdings. It should also be remembered that the percentage of <u>agricultural</u> land redistributed was small everywhere: 29.7 per cent in Rumania, 14.1 per cent in Czechoslovakia, and less than 10 per cent in Yugoslavia.[47]

The most immediate point to be made about the land reforms is that they may well have created more problems than they purportedly resolved. The two major problems of these rural areas after reform were inefficient productivity and overpopulation. The new farm units were too small to be effective producers for a market. Such problems might have been overcome by resort to cooperative efforts or some form of collectivist practices. Cooperatives were established through Europe, but their effect in the more strongly peasant areas of the east was limited. Collectivist patterns were almost universally condemned. For example, the original draft of the Rumanian land reform law proposed that the redistributed land should for technical reasons be given to village communities which would administer it collectively: the proposal was opposed violently by the peasants and hence quickly dropped.[48] The situation was worsened by the peasant insistence upon mixed farming rather than concentration upon cash crops. Productivity was low because the new owners had few mechanical tools with which to ease their labours. Many did not possess the necessary draft animals, and technical assistance, advice and easy credit were far from forthcoming. Moreover, land reform led to a disintegration of the role of nuclear villages and an emphasis upon isolated farmsteads. But the new farm units were not as integrated as in the more efficient holdings in the west. The hurried nature of the reforms and the small size of the new enterprises often meant that farm buildings were separated from the land they served: indeed, many of the new farms did not originally possess any buildings. One further complication was that the formal transfer of land to full peasant ownership was sometimes delayed for several years: in Yugoslavia this interim period was as long as fifteen years.[49] In a sense, therefore, the land reforms thwarted agrarian capitalism in Eastern Europe. The masses remained at the margin of commercial agriculture, while the land that previously had belonged to the large estates, and hence used for capitalist production, had largely been transformed into small enterprises with a domestic consumptive orientation.

The second major problem was rural overpopulation. It has been estimated that in 1930 61.5 per cent of the rural population of Yugoslavia was "surplus", that is, could not be fully employed and supported on the land by existing methods of production: other figures are 53 per cent in Bulgaria, 51.4 per cent in Rumania, and 50.3 per cent in Greece.[50] The facts of economic life meant that the small farm pattern introduced by the land reforms could be sustained only by the effective operation of the safety valves of emigration to the cities and reasonable government subsidies. Neither safety valve was sufficiently adequate to mitigate the strength of the atavistic agrarian commitment to uneconomic holdings. Rural overpopulation had consequences for the whole society. Where it was greatest, the less satisfactory land reform became as a solution. It resulted in peasant underemployment, which in turn tended to affect industry and also to depress industrial wages. The best way out of the dilemma was industrialization, yet the new governments proved unable to achieve this, and the peasants did not seem to want it.[51] In any case the peasants could rarely afford to purchase manufactured products: in Poland for example, peasants constituted almost twothirds of the population after 1918, yet they accounted for only 12 per cent of the total market demand for manufactured consumer goods.[52] Because of continuing overpopulation and extremely limited industrialization, the land reforms of the early twentieth century offered a remedy for only one generation, and even then it was only a partially successful cure. One indicator of overpopulation and of the effect of the reforms is the average amount of land available to each male actively employed in agriculture. These data are reported in Table 2.2. Most of the countries where the amount of land decreased between 1900 and 1930 had carried out land reforms. Those where the amount of land per man increased are in Western Europe, and possessed higher levels of industrialization and a stronger commercial agriculture.

 Alleviation could come only from the new governments. Many peasants thought that since their insistence upon private property coincided with the view of the urban middle classes, the latter would be their natural allies. However, the urban middle classes supported land reform not simply because it was in accord with their libertarian views of justice and equality, but because it enabled them to emerge as leaders of a mass movement. Kautsky's point about an urban intelligentsia is most germane here: "they press for land reform not because of anything it will do _for_ the peasant, but because of what it will do _to_ the aristocracy. The latter is the intellectual's only powerful

Table 2.2: Hectares of Agricultural Land per active male in Agriculture, 1900 and 1930

Country	1900	1930
Albania	6.9	14.8
Austria	5.3	6.3
Belgium	3.3	3.7
Bulgaria	6.9	4.1
Czechoslovakia	4.5	5.1
Denmark	8.9	7.2
Estonia	12.5	11.0
Finland	6.2	4.8
France	6.1	7.6
Germany	5.7	6.4
Greece	10.1	8.3
Hungary	5.4	4.7
Ireland	8.1	8.9
Latvia	12.0	9.3
Lithuania	8.0	7.0
Luxemburg	5.7	6.2
Netherlands	4.1	4.1
Norway	3.8	2.9
Poland	5.9	5.0
Portugal	4.2	4.3
Rumania	5.1	4.0
Spain	7.0	7.9
Sweden	6.9	5.8
Switzerland	5.7	5.9
United Kingdom	12.6	15.0
Yugoslavia	5.1	4.3

Source: Estimated from the data in Dovring, _Land and Labor in Europe_, pp. 66-67.

domestic enemy, and land reform strikes at the very root of its economic and social position".[53] Major governmental assistance terminated with the land reforms. The prime concern was rapid industrialization as a means of achieving economic autarky. Support for agriculture was given a low priority. The favoured position of urban groups was strengthened by the proximity of the Soviet Union, the example of Bela Kun, and the fears of indigenous Communist revolution. Moreover, the peasantry was regarded as the main source of government revenue. Rather than being the recipients of government assistance, the smallholders were forced to carry a large share of the burden of national taxation. Indirect taxation was especially heavy, usually in the form of state monopolies on articles of essential consumption such as salt.[54]

We could perhaps say that the novelty of ownership, their domestic orientation, and a seemingly inexhaustible capacity for endurance of harsh conditions enabled the peasants to tolerate their lot. More practical reasons, however, buttressed their at least passive acceptance of the new status quo. In few of the successor states was there sufficient land for all those who desired it. Given the amount of land available and the priorities selected, the set minimum levels for the size of holdings were hopelessly unrealistic. In most places the result was a considerable increase in the number of submarginal holdings.[55] Even after 1918 substantial numbers of unemployed and underemployed landless labourers still remained. Their numbers were clearly most critical in the two states which carried out only very limited land reforms.[56] But the continuing pressure of the landless only intensified the conservative nature of the new proprietors. Moreover, the reforms had been portrayed as nationalist measures. The new states were confronted not only with privileged minorities who owned land, but also with large numbers of other ethnic groups who had been equally oppressed in the past. These were not so fortunate in the redistribution of land: frequently, they were dispossessed of that they did own. These moves were most prominent in mixed border areas where governments encouraged colonization by "loyalist" elements: in Eastern Poland Poles were settled among the predominantly Ukrainian and Byelorussian populations, while

Serbs were moved among the Albanians of Macedonia, and Rumanians among the Bulgars of Dobrudja.[57] Such government policies simply emphasized that land reform was pushed through for nationalist and political rather than economic reasons.

Similar reforms did not occur in the older states of Western Europe. Many were already characterized by small owner-occupiers, and by capitalist agricultural enterprises. The issue of land reform did not occur either in countries such as Belgium which were typified by substantial numbers of tenants with reasonable security of tenure.[58] Some data on farm ownership and land tenure are given in Table 2.3. Time series data on farm size are difficult in obtain, especially for Central and Eastern Europe across the boundary changes of 1918. However, data collected by Dovring indicate relatively small changes in the <u>range</u> of farm size in Western Europe after the late nineteenth century.[59] Of course, large regional differences existed in several countries. For instance, by 1900 Germany was already an industrial country, yet as late as the 1920s the large provinces of the north-east - East and West Prussia, Pomerania, Mecklenburg-Strelitz and Mecklenburg-Schwerin - all had a majority of their population in communes of less than 2,000 inhabitants, with less than 20 per cent employed in industry.[60] Nevertheless, in Western European states industrialization and urbanization operated as powerful magnets for agrarian populations. The two possible exceptions were Ireland and those Mediterranean regions of Iberia and Italy where large estates (<u>latifundia</u>) predominated.

The survival of <u>latifundia</u> ensured the survival of a powerful rural elite and of a mass of landless labourers. These regions of Iberia and Italy may have experienced the same problems as those of the successor states, but for different reasons. LaPalombara describes government policy in Italy after the victory of the Liberals in 1878 as follows:

The policy of the government as far as the South was concerned encouraged an inefficient agriculture, did not significantly benefit the southern peasant or small landowner, and served to aggrandize the <u>latifondisti</u>, or exactly that socio-economic class in the South that had long neglected the problems of economic growth and modernization.[61]

Table 2.3: Structure of Land Tenure: Number of Farms and Farm Area (in percentages)[1]

Country	Number of Farms			Farm Area		
	Owner-operated	Rented	Other[2]	Owner-operated	Rented	Other
Austria (1930)	90	10	–	93	4	3
Belgium (1930)	43	57	–	41	59	–
Bulgaria (1934)	92	8	–	90	10	–
Czechoslovakia (1930)	80	20	–	90	10	–
Denmark (1949)	97	3	– (1946)	94	6	–
Estonia (1930)				87	13	–
Finland (1950)	98	2	–	98	2	–
France (1930)	75	20	5	60	30	10
Germany (1907)				86	13	–
Greece (1929)	81	6	13 (1950)	92	5	3
Hungary (1930)				82	18	–
Ireland (1930)				98	2	–
Italy (1930)	69	16	15	67	15	18
Luxemburg (1950)	81	19	– (1961)	81	19	–
Netherlands (1930)	46	54	–	49	51	–
Norway (1960)	92	8	–	88	12	–
Portugal (1950)	73	22	5			
Rumania (Regat 1913)				60	40	–
Spain (1952)	56	31	12 (1950)	64	22	14
Sweden (1930)	80	20	–	73	27	–
Switzerland (1960)				81	19	–
England and Wales (1950)	43	57	–	38	62	–
Scotland (1950)	27	73	–	42	57	–
Northern Ireland (1950)				100	–	–

Table 2.3 (continued)

Notes: 1. Owner-operated farms were the norm in the countries for which data are not available. The number of rented farms and their area would be somewhat higher in Poland and Hungary. In several countries, especially in the Mediterranean region, the number of owner-operators is often inflated to include manager-operated estates and sharecroppers. In several Eastern European countries the statistics are often unreliable.
2. Mainly sharecropped farms.

Sources: National statistical yearbooks; Dovring, Land and Labor in Europe pp. 150-152; B.M. Russett et al World Handbook of Political and Social Indicators (New Haven, 1964), pp. 241-242; Warriner, The Economics of Peasant Farming, pp. 20, 47; Spulber, "Changes in the Economic Structures of the Balkans", p. 367.

As in the successor states, Italian governments preferred to promote industry, as well as imposing a high protective tariff on imported grain. The tariff and public works programmes encouraged owners to concentrate on grain production rather than on crops more suitable for the climate and terrain. This policy reached its peak with Mussolini's attempt to achieve economic autarky in agricultural production - the so-called "Battle of the Wheat" - which committed the South even more deeply to grain production. Similar problems existed in the Spanish regions of Estremadura and Andalusia. Land reform proved impossible because of the kind of people who owned the land. Neither the state nor local municipalities possessed land that might be provided for the peasantry without expropriation. By contrast to pre-revolutionary France or Greece, the Church was not a major landowner: it had already been dispossessed. Moreover, by contrast to the successor states, ethnic minority elites did not own land, so that the repercussions of expropriation could not be absorbed by nationalist fervour and appeals. In addition, the amount of land owned by the aristocracy had declined steadily since the mid-nineteenth century, so that it too could not produce a significant amount of land for redistribution. The major source of expropriated land would have had to be that owned by the middle classes, or precisely that group which was closely identified with the political system: land reform would have been an attack upon the political system itself. Ireland was the only state of Western Europe where a major land reform occurred. The country was, however, similar to Eastern Europe in its struggle for independence from an imperial power. The major difference was that the reforms were initiated by British governments forty years before the island succeeded in winning independence. Nevertheless, the reforms bequeathed to Ireland a pattern of unprofitable individual smallholdings with most of the characteristics described above.[62]

In some senses the reforms carried through after 1918 were no different from those that had occurred earlier. All land reforms before World War II took place in predominantly agrarian societies. However, earlier reforms in the West were frequently motivated equally for economic reasons as for political reasons. Moreover, they occurred within more complex societies in which the monarchy, aristocracy, middle classes, and later industrial workers, were all involved. Eastern Europe did not possess this complexity. With the collapse of the empires, the way was open for small groups of middle class individuals to dominate national politics and economies. The aristocracy had been destroyed, the middle class was small and relatively homogeneous, the industrial working class was negligible or non-existent, the new dynasties were imported from outside and too weak to impose authority by themselves: all these factors distinguished Eastern from Western Europe, and also laid the foundations for an urban-rural dimension of conflict different to that in the West. No reform changed significantly the economic marginality of the eastern peasant or his status in society. Compared to the radical collectivist programme of the Soviet Union, the land reforms were _per se_ conservative measures whose main effect was to buttress the traditional orientations and way of life of the peasant. Perhaps the most significant point about the post-1918 measures is that they were not supported by accompanying agricultural reforms. Land reform affects only the redistribution of property, and perhaps also of income: agricultural reform refers to improvements in farming techniques and a subsequent increase in agricultural productivity. Agricultural reform without land reform may increase economic productivity while inducing rural social and political instability. By contrast, land reform without agricultural reform may be conducive to political stability while permitting a lower degree of agricultural efficiency and productivity. Many agricultural developments before 1913 were of the former type: after 1918 the successor states generally experienced the latter. With few exceptions, the economic productivity, efficiency and wealth of their rural areas declined dramatically.

6. Commercial and Peasant Agriculture

Generally speaking, it is possible to suggest that during the early twentieth century distinctions between the north-west and west of the continent on the one hand, and the south and east on the other remained and even intensified. The west was characterized primarily by a commercial agriculture with farmer capitalist enterprises, the east more by a peasant economy and domestic consumptive enterprises, many of which were even smaller than the minimum norms set by the post-war governments.[63] There were, however, notable pockets of peasant economy in the west. In France, for example, the structure of agrarian society determined by the French Revolution had changed only slightly: sheltering behind high tariff barriers and other protectionist measures, many French peasants had few incentives either to leave the land or enter more whole-heartedly into a competitive market.[64] Similarly, some smallholding areas in the east, notably Bohemia and Moravia, were as commercially inclined and efficient as any in the west.

The basis of agricultural commerce depended upon farm organization. The three patterns of organization that can be detected throughout European history remained after 1918. The basis of commercial agriculture in Western Europe rested upon its highly intensive nature. The most successful farms were large or medium-sized: deficiencies in size were compensated by widespread participation in cooperatives. Moreover, Western Europe had come to concentrate more upon livestock production - dairy farming as in Denmark or Switzerland, or meat production as in areas of Germany and France. Livestock was also the foundation of the viable small farms in Bohemia and Moravia. By contrast, the predominant pattern in Eastern Europe was extensive cultivation in peasant farms, involving at best a meagre subsistence level: the emphasis of the eastern farmer upon mixed farming to meet the various needs of his own family only helped matters to deteriorate. To be fair, however, it should be pointed out that self-sufficiency was often expected by governments. In Latvia, for example, it was a principle of governmental agricultural policy that each farm should be economically independent: the Latvian farmer was expected to meet domestic requirements from his own enterprise not only in food, but also in materials such as leather and wool for clothing.[65]

The third type of structure was extensive cultivation in estate farms with a large landless proletariat: this pattern remained characteristic of regions of Poland, Hungary and the Mediterranean littoral. In Italy a pattern of small farms appeared in the north after the expropriation of aristocratic domains. By contrast, land was acquired in the south by the middle classes, primarily from the abolition of the landholding privileges of the Catholic Church (manomorta). Thus Italy has been characterized by a dual pattern of economic development, a capitalist structure emerging in the north alongside the retention of patrimonialism and a landless proletariat in the south. However, the southern latifundia rarely operated as commercial farms using up-to-date methods and hired labour. Since labour was plentiful and capital scarce, the owners preferred to exploit the land by renting it out in small strips on short-term contracts. Hence, the region has been characterized by hardship, uncertainty, and discontent.[66] Similarly, most of the land in Northern Spain had already been acquired by small cultivators. The nineteenth century reforms reinforced their position. But in Estremadura, Andalusia and La Mancha, the desamortizacion (the drastic transformation of property relations after 1836) did little or nothing for the vast mass of labourers. They received none of the land taken from the Church, and their dependancy upon the estate owners became even greater.[67] Probably in no instance did a "peasant mentality" completely disappear. Vestiges of the old traditional ethos could survive quite happily in a more modern world. Earlier patrimonial patterns may endure quite functionally throughout dramatic social and economic changes. Conversely, the market economy played an significant role throughout Europe. But while it has been claimed that even in egalitarian Bulgaria as much as 35 per cent of farm output was sold to the market, an anthropologist could point out that although his Bulgarian villagers traded in the local market and paid weekly visits to the neighbouring town, their contact with and exposure to the outside world effected very few changes in the social and economic behaviour of the individual and the village.[68]

7. The Decline of Agriculture

The relative importance of the agricultural sector continued to decline after 1918 in all European countries. In some instances this development provoked relatively little political tension: elsewhere it caused conflict. Strong protectionist policies were both the symbol and cause of powerful agrarian political influence, whether this be exercised on behalf of large landowners as in Prussia, or small farmers as in France. In other cases foreign competition, selfhelp through cooperative movements, and governmental policies facilitated the economic modernization of agriculture. Thus, for example, Dutch and Danish farmers fared particularly well.[69]

The pattern of political influence depended very much on the historical developments in land tenure, and also upon the relationship of agrarian and urban groups. The crucial distinctions arise perhaps from the behaviour of the urban middle classes. Three general options were available for the middle classes: each was taken up in different areas of the continent in the late nineteenth and early twentieth centuries. In Western Europe the middle classes preferred urban life, and sought a career in industry and trade. Their interest in land was economic and in many cases this assisted in the modernization and commercialization of agriculture. In Eastern Europe, the land reforms had placed severe limitations on the amount of land a single individual could own: moreover, little governmental assistance was forthcoming for modernization. Land _per se_ stopped being a base for either political influence or economic prosperity. There were also few outlets in industry and trade: in any case, these were not regarded as prestigious occupations.

The middle classes here moved into politics and the bureaucracy, and were relatively disinterested in winning support from either industrial workers or peasants.[70] The political consequence of this cleavage between bureaucracy and peasantry is a necessary theme for the later discussion on agrarian parties. The third option was to buy land for reasons of political influence and social prestige rather than for economic profit: it was exercised most by middle class groups in Southern Spain and Southern Italy. Land reform became impossible under such circumstances as it would have been an attack upon the basic prop of the socio-political system. Here the agrarian population was further alienated from urban society and the national centre.

Furthermore, no country avoided the consequences of the fluctuating world economic situation. While capitalist farmers suffered from the cyclical character of a market economy, the more rural, weakly industrialized countries of Eastern Europe suffered even more from conditions characteristic of dependent, underdeveloped economies. Long before the great depression of 1929 reached Europe, agricultural conditions were extremely poor. Economic stagnation was a general condition which persisted throughout the interwar period, frequently worsened by the autarkic policies pursued by every government. Whereas the industrial base already achieved by the more highly industrialized countries gave them a certain economic strength, this base had not been achieved by the vast majority of the successor states. In addition, despite their fewer numbers, Western farmers left the land to a greater extent than their Eastern counterparts.[71] The huge agrarian populations of Eastern Europe actively hindered a more rapid industrialization. Populist and peasantist sentiments commonly expressed by political elites in Central and Eastern Europe were not the result of a belief that these would lead to the discovery of solutions to social problems, but rather a consequence of the tremendous agricultural problem and the size of the agrarian population. As Mitrany points out:

The irony of the eastern revolution was that the break-up of the large estates into millions of peasant holdings was presided over not by Populists but by those who stood for the industrial solution .... The division of the land had at once serious consequences for the towns and their industrial plans ... it tended at first to reduce the supply of food to the towns; it also reduced the supply of labor.[72]

Neither industrialization nor an efficient prosperous agriculture were achieved. That the chances of either were slim was apparent at en early date: the period of reconstruction in the Balkans was terminated as early as 1924 with the rapid fall of world farm prices.[73] Agriculture could not solve the many problems of the successor states, but in addition either the will or the capacity - or both - to undertake rapid industrialization were also lacking. Industrialization would have meant extremely high

Table 2.4: Proportion of National Populations Dependent upon Agriculture, about 1930 and 1960, and share of GNP originating in Agriculture, 1960 (in percentages)

Country	1930	1960	GNP	Country	1930	1960	GNP
USSR	87	48	22	Italy	49	27	17
Albania	80	68	43	Sweden	39	17	
Yugoslavia	75	50	27	Norway	37	18	12
Bulgaria	75	55		France	34	21	9
Rumania	72	67	33	Czechoslovakia	33	21	14
Lithuania	70			Austria	31	20	11
Poland	61	38	25	Denmark	29	18	14
Finland	58	25	21	Switzerland	24	14	
Estonia	56			Germany	23		
Portugal	56		26	East Germany			12
Spain	55	41	26	West Germany		10	6
Latvia	55			Netherlands	23	12	10
Ireland	53	37	25	Luxemburg		11	8
Hungary	51	37	23	Belgium	19	9	7
Iceland		40		United Kingdom	8	5	4
Greece	50	48	30				

Sources: Statistical Yearbooks; Warriner, The Economics of Peasant Farming pp. 20, 47; Spulber, "Changes in the Economic Structure of the Balkans", p. 367; Jackson, Estonia, p. 191; H. Seton-Watson, Eastern Europe Between The Wars, 1918-1941 (New York, 1964), pp. 413-417; Dovring, Land and Labour in Europe, pp. 131-135; Tomasevich, Peasants, Politics and Economic Change in Yugoslavia, p. 309; L.E. Howard, Labour in Agriculture (London, 1935), pp. 42-43; Russett et al World Handbook, pp. 172-179.

protective tariffs, large foreign loans, and yet more taxes upon the peasantry, as well as perhaps furthering the expansion of the recruiting grounds of Communism.[74]

Eastern Europe remained predominantly agricultural (see Table 2.4). The new proprietors lacked technical knowledge: agricultural education was limited and poor by Western standards.[75] Equipment was conspicuous by its absence: many peasants did not even possess a plough. The cooperatives did not fill this vacuum.

Moreover, the governments and peasants tended to be rather hostile to or suspicious of commercial practices and efforts. Cheap credit was almost impossible. In short, the predominant form of agriculture moved towards subsistence farming:

The Polish peasant economy, as an economy of very small holdings, was self-sufficient in the sense that the peasant had no real surplus for the market, and therefore to raise cash his family had to go underfed. These cash earnings were really insufficient to cover his most urgent needs for the market, still less his taxes and public services.[76]

In the 1930s the culmination of the world economic crisis and even stronger overseas competition in the markets of Western Europe led to even greater depression. By the 1930s the inadequacy of the land laws to deal with problems of dividing property or consolidating fragmented holdings arising from inheritance patterns (within Slav Europe, primogeniture existed only in Bohemia) had also caused many of the small farm units to degenerate into dwarf holdings. These problems were in direct contrast to much of the Western experience.

The dramatic decline in agricultural population has continued apace, especially in Western Europe. Most outstanding is Finland where the proportion of the work force in agriculture has declined at more than one per cent <u>per annum</u> (Table 2.4).[77] Britain is no longer unique in terms of an exceptionally low number of farmers. The post-1945 period has been characterized everywhere by vast industrial expansion, a continuing urban demand for labour that came in the first instance from an agrarian reservoir, and greater agricultural productivity from a widespread use of machines which, apart from the initial investment costs, are cheaper and more efficient than manpower. It was only in the 1950s that the burgeoning and diversified economy of modern pluralist society forced a complete reassessment of the value of "peasant" farming, not only among administrators and politicians, but also among smallholders themselves. In many ways, a more traditionally-oriented peasantry had succeeded in remaining relatively immune to the impact of industrialization: their presence continued to influence the politics, economies and cultures of European societies. But after World War II the exodus to the towns continued at an ever-increasing rate. Simultaneously, industry has penetrated rural areas, and ease of transportation has turned many rural areas into commuting dormitories of the cities.[78] Increased mechanization has resulted in what might be called the industrialization of agriculture. These developments have obviously effected both the internal structure of agrarian society and rural-urban relationships. Divisions between town and country can no longer be so politically salient as before, at least not in their traditional form. In economic terms this means acceptance of the cities and the commercial market. Mechanization has made large farmers almost indistinguishable from urban entrepreneurs. Many small farmers have a foothold in both the industrial and agrarian worlds. These factors suggest that agrarian groups in Europe have been acquiring new occupational characteristics and a new status as the rural strata of industrial society.[79]

CHAPTER 3   The Agrarian Response: Mobilization, Association, Representation

The most obvious political consequence of the changing nature of agricultural society was a rising wave of agitation and peasant unrest. It is not insignificant that greater agrarian unrest tended to occur in the period when pressures arising from over-population, legal reforms, industrialization, international economic competition, and the transition to a market economy were also at their highest. Peasant agitation took one of several forms. Most common was its reflection in a rising crime rate, especially against property: for example, such crimes became almost commonplace in Ireland in the late nineteenth century as imported cattle from England reduced the area of land under tillage for the peasants' own purpose.[1] This kind of anomic, undirected protest had a long heritage and is obviously the simplest response to increasing pressures and hardships. Peasants also more and more refused to pay taxes or to continue with redemption payments. In areas of large estates the most important, widespread and politically relevant object of peasant unrest was the landlord, who was seen as the principal barrier between the peasant and landownership. Also endemic were attacks against those outsiders identified as representatives of the system believed to be the cause of peasant hardship. Merchants were particularly vulnerable with an increase in prices of products required by peasants, or when the prices offered for agricultural produce fell dramatically. For example there was violence in many English market towns in 1795; poor harvests stimulated peasant assaults in France in 1828 and 1847;

and Italian graindealers were attacked in 1898. Moneylenders were frequent targets of agrarian protests. This situation helped to plough the ground for a more intense antisemitism that later characterized the Central and Eastern European countryside.[2]

Several revolts were directed against the cities and urban groups. Encroachments upon property or property rights, accompanied by oppressive taxes, were a common cause of agrarian agitation. Alternatively, as had occurred earlier, city domination and exploitation by a high level of urban control over agriculture through the requisitioning, registration and regulation of production, marketing and consumption led to outbursts of rural grievances. The appearance of an urban working class that demanded cheap food was a further stimulus of agrarian action: the urban authorities often attempted to neutralize the political threat of the working class by appropriating agricultural production to the detriment of the cultivators.

1. Problems of Organization and Leadership

Much of this agitation remained undirected and apolitical. The majority of agrarian uprisings were qualitatively different from urban unrest. They tended to possess no clear-cut intentions, programme, organizational unity, or a conscious direction. In particular, they still tended to be local in character and grievance, and "usually spread from one locality to another by contagion rather than by advance planning".[3] While agrarian uprisings often coincided with a more widespread political revolution, as in France in 1789, Germany and Austria in 1848, and Italy in the 1860s, the peasants were fundamentally disinterested in (and sometimes hostile to) the political objectives of the other objecting groups. Serious peasant uprisings were rarely preceded or followed by urban revolutions, while the latter seldom generated a significant rural response or support. After 1789 the French revolutions of 1830, 1848 and 1871 were almost exclusively urban phenomena: agrarian participation was negligible.[4]

The amorphous nature of agrarian unrest was buttressed by the absence of any expression of a coherent political ideology. In fact, ideologies tended to be violently rejected, as was the case of many Russian peasants in the late nineteenth century when confronted by efforts of the urban intelligentsia to generate support for a form of agrarian socialism. Ideologies with rural support did appear in Sicily during the Fasci agitation of the 1890s, when peasants accepted the political views of an urban socialist leadership, and in Andalusia after 1870 where many peasants came to accept and support some of the doctrines of anarchism.[5]

The phenomenon of populism in Europe (narodnichestvo) was an agrarian socialist movement that spread from Russia and aimed at building a progressive peasant society in regions of Eastern Europe. Essentially an urban movement, it remained to a large extent peculiarly Russian: even there it evoked only a limited response from the peasantry. Narodnik influences did appear here and there in Eastern Europe. As in Russia, the "populist" movements in Croatia, Bulgaria, Serbia, Rumania and Slovenia coincided with peasant agitation caused by a decline in economic conditions. But they remained weak, and were severely repressed by the central authorities.[6] Even in Russia the narodni were interested more in thought and ideology than in organization. The various harvest strikes and attempts to form a union in Hungary in the 1890s aroused only a limited response but were broken by the authorities by police methods and the introduction of non-Magyar workers. The same fate befell the narodniks in Galicia in 1901.[7] When it occurred, peasant mobilization in Eastern Europe was stimulated by nationalist aspirations rather than by agrarian socialism: the former held a promise of land reform and individual peasant proprietorship, while the latter possessed collectivist implications. Religion, too, fed into the nationalist struggle. In the Balkans, it was religion that provided the driving force. Adherence to the Orthodox and Uniate churches symbolized the major bulwark of resistance against the Ottoman overlords, and the priests, themselves recruited from the local communities, played important leadership, recruitment and communication roles in the fight for national independence.[8]

Movements of this kind were in a sense the direct descendants of the millenarian uprisings and cathartic outbursts of the past. Chiliasm, however, could offer only a manifestation of latent agrarian opposition. In other words, it can offer a vision and a myth, but it rarely provides an organizational framework for action: myths can provide unity, but by themselves they cannot organize the masses. Peasant uprisings in the early phases of industrialization, many of which possessed chiliastic overtones, disintegrated unless adequate leadership provided them with a more institutionalized organization. The same fate befell agrarian strikes. The agrarian ability to use the strike weapon was impaired by the paradox that such strikes were simultaneously more damaging and less disruptive than industrial strikes. The latter threaten a loss of output only during the duration of the strike. An agrarian withdrawal of labour, especially at sowing and harvest times, may lead to the loss of a whole year's output. At the same time, the isolation of the local communities reduced the likelihood of a cross-regional strike contagion. For obvious reasons, this enormous latent power could very rarely be used. It was a drastic step for cultivators and labourers to take, and in any case its consequences could not be tolerated by non-agricultural groups. Generally, then, agrarian movements were at first similar to their predecessors of earlier centuries, being little more than unstable and temporary alliances of semi-autonomous units. If the immediate objectives were not attained quickly, the agrarian upsurge rapidly lost momentum.

These considerations suggest two significant points. Where the only available avenue of political protest was direct action, the likelihood of an agrarian movement retaining momentum or developing an organizational framework was limited.[9] Activity entailed movement away from the locality, a step which contradicted the fundamental commitment to survival. Hence, the extension of the suffrage was of crucial importance for the possibility of rechannelling and stabilizing agrarian political action. Problems of organization and institutionalization took on different aspects, for they now primarily entailed mobilizing cultivators into organizations that at a minimum involved only joining a particular association or going along to vote in an election. In short, political action could involve only a minimal amount of dislocation for the individual. Moreover,

non-electoral or non-associational agrarian action was more
assured of success only if it could be related to a more general
political protest, or if it could be provided with effective
leadership.

As in the past, it was the wealthier cultivators more heavily
engaged in capitalist agriculture, who tended to stand forward
as leaders. Increasingly, however, leadership came to be
assumed by urban middle class elements which sought to channel
rural unrest for their own political ends, such as national
independence. Erhard Rumpf has demonstrated quite clearly that
in Ireland prosperity was a precondition for active rural
participation in the struggle for liberation from English rule:
the involvement of the poorest regions of the country was
limited.[10] These problems existed even in Norway, despite the
long tradition of independent peasant ownership and little
indigenous nobility. Peasant discontent over tax laws imposed
by Denmark in 1762 flared up into the Stril War of 1765.
Problems of organization did not disappear even when the "peasant
estate", established in 1814, won a majority in the estates-
assembly after 1830:

(The) determined opposition to central authority was the common
denominator of the policies of the peasants on entering the
political arena; beyond that they were frequently at loggerheads
and unable to act in concert. The Norwegian peasantry was
deeply divided by region and locality; there were fundamental
differences in economic conditions and rural traditions and the
unity achieved in opposition to the common enemy proved difficult
to maintain once the officials had been forced to give in and
submit to parliamentary control. The peasants had united in the
defence of the periphery against the center, but there was as
yet no positive ideology underlying their policies. Their outlook was basically local and provincial.[11]

These points help to explain the greater occurrence of agrarian
unrest in less industrialized, less wealthy countries and in
those regions characterized by large estates, as well as their
lower probability of success.

2. The Timing of Agrarian Unrest

The pattern and timing of the sequence of agrarian uprisings varied from country to country, but generally coincided with an increasing pressure upon rural populations. In Britain, where new industrial and market pressures came first, rural unrest continued until about 1850: ironically agrarian protest began to subside at a time when Britain, by the 1846 repeal of the Corn Laws, adopted a policy which by letting industrial production pay for imported food, actively assisted the contraction of native agriculture.

The major revolt in France occurred in 1789. Nearly all agrarian risings in France were radical, in that they attacked the monarchy, aristocracy and church. In the Vendée, however, the peasant counter-revolution fought for monarch and church: the Vendée peasants were to rally to the same cause again in 1815 and 1832. Nevertheless, the immediate targets of the Vendée uprisings were the towns and the urban merchants. Much of the region had been characterized by absentee landlords, rented farms relatively large by French standards, and isolated holdings. While the penetration of capitalist agriculture was limited, the strains experienced by the French economy were nevertheless also felt in the Vendée. The anti-urban, anti-capitalist attitude of the Vendée peasants made their protests similar in many respects to those in other French provinces.[12] The major cause of peasant unrest seems to have been eliminated in 1793 when a certain amount of expropriated land was redistributed among peasants. Although later agrarian uprisings occurred in a few poor regions, such as the Auvergne in 1843, the French peasantry remained fairly quiescent after 1793. While landhunger may have spurred many French peasants into action in 1789, the sale of lands expropriated from emigré aristocrats and the Catholic Church was not the origin of peasant property: that has a much longer history. It was the middle classes and the richer peasants who gained from the confiscation of property. Attempts by the urban revolutionaries to requisition produce, to place a limit on the price of grain, and to demand redistribution of land among agricultural workers all eventually forced richer and landed peasants into violent opposition to the Revolution.[13] For the peasants the French

Revolution simply turned <u>de facto</u> occupiers into <u>de jure</u> owners. Later economic conditions helped to rigidify the structure of French agriculture which sheltered behind tariff barriers long before protectionism became a general European phenomenon.

In Germany the south and west experienced unrest in 1848: the catalysts were two consecutive bad harvests. In Southern and Eastern Europe the main wave of agitation and violence did not occur until about 1870 when already deteriorating rural conditions slumped even more dramatically. In Italy the pattern was set by the agrarian revolt of 1867 against a new milling tax: after about 1800 there was always a revolt somewhere in Italy against taxes, the low prices of grain, or the lack of land.[14] Direct action became frequent in the Cis-Leithanian provinces of Austria-Hungary.[15] Anarchism took root in Andalusia by the 1870s.[16] Christian and Muslim Bosnians rose up against the Muslim landlords in 1875 following a crop failure and greater demands upon them. In Congress Poland revolutions against Russian suzerainty began to involve the peasantry for the first time: the two great revolts of 1830 and 1863 had hardly affected the peasantry. Successive outbreaks of agrarian violence occurred in Rumania until the great and successful uprising of 1907, which started typically as a protest in Moldavia against exploitation by Jewish urban tenants who had rented farms from estate owners.[17]

The growing pressures of overpopulation, industrialization, the penetration and internationalization of the market economy all led at some time in the nineteenth century to a major wave of agrarian unrest. Landlords and urban elites were frightened into either more oppressive measures or discussing the desirability of land reform, franchise extension and similar possibilities. The major significance of these combined pressures was that they were forcing a drastic change in the traditional agrarian way of life. Improved communications, the enforcement of taxation, the multiplicity of administrative offices, the spread of the market economy all increased the contacts of the individual cultivator with and his exposure to the outside world. They also implied a greater reliance upon that world for goods which earlier either were not needed, or not known, or had been produced domestically. Hence, these agrarian outbursts, in which the peasant sought to defend his traditional commitments, interests and resist encroachment were directed not only against the local lord but also against national governments and their policies. The target of agrarian unrest may have changed, but it was still centred around the land and its possession, redistribution and cultivation: "it was not the standard of living but the illusion of independence which the possession of property gives that separated the non-revolutionary from the revolutionary peasant".[18] Economically the new surge of agrarian uprest in the nineteenth century involves - as much as the capitalist transformation of the sixteenth century - a major watershed in the agrarian way of life: politically it marks a massive peasant intrusion into national politics.

Several factors contributed to the easing of the pressures upon agrarian life: they were simultaneously political and economic. One early alleviation, especially in regions of peasant smallholdings, was the abolition of redemption payments and feudal dues. This occurred at different times in different regions, ranging from France in 1793, through West Germany, North Italy and the Low Countries soon afterwards, Austria and Eastern Germany in the 1850s, to Russia in 1906.[19] At the same time, increasing industrialization could provide an outlet for surplus rural population. However, this solution applied only where the expanding urban areas were within reasonable communications range of rural regions. Some regions in Western Europe, such as Brittany, remained overcrowded, in part because they were still isolated and too distant from industrial centres. A study of peasant rioting in Russia in 1905 discovered that its distribution was explained only when the degree of urbanization of regions and the size of agricultural enterprise were taken into consideration. In the less urbanized regions of European Russia agrarian rebellion was related to aspects of rural structure. In more urbanized areas the cities offered alternative employment and a "refuge" from the deprivations caused by an inequitable land tenure system. Similarly, provinces with smaller peasant holdings displayed a much higher propensity for revolt than those with larger peasant farms.[20]

The consolidation of state territories made political

boundaries more impervious to mobility: this had serious
consequences for the future in those Central and Eastern regions
where the boundaries were later redrawn in 1918. For example,
in the area that was to become Czechoslovakia, Bohemia and
Moravia, ruled from Vienna, had a declining rural population
from the late nineteenth century, while neighbouring Slovakia,
ruled from Budapest, had severe overpopulation: there,
government pressures and what was virtually an international
boundary between it and the Czech provinces prevented the
surplus population being absorbed by the expanding Czech
industries.[21] Rural overpopulation remained especially severe
in the less industrialized regions of Southern and Eastern
Europe where the traditional social structure survived after its
legal buttressing had gone. Crops such as grain still tended to
dominate both production and diet: a largely consumption-
determined output limited market expansion by producing
relatively low surpluses and small amounts of money. The
problems were compounded by poor and unsystematic book-keeping
and by low levels of professionalization. Education was clearly
important in any developments leading towards agricultural
reform. Submersion in a capitalist economy benefited primarily
those cultivators who owned their own property - or had both
security of tenure and freedom of action - and operated
reasonably large holdings. In Eastern Europe the lowest level
of rural depopulation was in Hungary, which had the least amount
of land reform and the greatest proportionate number of landless
labourers: the greatest depopulation was in Bulgaria which had
the most egalitarian social and farm structure.[22]

3. The Political Response: Mobilization and Representation
Political activity in the form of organizational efforts and
economic demands upon central governments was more noticeable in
Western Europe. In any one region, moreover, it was dominated
by those cultivators who were more directly involved in the
capitalist market and who were aware of their predicament.
Attitudes towards the state underwent a marked change with a
change in the societal base from agriculture to industry,
demands for suffrage extension, and the continued build-up in

state activities. The state apparatus may still have been disliked or even feared but it also came to be regarded as an institution that farmers themselves could and ought to use to their own advantage.[23]

Nor surprisingly, political mobilization began among the large landowners. But by the late nineteenth century it had spread in Western Europe to the bulk of enterprise operators. In the east and south agrarian political mobilization had not advanced much beyond the confines of the large landlords and entrepreneurial managers. Here and there, attempts were made to unionize agricultural labourers and to use the weapon of the agricultural strike: these usually petered out because of the almost insurmountable obstacles involved, not least of which was the reluctance of farm labourers to join unions.[24] Overall, however, pressure for government assistance and for protection against imports through creating or raising tariffs was almost invariably instituted by the larger landlords or richer farmers, often in alliance with urban middle class elements. The classic example is Germany, where it was the Prussian Junker class who led the rural agitation for tariff reform. While the three-class electoral system in Prussia guaranteed the supremacy of the Gutsbesitzer east of the Elbe, the small cultivators of the Western Prussian provinces and other German states were reluctant openly to support a political organization, the Conservative Party, that was closely linked with the Prussian aristocracy. However, the depression produced problems common to both large and small cultivators, and facilitated a rapprochement between the two. Junkers took the lead in founding in 1893 the Bund der Landwirte, a political party which would hopefully mobilize the independent peasantry behind a set of demands similar to their own. The strength of the Bund was concentrated in the smallholding regions of Southern and Western Germany, where an aggressive posture brought rapid success, as well as east of the Elbe. By 1894 it had acquired 201,756 members: by 1914 membership had increased to 330,000 with only a slight majority residing west of the Elbe. The adoption of protection in Germany in fact slowed down the pace of agricultural contraction and prevented financial disaster, but it also froze the structure of German agriculture in a not entirely efficient mould, a fact which became apparent during World War I.[25]

Agitation for tariff reform followed similar lines in Sweden, where the protectionist debate stimulated political mobilization to a much higher degree than hitherto.[26] Political mobilization in Scandinavia was characterized by powerful urban-rural alliances until the early twentieth century: in their first phase these alliances tended to be radical oppositions to the general political policies and influence of the central bureaucracies and urban elites. By contrast, a number of conservative-oriented peasant organizations appeared in regions of consolidated small enterprises involved in commercial production - Hesse, Westphalia, and other areas of Western Germany, Belgium and the Netherlands. They were radical only where governments failed to accept their request for agrarian defence. In Italy the idea of protection received little support as long as the effect of foreign competition was limited. When tariffs were eventually introduced, they served more to hinder than to assist industrial and agricultural development, foreshadowing problems endemic to Eastern Europe several decades later.[27]

Significant legal and social barriers handicapped the election of peasants to assemblies or their appointment to official posts. A tradition of subservience, ignorance, the daily demands of their holdings, and a fear of reprisal, all had fed into a syndrome of withdrawal. Moreover, legal measures and illegal pressures were often employed even where enfranchisement had occurred. For example, the operation of the three-class electoral system in Prussia between 1849 and 1918 ensured that the political influence of the agrarian masses would be significantly less than that of the richer property owners and the <u>Gutsbesitzer</u>.[28] Electoral corruption and intimidation were widespread throughout rural Europe. In Bulgaria, for example, the mass of peasant landholders were frequently dissuaded under duress from voting by administrative officials. One estimate claims that during the regime of Stefan Stambolov (1887-1894) only 5 per cent of the electorate voted: intimidation, not lack of interest, was the major cause of the low turnout.[29]

Peasant candidates and representatives were most prominent in two distinct kinds of situation. They appeared when relations between the peasant and the local lord or state administration deteriorated so rapidly that there arose a spontaneous and almost unanimous demand for reform. Peasant participation in the 1848 rebellions in Austria and Prussia resulted in the return of peasants to the constitutional assemblies which then embarked upon an attempt to destroy the vestiges of manorial control and to replace it by a more equitable distribution of manorial lands. Similarly, Danish farmowners and large leaseholders occupied one-third of the seats in the new constituent assembly established after the unrest and reforms of 1848.[30] Russian peasants reacted the same way in 1905. Even in Britain, where the smallholding population was minute, the deterioration of conditions in the Scottish Highlands resulted in the 1880s in the establishment of a Crofters' Party which subsequently won almost every constituency in the region.[31] A major characteristic of this scenario was the subsequent decline in peasant representation after the initial burst of enthusiasm and a return to "normality": unless organizations were established on a durable basis, peasant interest in such activity tended to wane markedly.

A second and related background for peasant representation came from the establishment by governments of a curial system of voting and representation. The peasant estate, however, was limited in influence and not all representatives were themselves peasants. If, as in Austria after 1848, conflicts between peasantry and rural elite were resolved, then peasant interest in the curia declined. On the other hand, if issues between the curia remained unresolved, as in Russia after 1905, the peasants continued to be politicized. The use of the limited freedom granted under this type of franchise arrangement was, however, frequently accompanied by direct action and spontaneous revolt. In retrospect, the Swedish experience seems to have been unique. In Sweden the peasant estate had a pedigree of at least some success: at any rate, peasant politics were for long not based on popular upsurges, and instances of non-parliamentary discontent were rare.

By the closing decades of the nineteenth century peasant representation in assemblies was on the increase, both under the

auspices of these two scenarios and because of the growing
stimulus of capitalist competition. But there was a difference:
a new kind of representative had entered the lists. He was more
strongly oriented towards entrepreneurship, more interested in
the organization of agrarian associations and cooperatives, and
sought the parliamentary promotion of agricultural interests
through either specific agrarian parties or alliances with urban
groups. Nevertheless, the political organization of the rural
masses was both limited and slow. The barriers which mitigated
against exerting a political influence commensurate with their
size also operated against any meaningful increase in the numbers
of cultivators who sat in legislatures or occupied government
positions. Once again, France provides an excellent case study.
Weber pinpoints the politicization of the peasantry as one of
the major catalysts of change after 1870: the old localized
territorial politics were replaced by nation-wide alignments.
Peasant virtues were indeed extolled in the Third French
Republic: around 1900 just over 40 per cent of the population of
the so-called "Peasants' Republic" depended upon agriculture for
their livelihood. Yet in the fifth session of the Chamber of
Deputies (1889-1892) only ten of the 578 deputies were
agricultural cultivators by occupation. The agricultural lobby,
broadly defined, constituted a majority in the legislature in
the early Third Republic, yet while the notion of the peasant as
the backbone of the nation rapidly became an enduring cliché,
practising peasants and farmers were absent from the national
political stage before 1914, and scarcely present at the
regional level.[32] Peasant involvement in central affairs
remained at an even lower level in the agricultural east, even
where political reforms had taken place. As late as 1923 almost
80 per cent of the Polish population was dependent upon
agriculture, yet individuals who before accepting a government
position were employed in agriculture occupied only 1,225 of the
120,705 higher official posts in the central administration.[33]

4. The Economic Response: the Cooperative Movement
The major economic response was in many areas a massive
acceptance of the challenge of the laws of supply and demand.

More and more people began to buy land, for which they would often go into debt. Cooperative organizations appeared to assist the individual in all aspects of his economic cycle from offering credit to providing improved marketing services and outlets. In many parts of Western Europe the value of land dropped considerably during the immediate aftermath of the crisis of the 1880s: for some the importance of buying and selling land also declined. Renting became regarded as more profitable and respectable, since then the cultivator might be able to release more ready capital for other purposes. Furthermore, with the value or productivity of land rising where it is regarded as an article of commerce, the owner of land can be provided with a steady and comfortable income from his tenants without having to be concerned about the economics of production and management. There was also an improvement of farming methods, a general change from grain to livestock production, and a continuing specialization in a single agricultural product.[34] Denmark's switch to intensive dairy farming is perhaps the best example of the transition to new forms of agriculture. It has even been claimed that through this revolution agriculture became the major catalyst of Danish economic expansion: certainly, from the 1880s agriculture was the major source of foreign currency at the same time as the country became a net importer of grain.[35] But similar developments occurred in many regions of Western Europe. In France the wine industry was rescued from economic stagnation by policies of self-help and marketing developments.[36] After 1900 capital gained from the utilization of its extensive timber areas enabled Finnish agriculture to modernize and escape from its only recently established dependence upon grain production.[37] By and large, these economic trends did not greatly affect those rural regions in the east and along the Mediterranean which still suffered from overpopulation, limited industrialization, large landowners and masses of landless or unemployed labourers: here the first major response was agrarian unrest in the traditional manner. Only where commercial production had penetrated and enriched a number of the peasantry was there any movement for political reform by organized groups.[38]

It should not be surprising that psychological, cultural and economic differences among agrarian population and differing relationships with urban groups stimulated distinctive political reactions. The most appropriate terminology would seem to be that of Almond and Verba.[39] The peasant societies of Eastern Europe retained primarily a <u>parochial</u> culture, while a <u>participant</u> culture became more prominent among commercial cash-crop and livestock farmers. The key was organization. While political and cooperative peasant movements proliferated in Eastern Europe, perhaps to an even greater degree than in the west, peasant involvement was more limited. In one sense peasant political behaviour in Eastern Europe remained unchanged from the past. Voting participation did not bridge the gap between apathetic non-involvement and massive unrest. By contrast, commercially-oriented farmers were active in creating and participating in political and economic organization to defend their interests. The strength and vitality of agrarian organization distinguishes Western from Eastern Europe. Voting behaviour and political organization are the subjects of more detailed treatment in subsequent chapters. Here we may look briefly at the largely uncharted field of agrarian economic organization.

Working within a market economy confronted cultivators with problems beyond their control. Commercialization, no matter how limited its penetration of agrarian society, made the cultivator aware of his weak position <u>vis-à-vis</u> the buyers of his produce, the sellers of his utensils and equipment, and the bankers and moneylenders who provided him with credit. While political mobilization through the ballot box and political party membership might have provided a means of strengthening the position of agrarian society, the concept of organization appeared to be more relevant and necessary within this economic context rather than in the political one. There emerged a concern for developing agrarian cooperative organizations that could pool the resources of individual farm units in such fields as marketing and capital investment.

Cooperative efforts in agriculture have a lengthy history. Apart from such formalized structures as the <u>mir</u> and <u>zadruga</u>, there were, for example, various kinds of cooperative associations in Germany and the Netherlands which collaborated on drainage problems and projects. Similarly, several cooperative associations in Southern Europe dealt with irrigation problems. But these were all based upon the local community. Something new was required as the latter disintegrated under the twin impact of agrarian capitalism and bureaucratic standardization. Organized credit institutions were late in appearing: the characteristic relationship was an individual one between borrower and moneylender. But, for instance, from the late eighteenth century the owners of manorial estates (<u>Rittergüter</u>) in Germany were able to obtain from a credit institution letters of credit backed by the corporate liability of provincial and knightly associations. While the modern cooperative institution with a formal organization appeared only in the late nineteenth century as a response to the culminating political and economic problems that confronted the farmer, it was not until the twentieth century that the cooperative movement became truly established and important.[40]

The first agricultural cooperatives were established in Germany as savings and lending banks for their members. After 1846 the <u>Raiffeisen</u> banks were founded as a response to the current agricultural crisis: they employed a network of cooperative associations in order to achieve easier credit for a system of rural cooperatives. Indeed, such savings and loan organizations proved to be the most popular form of agrarian cooperation. The needs of the small cultivator were too trivial for the banks. Moreover, peasants were usually unable to offer the banks satisfactory collateral. Smallholders more often relied upon private moneylenders who charged high rates of interest, especially just before the harvest, when the peasants' economic resources were exhausted and their need of credit greatest. Clearly, peasants were reluctant to use loans carrying such a high interest burden for anything but immediate necessities. Hence, they were more disposed in the first instance to accept credit cooperatives.

Cooperatives began to mushroom with the entry of agrarian society into national political and monetary systems. The private and communal savings banks established in Scandinavia after 1850 were slowly transformed into credit institutions.

Purchasing cooperatives began to emerge after about 1870. The first cooperative in France was established in 1881 to buy fertilizers for its members.[41] The first Italian cooperatives were formed in the peasant region of Emilia between 1882 and 1886.[42] In the previous decade cooperatives had been formed in Denmark to buy cream separators, the invention of which had revolutionarized dairy farming. These associations were formed by both large and small farmers. A national farmers' union was established from regional federations in 1892, and a federation of smallholders in 1910, although the former rapidly acquired a dominant position in the cooperative movement.[43] However, cooperatives had a firm foothold in only a few countries by the close of the century. From Germany they spread through the Hapsburg domain, with village credit cooperatives first appearing in Austria in the 1890s, to the Balkans. Developments tended to be slower in Britain, although in Ireland Sir Horace Plunkett, a Protestant landowner from Meath, began a campaign for cooperatives in 1889. His promotion of the Irish Agricultural Organization in 1893 to set up dairy cooperatives and banks was at first resisted by the farmers themselves: by 1900, however, this resistance had been overcome and about 800 cooperatives were in existence.[44] In Belgium the first cooperatives appeared under the sponsorship of the Catholic Church and its Boerenbond. In Finland cooperatives did not become firmly established until the twentieth century.[45] Similarly, their growth in Southern Europe was slow and sporadic. Their greatest success was in Denmark where the movement attained a dominant position by the 1890s.

These associations grew fairly rapidly in the twentieth century.[46] Cooperatives tended to remain a peculiarly rural phenomenon. In Denmark cooperative associations began to appeal to urban elements only in the 1920s. By 1920 no less than 81 per cent of all cooperatives in Germany were agricultural organizations. However, the strength of agricultural cooperative cannot be measured simply by their numbers. For example, the large number of cooperatives in Germany (Dovring reports over 12,000 by 1900) emphasizes the local character of most associations: they were originally little more than a new form of sharing local resources. Moreover, they frequently were established to assist a particular kind of farming. In addition, only a minority of peasants usually joined such associations: the small size of most of them becomes immediately apparent. For example, about 90 per cent of the French peasantry did not belong to cooperatives. Wright has argued that

> if agrarian syndicalism before 1914 was useful to the peasants (who got cheaper fertilizer and some protection against the hazards of nature) and to the politicians (who got some dependable voting support), it did nothing to help the peasants influence political decision making, develop a sense of professional solidarity, or solve the fundamental economic and social problems of rural France. A few peasants gained some rudimentary experience in administering a cooperative or a mutual-aid society; but in the main, these managerial functions were left to the large landowners or to towndwellers initiated into the mysteries of book-keeping .... Right and Left alike favored undifferentiated organizations uniting all elements of the rural population, and both proclaimed the unchallengeable virtues of small ownership.[47]

Overall, the success of cooperatives was most complete in Western Europe, with Germany, the Netherlands and Scandinavia being most successful in enlisting their potential membership.

Quite apart from the difficulties of organizing isolated families and communities, and the problem of finding efficient administrators, cooperatives presented in some ways yet another challenge to the peasant, demanding that he subsume his individual enterprise within collective action and majority decisions. This is why in the early cooperative period many peasants preferred to join only credit associations, which existed to finance the cultivator as an individual. The fragmentary data collected by Dovring show that credit cooperatives remained more popular in the east, while marketing cooperatives became much stronger in the west. France is perhaps typical in that the strongest sponsorshop of cooperatives came from large landowners and richer peasants. Admittedly, they were also inspired by social Catholicism and the desire to insulate the peasantry from republicanism. Paternalism had been the hallmark of the first aristocratic-directed association, the Société des Agriculteurs de France, founded in 1868. But by the mid-1880s there were both republican and anti-republican cooperatives and syndicates - all, however, dominated either by large landowners or townspeople. The <u>Confédération Nationale des Associations Agricoles</u> of 1919 was the first serious attempt to achieve organized peasant unity, but its success remained very limited: the mutual hostility of the rival components made it difficult for them to make an effective national impact for several decades. Instead, organizational efforts were channelled into associations established to defend the interests of a specific kind of farming.[48]

Similarly, cultivators were reluctant to become members of organizations based in the cities. Industrial trade unions and union federations found it extremely difficult to recruit agrarian members. For example, even though the French Socialist Party early abandoned Marxist orthodoxy to champion small ownership, by 1936 the <u>Confédération Générale du Travail</u> could claim only 180,000 peasant members.[49] In Eastern Europe levels of industrialization were so low that unions were too weak to exert any significant political influence and so perhaps attract a rural following. In any case, many unions were completely disinterested in rural recruitment: outside the industrial working class there was only the petty bourgeoisie. Unions enjoyed significant agrarian support perhaps only in Northern Italy and Southern Spain.

The role of cooperatives has hardly been explored in the literature. We must, however, make a distinction between economic and political roles. Generally, the economic role of cooperatives was more important and their impact more considerable in countries and regions where farmers were more or less fully integrated into a money economy. The most prominent example is Denmark and its dairy cooperatives. While cooperative federations in many Western countries were allied or associated with specific political parties, their degree of autonomy was considerable. Moreover, cooperatives were active in all aspects of farming from giving credit to providing efficient marketing facilities. By contrast, the economic role of cooperatives in the new states of Central and Eastern Europe was generally limited. With the exception of Czechoslovakia, and perhaps also Bulgaria, where they did play a decisive role in both economic and political life, the cooperatives were backward and unable to alleviate agrarian conditions significantly: in fact, they frequently depended upon the state for funds.[50] They more often attempted to be all-purpose organizations, unlike the highly specialized structures geared to one particular economic activity which predominated in most areas of Western Europe.[51] In the east their major significance was more often political. In several instances cooperatives were directly or indirectly controlled by the state: in Rumania they even had to assume the role of tax collectors.[52] Overall, it was a relationship between the strong and the weak. Cooperatives were utilized by governments and were often seen by the peasants as instruments of central control rather than as associations working for the betterment of agrarian conditions. Frequently, the peasants found that their associations had acquired an urban leadership and were being used to further urban interests a paradoxical development that further contributed to urban-rural tensions.[53]

Furthermore, the formation and direction of agrarian cooperatives in Eastern Europe were nearly everywhere assumed by political parties: these in turn reflected significant social cleavages. Thus there were 37 cooperative federations in Yugoslavia, all associated with or controlled by political parties and all reflecting the salient linguistic, ethnic and religious cleavages in the new state.[54] Similar ethnic and religious federations appeared in Poland. Where religious cleavages were important, cooperatives were often managed by clerics and used to protect the position of the Church. In Slovenia the largest cooperative was controlled by the Slovene Populist Party: both organizations were directed by Catholic priests.[55] The Ukrainian cooperatives in Poland were associated with Ukrainian political parties and managed by Uniate priests.[56] In other words, cooperatives were treated primarily as adjuncts of political organization. While they may have indirectly gained economic benefits for their members, the <u>raison d'être</u> of cooperatives in Eastern Europe was more often to further the political interests of groups who frequently were disinterested in the betterment of rural living conditions and the creation of an efficient and economic agriculture.

5. Dimensions of Variation

This survey of European agriculture has ranged widely and rather superficially over a great number of themes. To detect some kind of pattern has perhaps led to the sacrifice of strict chronological veracity. But the pattern does exist. We may summarize its general thrust by saying first that before the consolidation of capitalism the stability of local communities had depended upon a kind of symbiotic relationship between peasantry and elites, whereby the latter received the benefit of peasant surpluses while leaving the peasantry a minimal security. The ways in which peasants sought to increase their security only partially included the maximization of profit. The political involvement of agrarian groups was essentially sporadic, unorganized, and localized in its extent. This social pattern was abruptly ended by the advent of the world economy and, later, extensive industrialization. The capitalist and industrial revolutions affected all countries, even those which still possessed a traditionally oriented society and a pre-industrial economic base. The repercussions of capitalism or industrialization did not respect national boundaries. With great improvements in transportation and communication, the market penetrated to a greater or lesser extent all geographical corners of the continent. Simultaneously, the filtering screens between local and national society were further weakened by the penetrative activities of national bureaucracies and their more effective regularization of life according to nationally standardized patterns and proscriptions.

The net effect of these developments was that individuals were cut loose from their customary relationships: the traditional social matrix could no longer survive unchanged, if indeed it could survive at all. Increasingly, agriculture became commercialized. The maximization of returns and the minimization of expenditure became of much greater importance.[57] Yet the victory of the market over the basic agrarian problem of subsistence depended upon land and labour being regarded as economic commodities which could lead to greater economic wealth. In turn, this depended upon the destruction or transformation of the existing social and cultural institutions and the establishment of new forms of organization and behavioural patterns.

The significance of the Industrial Revolution is that it was the period in which this transformation proceeded most rapidly and most extensively. Increasing and different forms of economic and political pressures enmeshed agrarian populations in national economic and political systems. From the 1870s onwards Europe could be divided perhaps as never before into advanced and underdeveloped agricultural regions. But both farmer and peasant, high-cost or low-cost farming, suffered to a degree previously unprecedented from the recurring gluts and fierce international competition that marked the establishment of a world economic market for primary products. The net result of these several cumulative pressures was that for the first time the agrarian masses appeared as a permanent political factor with latent possibilities for organization and political influence at the national level: political mobilization, according to Nettl, "is primarily a forced process of familiarization with politics".[58]

However, while the contagious effect of technological advances spread throughout the whole continent, industrialization in Europe did not mean the abolition of a peasant way of life or the destruction of peasant characteristics; nor, where they occurred, did comprehensive land reform or government regulations. While this was more clearly the case in countries which still possessed only low levels of industrialization, it was to some extent true everywhere: commercial and domestic subsistence agriculture are not exclusive dichotomies. Indeed, in a sense, political, social and economic change since the late nineteenth century transpired to preserve in part the primary characteristics of a domestic subsistence economy. The granting of the franchise enabled peasants to mobilize in defence of agrarian interests. Tariff protection led to a concern for autarkic national economies and helped to shield cultivators from some of the worst effects of the impersonal laws of supply and demand implicit in a commercial and market economy. The upsurge in nationalist sentiments and the resultant creation in Central and Eastern Europe of successor states out of the debris of the Hapsburg, Hohenzollern, Ottoman and Romanov empires brought wide-ranging land reform. In several instances the consequence was the consolidation of a large mass of subsistence level peasant smallholders.

This historical survey of economic developments in European agriculture and their affect upon agrarian political behaviour has been a story of how a kind of inner unity which existed at the beginnings of this historical period fell apart under the impact of different cultural, economic and political events and trends. The major conclusion to be drawn from this analysis is that the structure and situation of European agriculture in the twentieth century were determined by a particular combination of political events, cultural climate, and economic trends in each region. In turn, these presented each area of the continent with a particular set of economic problems, as well as influencing the style of political behaviour. Subsequent developments in the twentieth century have not had a similar crucial effect upon agrarian economic and political behaviour (if we except the collectivization of farms in most of Eastern Europe under the post-1945 Communist regimes).

Chapter 1 suggested that on the eve of the Industrial Revolution four major influences or constraints had shaped the variations in the structure of farming throughout the continent: the nature and strength of central political and bureaucratic penetration, the strength and proximity of cities, the structure of landholding, and the degree of involvement in a commercial market beyond that of the immediate village. The following two chapters have traced the later influences of and changes in the nature of these constraints in the nineteenth and early twentieth centuries. The discussion also combined the crucial questions of who is occupying the land and the size of holdings with the role of the urban middle classes and their relationship to the land. In this way the various issues such as protection and land reform which have agitated agrarian societies, as well as their resolution or otherwise, can be more easily understood. A rudimentary classification would place the majority of European countries and regions in one of three categories: owner-operated market farming and a commercial and industrial middle class; manorial systems and a landowning middle class: owner-operated subsistence farming and a bureaucratic middle class. In the period of mass politics the intensity of the urban-rural gap, the economic nature of farming, the density of the agrarian population, the economic situation and strength of urban groups, land tenure systems and fragmentation, the utilization of cooperatives and agricultural associations all served to continue these intra-European distinctions. We can now turn to how they affected agrarian political participation and involvement in twentieth century Europe.

CHAPTER 4 Agrarian Political Participation

The level of participation in politics by individuals and social groups is variable. Even in a political system where the social and legal thresholds barring the political mobilization of the masses have been overcome, only the political elites are deeply involved in political activity on a continuous basis. The participation of the average individual remains only partial and sporadic. In an intensive study of political participation Lester Millbrath proposed a scale of political involvement in order to identify different degrees of participation. This scale runs from such spectator activities as trying to influence someone's vote to working actively for a party organization or attempting to seek political office.[1] The levels of political participation suggested by Milbrath are clearly applicable only to stable and structured political systems where competition is waged primarily or exclusively in the electoral arena. They do not take into consideration such forms of direct action as demonstrations, riots, or revolution. Direct action has historically been the most common form of agrarian political activity. The extension of the suffrage to the agrarian masses presented them with an alternative channel of political expression. Logically, of course, the two channels of direct and formalized activity are complementary, not exclusive. Franchise extension simply meant a lengthening of the continuum of options available to cultivators. The remaining chapters take up the theme of the use made of the new field of electoral and party politics. First, however, we shall concentrate upon agrarian electoral _participation_, that is upon the _degree_ to which cultivators utilized this alternative channel.

A comprehensive analysis of the level and degree of participation would include influence upon and penetration of national and local leaderships, the degree of activity within political organizations, and the patterns of informal network and opinion leadership within small, localized groups. A systematic analysis of European agriculture along these lines would be a fascinating field of study. However, it lies beyond the more limited parameters of this analysis which more modestly is concerned only with the question of voting and non-voting. We shall also concentrate upon the late nineteenth and early twentieth centuries. As these decades were the period of the major transition towards participant politics in Europe, it may intuitively be assumed that turnout variations were more likely to be greater than in the post-1945 period when electoral mobilization had more closely reached saturation point.

1. Turnout: A Rural Lag?

The historic isolation and "peculiar" economic activities of agrarian populations have provided the basis for several interrelated hypotheses about the level of turnout in rural as compared to urban regions. It was Marx's thesis, for example, that the isolation and dispersion of farmers prevented them from acquiring a political class consciousness similar to that of urban workers: he saw an agrarian mass formed "by simple addition of homologous magnitudes much as potatoes in a sack form a sackful of potatoes".[2] However, in the past century improved educational, transport and communications facilities have overcome to a great extent the geographical barriers impeding cooperation and organization in rural areas. The previous discussion on the emergence of agricultural cooperatives emphasized the potential importance and political influence of these organizations. We might, indeed, hypothesize from the European experience that political activity is highly correlated with market involvement and the pressures of capitalism. Industrialization and urbanization, it might be said, are epiphenomena of the expansion and intensification of capitalist practices. In this way it perhaps becomes easier to avoid the simple juxtapositions of urban-rural and agriculture-industry and to understand the continued momentum of the thesis that urbanization and industrialization entail higher levels of political participation.

Two important studies published in the interwar period suggested that within any one country electoral turnout was higher in the towns than in the countryside, and/or that countries with a predominantly agrarian population will possess lower levels of electoral participation than those with a strong industrial base.[3] In more recent years these themes have continued to be emphasized by political scientists and sociologists.[4] A more sophisticated approach is that of Stein Rokkan, who has recast the hypothesis in developmental terms. His concept of a <u>rural lag</u> in mobilization, based upon an intensive study of Norwegian developments, is built upon a time series of data illuminating the social and geographic nationalization of the political system: changes in the formal criteria determining who are permitted to participate, the mobilization of the newly enfranchised in electoral competitions, their entry into direct political participation, and the penetration of national political parties into all geographical areas of a country and into local and municipal electoral contests.[5]

On a cross-national level, however, the picture is somewhat confusing. In his work on urbanization, for example, Thompson's thesis that urbanization is correlated with higher turnout is not supported entirely by the data he employs. Urban turnout in Spain was higher than rural turnout, but the opposite was true of Italy in 1919, and also of Britain, while the data on Germany and France show negligible urban-rural differences.[6] We shall first attempt to clarify the picture with a country by country survey of electoral turnout. Survey data, of course, is almost totally non-existent for the period that interests us. Therefore the discussion must be based upon the statistics contained in official publications. The value of these is limited for only rarely do they include occupation as a category: we cannot, therefore, easily determine the turnout rate of cultivators. In general then, our discussion must be built upon the participation rates of urban and rural areas. Because it has been widely accepted that rural women have been exceptionally immune to regularized forms of participation, sex has been included as a variable in the analysis.

Table 4.1: Urban and Rural Turnout in Norway (in percentages)

Election	Urban Turnout	Rural Turnout	Urban-Rural Difference
1897	77.7	67.8	+9.9
1900	62.8	51.6	+11.2
1903	64.7	48.7	+16.0
1906	70.7	58.7	+12.0
1909	72.9	59.0	+13.9
1912	72.8	61.1	+11.7
1915	69.4	54.9	+14.5
1918	71.3	54.9	+16.4
1921	76.9	64.0	+12.9
1924	80.1	65.4	+14.7
1927	76.9	64.3	+12.6
1930	81.6	75.7	+5.9
1933	81.8	73.9	+7.9
1936	87.5	82.4	+5.1

Source: Adapted from Rokkan and Valen, "The Mobilization of the Periphy", Table 1.1.

The most detailed studies have been done in Scandinavia, where a wealth of data is easily available from official sources. Electoral participation in Norway was consistently higher in the towns than in the countryside (Table 4.1). The limited enfranchisement of women in 1907 (with universal suffrage in 1913) did not radically affect the urban-rural difference in turnout. Turnout levels were very low until 1894 when political mobilization increased dramatically with growing economic problems and the prospects of a struggle for independence from Sweden. But the decisive rural breakthrough did not occur until 1930. After 1945 the urban-rural difference in turnout has stabilized around the margins that first appeared in the 1930s. Ecological analyses also emphasize the persistence of these differences: turnout is consistently higher in industrial and suburban communes. Similar urban-rural differentials have been characteristic of Norwegian local elections and of the two advisory referenda of 1919 and 1926 on the question of the prohibition of alcohol.[7] In a country like Norway where topography is such an important constraint upon organization and communication, the distance that the voters had to travel to the polling booth could become a significant factor hindering high rural turnout.

Table 4.2: Urban and Rural Turnout in Sweden: Selected Elections

Election	Men			Women		
	Urban	Rural	Difference	Urban	Rural	Difference
1866	40.5	15/16	+24.5/+25.5			
1881	45.2	19.5	+25.7			
1887 I	62.9	48.1	+14.8			
1908	70.0	57.4	+12.6			
1911	63.0	55.5	+7.5			
1921	62.2	61.9	+0.3	50.5	45.5	+5.0
1932	74.0	72.7	+1.3	65.6	60.6	+5.0

Source: Rokkan "Electoral Mobilization", p. 261.

Similar trends have been apparent in Sweden (Table 4.2). The urban-rural differential decreased markedly with the major suffrage extensions of 1909 (manhood suffrage) and 1921 (universal suffrage). A further upsurge in rural turnout after 1932 was due to a successful mobilization of rural workers. Urban-rural differences were more noticeable among women. Urban turnout was higher than rural turnout in local elections and referenda.[8] The Danish pattern is less clear. In general, turnout declined with increased distance from Copenhagen, with the lowest returns found in the agricultural districts of

Northern Jutland. Högh has further suggested that turnout decreased with geographical distance from the polling station, and increased with the possession of economic resources. However, urban turnout as a whole was only marginally higher than rural turnout, and on several occasions the turnout in Copenhagen was as low as or even slightly lower than in rural Denmark.[9] Reykjavik has been the only proper urban community in Iceland: turnout there was usually substantially more than ten percent above the national figure.[10] By contrast, no clear pattern emerges in Finland. The sudden and drastic reforms conceded by Russia in 1906 permitted a rapid mobilization of both urban and rural populations. Since 1907 turnout in Finland has remained at a very high level: on frequent occasions, especially in the early period, it has been higher in the countryside than in the towns (Table 4.3). Once again, urban-rural differences were more marked among women. In local and presidential elections, however, urban turnout levels have been markedly higher.[11]

Table 4.3: Urban and Rural Turnout in Finland 1908-1930

Election	Men			Women		
	Urban	Rural	Difference	Urban	Rural	Difference
1908	66.1	69.3	-3.2	59.2	60.6	-1.4
1909	64.6	71.4	-7.0	59.4	60.8	-1.4
1910	63.7	65.1	-1.4	57.7	55.4	+2.3
1911	60.4	65.9	-5.5	52.4	55.3	-2.9
1913	54.4	56.1	-1.7	45.2	47.0	-1.8
1916	54.5	61.0	-6.5	45.0	52.7	-7.7
1917	69.9	73.6	-3.7	66.6	65.6	+1.0
1919	64.8	70.3	-5.5	70.0	64.0	+6.0
1922	65.8	62.5	+3.3	59.0	53.5	+5.5
1924	62.0	61.7	+0.3	57.9	52.6	+5.3
1927	62.0	59.2	+2.8	54.5	51.9	+2.5
1929	57.3	60.0	-2.7	50.9	52.4	-1.5
1930	68.5	68.6	-0.1	66.6	62.8	+3.8

Source: Adapted from Tingsten, Political Behaviour, p. 22.

Data on Eastern European countries are limited. Moreover, the quality of much of the data that is available is such that they must be treated with caution. In addition, while the actual manipulation of election results might have been a rare occurrence, strong official pressure upon electors not only to vote, but also to vote for a particular party was not an infrequent phenomenon. In such circumstances high turnout figures may be less an indicator of political mobilization than a measure of the efficiency of the administrative apparatus in controlling and directing the electorate.

Some data are available for Latvia, Estonia, Poland and Bulgaria. In Latvia turnout in the 1920s was substantially higher in the towns: in 1925 urban turnout was 80 per cent, while rural turnout was only 67.7 per cent. However, electors could vote in any polling district: many rural residents also worked in the towns and voted there.[12] By contrast, rural turnout in neighbouring Estonia was as high as in the cities: rural men in particular participated to a higher degree than their city brethren (Table 4.4). On the whole the highest turnout was recorded in the towns. These, however, held only 17,625 electors (an average of just over 1,000 each) out of a total electorate of 721,670 in 1932, as compared with 217,084 in the cities and 486,961 in rural districts. They were primarily small towns which, if not agrarian, were at least semi-rural in character: but the distinction between city and town was

Table 4.4: Urban and Rural Turnout in Estonia 1923-1932

Election	Men			Women		
	Cities	Towns	Rural	Cities	Towns	Rural
1923	66.5	69.3	74.8	62.6	64.8	63.0
1926	74.4	72.7	78.5	72.2	73.5	69.3
1929	71.6	76.3	74.8	65.5	71.6	64.8
1932	72.0	75.8	72.6	66.8	70.7	60.6

Source: Riigi Statisika Keskbüroo, II Riigikogu valimised (Tallinn, 1923); III Riigikogu valimised (Tallinn, 1927); IV Riigikogu valimised (Tallinn, 1929); V Riigikogu valimised (Tallinn, 1932).

determined on administrative, not demographic grounds. Estonia also held four referenda between 1923 and 1933. Turnout again fluctuated. In the referenda concerning the introduction of religious teaching in schools and on the constitutional extensions of executive authority, rural turnout was higher than urban: the reverse was true of the two referenda in 1933 concerning constitutional reform.[13] Similarly, no clear pattern emerged in Poland. In 1922 urban turnout was 72.7 per cent, compared to a rural figure of 66.1 per cent. The reverse occurred in the 1926 election: urban turnout was 75.8 per cent, and rural turnout 79.6 per cent.[14] By contrast, rural turnout in Bulgaria was persistently higher than urban levels throughout the whole period of "competitive" politics: indeed, from 1923 onwards agrarian mobilization had almost reached "saturation" point (Table 4.5). Why Bulgaria had such a high agrarian turnout is, of course, another question.

Table 4.5: Urban and Rural Turnout in Bulgaria 1913-1931

Election	Urban	Rural	Difference
1913	47.9	57.0	-9.1
1914	52.8	71.3	-18.5
1919	45.3	57.6	-12.3
1920	61.8	82.0	-20.2
1923 I	77.6	89.3	-11.6
1923 II	74.1	90.0	-15.9
1927	72.7	87.8	-15.1
1931	78.1	87.4	-9.3

Source: Statistique des élections des députés pour l'Assemblée nationale ordinaire 1915 (Sofia, 1916), s. xii; Statistique des élections des députés pour l'Assemblée nationale ordinaire 1928 (Sofia, 1929), p. ix; Annuaire statistique du Royaume de Bulgarie (Sofia, 1933), p. 375.

Similar mixed findings emerge from other countries. For Ireland Chubb has constructed a not entirely satisfactory classification of constituencies: Dublin and its immediate environs (Dublin county, Dun Laoghaire and Rathdown), the most isolated and mountainous regions of the west (Donegal, Mayo, West Galway, and Kerry), and the rest of Ireland. His figures do emphasize that between 1923 and 1938 turnout in the more urbanized area (median 67.8 per cent) was usually only slightly lower than in the most isolated regions (median 69.2 per cent), but persistently lower than in the rest of the country (median 74.3 per cent).[15] Participation outside Dublin increased dramatically in the 1930s with the coming to power of De Valera and the Fianna Fail party. In the first Austrian Republic turnout in Vienna was generally less than in any other province.[16] Tingsten analyses occupational data from the official examination of the 1907 election in the Cis-Leithanian part of the Hapsburg Empire: these are summarized in Table 4.6. The higher figures for Vienna here may be discounted since compulsory voting had been introduced in the city, but not in Bohemia and Galicia. The important point is that the turnout figures for the various agricultural groups compare favourably in each region with those for other groups. In particular, turnout by farm owners is higher than the regional average in each instance. These figures are perhaps also useful for appreciating the limited urban-rural differences in post-1918 Czechoslovakia and Poland.

Compulsory voting was introduced early in the Low Countries: it seems to have had the effect of limiting variations in turnout. Historically, however, turnout in national elections was slightly higher in rural areas. On the other hand, the nationalization of party competition in local elections seems to have occurred earlier in urban communes: in the 1921 Belgian local elections 70 per cent of the uncontested seats were in communes with less than 1,000 inhabitants.[17]

No apparent urban-rural differences appeared in Italy between the extension of the suffrage and the Fascist seizure of power. A recent study of survey responses also found no significant differences in participation between the smallest communities in the Italian South and the large industrial cities of the North.[18] Reliable French data are difficult to obtain. However, most observers suggest that variations in turnout are negligible.[19] Data from Switzerland vary somewhat from canton to canton: in general, however, participation tended to be higher in the more agricultural districts than in industrial and urban districts.[20] A rural lag in mobilization was present in early national elections in Germany. But rural turnout reached unprecedented heights in the early 1930s when the Nazi party (NSDAP) achieved its breakthrough to become a prominent mass party. The Federal Republic of Germany after 1949 has evidenced no unambiguous difference between urban and rural turnout levels.[21]

Several general observations may be made at the conclusion of

Table 4.6: Turnout in Vienna, Bohemia and Galicia 1907, by Occupation

Occupation	Vienna	Bohemia	Galicia
INDUSTRY			
Managers, owners:			
large enterprises	88.6	80.9	80.2
small enterprises	94.4	84.6	82.0
Workers:			
large enterprises	90.0	90.3	82.7
small enterprises	90.7	80.4	78.3
TRADE AND TRANSPORT			
Managers, owners	91.8	78.7	79.3
Workers	88.6	77.4	75.2
AGRICULTURE AND FORESTRY			
Independent	92.9	87.7	87.5
Salaried	81.9	79.9	79.5
Workers	84.9	83.2	78.9
Häusler[1]	-	86.7	80.5
TOTAL ELECTORATE	91.1	84.7	84.7

1. Small Cultivators who owned some land, but who were also employed on neighbouring large estates as day-labourers.

Source: Adapted from Tingsten, Political Behaviour, p. 152.

this country by country survey. Superficially, increasing urbanization and increasing electoral turnout do seem to appear together. However, the coincidence does not necessarily mean that they are causally related. Much further empirical research would have to be done before the hypotheses could be verified or rejected. Similarly, the proposition that turnout will be substantially lower in predominantly agricultural countries is not particularly useful. To reinforce the discussion to date,

Table 4.7: Proportion of Population Dependent upon Agriculture around 1930, and Median National Electoral Turnout 1920-1930

Country	Dependent on Agriculture	Median Turnout
Yugoslavia	75	71.1
Bulgaria[1]	75	82.2
Rumania[1]	72	76.5
Poland	61	74.8
Finland	58	57.4
Estonia	56	69.3
Latvia	55	80.8
Ireland	53	75.6
Sweden	39	54.7
Norway	37	68.9
France	34	83.0
Czechoslovakia[1]	33	91.3
Austria[1]	31	88.1
Denmark	29	77.8
Switzerland[1]	24	77.8
Germany	23	78.8
Netherlands[1]	23	91.4
Belgium[1]	18	92.8
United Kingdom	8	76.1

1. Denotes countries with compulsory voting. In Switzerland and Austria compulsory voting was in force in only some of the cantons and provinces. Other countries have been excluded from the table because of the lack of either electoral or social structure data.

we present data on national turnout figures and level of agricultural dependency around 1930 (Table 4.7). It might be added that statistical tests failed to produce any meaningful correlation between the two sets of data, though of course they represent such a high level of aggregation that any kind of assertive generalization must be hedged around with qualifications. Moreover, there have always been a number of problems connected with the calculation and ecological analysis of turnout. These further limit the value of any interpretation of the data:

1. Quite apart from the rules determining who can or cannot vote, turnout may be affected by the practical operation and consequences of different kinds of electoral systems. It may for instance be higher under proportional systems, since there the likelihood of the existence of safe seats is much lower than in majority systems. In constituencies with a hegemonic party, many electors - both supporters and opponents of the dominant party - may believe that the result is a foregone conclusion and so stay away from the ballot box. During the period under consideration, most countries had adapted a system of proportional representation with party lists. Two exceptions were Britain (simple majority system) and Ireland (single transferable vote). These two countries did have a lower turnout than most, but only marginally so.

2. The median refers to the aggregate turnout in each country as a whole, and not to the results of individual electoral districts. Hence, the figures refer only to <u>contested</u> elections. Where there was no contest, as for example, was the case in several British constituencies, the turnout level was accordingly reduced. On the other hand, it could be hypothesized that contests in every British constituency throughout the period might not have raised turnout levels significantly. An examination of constituency electoral data in the interwar decades showed that turnout tended to be persistently lower in contested safe seats (defined in terms of a victory margin for one party at the previous election of at least twenty per cent) than in more competitive constituencies.[22]

3. Third, the level of turnout may depend upon whether women have been enfranchised. It is now a part of conventional wisdom

that women are less likely to vote than men. This, it could be assumed, might be even more probable in the early twentieth century, given first that societies were still heavily impregnated with a traditional ethos about the social role of women, and second that political mobilization was still in a diffusion phase. The data in the previous tables indicate that female turnout in urban areas tends to be some five percent lower than male turnout, and frequently ten per cent or more in rural areas. Thus, it might also be expected that turnout would be higher in countries with only a male electorate. The importance of this point is difficult to assess, in that of the countries involved Britain had a partial female franchise until 1928, while Belgium and some Swiss cantons employed compulsory voting. However, if we compare the median turnout in France and Belgium in the 1920s, when the electorate was entirely male, with that in the post-1945 period when women were granted the right to vote, no meaningful differences emerge. In short, possible differences in the propensity to vote between men and women are not apparent at this level of aggregation and comparison.

4. Finally, the table is complicated by the existence of compulsory voting in a few countries. Compulsory voting should obviously increase turnout levels considerably, as for example it did in Belgium, the Netherlands and Czechoslovakia. However, the relatively low figure for Rumania illustrates that compulsory voting is rarely fully effective. If that were so, there would be no variation in turnout. Several factors limit its effectiveness. For example, people may have died or moved to another locality between the compilation of the electoral register and voting day, or they may be ill and house-bound. Again, distance from the polling booth or kind of occupation may make them disinclined to make the journey to vote, while some individuals may dislike the available choice of parties and candidates so much that they are willing to incur whatever legal and financial penalty is imposed for non-voting, rather than vote.[23]

2. Influences upon Turnout

These are important considerations. However, their significance is at least not immediately apparent at this high level of aggregation and comparison. The immediate point is that, although in many countries urban groups participate in elections to a greater extent than rural groups, a corresponding generalization about variations in turnout does not seem to be entirely appropriate or applicable. Similarly, the notion of a rural lag in mobilization does not seem to be universally appropriate. It is much more probable that variations in turnout levels in each country, and changes over time, can be explained best in terms of the overall social structure and political events in that country. The virtue of Rokkan's use of the concept of rural lag in mobilization is that it is firmly grounded in an exhaustive empirical analysis of Norwegian political circumstances and developments. Unfortunately, few countries have such a multitude of accessible and relevant data as Norway and Sweden. We propose to discuss here only some of the factors which may explain variations and diachronic changes in electoral turnout.

First, it is immediately obvious from several of the tables presented earlier that variations in electoral participation by men and women account substantially for lower rural participation in several countries. This is the case in Sweden and Estonia, and to some extent it is also true of Norway, Denmark, Iceland, and at least some areas of Germany.[24] The much lower turnout of rural women is a phenomenon that has occurred in most European countries. It is perhaps explainable in terms of the traditional norms of the society governing the status of women, the greater traditionalism of the countryside, and the even greater isolation of rural women, not only from national society, but also from much of the daily life of the rural community. In addition, the introduction of compulsory voting can be important in levelling out variations in turnout. It is interesting to note that in the First Austrian Republic the highest turnout was in the two rural provinces of Tirol and Vorarlberg, which were the only two provinces to introduce compulsory voting. Female participation in elections was also substantially higher than in the country as a whole.[25]

Furthermore, differences in turnout that do exist between towns and countryside may not necessarily be due to their urban or rural character. Other dimensions of social structure may be more important than urban-rural divisions in determining rates of electoral participation. What are the consequences, for example, if religious or ethnic divisions coincide with the urban or rural character of regions. A most striking illustration of how religion is correlated with strong variations in levels of turnout comes from the rural <u>Kreise</u> (communes) of North-west Germany during the Weimar Republic (Table 4.8). The political fragmentation of Germany at the time of the Reformation produced in this corner of the country <u>Kreise</u> which have remained predominantly Catholic or predominantly Protestant ever since: in each commune the majority religion was supported by at least eighty per cent of the population. Turnout in the Protestant <u>Kreise</u> remained low until 1930 and the rise of the NSDAP: by contrast, the Catholic <u>Kreise</u> retained a consistent and high level of participation throughout the lifetime of the Weimar Republic. In fact, at the regional level the lowest turnout figures in Weimar Germany were recorded by those constituencies which were more distant from Berlin and industrial Germany in

Table 4.8: Turnout in Catholic and Protestant Kreise in Oldenburg and Ostfriesland in the Weimar Republic (in percentages)

Election	Catholic Kreise	Protestant Kreise
1920	87.9	68.7
1924 I	86.3	63.6
1924 II	86.2	66.5
1928	82.4	63.6
1930	86.6	73.0
1932 I	85.8	83.9
1932 II	82.6	80.1
1933	88.0	86.7

<u>Source</u>: Data extracted from the ICPSR data set: Germany in the Weimar Republic (ICPSR 042)

social rather than urban terms: Oppeln and Posen which possessed a fairly large Polish minority, and Baden, Württemberg and Bavaria which retained a lively memory of political independence and a sense of cultural identity. Similar examples can be found in many areas with mixed religious or ethnic populations. Where it has conceived of itself as being in a state of siege, or where it has faced powerful opponents, the Catholic Church has persistently argued that non-voting will in fact harm the Church in its struggles against other religions, atheism, communism or secular authority. Religions, and Catholicism in particular, have proved to be extremely successful mobilizing agencies - not least in raising rural participation to a level at least equal to that of urban areas.

Finally, there is the question of occupation. Rural populations clearly contain people who are not employed in agriculture. Similarly, they may contain several different kinds of agrarian groups. Participation rates may vary from group to group. Lipset, for example, hypothesizes that electoral participation will be higher among commercial-crop farmers than among peasants or subsistence farmers.[26] This thesis also has a long history, and is based on the one hand upon the awareness of commercial farmers of their exposed position in the market economy and the relevance of governmental policies, and on the other upon the absorption of the subsistence peasant with the more immediate concern with survival: the pressures of life leave the poor peasant with little time or energy to spare for political activity, especially if this entails travel away from his holding.[27]

The major problem is to operationalize the concepts of commercial farmer and subsistence peasant. As we have argued, even after 1900 every European cultivator possessed to a greater or lesser extent characteristics of both types: the argument to date, however, does not suggest the presence of any clear cross-national pattern. Contemporary survey analyses could have offered an opportunity to assess this question more accurately. However, very few surveys are satisfactory in distinguishing between various categories of agricultural occupation, let alone in including those questions necessary to determine the degree to which an individual cultivator is integrated in a market economy. It was argued earlier that with suffrage extension agrarian political mobilization changed significantly: with the franchise, participation involved at a minimum only voting in elections, which did not entail leaving the land for appreciable periods of time. Hence, a new opportunity became available for the political parties to enlist the support of agrarian populations. Education levels might also be important in that better-educated people are more likely to vote. Levels of education are generally higher in urban areas than in rural areas. Rural inhabitants may therefore be less able to appreciate the value of voting. Moreover, a low rural turnout might be expected when the rural areas feel themselves to be "disfranchised" because all the political parties are seen as city parties espousing urban interests. In other words, low rural turnout may equally reflect the inability of political

Table 4.9: Turnout of Agricultural Occupational Groups in Sweden 1928

Occupational Groups	Men		Women	
	Number	Turnout	Number	Turnout
SOCIAL CLASS (total electorate)	64,417	84.7	67,529	83.4
Estate owners	1,894	89.5	1,933	86.2
SOCIAL CLASS II (total electorate)	494,135	75.7	487,114	66.9
Farmers	214,921	79.4	208,112	66.2
Tenant farmers	40,331	77.2	34,791	64.1
Farmers' sons working on the family farm	48,709	69.2		
SOCIAL CLASS III (total electorate)	658,701	69.4	591,282	58.1
Farm foremen	11,140	72.7	7,833	66.9
Crofters	50,114	66.1	51,697	51.0
Farm labourers	82,866	60.8	43,473	54.7
TOTAL ELECTORATE	1,217,253	72.6	1,145,915	62.7

Source: Adapted from Riksdagsmannavalen åren 1925-1928 (Stockholm, 1928), pp. 49 ff.

parties to penetrate and mobilize rural society (or their disinclination to do so) as the political disinterest of the rural population.

Be that as it may be, there is sufficient data to suggest that participation increases with landownership. Sweden is one of the few countries where official statistics have shown the voting rates of different socio-economic categories. Table 4.9 clearly illustrates the low turnout rates in 1928 of agricultural labourers compared to those of farm owners. The variations between the categories are not substantially different in other Swedish elections in the interwar period: farmowners have a consistently high turnout, while farm labourers have a persistent record of substantial non-voting. Survey data on turnout are notoriously unreliable. However, bearing this constraint in mind, we do find that post-1945 survey data for several countries corroborate the finding that farm labourers have an exceptionally low rate of political participation. In post-1945 Denmark, for example, their turnout rate was the lowest of all the groups examined.[28] A survey in West Germany in 1953 found that 90 percent of farmowners claimed to have voted in the previous election: this was the highest positive response in the sample. By contrast, the farm labourers were the most apathetic group: a secondary analysis of the same data found that 48 per cent expressed indifference to the outcome of the election.[29]

3. Variations and Diachronic Change

All these factors feed into each other. What counts is the particular constellation of forces in each country. Above them all stands one issue which may dramatically affect rural turnout: the impact of social, economic or political crisis upon the rural electorate. The agrarian population may be mobilized to achieve some economic or political gain, such as land reform, which is seen as immediate to their interests. Similarly, high turnout rates may be a reflection of agrarian determination to defend some recently acquired gain. The wave of russification in Finland between 1894 and 1906 heightened political awareness, and in the decades following 1906 the highest levels of turnout in rural Finland came shortly after the struggle against Russia in 1906 and just after the Civil War of 1917-1918 and the land reform of the same years. In several East European countries turnout declined somewhat from the level reached in the first elections following the land reform. The Finnish pattern seems also to be followed by Latvia. The highest turnout there occurred in 1920 and 1922. Not only was this probably influenced by the recent land reform and the proximity of the Soviet Union: the presence of Riga, one of the largest industrial cities in the Tsarist Empire, was perhaps also a significant factor. We pointed out in the previous chapter that there was a considerable level of Bolshevik sympathy in Latvia. By contrast, turnout in neighbouring Estonia was much lower. Despite the mobilizing effect of the turmoil of 1917, there appears to have been rather less urban-rural tension, and the city of Tallinn was in no way comparable to Riga in either size or importance.

Political upheavals may have been frequent in European history. Nevertheless, they are not exactly everyday occurrences. Throughout the centuries the most common stimulus of agrarian unrest and mobilization has been economic crisis. The latter continued to serve as the fundamental motor force that drove cultivators towards greater participation through the alternative channel of the ballot box. Generally, the economic condition of European agriculture remained serious, and even deteriorated throughout the 1920s: the great depression at the end of the decade generated an even greater agrarian crisis. In most of Western Europe the most significant rural breakthrough since the beginnings of mass politics occurred in the late 1920s and early 1930s: Norway and Sweden are by no means exceptional in this respect. The most dramatic instances of a sharp upsurge occurred in Germany. Catholic farmers had already been successfully mobilized by the Zentrum party, but, as was demonstrated in Table 4.8, turnout in Protestant agrarian regions of Oldenburg and Ostfriesland remained low until 1930. Similar examples can be found throughout Protestant Germany.[30]

Increases in rural participation may be spontaneous developments arising from social circumstances. Alternatively, they may be the result of specific activity in rural areas by political parties. In either instance political organization and commitment become important variables in maintaining levels of participation. We shall turn to the question of the direction of the rural vote in the next chapter. Here it will suffice to emphasize that the political impact of upsurges in rural political participation is no longer as salient as in the past. Historically, agrarian uprisings always carried an implicit or explicit threat to the survival of regimes. States, regimes, governments all were extremely vulnerable to a disruption in the food supply. But with the consolidation of a world economy, continuing technological innovation, and an increase in the resources at the disposal of the state, the threat of a break in this most vital of life-lines receded somewhat. Yet rural upsurges in turnout in the era of mass politics could still dramatically upset the balance between political parties and so possibly affect the stability of regimes. Continuing mobilization, however, has diminished significantly the likelihood of similar consequences, especially after 1945 with the continued decline in the numbers employed in agriculture. In any case levels of turnout in rural areas are considerably higher than in the past. The major consequence for party support of rural volatility is based less upon previous non-voting and more upon the transference of agrarian votes from one party to another, or to a new party entering the system. These questions will also be examined later. Here it may be pointed out that in many instances the persisting mobilization of rural support is not as constant or "frozen" as urban mobilization. On the other hand, new parties which have entered the political arena after the consolidation of a structured mass party system have almost always originated and gained most of their support in the cities: even the so-called Boerenpartij in the Netherlands gained most of its votes in urban areas. The one major exception is the Finnish Smallholders' Party of the 1960s which specifically appealed for and obtained support from the small farmers and cottars of Northern Finland. In many rural areas the party process of structurally consolidating the vote is still continuing.[31] To a limited degree, therefore, lower levels of organization and institutionalization in rural Europe, and an inherent potential volatility that arises from the cultivator's "peculiar" economic exposure, do give the agrarian population a political character and significance similar to

CHAPTER 5   Agrarian Political Behaviour

Class is everything, the rest mere ornamentation: a common assumption about the nature of politics, but one which at least superficially does not fit very easily with the agrarian world. To employ the phraseology of class politics unreservedly to the political preferences of farmers is to invite ambiguity. One useful measure of voting solidarity by social groups is Alford's index of class voting: "subtract the percentage of persons in non-manual occupations voting for Left parties from the percentage of persons in manual occupations voting for Left parties."[1] The index can vary from -100 to +100: an index score of zero indicates that the variables are totally unrelated. This index can be developed to measure the strength of relationships other than class and politics by similarly dichotomizing both independent social structure variables and party preferences. Arend Lijphart has applied such an index to the relationship between urban-rural divisions and conservative voting. The data in Table 5.1 show a low correlation between rural residence and conservative voting. There was, for example, almost no correlation between the two variables for Norway, and a small negative one for Sweden: the highest correlation of +22 was found in Austria.

One major problem associated with these data - and indeed with most survey data - is that rural and urban populations are classified in terms of the population size of the city, town or village in which the respondents reside. For this reason it is often difficult to determine the real farming vote. In addition, the possible proximity of large urban centres is frequently

Table 5.1: Indices of Urban-Rural Voting for Conservative Parties

Country	Year of Survey	Index
Austria	1967	+22
West Germany	1959	+17
Italy	1959	+12
France	1956	+11
Britain	1959	+10
Netherlands	1956	+10
Belgium	1956	+7
West Germany	1956	+6
Norway	1957	+2
Sweden	1955	-8

Source: A. Lijphart, Class Voting and Religious Voting in the European Democracies (Strathclyde Survey Research Centre Occasional Paper 8: Glasgow, 1971), p. 8.

ignored. Internal differentiation of the agrarian population is even rarer. Survey and ecological data simply do not contain sufficient information on aspects of agrarian structure such as landownership, size of enterprise, wealth and capital assets (or debits), and the ratio in which produce is distributed between domestic consumption and sale on the market. Any systematic discussion of the relationship between agrarian structure and voting behaviour must do so therefore at a fairly high level of generality. What does seem clear from the evidence is that the rural vote can be spread across a great number of parties: generally, an analysis of only the farming vote does not suggest a radically different pattern. To take only one example from Europe, the farming vote in Italy is distributed (admittedly in varying proportions) among all parties from the Communists (PCI) to the neofascist Social Movement (MSI). This single example also illustrates the limitations of such indices as Alford's in that they must perforce dichotomize both parties and votes. Dichotomization may be of less value in analysing the agrarian vote, for it is this diversity in voting behaviour which seems to distinguish agrarian groups from other elements in society, whose political responses have been, nationally and cross-nationally, much more uniform in particular historical and socio-economic contexts. However, the bond between parties and farmers may appear to be unusually weak because it is incorporated into a class nexus which is derived essentially from urban life, and because most parties are urban-based. Farmers may not be qualitatively different from other groups, once allowances are made for the constructs of the agrarian world, and we begin by isolating those elements of agrarian structure which seem to have political significance. The overview of political and economic developments in rural Europe shows that the term "cultivator" encompasses a wide and complex mosaic of social and economic groups. For example, even in the so-called homogeneous peasant society of Southern Italy, considerable differences in life style and status exist between the various kinds of peasants and the nature of their land tenure, especially between ordinary peasants and those acknowledged as belonging to the peasant elite (<u>massari</u>): in the last resort, the measurement and perception of status revolve around the questions of land, its occupation and its use.[2]

There are perhaps not many points upon which there is general agreement among agrarian groups: a minimum list would include a concern with landownership or complete security of tenure, an interest in achieving high and stable prices for their product and/or labour, and a desire for easy and cheap credit terms. The means by which farming groups seek to obtain or defend these political goals will vary according to the structure and attitudes of the agricultural community, and with the intensity and nature of their involvement within the market economy. The structuring of the party system and the strategies adopted by party leaders also become significant variables. If, for example, there is a low level of internal differentiation among the agrarian population in a region, a cohesive rural response may be much more likely. However, rural political action may be influenced as much, if not more so, by urban political behaviour. Since the focal point, control, membership and support of most European political parties rapidly became urban-based, rural political behaviour may have been more a reaction to urban-oriented and urban-inspired policies.

Competitive party systems became the major means of assimilating rural groups into national politics. Clearly, the nature of the channels offered by the parties depended upon the nature of the party systems; that is, on the number, size and outlook of the parties. However, the ability of any party system to assimilate new groups that newly enter the political process depends also upon the concurrence and acquiescence of the dominant social groups in the diminution of their political influence. Thus if parties are eager to acquire rural support, they ought to be prepared to adapt their economic policies and programme to accomodate various agrarian requirements such as greater capital and investment provisions, land reform, or guaranteed price support systems. On the whole, agrarian commitments and demands are not translated into a political Weltanschauung: their expectations and needs are fairly specific. Hence, if their demands are satisfied, agrarian groups may well lapse back into a quiescent and non-political role. A further influential factor that has to be considered is that irrespective of their economic demands on the political system, the social and cultural values of rural groups typically retain a highly traditional flavouring. These tendencies create two major problems for political parties. Lower rural levels of political involvement entail a continuing problem of mobilization and organization in rural areas. Moreover, where a rural population is normally quiescent, its periodic entry into competitive party politics in significantly greater numbers may not take the same directions or benefit the same parties each time it occurs. In short, such sporadic eruptions may dramatically upset the balance of competition between the parties. One further point ought to be mentioned. We have suggested that the issue content of agrarian demands is typically particularistic and practical, but this may be valid only where the issue content relates specifically to agricultural questions. Where the issue content becomes complex and general, it more often escalates towards a conglomeration of panaceas that ignore the realities and limitations of both the social structure and the political process. A heightened agrarian political awareness may thus simply turn potential into real volatility: such vestiges of past chiliastic tendencies stress the basic continuities of rural life.

Economic problems and issues constitute the mainspring of agrarian political activity. Where, therefore, a competitive party system is free of religious, regional or linguistic-ethnic cleavages, the major question for farming groups is simply which party or parties are most sympathetic to their economic demands. If, for example, "left" parties call for either land nationalization or for cheaper food for industrial workers, cultivators may feel it necessary to support more conservative parties: these in turn may then directly appeal for rural electoral support. One reason for the inability of many Socialist parties before 1914 to win more rural support (in addition to their urban origins) was precisely their policies favouring cheaper food prices for urban workers and the public ownership of land. However, if a later revision of conservative or radical party policy appears to affect rural interests, or if farmers turn to demands for increased government aid or regulations, agrarian groups may switch their allegiance quite easily. Again, if no established party seems to offer a viable alternative, farmers may turn to new or "flash" parties and political movements that seem to offer a better bargain. Such temporary movements have not been uncommon among farmers, and they are in the same tradition as many historical expressions of agrarian direct action. A final alternative would be for cultivators to reject all available party options as inappropriate vehicles for agrarian demands. Short of remaining as gadflies on the fringes of the regularized political process, the only remaining option is a party of their own.

Substantial electoral volatility and a tendency to seek out the best political bargain from the parties have been frequently remarked upon as characteristic of agrarian populations. These features derive partly from the relatively exposed position of the agricultural producer in a market economy and the more explicit relationship which can be perceived between government policies and the cultivator's own economic well-being. Whereas a direct relationship between legislation and administration on the one hand, and wage levels and working conditions among urban groups on the other, is both complex and usually appreciated only indistinctly, a similar relationship between policies and agricultural prices and credit is, at least to the farmer, more immediately apparent. The farmer is closer to his product in all its stages from planting to marketing than either urban workers or owners and managers of enterprises employing more than a handful of employees. More than is the case with most occupations the farmer stands in a one-to-one relationship with both the government and the purchaser of his produce. Such a clear perception by agrarian populations may be a major reason why so many observers have commented upon the intensity of the rural reaction to economic difficulties: "the farmer reacts to economic pressure with political protest, yet the response has an explosive quality - great force without duration - which is unique".[3] Moreover, there has been historical antipathy towards organization in rural Europe. Such hostility is substantially greater where the organizations are clearly based in the cities. Hence, the low level of organization in rural areas may weaken a collective rural response to economic problems: a variegated political reaction is much more probable. An individualistic reaction to economic situations is made more likely by the internal differentiation of, and the isolated nature of households in agrarian society. Differences in crop production, the size of farm, the quality of land, productivity levels, and economic viability all mean that the economic climate will affect individual farmers in different ways.

The purpose of this chapter is to see if there are detectable cross-national tendencies in the electoral behaviour of agrarian groups. Two general approaches are available. The more common procedure has utilized party systems to study the relative support given to political parties by different social groups. Alternatively, it is possible to take the individual political party as the unit of analysis and look at the distribution of each party's support among various social groups.[4] We propose to study both how the agrarian electorate distributes its vote among political parties, and the proportion of the support of each party that comes from agrarian groups. But only the first theme will be taken up here: the second is deferred to a later chapter. As far as is possible, the analysis will focus upon the early twentieth century, but because of a relative paucity of information from this period, we shall also draw upon data from the post-1945 era, which of course is much better served by the sample survey, and from which we may perhaps deduce a more exact map of the contours of agrarian political behaviour. A greater reliance upon data from recent decades inevitably means a focus upon Western Europe as the region in which competitive party systems survived. However, the relegation of Eastern Europe to the wings is not as serious as might first seem apparent. Before 1940 most of these societies were overwhelming rural with a fundamentally monochromatic agriculture. A superficial examination of election results would suggest that most parties received a substantial agrarian vote. We may quote the example of Estonia where all the significant parties except the "landlords" party - but including the Socialists - received anything from 50 to over 90 per cent of their vote from rural areas. The politics of Eastern Europe will be considered in some detail later, when we turn to the theme of agrarian political parties. For the moment it might be enough to suggest that non-economic factors were at least as equally important as economic cleavages in the formation and operation of the party systems in this region.

Let us begin, then, by looking at post-1945 Western European data, to see if they suggest any kind of pattern upon which the rest of the discussion can hinge.[5] But first, a word of methodological warning. One deficiency is simply the reliance upon data that were collected without cross-national comparisons in mind. Comparability of data across countries is always a major problem of political research, particularly in secondary analyses. Both social structures and party systems vary greatly from country to country. Comparability is also affected by the time factor: without conducting an original cross-national study, it is almost impossible to guarantee that the data have been collected in different countries at the same time, or at a similar stage of development in each country. Furthermore, both the operationalization of social structure variables and the questions soliciting the respondent's party preference may vary considerably from survey to survey. The criteria governing the use of survey data here are entirely eclectic and, hopefully, pragmatic. There is a general paucity of data which include either farmers as a separate category or which permit some differentiation between agrarian groups. Data on rural or urban residence are also considered, but their value is limited because of the way in which rural or urban residence is generally measured in surveys. Finally, there is an insufficient number of surveys in European countries to permit any rigorous consideration of the developmental aspects of agrarian voting. However, no meaningful trends or fluctuations other than those discussed here emerged from an analysis of whatever data were available.

1. The Political Preferences of Agrarian Groups

If it is true that the diversity within rural society may be nearly as great as that within urban society, then it might be expected that groups distinguished in terms of the ownership or non-ownership of land, patterns of land tenure, or relationship with the market would possess different patterns of partisan support. The easiest source of such information is survey data. As pointed out, there is a general paucity of data which permit any internal differentiation among the agrarian population. The evidence therefore should be regarded as suggestive rather than conclusive. Nevertheless, some clear cross-national trends do emerge from a comparison of different farming categories. It seems pointless to present extremely bulky tables of data that are already easily available in other sources: instead we shall present only a summary table of those parties which receive the support of a significant proportion of the agrarian electorate. The available data suggest that large farmers are more likely than small farmers to vote for conservative parties, and that farmers in general tend to prefer conservative or centrist parties in greater numbers than agricultural workers (Table 5.2). Hence, within the terms of reference of the structure of rural society, the left-right continuum of party support by working class and middle class voters within urban society is reproduced to some extent within the countryside. The dichotomy, of course, is not very neat, not least because of the presence in some countries of agrarian parties. The social bases of the latter's support is a specific theme of a later chapter. We propose here to pretend that agrarian parties do not exist, and to structure the discussion around the classic left-right continuum of political sociology.

Table 5.2: The Distribution of Agrarian Support among Political Parties in Western Europe after 1945

Level of Support	Agrarian Groups	Country	Political Party
70% or more	Farmers	Belgium	Christian Socialist
50-70%	Farmers	Finland	Centre (Agrarian)
		France	Conservative (4th Republic)[1]
		Ireland	Fianna Fail[2]
		Norway	Centre (Agrarian)
		Sweden	Centre (Agrarian)
	Farm workers	Italy	Communist
		Norway	Labour
		Sweden	Social Democrat
40-50%	Farmers	France	Conservative; Communist (4th Republic)[2]
		W. Germany	Christian Democrat
		Ireland	Fianna Fail; Fine Gael[1]
		Italy	Christian Democrat[2]
		Netherlands	Catholic
		Switzerland	People's (Farmers', Traders' and Citizens')
	Farm workers	Finland	Social Democrat
30-40%	Farmers	Italy	Christian Democrat; Communist[3]
		Norway	Labour; Centre (Agrarian)
		Switzerland	Christian Democrat
	Farm workers	France	Communist (4th Republic)
		Netherlands	Catholic

Table 5.2 (Continued)

Level of Support	Agrarian Group	Country	Political Party
20-30%	Farmer	Ireland	Fine Gael[2]
		Italy	Christian Democrat; Liberal[1]
	Farm worker	W. Germany	Christian Democrat; Social Democrat
		Netherlands	Labour; Christian Historical Union
		Sweden	Centre (Agrarian)

Notes:
1. Wealthy or large farmers.
2. Poor or small farmers.
3. Sharecroppers and tenants.

Sources:

Belgium: K. Hill, "Belgium": Political Change in a Segmented Society", in Rose, Electoral Behavior, p. 83.

Finland: Allardt and Pesonen, "Cleavages in Finnish Politics", p. 342; Pesonen, "Finland", p. 294.

France: Lipset, Political Man, p. 225; J. Stoetzel, "Voting Behaviour in France", British Journal of Sociology 6 (1955), pp. 118-119.

Germany: J.J. Linz, "Cleavage and Consensus in West German Politics: The Early Fifties", in Lipset and Rokkan, Party Systems, p. 287.

Ireland: Nusight, October 1969, pp. 78-84; J. Whyte, "Ireland: Politics Without Social Bases", in Rose, Electoral Behavior, pp. 631-632.

Italy: Lipset, Political Man, p. 227, G. Poggi, Le preferenze politiche degli italiani (Bologna, 1968), p. 27.

Netherlands: A. Lijphart, The Politics of Accomodation (Berkeley/Los Angeles, 1968) p. 29.

Norway: A. Barton, "Sociological and Psychological implications of Economic Planning in Norway", doctoral thesis Columbia University, 1954, p. 313; H. Valen and S. Rokkan, "Norway: Conflict Structure and Mass Politics in a European Periphery", in Rose, Electoral Behavior, p. 334.

Sweden: N. Stjernquist, "Sweden: Stability or Deadlock?", in R.A. Dahl (ed.), Political Oppositions in Western Democracies (New Haven, 1966) p. 127; B. Särlvik, "Sweden: The Social Bases of the Parties in a Developmental Perspective", in Rose, Electoral Behavior, p. 409.

Switzerland: Der Schweizer Wähler (Basel, 1963), p. 10; H.H. Kerr, Switzerland: Social Cleavages and Partisan Conflict (Sage Professional Papers in Contemporary Political Sociology, I 06-002, London/Beverly Hills, 1974), p. 11.

Substantial rural support for radical parties is particularly notable in Finland, France and Italy. Communist (and early Socialist) rural strength in Italy has been especially prominent among the tenant farmers, sharecroppers and farm labourers of Central and Northern Italy, mainly in the provinces of Emilia-Romagna, Tuscany and Umbria. They were early supporters of liberalism and republicanism, and possessed by the late nineteenth century a fairly well-developed agrarian socialism. In turn, socialist sympathies derive considerably from a pronounced anticlericalism that may be traced back at least to the eighteenth century when much of the area was under papal control and landownership. After the eighteenth century, moreover, much of the land passed under the control of urban bourgeois groups.[6] These provincial fortresses of radical strength are characterised by the _mezzadria_ and sharecropping agriculture: the most radical province of Emilia-Romagna, moreover, contains a substantial number of farm labourers. Communist voting has also been aided by the strength and efficiency of the party's organization with its network of cooperative and lending facilities: "it is ironic that the Tuscan sharecropper is attached to the PCI (Communist party) in large part because its economic service agencies allow him to make a profit".[7] North-Central Italy supports Paige's general hypothesis that extreme radicalism is strongly correlated with sharecropping.[8] Certainly, the persistent leftist orientation of the region contrasts strongly with the more rural South with its large estates and mass of day labourers (_braccianti_). There, Communist support has grown from a much weaker base at the same time as the large landowners have moved towards unambiguously conservative parties, such as the Liberals.[9] The southern peasants to a greater extent than in the more industrialized North have become the largest element (42 per cent) in the Communist party membership: since most of these are _braccianti_ the party has placed a strong emphasis upon land reform. Yet the PCI does not enjoy the same dominant position in the South: in part this may be a result of its weaker organization and cooperative network, which have had to struggle against a more atomistic societal fabric.[10]

Similarly, some of the largest concentrations of Communist votes in France have been found in _départements_ which are essentially rural. In 1951, for example, the Communists won over 40 per cent of the votes in Corrèze: in 1956 the party gained 46 per cent of the vote in nearby Creuse (86 per cent agricultural).[11] In both instances the level of Communist support was higher than in the industrial areas of the north or the famous "red belt" around Paris. There is in fact a swathe of rural départements along the northern and western slopes of the Massif Central which possess several things in common. All tend to have a high Communist vote and/or a more general "radical" orientation. All are characterized by subsistence enterprises with a strong emphasis upon domestic consumption. Sharecropping and the métayer occupy a prominent position in the agrarian structure.[12] Anticlericalism is exceptionally strong, the presence of the Catholic Church is almost non-existent, and historically there seems to have been a historical leftism, which Schram suggests goes back to the Reformation, that has produced a tradition of support for the most radical tendance and opponent of the regime.[13]

Extensive rural support for the Communist party in Finland has been most prominent after 1945. In view of the country's proximity to the Soviet Union, and the tense relationships between the two states after 1918, the Communist strength in Finland might be thought to be somewhat puzzling. Intuitively, one might expect that patriotic feeling would generate a powerful anti-Communist atmosphere. But as in Italy, the Communist vote is the heir of earlier traditions of socialist voting. In the north and east of the country the Communist vote comes primarily from smallholders who usually must gain additional income from employment as foresters. The propensity of left voting among isolated groups with marginal incomes and/or hazardous occupations has been commented upon by Lipset.[14] The forests of Sweden also appear to have served as a core for that country's much smaller Communist party. One study showed that of the 25 communes with the highest communist vote, no less than 13 were "classic" forestry areas, while many of the remainder had a large population dependent upon forestry: by contrast, the party made scarcely any headway in the primarily farming communes.[15] Erik Allardt has tried to distinguish this rural Communism in Finland from the more typical support of industrial workers. He has argued that the northeastern variety derives from economic insecurity, isolation, and recent and rapid modernization leading to improved opportunities for comparisons with other groups, and hence to an increased sense of relative deprivation. At the aggregate level he sees Communist strength associated with unemployment, high voting activity, and low levels of religious activity. The party is strong where traditional values have recently declined, economic change is rapid, insecurity dominates, and where migration is common. However, an equally strong factor may have been the sudden mobilization of rural society by the Socialist party in the first decade of this century as an expression of the struggle against Tsarist suzerainty. This may have dissipated somewhat because of the 1917-1918 civil war, but even so Socialist support in many areas of rural Finland remained strong in the 1920s.[16]

Similar strong leftist rural support originally existed in other areas of the Russian Empire that subsequently became independent. Bolshevik support was high in the rural areas of the Baltic provinces in the crucial election of 1917.[17] In the Constituent Assembly elections of 1919 the Estonian Social Democrats gained 37 per cent of the votes, a moderate Labour Party won a further 25 per cent, while the Peasant League could win only four per cent. Throughout the 1920s the Social Democrats kept over 20 per cent of the votes in rural areas, though by 1932 this had fallen to 17.7 per cent. Similarly, in the rural province of Vidzeme the Latvian Social Democrats won no less than 60 per cent of the votes in the elections for a Land Council in 1917, compared with 33 per cent for the Farmers' Union. After 1919 the fear of the Soviet Union and its collectivization policies, coupled with the pressure for land reform along collectivist lines by the native Marxist parties, alienated them from the rural masses.[18]

One general thesis in the literature has been that ethnic minorities are more susceptible to Communist claims. But, as Burks points out, some minorities in Eastern Europe were not attracted by Communism: however, he does also demonstrate that the greatest Communist support in the region did come from rural areas which were both inhabited by minorities and suffered from extreme conditions of economic poverty.[19] Yet the "radicalism" of territories such as the Polish Kresy and Czechoslovakian Ruthenia may have been partly due to an ethnic identification with the Russian. The generalization may well be true only where other dimensions do not complicate the picture. The fact that several economically depressed minorities did not follow a radical line suggests an equally important role was played by ethnic and cultural identities, earlier traditions of socialization and institutionalization, and the geopolitical landscape of interwar Europe.

Critical junctures like the Finnish civil war may have been important in determining or changing voting allegiance. Yet many countries have avoided such turmoil. Even where severe unrest prevailed, the agricultural population may not have succumbed to leftwing mobilization. For example, in the Bavarian "revolution" of 1918-1919 several Peasant Councils were formed. However, these were supported by only a few peasants in Upper and Lower Bavaria who had already been mobilized by the <u>Bayerischer Bauernbund</u>. The other peasant organization - the local sections of the <u>Bund der Landwirte</u>, dominated by larger landowners, and especially the huge Catholic peasant organization - were hostile to the whole idea of Peasant Councils and their aims. However, these councils were by and large totally ineffectual and, far from demanding radical measures such as collectivization, contented themselves with supporting policies for confiscation of a few large estates and for the expansion of public services in the countryside.[20] One distinguishing feature to be borne in mind is the <u>attitude</u> of parties and their <u>willingness</u> to penetrate rural society in their efforts to mobilize more voters. In Bavaria, for instance, the Social Democrats were basically disinterested in the peasantry: the party considered them to be reactionary and was not prepared to permit the Peasant Councils a voice as important as that granted the workers' and soldiers' councils. Again, we can see that abrupt rural mobilization occurred in Norway just as it did in Finland, but while the initial "politics of cultural defence" survived in South-West Norway, a pattern of class politics emerged in the more hierarchically structured communities of Finnmark and other northern provinces.[21] What is important is that the Norwegian Labour Party was willing to accept and attempt to increase its rural voting support. This active and pragmatic rural strategy of the Labour Party contrasts strongly with the German Communists (KPD) and Socialists (SPD) who had little rural organization and, moreover, seemingly little inclination to attempt the political mobilization of rural areas: instead, they tended to regard all rural dwellers as petty bourgeoisie.[22] Institutionalization of voting support becomes an intervening variable between a party's behaviour and its social following.

So far we have reviewed those factors which increase the likelihood of rural support being given to left-wing parties. The limited data available from national surveys suggest that generally the strongest rural support for left parties comes from landless farm labourers. In contemporary Italy, for example, the large landowners have tended to support the Liberals or Monarchists, and farmer owners have been overwhelmingly found in the ranks of the Christian Democrats: by contrast, farm labourers and sharecroppers have supported more radical parties, particularly the Communists. The general outline of this spectrum can be found in several countries. That landownership *per se* is not a sufficient factor is illustrated by the problem of tenancies. Owner-tenant relationships seem also to revolve as much around the issue of economic security as market orientation.[23] The radicalism of sharecroppers in France and Italy is juxtaposed by the conservatism of wealthier, more secure tenants. In his classic study of the west of France, Siegfried points out that while historical reasons and status differences have isolated them from the great landlords, the larger *fermiers* of Normandy loyally supported various forms of conservatism after 1871.[24]

Labourers and sharecroppers, then, form the largest potential rural reservoir of radicalism, a reservoir that can most easily be tapped where they are together in large numbers in both their daily occupational activities and settlement patterns. Yet the degree of political involvement of farm workers is extremely limited. Historically, it has proved very difficult to unionize farm workers, and studies of Italy, Germany and Spain in the early twentieth century suggest sudden, frequent and dramatic fluctuations in the membership of organizations catering for farm labourers and poor tenants.[25] There is no reason to deny the probability of a similar volatility in political mobilization. The previous chapter indicated that levels of political interest and turnout rates among farm labourers are among the lowest of all social groups. Alternatively, the mobilization of labourers may take a very different path: where this is so, the political influence of the great landlord or owner has probably been paramount. In pre-1918 Germany, East Elbia was a stronghold of the Conservative party. That this party was formed by and worked for the great landowners is beyond doubt: of its representatives in the Reichstag, at least 50 per cent were <u>directly</u> related to agriculture, and some 60 per cent were either <u>Rittergutsbesitzer</u> (noble estate owners) or <u>Gutsbesitzer</u> (landlords). Yet the size of its vote indicates that it must have been supported by substantial numbers of farm labourers.[26] Krehbiel has similarly noted that in the decades following the Reform Act of 1884, areas of large estates in England were among the staunchest Conservative areas.[27] Until the Liberal Unionist schism, Conservatives in the liberal fortress of Scotland could generally hope to win only a few constituencies such as Bute where the great landlord, himself a Conservative, could prevail upon his tenants and workers.[28] The conservatism of some regions of the West of France was attributed by Siegfried to the political influence of the landlords, which peaked where they were themselves local residents in areas characterized almost entirely by large enterprises divided into relatively small tenancies.[29]

By contrast, in regions where patterns of settlement have meant that both small cultivators and labourers live, not on isolated farmsteads, but in central villages or even agro-towns - as in parts of Southern Italy and Andalusia - political orientations have been radical. In Southern Italy the Communist vote is weak in the smallest villages and highest in the agro-towns of over 20,000 population.[30] This political support may be due not only to land-hunger, economic poverty, strip-farming, and insecure short-term contractual arrangements, but also perhaps to the greater likelihood of a community consciousness of relative deprivation. The most salient characteristics of rural life in Southern Italy have been its economic marginality,

poverty, and domination by cities. The sense of deprivation
may in fact be more important than extreme poverty in stimulating
political militancy. Class distinctions in the <u>latifundia</u>
regions may create an atmosphere of labour militancy which is
attracted to revolutionary organizations because the aristocratic
and middle class landowners are so closely identified with the
state as well as the existing local social structure.[31]
Concentrated settlement may make their mobilization much easier,
especially where reinforced by both migration flows that do not
break traditional familial links, and effective communication
channels. The heaviest Bolshevik support in rural Russia in
1917 came precisely from those regions that had a direct railway
link to cities or had experienced heavy migration to urban
areas.[32]

A polarization of political support is more likely in areas
of large farms with hired labour. A high degree of radicalism
among farm labourers is paralleled by a more intense conservatism
among owners. Heberle's comments upon the politics of East
Schleswig-Holstein, a region of large enterprises and advanced
commercial agriculture, show the relationship between this style
of agricultural activity and high levels of support for the
conservative DNVP. But at the same time the largest pockets of
Socialist and Communist support were also associated with this
area of large estates. This polarization contrasted strongly
with the adjacent <u>Marsch</u> region of small commercial enterprises
which in the 1920s supported either bourgeois liberalism or a
regional agrarian movement (which functioned very much as a
pressure group) before heightened insecurity and the shock of
depression pushed it into the Nazi camp.[33] A similar pattern of
rather extreme conservative and radical politics has been noted
in areas of France and Italy with large concentrations of hired
labour.[34] Similarly, a distinctive behavioural pattern of
smaller farmers seems to be common. Under "normal" circumstances
these agricultural operators are influenced primarily by
agricultural economic considerations. Lacking the high status
and historical tradition of connections with the state that tend
to be possessed by the great landowners, they nevertheless are
deeply suspicious of any political philosophy that seems to
threaten private ownership or secure tenure of individual

enterprises. A more middle of the road stance may also under certain conditions push them towards the formation of specific parties for agrarian defence. Alternatively, in times of stress their exposed economic position may persuade them to shift towards a totally different political alternative. In Schleswig-Holstein the small farmers moved en masse behind the NSDAP after 1930, and a similar tendency can be seen in parts of Northern Italy.[35]

Overall, then the relative numbers in any one area of owners and labourers will join with forms of employment and degrees of economic security to affect political identification. We might in passing note also the contagion of the proportionate strength of the competing parties. In Italy, for example, there is a tendency for greater than average support by farmers for the Christian Democrats, and labour/sharecropper support for the Communists, in areas where these parties enjoy a very high degree of support.[36] Where the number of labourers is small, the prevailing political feeling may be that of the farmowner. The number of labourers per enterprise is small, and if only a handful or less they tend to stand in a much more personal relationship with the owner, live on the farm, and are more likely to accept the farmer's values. Linz comments on the presence in the Italian Romagna of many such labourers who even participate in the economic management of the enterprise and who tend to be politically divorced from the mass of day labourers.[37] This type of situation is perhaps most likely in regions of isolated farmsteads and small hamlets. Isolation is similarly important for small enterprises operating on the margins of capitalism, for, as Siegfried notes, the political independence that ownership and isolation imply is valid only where the small operators are not forced to seek additional income (either on large estates, or in industry) in homogeneous regions characterized by this form of agrarian structure.[38] By contrast, a divorce between place of work and place of residence seems to increase the likelihood of "class" politics. Heberle argues that the polarized politics of the Marsch zone were assisted by the settlement pattern, where "the farmers live on single farm-steads with spacious buildings in the midst of their fields and pastures; the poor, the working-class people in the villages and in small line-settlements along the dikes and the edge of the Geest".[39]

Alternatively, it might be that in more integrated regions of small enterprises and few labourers, the farmowner will feel less threatened by a mass of land-hungry labourers; and that therefore radical parties will be more successful in attracting the electoral support of the farmowners. However, radicalism in this context is less economic than it is political. The existence of integrated regions of farmer-capitalist enterprises more or less means the elimination of internal agrarian cleavages and transfers the focus of opposition to the cities. Market forces become pre-eminent, and urban groups are on hand to be blamed for catastrophe. The importance of the capitalist economy and its vagaries helps explain the greater volatility of this farming group, and the simplified urban-rural contrast perhaps lies behind the greater probability of the generation of agrarian-specific parties or a flight to <u>politically</u> radical parties, most notably fascism. As a rider, it may be added that in the early phases of this symbiotic relationship between town and countryside, those urban occupations with whom the farmer was engaged most frequently were filled to a not inconsiderable degree by Jews; antisemitism became another facet of the politics of the countryside in the early twentieth century. But overall, it is a limited number of landless labourers which defines the restricted clientele of radical parties. Throughout the twentieth century migration from rural areas to the towns and the mechanization of agriculture have led to a steady decline in the numbers of hired labourers. The contraction of agriculture may not only have produced a more homogeneous countryside: it also has reduced opportunities for radical parties to gain rural support as well as diminishing the electoral value of the latter.

A further vital factor that distinguishes between various kinds of enterprise would seem to be the characteristics and structure of farming organizations. Farming unions and cooperatives tend to be led and dominated by larger wealthier cultivators. Peasant organizations and cooperatives in France and Germany at the end of the nineteenth century were usually dominated by larger landowners, and served the latter's interests rather than those of the poorer peasants. Only after 1918 did there appear in France any kind of agrarian organization with a radical orientation: nevertheless, the major associations have been dominated by larger farmers.[40] Denmark is one of the few countries with more than one viable national cooperative federation, each appealing to and catering for a different size of farmer. Where farming organizations are dominated by large owners, they may, other things being equal, be more likely to support conservative parties. As a consequence, "organizational contagion" may induce poorer, smaller farmers also to accept the views of the organization and to support conservative parties. In Ireland, for example, irrespective of the size of farm and degree of capitalist involvement, farmers who belong to farming associations tend to prefer the more conservative Fine Gael party rather than Fianna Fail.[41] Again, in Italy the support of near-subsistence farmers for the Christian Democrats seems to be a function of their almost complete financial dependence upon the semi-public <u>Federconsorzi</u> (Federation of Agricultural Consortiums). Not only is this body controlled by the Christian Democrats: it is also under the domination of the Christian Democrat association of small farmers, the National Confederation of Direct Cultivators. It is estimated that about 80 per cent of small Italian farmers belong to the latter, while only about ten per cent are enrolled in the Communist affiliated Peasant Alliance.[42]

It is clear that one major restraint upon agrarian voting patterns is the greater traditionalism of the countryside. The persistence of traditional conservatism is often manifested through a greater religiosity and a concern with moral issues and values. Personal, family and local loyalties are buttressed by a strong religious belief and are clothed in historic ceremonial rites. The survival of traditional conservatism is especially true of small enterprises at the fringes of the capitalist economy. They are more removed from market pressures and less readily perceive the direct consequences of specific governmental policies. However, isolation does not preclude prejudices against "the government" in the abstract. Such conservative areas may on occasion burst into revolt. In Norway the Fascist appeal succeeded less in regions of large farms with many labourers, and was rejected by the more strongly religious small farmers of the southwest: its limited strength lay more in homogeneous areas of marginal enterprises in the southeast which had shed much of their religiosity. Occasionally, the violence of the eruption is such that the traditional underpinnings vanish almost overnight as the agrarian electorate veers towards radical extremes - the case of several regions of France, Central and Southern Italy, and Northern Finland. Overall, however, it is simply a particular set of historical circumstances that produces a persisting framework of points of reference. The symbolic language generated may have little or nothing to do with religion. In France the symbolic language has buttressed a radical political tradition, which through the decades has turned some rural regions towards the most radical political alternative. As each alternative became assimilated into the system, - from Radicalism through to Communism - so the electorate looked elsewhere for a refurbishing of its faith. That even agrarian support for the Communist party is contingent rather than institutionalized was underlined by the fact that there were indications of a high Poujadist vote in the 1950s in many rural Communist fiefs.[43]

There does, however, seem to be a major distinction between Protestant and Catholic cultures. In the former a powerful emphasis upon individual morality is a persistent issue orientation, frequently arising from a continual reframing of political issues in moralistic language. There exists much evidence to suggest that agrarian society is more likely to favour such measures as the prohibition of alcohol, illiberal divorce laws and a ban on gambling. The clearest instance of such attitudes is the issue of teetotalism in Scandinavia and Estonia as a significant political force in the early twentieth century. The great increase in rural turnout in Norway in 1930 occurred during an election campaign in which such issues were prominent.[44] An appropriate measure of the rural emphasis upon moral values is the series of referenda held after 1918 upon the desirability of prohibiting the manufacture, sale and consumption of alcohol: these clearly demonstrate that rural populations were more strongly in favour of teetotalism. In Sweden the issue of prohibition even split the Liberal party in 1923: most of the support for the new "dry" faction came from rural districts.[45] The question of alcohol remains a salient political issue today, particularly in Norway.[46]

Religion and its values have been taken more seriously in rural areas. Underlying these moralist and religious beliefs is the general phenomenon that innovation tends to be diffused from city to countryside. Hence, agrarian groups retain traditional and older ways of living and thinking for longer periods of time. The strength of moral asceticism in Protestant countries is not surprising, for the religious creed itself stresses asceticism. By contrast, rural traditionalism in Catholic Europe does not necessarily entail a moralistic and austere bias. As a network of inter-related organizations, the Catholic Church itself actively provides the underpinnings of rural traditionalism. The core agrarian areas of radical parties in France are characterized not only by the weak position of the Church, but often also by a militant anti-clericalism. Some of the most rabid Catholic areas of western France are <u>fermier</u> (tenant) regions where the local presence of the Church has been pervasive throughout the social fabric. On the other hand, the post-1945 MRP (Christian Democrat party) found more rural support in Western France in churchgoing areas of small owner-occupiers.[47] In Belgium, the degree of religious commitment seems to operate as a powerful intervening variable on agricultural behaviour. Practising farmers overwhelmingly support the Christian Socialist party: non-practising farmers to an equally high degree give their support elsewhere - to the Socialists in Flanders and the Liberals in Wallonia.[48] Similarly, the more devout cultivators of Moravia were staunch backers of the Czech Populist (Catholic) party, in strong contrast to the more secularized farmers of Bohemia.

2. <u>The Politics of Different Kinds of Agriculture</u>
Occupational differences between farmers and farm workers influence their voting behaviour. A further electoral distinction derived from agricultural social structure may be related to agricultural activity. The historical differences between those farmers who produce crops commercially for the

market, and those who are more oriented towards a subsistence level and domestic self-sufficiency seem to have survived into the period of electoral politics. The data for France for example show that share tenants have been more left-wing in their voting behaviour than cash tenants. Two general points may be made. First, the operator of a domestic consumptive enterprise, because of a nexus of social traditions and his prime economic interest, seems to be more inclined than the farmer-capitalist to vote for conservative parties; and second, he is more likely to be a political non-participant. Nevertheless, in times of severe economic depression, when retrenchment alone appears insufficient to ensure his family's survival, the marginal cultivator may swing violently towards radicalism. However, the political parties which attract peasant support in periods of agricultural crisis may not necessarily be left-wing in class or urban terms, but are more often radical in the sense of being anti-system or at least anti-establishment. These hypotheses are difficult to test: the quality of survey data is such that no assessment of the "capitalist" or "subsistence" characteristics of individual respondents is possible. Even a crude classification of regions on the basis of aggregate data would be very difficult.

While all farmers are concerned with the maintenance of income levels and the availability of easy, cheap credit, and while all may look towards governments and parties to guarantee these, political differences may arise because of varying attitudes held towards the land. Landless labourers may desire land, but their aspiration may well be for individually-owned holdings. This means for instance that they may be resistant to the appeals of Communism. On the basis of limited and rather unsatisfactory data from Bulgaria (1923) and Slovakia (1928) one author has argued that Communist mobilization in Eastern Europe, contrasting somewhat to its successes in France and Italy, was more effective among cash farmers than among dwarf and landless peasants.[49] The more conventional view is that for the peasant, landownership (or the secure occupation of land) dominates over all else, while for the commercial farmer the land is more a means to an end, of satisfactory prices for his produce. It is the effect of the laws of supply and demand in causing fluctuations, at times severe, in price levels which makes the commercial farmer both more insistent upon government action (thereby perhaps favouring more radical parties) and more likely to "sell" his vote to parties which promise action in this field. In his review of Catholic parties in Southern Europe Burks comments that "crop diversification coupled with intensive cultivation based upon manual labor tends to be characteristic of Catholic, i.e. Conservative strongholds ...... The rural population of the radical areas, on the other hand, is characteristically engaged in the production of a single crash crop. The price of the crop fluctuates with the vagaries of the international market."[50] The Catholic areas were, moreover, characterized by relative isolation (being mainly mountainous), relatively distinctive ethnic traits, less urbanization, and middle class dominance in Catholic political organizations. Yet one should be wary of over-generalization. One of these areas, Brittany, has been a great mix of traditional conservative, Catholic, and republican sentiment.[51]

The market and commercial considerations can be equally important for the domestic consumptive enterprises. One need not be heavily involved in capitalist activities to feel or suffer from the consequences of the capitalist system. En masse, subsistence cultivators may be politically passive and enmeshed in a more stable structure of local relationships that to some extent shuns the outside world. Yet a complete divorce is never possible. The grand march of economic events may have political consequences similar to those of the capitalist farmer. The difference is more one of degree: the commercial farmer is simply more deeply and continuously engaged in the market. In short, the greater the susceptibility of cultivators to capitalist forces, the more likely they are to seek alleviation and protection. In the era of centralized government, their search inevitably finishes with the government. Moreover, demands - for example either for tariff barriers against foreign competition or for price support schemes for native produce - will push agrarian groups into alliance with some urban groups and into opposition to others. Tariff schemes have been widely popular in Europe since the late nineteenth century. They can, however, give rise to anti-rural feeling among urban working class groups who may see protective tariffs as the cause of high and rising food prices. On the other hand, price support schemes have frequently been frowned upon by urban business groups, perhaps because of their general opposition to government intervention in the economy and movement of prices.

It is the agrarian reaction to both its own social structure and economic situation which determines which policy is sought by agrarian groups, and this will obviously vary from structure to structure and from country to country. In Sweden, for example, the basic sympathy which the Social Democrats had in the 1930s for guaranteeing agricultural prices not only enabled them to attract a significant rural support, but also persuaded the Agrarian party that entrance into a government coalition with the Social Democrats would help advance the economic interests of their own supporters. An interesting aggregate analysis which illustrates the importance of the market in influencing political behaviour is Rumpf's attempt to explain nationalism and radicalism in Ireland in terms of socio-economic factors. He detects an east-west gradient corresponding, among other things, to differences in the size of farms and the kind of agriculture pursued. In the north-east of the Irish Republic the large farmers were largely quiescent in the independence struggle, and during the Civil War were in favour of the Free State rather than the Republic solution. Ater 1923 they voted heavily for Cumann na n'Gaedheal (later Fine Gael). Their position was determined to a considerable extent by the fact that they exported cattle direct to England and hence were very much dependent upon the British market for their economic well-being. By contrast, nationalist and republican sentiments prevailed over economics among the smaller farmers of the west, who were not so involved in commercial farming and had no direct connection with the British market: what few cattle they sold were to the large farmers in the east for fattening prior to export. The dairy farming region around Cork offers a striking corrobation of the thesis. Before 1923 it had been a hotbed of nationalist activity. But once the British government had assured political independence in principle, the political motivations of the dairy farmers sprang primarily from economic considerations: since they also exported produce direct to Britain, the area was in favour of the Free State.[52]

One further explanatory factor in determining rural voting behaviour may enable to distinguish between various kinds of farmer capitalist enterprises. Evidence from Anglo-American countries suggests that variations in political behaviour are correlated with different kinds of crops produced for the market.[53] The commitment to a market economy usually means a concentration upon the production of a single crop, and this increases the vulnerability of the farmer to the vicissitudes of the international market. Specialization of production obviously means that not all farmers will experience similar fluctuations at the same time. We may hypothesize that those farming groups that are most susceptible both to international competition and variations in crop yields may be more inclined towards radical voting and more likely to accept the idea of government involvement and regulations. North American evidence suggests that more radical politics are to be found among wheat farmers. In France those northern regions which grow wheat by means of extensive techniques have tended more to support leftist parties. By contrast, Fauvet suggests that meat, and especially dairy regions are conservative.[54] In his excellent study of Seine-et-Marne, Bernard suggests that the radicalism of the wheat and sugar beet areas is a function of the presence of large numbers of labourers.[55] The same is probably true of the wheat-growing areas of the Italian Po valley.[56] But even the cantonal agrarian parties of Switzerland, which traditionally have been conservative, always united with the left parties on the wheat monopoly issue.[57] On the other hand, the stronghold of the Spanish Right in the 1930s lay in the Kingdoms of León and Burgos, where many of the provinces relied heavily upon wheat-growing. However, in contrast to the larger estates of Seine-et-Marne these were strongly Catholic areas with medium to small enterprises, including some cash tenancies.[58]

Can we say from the limited evidence that crop-producing areas are likely to be more radical than stockraising or dairy areas? The data are insufficient to support or invalidate such a hypothesis. It could, however, be agreed that livestock production, especially dairy farming, can lead to a certain diversification in the end products which, as for example in

Denmark, result in associated rural industries. Moreover, before the development of efficient refrigeration, commodities such as butter and milk had a short life, and therefore producers were to some extent shielded from geographically distant competition. A further reason could be the greater susceptibility of crops to climatic hazards: this is especially true of the situation of wheat in the temperate zones of the world. But we should also remember that the contrast between France and Spain indicates the importance here also of the size of enterprise and the size of the hired work force. At a minimum, it seems clear that capitalist involvement and specialization upon one product may push cultivators into periodic protest movements, authoritarian as well as radical: their political involvement, moreover, may be highly unstable. Once again, we can refer to Heberle's excellent regional study. The cattle and dairy farmers of Schleswig-Holstein, previously unhappy about the war economy measures of the imperial government, turned after 1918 to liberalism and the Weimar coalition. But once it was clear that the new government was determined to follow a cheap food policy and retain the wartime measures, the farmers abandoned their party allegiance and founded a new regional agrarian movement, the Landespartei. By the end of the decade, with the failure of all governments to satisfy their aspirations, they were turning towards the NSDAP.[59]

3. Conclusion: Parochial Conservatism and "Entrepreneurial Radicalism"

On the whole, the radicalism of the cultivator is not in favour of state control, but at the extreme looks for a redistribution of land or extensive governmental aid <u>within</u> a framework of private property. Despite at time strenuous efforts by Communist or Socialist parties in Europe, their attempts to win over the agrarian population have rarely met with significant success on the basis of their economic programmes. For example, the Socialist Congress at Breslau sought support by promising state crop insurance and state ownership of mortgages, but with little avail. A single peasant group, from the Belgian Ardennes, participated in the Socialist Internationals in the nineteenth century: with "simple peasant sense" they told the assembled delegates that "it will be difficult to build up Socialism on the soil of old Europe" and proposed instead a "general emigration to America".[60] Again, during the brief existence of the Peasant Councils in Bavaria, one report from Upper Franconia said: "Our local peasant council was founded in the critical days of November to prevent a foundation by the Social Democrats so that radical elements would not pester us. No real activity was intended and until today virtually nothing has been done".[61]

Essentially, then, conservatism or radicalism in the rural context mean very different things than in the urban context. Conservatism is social and parochial conservatism, not economic laissez-faire. Farmers may vote for conservative parties, but may still desire government invervention, regulation and financial support. Radicalism can mean different things to landless and landed. In most parts of Europe labourers may vote for radical parties as a protest against their condition, but the basic remedy is frequently seen not as being economic betterment through higher wages, but the acquisition of land. It tends therefore not to be radical in the sense of wishing any other kind of fundamental reforms of the social structure. Radicalism among owner-occupiers, especially those heavily involved in commercial farming, is even less a critique of prevailing social patterns. A recent study of Italy points out that the Catholic organization of small farmers (Coldiretti) possesses the most implacable anti-Communist attitude of all the Catholic organizations: yet its opposition to the Communist party derives less from the latter's anticlerialism, than from its implicit hostility to private property.[62] The phrase "entrepreneurial radicalism", coined by Hofstadter to describe the American experience, seems to be the most succinct description of this style of political behaviour which is almost solely concerned with economic satisfaction within a system of private ownership of land.[63]

CHAPTER 6   The Formation of Agrarian Parties

Attempts to organize agrarian interests and political movements are not only contemporary phenomena: they constitute a not entirely insignificant thread throughout the whole course of European agrarian history. Agrarian structures, their forms of social organization and styles of activity have revolved around the institution of land, its ownership, and its utilization. Modern agrarian movements are essentially still built around the same preoccupations. Cultivators have been forced or led into the national political arena because of the overriding agrarian concern with landownership and/or the consequences of market involvement. While the two are inextricably intertwined, perhaps the question of land occupation must be settled first: only then maybe can market considerations emerge in their own right. The discussion of the post-1918 redistribution of land in Eastern Europe demonstrated that the mobilization of the landless and dwarf peasantry was not particularly essential for the introduction of land reform. However, if it is to be successful, land reform must serve as the catalyst for peasant mobilization. The establishment of agrarian political associations becomes of paramount importance: it may well be the most important political consequence of agricultural reform movements.[1]

However, in most European countries the rural entry into national electoral politics resulted in agrarian support being spread among several political parties: only occasionally has one party received a majority of agrarian votes. In Western Europe today, agrarian votes without exception constitute only a minority of most parties' support: many political parties may be sympathetic towards rural claims, but their primary <u>raison d'être</u> was not and is not agrarian. By collaborating with larger, broadly-based national parties, farmers and farming organizations have been able to surmount the barrier of spatial isolation: this is equally true where farmers, although a minority of the national electorate, dominate a certain area of the country. For several decades agrarian populations in Western Europe have been permanent social minorities. The limited size of the agricultural sector and its social and economic distinctiveness are major reasons why agrarian politics often appear to be ambiguous or even opportunistic. Where the dominant social groups refuse categorically to accommodate rural interests and demands, agrarian groups find that the opportunities of achieving their goals through the established political processes and institutions are extremely limited. Such situations conform to the "symmetrical and asymmetrical" types described by Dahl.[2] They may impose particularly severe strains where farmers are geographically concentrated. Alternatively, where cultivators are an electoral majority, the political power that could come from numerical superiority may or may not be realized, depending upon the degree of internal homogeneity and possible conflicts.

Let us pursue the former scenario in a little more detail. Farmers may feel obliged to form their own political party to espouse their interests. Alternatively (or even simultaneously), they may be driven towards direct action. The latter has a long and significant history in Europe: indeed, it has been the most typical expression of agrarian political activity. The numerous instances of direct action by European farmers in recent years indicate that it still serves an important purpose for agrarian society. The consequences of a permanent minority position for a party frequently lead it towards extremism. Admittedly, the theoretical and empirical literature dealing with this subject explicitly or implicitly refers to intensely ideologically motivated parties or to those springing from religious, ethnic or linguistic minorities. However, there is no logical reason why the consequence for farmers should be different: we have already indicated the propensity of farmers to support extremist movements in times of stress. Duverger has aptly summarized the consequences as follows:

> Permanent minority parties tend towards opposition. Expressing an opinion which is, they feel, not that of the nation and which has little support, they are led into an attitude of protestation and intransigence by the same psychological mechanism which leads an inferiority complex to show itself in aggressiveness...... When they are supported by a homogeneous and solid fraction of the population - a geographical or religious minority - the tendency is even more emphasized, for outbidding and violence are ways of retaining their basic supporters, of maintaining their separation from the national community, of keeping their individuality and their heteredoxy unsullied. If a party is clearly in a minority in the country as a whole but in a majority in certain districts its attitude becomes autonomist or even secessionist.[3]

Only a little rephrasing is necessary to see how this statement could apply to agrarian society and politics.

1. The Establishment of Agrarian Parties

The size of the agricultural population and its relationship with urban groups are important in considering the possible emergence of agrarian groups. It is easy to appreciate the difficulties facing such a potential party in contemporary Europe because of the small size of the agrarian populations and the strength of institutionalized party systems. It is more difficult to plot the possibilities in earlier periods when mass parties were only beginning to emerge and to consolidate themselves, and when the agricultural sector was significantly larger than it is now. In most of the countries of Europe, a majority of the population resided in rural areas and was dependent upon agriculture for its livelihood until fairly recently.

After about 1850 the growth differential between European urban and rural populations increased dramatically. The mix of a large rural population and rapidly growing cities has characterized the urban-rural dimension of political behaviour in transitional societies. In the concurrent phase in Europe of suffrage expansion and political mobilization the crucial institutionalizing role was played by political parties. However, as befits organizations which are essentially modern conceptions political parties have usually been urban creations with their leadership and activists recruited primarily from urban areas.[4] But in many countries parties can become mass organizations only through the mobilization of the countryside. Hence, political parties and the party system can provide an institutional structure linking rural with urban society. The bridging of the urban-rural gap may not be completed for one or two possibly complementary reasons. In the first place, agrarian society may reject the urban overtures out of hand. Alternatively, urban politicians may not be able to make the psychological adjustment necessary to understand the rural situation: they may not be capable of replacing their "modern", urban values and concepts by (or joining them with) the more traditional commitments of rural areas. These tensions may increase as the decline in the agricultural population continues, for at the same time the level of agrarian political participation may increase.

The net result of such developments may be attempts to form parties that would specifically defend agrarian interests. Among those European countries which have a long history of competitive party politics from the introduction of universal male suffrage to the present day, only in Scandinavia have such agrarian parties proved to be durable and electorally significant. In their review of cleavage development and party formation in Western Europe Lipset and Rokkan detail two developments from their Parsonian-inspired model: parties for territorial defence and parties for agrarian defence. Building primarily upon the empirical cases of Britain and Scandinavia, they trace the origins of parties for territorial defence back to the nation-building process and the Reformation, comparing the urban-rural alliance within British Conservatism with the centre-periphery division in Scandinavia where the Right remained essentially urban.[5] The problems of fitting a mass of empirical data into a parsimonious model are amply illustrated by this comparison. For when they refer to Britain the authors are essentially describing England. The British periphery experienced rather different developments. For example, as late as the nineteenth century rural Wales was typified by an economic dependence between small tenant farmers and the aristocracy, accentuated by sharp religious differences between the two. In the nineteenth century the landlords became urban residents, and the security of tenure of their tenants decreased significantly. In many ways the Welsh social situation approached that of Scandinavia yet the political expression of intra-rural and urban-rural cleavages was rather different.[6]

Lipset and Rokkan's model predicts that agrarian parties are most likely to appear in systems where there is a close alliance between the nation-builders (N) and the urban economic elite (U): these are the four N-U cases in their eightfold typology of alliances and oppositions. But in three of the four cases the opposition of the peasantry to the cities is closely related to their rejection of the religious or moral value of the urban nation-builders. These considerations lead the authors to opt for the emergence of landowning-religious nonconformist alliances in Scandinavia and a landowning-Catholic alliance in France and Italy: no basis existed for an agrarian-religious alliance in Belgium since the Catholic Church was influential in both the cities and the countryside. Only in Scandinavia did agrarian parties emerge. The construction of alliance options which affected the direction of rural political mobilization can only be understood in terms of the structure of agrarian society at the time of suffrage extension. Lipset and Rokkan suggest that the most important consideration is the concentration of resources for the control of political mobilization, and the relationship of the pattern of landownership and tenure to the size of farm units. They conclude that agrarian parties will appear when four conditions are present: where the cities and industrial centres are numerically weak when the suffrage is decisively extended; where the bulk of the agrarian population is employed on small or medium-sized farms either owner-occupied or with legal security of tenure; where significant cultural barriers exist between town and countryside, with strong resistance to the incorporation of agricultural production in an urban-dominated market economy; and where the Catholic Church is without significant influence.

It is not the intention here to object to this interpretation <u>per se</u>, but rather to explore it in greater detail and with a larger number of empirical cases. If we consider party formation in Europe as a whole from the late nineteenth century onwards, we find that attempts to establish agrarian parties were made in nearly every country. Most succeeded either for a short while or with a limited segment of the agrarian electorate. But throughout Eastern Europe such parties played a prominent role in their country's development and politics before 1940. Yet at first glance it would seem that some of these agrarian parties were different from those which established themselves in Scandinavia. We shall consider both the activities of these parties and their place in the party system, as well as the social structure conditions which deter rural voters from becoming integrated within urban-dominated parties and encourage them to form exclusively agrarian parties.[7]

The theoretical and empirical literature on political parties is vast. Discussions attempting to typify parties have always paid particular attention to their origins, for the circumstances surrounding their birth clearly have a significant influence upon later developments. Party origins have traditionally been discussed under three headings: institutional theories examining parliamentary and extra-parliamentary origins; developmental theories that focus upon the wider aspect of modernization; and crisis theories that relate to critical junctures which countries experience at the historical moment in time when political movements emerge.[8] Despite the flood of literature, which makes it almost impossible to discuss political processes and relationships in a country without referring to its party system, there is as yet no universally accepted answer to the problem of what constitutes a party: nor has there been established any theoretically meaningful definition of a minor or a significant party.

Perhaps the most important consideration to bear in mind is that political organizations are movements adapted to or reflecting local conditions. The social and economic environments of the countries discussed here are so disparate that it does not seem to be entirely appropriate or useful at this point to offer any kind of structured definition of the term "party", as this might well exclude from consideration certain significant political manifestations. At a minimum, a party may be said to be a political movement which describes itself as such and which is generally regarded as a party by the political actors and electorate. Hence we are not overly concerned with organizational aspects, at least in the first instance. It means that any group, no matter how loosely organized, seeking to obtain governmental office can be regarded as a party. The inability of personal groups to secure a permanent organization may be equally important a consideration in some countries as strongly structured parties in others. The approach to agrarian parties is equally eclectic. Agrarian parties can be regarded as those which demonstrably obtain the vast majority of their support from the countryside, claim in their programmes and other pronouncements specifically to represent agrarian interests, and/or simply include in their title some term as agrarian, peasant or farmer. Three important considerations must be noted. First, in some countries all parties will obtain most of their votes from the countryside. In such circumstances all three criteria listed above can be used to differentiate "agrarian" parties from the remainder. Second, the comparison of parties which claim to possess a similar set of ideological doctrines or even simply possess a similar title does not mean a kinship between them, or that there is an essential sociological similarity between the sets of beliefs and organization when viewed within the context of political action and behaviour. Any differences that exist will emerge in the analysis. Finally, we are primarily concerned with the late nineteenth and early twentieth centuries, the era of mass political mobilization in Europe and of the formation of political parties. It might well be that to some extent the material has been anticipated by the earlier historical analysis of the political development of agrarian society in Europe. Hopefully, however, there will not be a simple repetition, as the present intention is to view social, cultural and economic developments in terms of their influence upon the likelihood of the appearance and survival of political parties for agrarian defence. In particular, the focus will be upon the 1920s, for this decade was the heyday of the competitive party system in Europe. Because of their numeral size in most countries cultivators could have dominated electoral politics. The years after 1918, with the expansion of the suffrage, marked the greatest opportunity for forming and managing parties in a "free market" situation. By the end of the decade, the storm clouds of authoritarianism had gathered over the continent, and one country after another passed from a greater or lesser degree of genuine competitive electoral politics to some form of dictatorship. Because there is less opportunity for a party to manœuvre under an authoritarian regime, these new political structures are only of ancillary interest from our point of view. Moreover, such an emphasis implies an interest primarily in parties that contested elections. This is a reasonable proposition, for electoral participation assumes a minimum level of support juxtaposed with a maximum degree of visibility.

Based almost entirely upon electoral data (the major exception being Albania), Table 6.1 is a summary list of European agrarian parties, as well as a crude attempt to indicate their approximate strength and political tendency. Variations across these parties will be the theme of this and the next two chapters. With the exception of Portugal the table indicates a complete absence of agrarian parties only in some of the most industrialized and urbanized countries - Britain, Belgium and Luxemburg.[9] The Netherlands might also be included in this category, for the agrarian party that emerged in 1920 was a one-man party. One of the few new European parties of recent decades to win parliamentary representation was the <u>Boerenpartij</u> (BP) of the 1960s. However, this Dutch party was not strictly agrarian. It was founded in 1958 as a reaction against what was thought to be too much government interference in private life. Its original appeal was probably intended to be towards farmers because they were opposed to the growing activities of the <u>Landbouwschap</u> a semi-governmental agency possessing regulatory and taxation powers in the field of agriculture. However, the party reflected more a general unrest and dissatisfaction about the operation of public affairs as well as protest against social and economic change: the majority of its support came from urban areas.[10]

Small agrarian parties have appeared from time to time in all other countries which after 1918 had less than 50 per cent of their population dependent upon agricultures. But outside Scandinavia with its enduring farmers' parties, Western Europe

Table 6.1: The Universe of European Agrarian Parties

Country	Party and Approximate Date of Origin	Average Electoral Strength	Political Tendency
Albania	Agrarian Democrat 1918	(large)	peasantist
Austria	Landbund 1918	very weak	conservative
Belgium	-	-	-
Bulgaria	Agrarian Union 1889	large	peasantist
Czechoslovakia	Czech Republican 1896	medium	moderate
	German Bund der Landwirte 1920	weak	moderate
	Magyar Agrarian 1920	very weak	moderate
	Ruthene Autonomous Agricultural Union 1923	very weak	peasantist
Denmark	Venstre 1888	large	moderate/conservative
Estonia	Agrarian 1917	large	conservative
	New Settlers 1921	medium	moderate
	Smallholders 1923	very weak	moderate
Finland	Agrarian (Centre) 1906	large	moderate
	Smallholders 1962	medium	radical
France	Agrarian 1928	weak	conservative/catholic
	Peasant 1948	weak	conservative/catholic
Germany	several regional parties from the 1890s	all very weak	all conservative
Greece	ephemeral groups	very weak	peasantist
Hungary	(Christian Smallholders 1920)	majority	conservative
	Independent Christian 1931	weak	conservative
Iceland	Progressive 1916	large	moderate
Ireland	Farmers 1923	weak	conservative
	Clann na Talmhan 1938	weak	moderate
Italy	Peasant 1946	very weak	moderate
Latvia	Peasant Union 1917	medium	conservative
	New Farmers 1923	weak	moderate
	Latgalian Christian Farmers 1919	weak	catholic
	Latgalian Progressive Farmers 1919	very weak	moderate

Lithuania	Peasant Union 1919	medium	catholic
	Farmers 1925	very weak	moderate
Luxemburg	-	-	-
Netherlands	Agrarian 1920	very weak	conservative
	Farmers 1958	very weak	radical
Norway	Agrarian (Centre) 1920	medium	moderate
Poland	Piast 1913	medium	moderate
	Wyzwolenie 1915	medium	peasantist
	Ukrainian Peasant 1920	very weak	peasantist
Portugal	-	-	-
Rumania	National Peasant 1926	large	peas./moderate
	Numerous small groups	all very weak	all political tendances
Spain	Agrarian 1931	very weak	conservative
Sweden	Agrarian (Centre) 1921	medium	moderate
Switzerland	Farmers, Traders & Citizens (People's) 1920	medium	conservative
United Kingdom	(Crofters 1885)	(very weak)	(radical)
Yugoslavia	Croat Peasant 1904	medium	peas./nationalist
	Serb Agrarian 1918	weak	peasantist
	Slovene Agrarian 1924	very weak	peasantist

Note: Average Electoral Strength

Majority, 50% or more
major, 35-50%
large, 20-35%

medium, 10-20%
weak, 5-10%
very weak, less than 5%

witnessed no significant nationally-based agrarian parties. In Germany all the several agrarian groups that appeared between 1870 and 1933, including the Bund der Landwirte, were regionally oriented. After 1918 the East Elbian upper classes lost their control of the Bund, which fragmented into unambiguous regional and special interest groups, such as the Württemberger Bauern- und Weingärtnerbund und Bund der Landwirte. These were electorally successful usually only where they allied themselves with larger national parties. Their parliamentary candidates were often listed with those of the larger parties in published results: hence, their exact strength is difficult to assess.[11]

Fleurant Agricola's Parti Agraire of the Third French Republic and its Fourth Republic successor, the Parti Paysan, were in essence confined to certain strongly Catholic areas, particularly the Cevennes where both parties originated: the latter, however, succeeded in establishing organizations in one-half of the départements by 1950. In their relations with other groups these two parties cooperated very closely with conservative, more urban oriented tendances.[12] A small Italian Peasant Party failed to break out of a few Southern provinces whose particular interests it espoused.[13] In Switzerland also, small agrarian parties failed to extend themselves beyond certain cantons: the same is true of the Farmers, Citizens and Traders party (now the People's party) which seceded from the Radicals in 1920.[14] Of the successor states in Eastern Europe only Czechoslovakia falls into this economic category. Here each ethnic group tended to produce a sub-cultural party system that contained, among others, an agrarian party. After the Socialist-Communist split in the early 1920s the Czech Republican party (agrarian) became the largest party in the country (but never winning more than 15 per cent of the votes) and the lynchpin of all government coalitions.

It might be assumed that a prime factor influencing the foundation of a significant agrarian party would be a large agricultural population. But meaningful parties were not a necessary consequence of even a majority of a population dependent upon agriculture. In the more agricultural states of Eastern Europe, agrarian parties emerged in every country except Greece. In the three countries of Western Europe which fall in this category, agrarian parties apparently failed to emerge in Portugal and had only a limited electoral appeal in Spain and Ireland. In both cases the agrarian parties were regionally-based. This perhaps is not surprising in Spain, an imperfectly integrated society. The Agrarians, while hoping to establish themselves as a national party, were essentially limited to the wheat farmers of the Castiles and León: in any case, they rapidly passed into the relatively loose coalition of CEDA (Confederación Española de Dereches Autónomas).[15] In Ireland the interwar Farmers' Party was confined to the large farmers in the northeast of the country, while the later Clann na Talmhan appealed only to the small farmers in the western provinces of Connacht.

2. The Agricultural Basis of Agrarian Parties

Agrarian parties, then, were more likely to emerge in countries with a majority of the population dependent upon agriculture. The deviancy of Ireland, Spain and Portugal is perhaps to be explained in terms of other social structure variables, especially religion. The failure of *any* meaningful party in interwar Albania seems simply to be due to the total lack of political maturity. Before the seizure of power by Zog, an extremely rudimentary party system operated less within a nationally integrated political system than within a loose and localized tribal structure differentiated along religious and quasi-ethnic lines, more reminiscent of backward African areas at that time than Europe.[16]

The most interesting deviant case is Greece. Three reasons may be advanced why Greece, alone of the heavily rural states of Eastern Europe, did not give birth to an agrarian party. First, the country experienced early commercialization, aided perhaps by the total unsuitability of large areas of its territory for any form of agriculture. The early appearance of a strong merchant class affected all segments of Greek society: the urban-rural gap was not as great as in the neighbouring Balkan societies. Perhaps because of these factors the peasants' commitment to the land was never complete. The influence of mercantilism meant that for many the land was viewed to some extent as a marketable commodity. In addition, attitudes to the land are in many ways reminiscent of the hostility of Andalusian or Sicilian peasants noted by anthropologists.[17] Second, the influence of the traditionally strong Greek cities and also that of nearby Constantinople may have contributed to the survival of nuclear villages in which leadership was provided by local priests and prominent peasant landowners. The villages, moreover, were linked to the national centre through strong administrative and familial networks. Finally, the relatively early independence of Greece may have been contributory. The flames of agrarianism spread through Eastern Europe in the late nineteenth and early twentieth centuries in part as an expression of nationalist resentment against imperial rule and landownership. Greece, however, was already independent, with a long-established pattern of peasant occupation of land. Moreover, politics had already been institutionalized under urban leadership. Although the key to understanding Greek political development was a vast patronage system which entailed buying votes (through for example the control of debts and credit), it was an institutionalized system where clientelist arrangements did provide the rural masses with several benefits.[18]

Enduring agrarian parties were likely to appear in countries with no more than a substantial minority of the population dependent upon agriculture only when two subsidiary factors were present: where the structure of land tenure and farm size was one of small owner-occupied enterprises with a strong or increasing capitalist involvement. Land tenure systems were of crucial political significance at earlier critical junctures of European agrarian history. This applies with equal force during the early stages of suffrage development. In rural England, Prussia and France the electoral reforms of the nineteenth century strengthened the political influence of the aristocracy and gentry, Gutsbesitzer, and notables. Obviously, in such circumstances retention of the traditional rural stratification pattern with its deferential component could prevent the emergence of broadly-based agrarian movements. By contrast, the decisive thrust towards political modernization in Scandinavia came about through the mobilization of a freehold peasantry.[19] The nearest empirical case to these conditions for the emergence of an agrarian-based party is Denmark, which by the 1880s had an agriculture fully involved in commercial farming, but these conditions apply also to the other Scandinavian countries. Switzerland and Austria were similar cases, but did not produce nation-wide or enduring agrarian parties: the failure of the latter will have to be explained in the light of other factors. Czechoslovakia would also perhaps fall in this category, especially if we consider only Bohemia and Moravia-Silesia where a pattern of productive commercial farming did exist and which were the provinces where the Czech Republicans drew a disproportionate share of their electoral support.

Two further points may be added. Agrarian parties were more

likely to arise in countries which possessed a more traditional peasant society, where land-hunger was strong, enterprises were small and domestic-oriented, and where there was a powerful parochial nexus of social and cultural traditions. For example, Pešelj has argued that before 1945 peasant Europe stood "for that part of the continent which is devoted to agrarian production under the system of small and medium holdings and in which farming represents a tradition, a civilization, and a way of life .... in which by far the greatest portion of the population is peasant and forms a group whose economic, social, and cultural aspects have been genuinely preserved".[20] The countries which Pešelj regards as constituting peasant Europe all produced agrarian parties. Where there is this kind of rural society, urban-rural conflict is also likely to be great. In addition, most of these European nations were unified or gained independence only at a late date. Centralizing pressures, such as the desire for rapid industrialization, the emergence of an ambitious professional urban middle class, and the need for an effective state administration, all may cause a political reaction among the peasantry, driving them in the same direction as the quest for landownership. We have already dealt with the various facets of this situation: an economic policy favouring industrialization, inadequate national financial resources, a cultural challenge to peasant traditions. The granting of political participation generally occurred simultaneously with a redistribution of the land: agrarian parties, where they appeared, had both something to defend and the means to do so. Egalitarian rural conditions certainly apply in the Balkan peninsula, and to a lesser extent in Czechoslovakia, Finland and the three small Baltic states. However, the translation of these social conditions into political divisions resulted sometimes in more than one agrarian party, separated either by different cultural bases - for example, religious or ethnic differences - or by economic divisions among the cultivators themselves.

3. The Urban-Rural Basis of Agrarian Parties

The urban-rural continuum also distinguishes Eastern Europe from the West. In Western Europe urban influences tended to be more widespread. Moreover, greater urbanization and technological advance meant not just a reduction in the agricultural share of the population, but also a constant diminution of the traditional social structure and values of rural communities. In particular, Western European farmers became committed earlier and to a far greater extent to commercial farming. If peasantism refers to a greater commitment to domestic consumption and a more tenacious attitude towards landownership, then it remained an outstanding characteristic of all Central and Eastern European societies (with the exception of the Czech provinces) right up to World War II.

The existence of multiracial empires throughout most of Central and Eastern Europe until 1918 also helped to preserve a wide gulf between town and countryside. In most regions landowners and government officials were of a different ethnic group from the rural masses: particularly in the Ottoman Empire these elite groups had little attachment to the areas, sometimes being seconded or resident for only a short period of time. In most areas the expansion of empire over the centuries had resulted in the elimination of the indigeneous rural aristocracy, except where the latter adopted the religion of the conquerors (for example, the Bosnian landlords were converted to Islam) or renounced their nationality (for example, the old Lithuanian aristocracy survived because it became "Polonized"). The imperial expansion reached its zenith in the nineteenth century at the precise point in time when new nationalist forces appeared to challenge its supremacy. The presence of imperial power introduced two further factors limiting urban contagion of rural life: the educational gap between town and countryside remained very great, and the elite language of the government and the cities was different from that of the peasant. It is interesting to note that land reform as an integral part of the nationalist revolution failed or was significantly weaker in the two countries, Poland and Hungary, in which the traditional native aristocracy had survived to take the lead in the nineteenth century struggle for national independence.[21]

Ethnic distinctiveness was also marked in the towns of Eastern Europe. It is easy to overrate the alien presence in the commercial occupations of the cities and towns. Yet, historically, entrepreneurial tasks had been undertaken by Greeks, Italians, and above all Jews. In 1910 Jews comprised only 5 per cent of the Hungarian population, yet they made up 22 per cent of all industrial salaried employees, 54 per cent of the self-employed trades, and 85 per cent of the self-employed in banking and finance: Budapest was 20 per cent Jewish.[22] Similarly, 80 per cent of Polish Jews were urban dwellers and tended to dominate trade and service occupations. Many small towns had a Jewish majority, while Jews made up 30 per cent of the population of Warsaw (compared for instance with only 5 per cent in Berlin in 1920).[23] The wealthy Jew may be a figment of the imagination, but he loomed large in the minds of eastern cultivators simply because of the prominence of Jews among the merchants and money lenders with whom they had to deal. It is always easy to direct resentment against an alien, and no less so in interwar Europe. Jews, usury and urban vices could be lumped together as barriers to agrarian progress. Rothschild, in fact, goes so far as to comment that "it appears that the only really potent internationalistic ideology in the area at that time was neither Marxism, on the left hand, nor dynastic loyalism, on the right, but anti-semitism based on both conviction and expedience".[24]

The late establishment of national states, the late persistence of quasi-feudal tenure systems, and a more distinctive urban-rural gap helped to distinguish Eastern from Western Europe, where there was earlier national integration and/or centralization, with an administrative apparatus tying the countryside more closely to the towns. Urban life - even in a sense that of its ghettos of poverty - was far removed from the distinctive socio-economic structure of the East European countryside, characterized nearly everywhere after 1918 by small domestic consumptive enterprises relying almost exclusively upon family labour and somewhat marginal to the capitalist economy (but while still being exposed to the full weight of its consequences). Before 1918 much of the land in large estates had been held by ethnic minorities: Phanariots in Moldavia and Wallachia, Magyars in Transylvania and Slovakia, Germans in Bohemia, Moravia and the Baltic provinces of Russia. Rural politics therefore had been concerned less with the socio-economic and political reforms that agitated the urban bourgeoisie and working classes, but more with land redistribution. On the one hand, the overwhelming weight of the agricultural problem made "internationalist" peasantist or populist ideologies directly relevant: on the other, the ethnic presence meant that the prevailing conflict became identified with the nationality question. Short of mass assimilation, exodus or genocide, the ethnic problem remained untouched by the redrawing of political boundaries. The nationalism of nineteenth century Europe was transcribed later into a kind of xenophobic supernationalism, a state of mind that was influential in the rise of various fascist movements - not least in Eastern Europe. The consequences of the interplay between nationalism and fascism for the formation and survival of agrarian parties in these vital decades of mass mobilization will be taken up later. First, however, we will look at the urban-rural dimension of agrarian populism.

Peasants could be mobilized by urban groups in the struggle for national independence, but only in return for the promise of land tenure. And because of this rural obsession, urban parties had found it difficult to penetrate widely into the countryside. In Moldavia and Wallachia the Peasant Party (Partidul Tărănesc) had been established in the villages (with some support from urban intelligentsia) shortly before World War I. Its original ideology mirrored the views of the Russian narodni in its mystical belief in peasant communality: its presence hindered attempts by the urban-led Liberal and Conservative parties to spread out from their elite base.[25] The difficulties of rural penetration by purely urban parties increased immediately after 1918 when the new peasant owners were persuaded to organize themselves politically to defend their newly-acquired property. Agrarian parties had appeared before 1914: the Bulgarian Agrarian Union in 1899, the Czech Agrarians in 1896, the Croat Peasants in 1904. However, with the exception of Bulgaria where the Agrarian Union won 14.4 per cent of the vote in 1911, these parties had no real strength until after 1918. The Bulgarian party first appeared as a protest against a government proposal to take a tithe of every harvest. But even in this country, which already possessed a well-defined territory and an egalitarian rural structure, the greatest increase in Agrarian Union support came only after World War I. By confirming a basic rural social structure of smallholdings geared more for home consumption, the land reforms helped to maintain an urban-rural gap which was reflected in political life.

These historical developments led to a particular kind of urban-rural cleavage, where peasantism could be developed as a distinctive ideology. The minority position of the politically active urban groups also gave their political activity an anti-rural tinge. Moreover, the growing urban middle classes proved to be very different from Western bourgeois groups in their social and psychological composition. Whereas the middle classes in Western Europe tended more towards entrepreneurial characteristics, their Eastern counterparts depended to a greater extent upon government employment, patronage, corruption, and government contracts and subsidies. Typically, when a party or coalition left the government there was either strong business approaches to the new government for favours or a considerable turnover of government contracts, the state everywhere being the largest capitalist enterprise.[26] The dominant urban groups were professional people -lawyers and intelligentsia - who sought protection within government services rather than seeking economic profit in trade and industry. Furthermore, as one writer has commented, "the dispossessed landed class had to seek refuge in civil and military positions and in industry, trade and banking".[27] The numbers of people in these occupations grew far beyond the countries' requirements and resources. In general, there was a superfluity of bureaucrats, and the state's role as an employer received greater emphasis than its task of developing the national economy, an attitude which reflected the middle class concern for job security within the bureaucracy. Even so, the state apparatus could not absorb the rapidly growing army of university graduates, especially lawyers. It is perhaps indicative of the widespread insecurity of life outside agriculture that in the 1927 Bulgarian election there were no less than 40,000 candidates for the 273 Sobranje seats. This "surplus" middle class population was sustained by taxes primarily extracted from the peasantry who, however, tended to view this apparatus with as much suspicion, if not hostility, as they had those of the old empires. Many peasant families nevertheless attempted to secure a university education for at least one son.

While later on he might be able to award favours or some protection to his family, these graduates more frequently divorced themselves completely from their peasant background, while being qualified for occupations which the countries could not provide.[28] A common hypothesis in the literature of political development is that a premature or too rapid expansion of the bureaucracy compared to that of the political system is injurious to the consolidation of stable and effective politics. For example, Riggs discusses the relationship of bureaucracies to party systems, interest groups, legislatures and electorates, and argues that the merit system of bureaucracies weakens a basic support of a developing party system. When parties are unable to indulge in a spoils system, their effectiveness is weakened.[29] While this is true to some extent in Eastern Europe, the systems were equally undermined by the opportunistic nature of the bureaucracies, which themselves operated the largest spoils systems.

The example of Rumania is particularly outstanding. The post-war reforms swept away the old Conservative Party, composed almost entirely of large landowners: its electoral power before 1918 had been due exclusively to the rigid property qualifications determining the suffrage. For over a decade after 1918 the country's politics, economy and administration were dominated by the National Liberal Party, irrespective of which party or parties happened to form the government. The National Liberals were in firm control of the banks and other financial bodies as well as being soundly entrenched in the state apparatus. The autarkic Liberal policies were designed to promote industrialization at the expense of the new peasant class. Moreover, in Rumania more than in any other eastern country, the urban professional and middle classes abandoned their own culture in a facile attempt to imitate Western (in this instance French) culture.[30] This kind of urban-rural distinctiveness and tension was present even in Bulgaria, the most egalitarian peasant society in Eastern Europe. Of the successor states only in Czechoslovakia was this kind of cleavage weaker in its saliency. The Czech Republican party, however, was more interested in the commercial farmers of the western provinces than in the Slovakian and Ruthenian small-holders, and was also more representative of the Czech population as a whole: it even succeeded in becoming the second largest party in Prague.

It was the intensity of this cleavage between town and countryside which lent itself readily to an ideology of peasantism. Peasantism was not identical to populism, although descended directly from the ideas of Russian populism. The narodnichestvo had reacted against the impact of Western capitalism and had argued that they could hasten the inevitable course of history by bypassing the capitalist stage of development, that the future of the masses (only implicitly the peasant masses) could be assured only by effective leadership, which presumably would be provided by the intelligentsia, and that the "good" society could be secured only by the destruction or total overhaul of the existing state. By contrast, peasantism in twentieth century Europe was a reaction not only to Western capitalism, but also to Russian populism. It redefined the "small man" more specifically as the peasant, and proposed that the society and its institutional structure should be based upon peasant relationships and work. It asserted that the peasants were the class who should occupy the leadership of the political society, not simply because of their electoral preponderance, but because of their possession of superior moral and spiritual values. These beliefs about the peasant mystique were elevated to the status of an irrefutable historical myth. While they were mixed with socio-economic concerns and a powerful emphasis upon nationalism and liberation from all forms of foreign domination, rural life was praised as the ideal, and urban society was condemned as parasitic and evil.[31]

The new agrarian parties stressed their adherence to the principles of private property, their hostility towards Marxism, especially Communism, and opposition to any expansion of governmental involvement in economic affairs except where such policies were intended to remedy current practices that militated against agrarian interests. Few peasantist leaders succumbed to Krestintern overtures, apart from two Bulgarian leaders who accepted the idea of a "popular" worker/peasant alliance, and Stjepan Radić, head of the Croat Peasants, who however left the Krestintern only one year after joining it in 1924.[32] Paradoxically, the more committed peasantists frequently emphasized the notion of class conflict in Marxist terminology, even when they were reiterating their belief in the institution of private property. This was the position of the Croat Peasants before 1914. The party was also fundamentally anticlerical, although not essentially antireligious: but by the 1920s it had reached an uneasy modus vivendi with the Catholic Church in Croatia.[33] A gradual moderation or even abandonment of peasantist ideology typified most of these parties: the Rumanian Peasants had moved a long way from their narodni inspired origins even before their merger with the Transylvanian Nationalists in 1926.[34] When in office in the early 1920s the Bulgarian Agrarian Union ignored all urban groups entirely, and advocated only secondary industries in the countryside: yet by the late 1920s a new generation of party leaders was seeking an alliance with industrial workers.

Perhaps the major difficulty was that few parties had clarified their position and beliefs to the extent of having a consistent and systematic programme. Whether moderate or radical they simply sought to preserve traditional peasant culture, and tended to view urban-rural differences as a struggle between good and evil, between an agrarian utopia and the despoiling materialism of both capitalism and socialism. The peasant mystique was not a new invention, and even the conclusions drawn from it were similar to the organic exaltation of Russian populism. Radkey's description of the latter as less an ideology and more a state of mind is also an apt summary of peasantism.[35] In turn, the ideological commitment or prejudices of peasant parties, a commitment which in many ways refused to come to terms with contemporary economic problems and issues, proved to be a stumbling block when these parties were faced with the task of planning and sustaining a governmental course of action.[36] In particular, the parties' attitudes made it difficult for them to tackle the problem of industrialization or to consider the practicality of any kind of cooperation with industrial workers.

On the other hand, because political competition, occupation of governmental and administrative offices or even simply organizational ineptitude, meant that sometimes agrarian parties were forced to compromise their "ideological" commitments or were sometimes unable to satisfy peasant demands, the anti-urban, anti-capitalist and anti-labour sentiments of the rural population could be mobilized in the name of peasant virtues by more nationalist-authoritarian or nationalist-fascist parties. Indeed, there is a strong link between the peasant attachment to the soil, the emphasis upon peasant virtues by many agrarian parties, and the irrational mysticism which was a hallmark of much of European fascism. Events in the 1920s and 1930s demonstrated that the chiliastic atavism of rural Europe was far from dead. For example, in his outstanding study of Rumania Henry Roberts points out that the philosophy of Stere, one of the most prominent theorists of peasant populism and extremely influential in the early stages of the Rumanian party, contains the seeds of irrational and mystical authoritarianism:

Along with his desire for rural democracy and a rustic economy, there is also a persistent note of organic nationalism with its eloquent love of the 'national genius' embodied in the Rumanian peasant, its fear of the alien cultural and economic intrusion of the Jew, its belief that Rumania had its own particular destiny to fulfil, and its desire to avoid the 'Golgotha of Capitalism'. In Stere, these elements appeared in a relatively moderate and balanced guise, but taken together and intensified they closely resemble the driving impulses of the Iron Guard. The connection between certain aspects of populism and the Rumanian fascism of Codreanu is not accidental .... Therein lies the danger of this type of populism: in so far as it failed to provide a solution to Rumania's social and economic questions, it is apt to erupt into a wildly irrational and negative movement.[37]

The affinity with the better-known German and Italian fascist movements is apparent.

4. Urban-Rural Divisions, Political Institutionalization, and Fascism

Although the rise and support of fascist parties are not central to this study, it is worth digressing at this point to consider their importance in European political development, for even in many of the longer established, more institutionalized party systems of the west, the fascist phenomenon succeeded in achieving a significant level of disruption. The effect upon the more weakly structured party systems of the east was even greater.

The fascist phenomenon serves essentially to illustrate the continuing importance of some of the themes stressed as basic in European agrarian history, notably resistance to modernization and organization, hostility towards the cities, and the challenges posed by capitalism. It also illustrates some of the problems attendant upon the formation and survival of agrarian parties.

Clearly the most research has been done on the two fascist movements that succeeded in gaining power without external assistance. In Germany, the Nazi appeal was overall more successful in rural areas of smaller enterprises. Thus Heberle points out that in Schleswig-Holstein the NSDAP emerged as the dominant party in homogeneous regions of small family farms before 1932, while larger farmers and farm labourers were more reluctant to vote for the party. Heberle's thesis is confirmed by Franz' analysis of Niedersachsen: the Nazi breakthrough occurred first and most significantly in more marginal rural districts which had been less integrated into the national party system and had preferred the regional Hannoverian party. In Bavaria and Hesse also the Nazi vote came primarily from relatively egalitarian rural areas which had earlier supported regional and agrarian parties hostile to centralization.[38] While Italian Fascism became primarily an urban phenomenon, the Po valley with its small property owners and tenant farmers was later commemorated by Mussolini as the birthplace of the Fascist movement. After the 1919 armistice the area had been the scene of violent clashes between farmers and the Socialist Party, which saw rural Italy as a mainspring of a Marxist revolution. In turn, farmers looked to fascism for protection against the Marxist threat.[39]

Elsewhere in Western Europe fascist parties equally made their strongest appeal in the countryside. In Belgium the Rexists won 29 per cent of the vote in 1936 in Luxemburg, the most rural Walloon province, while throughout the 1930s the Flemish National Front reached 40 per cent in some rural Flemish cantons. The organizational strength of the Catholic Church may be seen as an important factor in hindering the rural expansion of the Flemish Nationalists, while its weakness in Wallonia made the mobilization of farmers by the Rexists easier.[40] In Spain small farmers in Léon and Old Castile seem to have been attracted by the fascist approach. Quisling's appeal in Norway was also greatest in areas of small farmer-capitalist enterprises.[41] In France the peasantry could choose from among several such movements. One of the more important, the <u>Front Paysan</u>, appeared in 1934 as a merger between the various peasant defence committees and Greenshirt movement led by Henri Dorgères, and the <u>Parti Agraire</u>. Like other new agrarian movements of the period the <u>Front</u> was aggressive and somewhat mystical in its expression of anti-urban sentiments. Dorgères' strength lay in Normandy and Brittany and so complemented rather than competed with the more southerly <u>Parti Agraire</u>. After a few agrarian leaders left the following year, the remainder developed close ties also with the authoritarian <u>Croix de Feu</u> and the fascist <u>Solidarité Française</u>. The two agrarian groups healed their schism in 1939, only to split again in 1940 with the vast majority merging once more with Dorgères' Peasant Defence League, and supporting Pétain.[42] The Austrian <u>Heimwehr</u> was originally a limited vigilante movement among the peasantry in several border regions, especially in Carinthia: it had no clear aim beyond protection against border raids. Yet it soon became imbued with the traditional rural shibboleths. The great symbol of rural oppression was Vienna, with its large Jewish population dominating financial life and its politics dominated by the Socialists. The <u>Heimwehr</u> acquired military trappings in part as a rural reaction against the Socialist control of the official army (<u>Volkswehr</u>) after 1918 and the party's attempt to turn the army into a party guard during the opening years of the First Republic.[43]

Generally, the fascist appeal in the West European countryside was limited by the smaller numbers of cultivators and by the greater institutionalization of the party system. Germany, especially the Protestant regions, with its multitude of regional, agrarian-oriented parties, is perhaps more like Eastern Europe where institutionalization was very weak or non-existent, and where societies were essentially agricultural. The new peasant parties, where they fell back upon a populist tradition, ironically stressed the one latent feature of rural life which they wished to neutralize. The revolutionary potential reappeared whenever the agrarian parties failed to react to the current economic problems of the peasantry. The emphasis upon folk ideology as expounded by the Croat Peasants or the Rumanian National Peasants was only a short step away from more pronounced views on romantic nationalism, antisemitism, capitalism and socialism. Fascist groups found it easy to appeal to the small landowners and labourers with their economic debts and problems, their desire for land or more land, their resentment of the favoured position of the cities, their hostility towards the large state bureaucracies, and their susceptibility to nationalist appeals: the way had already been prepared by the agrarian parties. The fascist movements of Eastern Europe adopted exotic names springing from their own obsession with mysticism: Iron Guard, Thunder Cross, Scythe Cross, Arrow Cross, Legions of the Archangel St. Michael. Yet, some were also prepared to work hard for their support. In Rumania, instead of relying upon promises of future action and political pressure, the Iron Guard, which also preached agrarian not industrial capitalism, went into the fields in 1931 to help the peasants bring in the harvest.[44] In competing with a more aggressively nationalist party, peasant parties lost. In most instances fascist support came from areas which had traditionally been centres of agrarian radicalism and core areas of support for the agrarian parties. In Rumania a majority of the National Peasant leadership under Iuliu Maniu eventually decided to merge with the fascists rather than compete with them, in order to contest the power of their urban "enemies", King Carol II and the National Liberals.

Of the new states in Eastern Europe, only in Czechoslovakia, Yugoslavia, Estonia and Latvia did the agrarian parties succeed in resisting the fascist nationalist challenge. In the Baltic states the agrarian parties "averted" the threat by seizing dictatorial powers themselves and, at least in the case of the Latvian party and its para-military arm (the Aizargi), acquiring the trappings of their competitors.[45] In Croatia and Czechoslovakia the greater organizational strength of the agrarian parties was probably a contributory factor. The success of the Croat Peasants in holding off the threat of the Ustashe may also be attributed to their own strong nationalist position and to the extreme nihilist views of the latter.[46] The lack of institutionalization was a major feature of Eastern Europe societies and parties: for example, the Rumanian National Peasants did not consider establishing ancillary party organizations until 1934.[47] Political parties were "more often a matter of personal following than of program and organizational or educational endeavor ..... Personal magnetism and demagogic skill brought more than one ... unemployed intellectual forward as the leader of a successful ... political group".[48] Moreover, the Fascist success in Germany and Italy later contributed to the creation by royal or bureaucratic dictatorships of "parties" that incorporated elements of fascist-nationalism.[49]

In most areas there was a close symbiotic relationship between leaders and parties. The leadership of nearly all parties consisted of urban lawyers and intellectuals. Parties were often for one generation only, disintegrating with the demise of the original leader, unless successors were groomed from within his family: for example the Bratianu family controlled the Rumanian Liberals for almost a century. Stoianovich concludes that "the significance of the death of a party leader, when it came after a full life, lies in its symbolization of the approaching end of the generation that made and nurtured the party and, therefore, of the party itself".[50] The significance of this party structure for the agrarian parties was that their original leadership was passing from the scene precisely at the point in time when the fascist movements, usually led by younger men, were making their appearance. Without an institutionalized structure, the parties found it difficult to keep their support or remain loyal to their original principles.

The rise and immediate success of peasant mobilization in Eastern Europe had frightened the dominant social groups. If properly mobilized and organized the peasants might have been the decisive political force in these countries. Their failure to do so was due in no small degree to an inability to organize effectively and the absence of an institutionalized party system: the result was the gradual integration of many agrarian parties into and their subversion by a political system dominated by the urban middle classes. These points go a long way towards explaining the relationship between peasantism and fascism, and the problems of party formation and survival. Politics in these societies was strongly sculptured by an accentuated cleavage between urban bureaucracies and agrarian peasantism.

5. The Formation of Agrarian Parties in Southern and Western Europe

It is the intensity of this rural-urban cleavage which distinguishes Eastern Europe, where agrarian parties did arise, from those areas of Western Europe, especially the Mediterranean fringe, where substantial landless rural populations and a similar type of capitalist-marginal society also existed. One particular characteristic of the Mediterranean agricultural area is a surprising degree of urbanization: the typical settlement pattern is one of large villages and even agro-towns. The rural population has tended to live in these centres and travel long distances each day to and from their work in the fields, whether they be owners or hired labour. Historically there has been in these areas relatively greater urban-rural communication, buttressed by a traditionally strong stratification system. This prevented the development of significant alienation along a simple urban-rural dimension. Two important consequences arose. First, it tended to make penetration by urban influences easier, and hence easier institutionalization by urban parties. Second, the retention of local rural stratification structures resulted in the emergence of clientele politics or <u>trasformismo</u>.

Moreover, the social structure of these areas in the period of mass politics has been quite different from that of Eastern Europe. They have been characterized by uneconomic dwarf holdings existing alongside or within large <u>latifundia</u> owned mainly by a "landed" middle class that emerged after the nineteenth century liberal attack upon Church property, and employing large numbers of agricultural labourers, often on a seasonal basis. The peasant parties of Eastern Europe did not appear as significant political forces until after the land reforms: they were in the first instance agents for carrying out and defending land redistribution. The absence of land redistribution in the Western Mediterranean hindered the emergence of agrarian parties. Moreover, the relationship between landowners and labourers was not simply economic. In Southern Italy, for example, the landowners were not just the employers of labour: they also fulfilled professional duties in the capacity of lawyers, doctors or bureaucrats. These relationships were not necessarily face-to-face. Nevertheless, they were sufficiently obvious for the peasants to be aware of the configuration of influences imposed upon them by the stratification structure.[51]

It would seem therefore that the extent of urban-rural integration, of the penetration of urban culture into the countryside, is important in explaining the ability or failure of urban-based political movements to mobilize the countryside under their own banners. In addition, the socio-economic structure of the agricultural population was a powerful conditioning factor for the development of agrarian parties. These two facets of society have distinguished Eastern from Western Europe throughout history, as Palmer has emphasized in his stately review of eighteenth century society and politics.[52] In Western Europe closer links between town and country involved the rural upper classes and landowners in the issues that dominated national politics in the period of mass mobilization: constitutionalism and the form of government, church-state relations, suffrage extension. Moreover, an indigeneous rural elite was common throughout Western Europe. Through landownership and capitalist involvement, many farmers followed the same path. A corollary development in areas typically possessing large numbers of landless labourers was that the rural proletariat proved receptive to new radical ideologies and programmes springing from the expanding industrial working class. Particularly in less economically viable regions, nineteenth century political liberalism, followed by socialism, anarchism and later communism, became attractive to the rural masses. The likelihood of these protest ideologies establishing themselves in the countryside was further determined by the structure of agriculture in different areas: the distribution of property, the pattern of land tenure, and the ratio of landless to landowners.

One further consequence was that frequently those agrarian groups who opposed the new protest movements also proved willing to accept an alliance with like-minded conservative groups in the towns and cities. Hence, various urban conservative tendances also looked for rural support. The same is true of religious movements which sought to prevent the secularization of society by organizing a national network of clerical-directed associations in which the more traditional and religious countryside would play a crucial role. In a similar manner, extremist and fascist parties in the twentieth century could successfully attempt to forge an urban-rural alliance. All this meant that in such circumstances it was very difficult to establish agrarian parties, particularly those which wished to act less as pragmatic interest groups than on the basis of some kind of peasantist ideology.

All these points are well illustrated by the experiences of Spain. The non-assertion of a national agrarian movement in the formative political period and its later absence during the rural economic crisis of the 1930s are due to a combination of all these factors. After the Restoration political power in the <u>latifundia</u> regions (and even in some <u>minifundia</u> regions like Galicia) rested with large landowners who had strong connections with urban groups. By contrast, the freehold and leasehold peasants in the linguistic peripheries, particularly the Basque territories and Catalonia, embraced either ethnic nationalism or Carlism as a defender of religion and tradition in opposition to the liberal-dominated centralizing governments in Madrid. Attempts to form specifically agrarian parties among the <u>foreros</u> of Galicia and the <u>rabassaires</u> of Catalonia failed completely.[53] Later, many of the discontented peasantry associated themselves with various urban-led republican movements opposed to the establishment of the Restoration, or with regional autonomist movements in the peripheries: the appeal of the latter went beyond the conventional ethnic minorities to appear in such regions as Galicia and Levante. On the other hand, in Andalusia and other <u>latifundia</u> regions the poorest peasants and labourers were successfully mobilized by anarchists, or within a Socialist federation of farm labourers. Except during the short-lived First Republic of 1873, when Pi y Margall attempted to introduce a legislative package dealing with land reform and agricultural wages, the urban-based republican parties and politicians were basically disinterested in the problems of the <u>latifundia</u> regions. In effect, the local <u>caciques</u> were left in control of a clientelist system of politics. Alienated from urban society and all political parties, the seasonal workers of Andalusia provided the original core support of Spanish anarchism. It was only where there were farmer capitalist enterprises without the complications of religious issues, ethnicism, or traditional regional autonomy that an agrarian movement stood much chance of success. In the Castiles and the Ebro valley the wealthier farmers had protested vigorously in 1900 against government taxation by establishing defensive associations. These regions were later the home of the Agrarian Party, and also of the most effective agricultural cooperatives in Spain. However, this agrarian party never established itself either beyond its original home or as a significant independent force in the Cortes. With the increased economic and secularization threats of the 1930s, it willingly allowed itself to be integrated within CEDA, which could rely upon an organizational base already established by the Confederación Nacional Católica Agraria (CNCA).[54]

The difficulties surrounding the ability to form agrarian parties were greater where the development of political mobilization and participation occurred earlier, or where other dimensions of social cleavage were politically more salient than the urban-rural. This is true generally of Western Europe. In most areas of the west where agrarian-specific parties appeared, they were - like the Parti Paysan in France or the Agrarios in Spain - confined to specific regions or localities, often representative of particular crop interests, related to non-agricultural factors, and usually forming part of a broader, loose political grouping, at least at the legislative level. We have seen that the Spanish Agrarios eventually merged with CEDA: indeed, before the merger their internal cohesion really existed only at the parliamentary level where it was forced upon them by institutional regulations stipulating the minimum size of groups entitled to representation on parliamentary committees. The Agrarians drew their support primarily from the wheat farmers of León and the two Castiles, which produced over 40 per cent of the country's wheat. Their main demand seems to have been for state intervention in agriculture to help preserve private property. They objected to the land reform bills of the 1930s: though small in numbers, they displayed considerable parliamentary skill and tended to win most of their legislative battles. CEDA itself had a strong agrarian element, drawing strength generally from the successful organization of smallholders after 1917 by CNCA, which claimed 600,000 members by 1920, and from the more conservative <u>Accion Nacional</u> (later <u>Accion Popular</u>), as in Salamanca and Guadalajara.⁵⁵ Similarly, the French <u>Parti Paysan</u> was very much part of the conservative bloc in the National Assembly and relied very much upon Catholic support. The several regionally-based agrarian parties of the Weimar Republic arose from dissatisfaction with the national party system. Their short lifespan ended when a new party, the NSDAP, emerged to forge an urban-rural alliance.⁵⁶

Scandinavia was the one area of Western Europe where durable national agrarian parties appeared. While today agriculture is commercialized and market involvement is high, these countries, apart from areas of Denmark, were characterized historically by a pattern of scattered and isolated medium and small owner-occupied farms: economic and social differences between large and small farmers were limited. In addition, the characteristic dimension of political conflict in the nineteenth century was between town and countryside. The catalyst of the conflict was the political mobilization of the peasantry, buttressed by their reaction to urban domination in politics and administration, their fundamentalist opposition to a more rationalist and tolerant stance by the state Lutheran churches, and the problems caused by their entry into the money economy. In Norway too there was the emergence of a language dimension that fed into the other social divisions.⁵⁷

Moreover, these countries succeeded in preserving a genuine folk culture based upon a traditional way of life. While they already possessed a compulsory system of elementary education - Denmark by 1800, Norway by 1827, Sweden by 1842 and Finland by 1866 - rural political mobilization was stimulated in the late nineteenth century by political socialization processes that were initiated through an independent network of folk high schools. This is most apparent in Norway where the high schools, founded in the 1860s and aided by the political movement known as the "Friends of the Peasant" (1865-1879), played an important role in the countryside, and also came to be significant recruitment centres for the militants in the rural political counter-culture, and so feeding directly into the foundation of rural-based political parties.⁵⁸ Throughout Scandinavia the crucial political conflict was between urban elites and farmers.

Few ties existed between town and countryside, and even these were tenuous: this was particularly true of Norway where the cities were identified with foreign domination. Only in areas of large estates - in parts of Jutland, Scania and South-West-Finland - was the urban-rural gap partially bridged: the political influence and local social status of the landowners enabled them to forge links with urban conservative parties in the opening phases of national politics. In Finland before 1906 the Finnish Party dominated the clerical and peasant estates, while the Swedish Party was supreme among the nobility and burgesses.

As in Eastern Europe the conflict was originally contained within a liberal-conservative struggle. A comparison of Denmark and Sweden is instructive. The institutional heritage of Danish absolutism and the Swedish curial structure determined the framework within and around which political conflict occurred. Hence we find different developments in the mobilization of the peasantry. Although the Swedish peasants had had a long tradition of independent representation in the curial assembly, they became part of the country's first liberal movement, the Lantmannaparti, which after 1866 dominated the second chamber of the Riksdag through its linking of agricultural interests with a more widespread populist resentment against the central bureaucracy. In Denmark the closing years of the era of royal absolution were marked by concessions to the peasantry as the monarch sought to contain the nobility. These concessions and the emergence of rural-based "popular" movements provided a basis for future political action. An alliance between peasants and urban liberals spawned the Venstre which established itself as a durable and effective organization in the parliamentary struggle. The party was strengthened by the work of the folk high schools established in the 1840s, a religious revival in the countryside which opposed urban latitudinarianism, and farmers' grievances about their tax burdens and military liability. A similar struggle occurred in Norway. By contrast, in Sweden the assimilation of the Lantmannaparti within the political system led to its disintegration in 1887 over the issue of protectionism. Though the factions reunited in 1895, in practice as a conservative party, they differed on so many issues that

the party's collapse after 1904 was not perhaps a surprise.
Political life was characterized by a variety of temporary
alliances within the Riksdag, and the slow growth of mass
organized parties outside the parliamentary arena. The Danish
Venstre succeeded in welding its urban-rural alliance into a
permanent organization: its rural orientation became perhaps
more pronounced after the secession of the Radical Venstre in
1905. By contrast, the old independence of the Swedish farmers
reasserted itself: increasingly unhappy in a newly-forged
coalition, they eventually seceded over the marked urban-rural
clash of interests in the commodity market to form their own
party, (though almost all the Agrarian deputies in 1917 had no
previous legislative experience). Similarly, in Norway the more
market-oriented farmers who had helped to found the Venstre and
had established the Norsk Landmandsforbund in 1896, became
progressively discontented with the Venstre. In 1920 they
decided to turn their own organization into a political party.[59]

It should be noted that Kevin Cox has explained the Liberal
strength in Wales in much the same terms as the Scandinavian
counterculture: the predominance of small farmers, an egalitarian
class structure, and linguistic, religious or cultural opposition
to central structures.[60] The crucial distinction between Wales
and Scandinavia is the important institutional variable.
Admittedly, Wales was a small appendage to the English giant.
But the gradual extension of the suffrage is a marked contrast
to Scandinavian struggles. Moreover, the disintegration of the
original urban-rural alliance and the consolidation of separate
agrarian parties in Scandinavia occurred with growing pressures
for electoral reform and the eventual introduction of proportional
representation. It was only when Liberal interests were unable
to offer the farmers satisfaction, or turned to give priority to
urban, industrial interests that the farmers were stimulated to
establish their own political organization. In Norway the
farmers also found themselves no longer able to accept the
cultural policies of the Left (which had also annoyed the Norsk
Landmandsforbund by trying to establish in 1913 a smallholders'
union), and were worried also by Socialist efforts among agricultural and forestry workers. Ancient antagonisms prevented a
rapprochement with the urban-dominated Right. The vigorous

interest associations which they had already established were available for use as the organizational basis of a distinctive party: the change was simply regarded as a tactical alternative to achieve the same ends.[61] Similar considerations encouraged an agrarian secession from an increasingly urban-dominated Radical party in some Swiss cantons, especially Bern: it was only later that the farmers sought a wider base by attempting to become a broad middle class party.[62]

At the time of the rural breakthrough in politics the Scandinavian cultivators possessed an agricultural social structure somewhat similar to that of pre-1945 Eastern Europe, with the urban-rural conflict as a salient political dimension of cleavage. However, in terms of political attitudes and behaviour, these Scandinavian parties were probably more like the localized agrarian parties elsewhere in Western Europe than the typically peasant parties of the east. The critical distinctions derive from a stronger organizational base and greater party institutionalization: these political features may in turn be due both to a greater level of literacy and political awareness, and a greater participation in the commodity market. Governments came to be seen not as the creatures of an urban devil and hence to be opposed outright, but as a tool that could be controlled or influenced on behalf of agrarian interests. The Scandinavian agrarian parties were less "peasantist" than "farmers" or interest-group parties.

6. The Cultural Basis of Agrarian Parties

So far we have considered the likelihood of the emergence of agrarian parties only in relation to agricultural or rural characteristics. But cleavages along other dimensions of social structure - linguistic, ethnic, religious, or class - may take precedence over or subsume these characteristics. For example, the Norwegian Agrarian Party established its firmest base in the East and Trondelag regions in rural areas which were sufficiently removed from the influence of Oslo, but which also avoided cultural issues of religion and morality, as in the South-West, or a strong rural stratification system and insecure livelihood which in Finnmark led to the pre-eminence of class politics.

Table 6.2: The Ethnic-Linguistic Homogeneity of European Countries

Country	Ethnic-Linguistic Groups (in percentages)
Albania	Albanian 92
Austria	German 99
Belgium	Flemish 58, French 41, German 1
Bulgaria	Bulgar 87, Turkish 10
Czechoslovakia	Czech 46, Slovak 21, German 22, Magyar 5, Ukrainian 4, Polish 1
Denmark	Danish 99
Estonia	Estonian 88, Russian 8, German 2, Swedish 1
Finland	Finnish 91, Swedish 9
France	almost entirely French
Germany	German 96
Greece	Greek 98
Hungary	Magyar 75, Rumanian 8, German 8, Ukrainian 4, Slovak 1
Iceland	Icelandic 99
Ireland	Irish 100
Italy	almost entirely Italian
Latvia	Latvian 73, Russian 11, German 4, Polish 3
Lithuania	Lithuanian 84, Russian 3, Polish 3, German 1, Latvian 1
Luxemburg	German
Netherlands	Dutch
Norway	Norwegian 100
Poland	Polish 69, Ukrainian 10, German 3, Byelorussian 4
Rumania	Rumanian 72, Magyar 8, German 4, Ukrainian 3, Russian 2, Bulgarian 2
Spain	Spanish majority: strong Basque and Catalan minorities
Sweden	almost entirely Swedish
Switzerland	German 72, French 20, Italian 4, Romansch 1
United Kingdom	English 81, Scottish 11, Welsh 5, Irish 3
Yugoslavia	Serb 43, Croat 23, Slovene 9, Bosnian 6, Macedonian 5, German 4, Albanian 4, Magyar 3, Rumanian 1

Note: Some of the figures for Eastern Europe must be treated with caution, as the strength of the minorities tends to be underestimated.

Table 6.3: The Religious Composition of European Countries (percentages)

Country	Catholic	Protestant	Jewish	Orthodox	Uniate	Moslem
Albania	10	-	-	25	-	65
Austria	90	6	-	-	-	-
Belgium	97	-	-	-	-	-
Bulgaria	1	-	1	84	-	13
ˣCzechoslovakia	74	8	2	1	4	-
Denmark	1	97	-	-	-	-
Estonia	-	78	-	19	-	-
Finland	-	95	-	2	-	-
France	95	2	1	-	-	-
Germany	33	66	-	-	-	-
Greece	1	-	-	95	-	2
Hungary	65	27	5	1	2	-
Iceland	-	98	-	-	-	-
Ireland	95	5	-	-	-	-
Italy	99	-	-	-	-	-
Latvia	24	57	5	9	-	-
Lithuania	81	9	8	3	-	-
Luxemburg	95	1	-	-	-	-
Netherlands	40	56	-	-	-	-
Norway	-	95	-	-	-	-
Poland	65	3	9	12	10	-
Portugal	92	-	-	-	-	2
Rumania	7	7	4	73	8	1
Spain	99	-	-	-	-	-
Sweden	-	95	-	-	-	-
Switzerland	42	57	-	-	-	-
United Kingdom	8	90	-	-	-	-
Yugoslavia	37	2	-	49	-	11

x 5 percent of the population belonged to the Czech Catholic Church

Sources: Statistical Yearbooks; RIIA, <u>The Baltic States</u> pp. 30-36; Seton-Watson, <u>Eastern Europe Between The Wars</u>, pp. 413-417; Rothschild, <u>East Central Europe</u>.

Here we shall review the significance of religious and linguistic-ethnic divisions. In order to facilitate cross-references to other tables and data, the religious and linguistic structures of European countries in the interwar period are given in Tables 6.2 and 6.3.

It has been suggested that "in a competitive party system, the social .... separation of communal groups encourages the development of communally-based political institutions and strategies".[63] Each community tends to possess its own history, separate social institutions, and distinctive customs and behavioural practices. Communal identity and cohesion may be due not only to a peripheral or isolated situation, but also to the policies pursued by the state. The community, in short, may become an obvious base for political operations. However, language and ethnic divisions appear to be important as the base of a single distinctive communal party only where the linguistic-ethnic minority is relatively small, as in Finland: smallness places a high premium upon solidarity. In most instances, such minorities reside in rural areas. Logically, there is no reason to deny the likelihood of this pattern emerging where these are large ethnic minorities: moreover, ethnic problems tended to occupy centre stage in many of the new states of Central and Eastern Europe, even though they were frequently exploited as scapegoats by governments anxious to distract attention away from other serious socio-economic tensions and deficiencies. Empirically, however, we find in these imperfectly integrated European states with substantial minorities that either the ethnic cleavage coincided with other cleavages, especially religion, or that the linguistic groups generated <u>complete party systems</u> of their own. This is generally the case in Eastern Europe, examples being the Germans and Magyars in Czechoslovakia, and the Jews and Ukrainians in Poland. These sub-cultural party systems often included an agrarian party. The notion of ethnic party systems seems to go against the logic of politics in plural societies.[64] However, we shall be concerned with offering some possible explanations only insofar as they help to understand the formation of agrarian parties.

A salient religious cleavage or the involvement of a church in political organization more clearly appears to be instrumental in preventing the ignition of an urban-rural conflict. The link between a church and an ethnic minority, for instance, tends to be particularly strong in fairly homogeneous rural communities which were linguistically distinct from the national society. The lower clergy were usually recruited from the ethnic minority and were also accepted as a local elite who could use the minority language in their daily activities: in this they were distinctive from other elites who frequently could speak only the majority language. For example, in Rumania the peasants avoided domination by the Orthodox hierarchy because its use of Slavonic and later the Greek language made its teaching largely alien to them.[65] The complex relationship between religion, class, ethnicity and agriculture in the Basque peripheries of Northern Spain has been described as follows:

The victory of the towns over the country in the two Carlist wars sowed the seeds of present-day nationalism in the minds of the peasants of Viscaya and Guipuzcoa who were Carlist to a man. These peasants, who were twice repulsed before Bilbao after having twice besieged it, and who had seen the moral leadership of the region pass to the cities, and to cities which contained a majority of non-Basque citizens, had ended by giving way to an understandable frustration-complex. Impotent to impose their absolutist ideal of Spain, not even on the principal cities in their own region, they had reacted by turning to racialism and separation. That the Carlist from Alava and Navarra was not affected by a similar aberration confirms this idea .... since neither in Alava nor in Navarra are there great cities, or any Liberal tendency of importance.[66]

The Carlist strongholds in Alava, Navarra and parts of Catalonia were characterized by a linguistic minority, an absence of cities, a strong Catholic Church, and a more or less egalitarian agrarian structure of medium or small owner-occupied farms.

Overall, agrarian parties were much more likely to appear in Protestant or Orthodox societies than in Catholic societies. Protestant and Orthodox churches were much more nationally-oriented than supranational, and placed less emphasis upon the collective nature of religious behaviour. The way in which Protestantism is regarded as having contributed to an emphasis upon individualism, personal responsibility and self-reliance has been noted by many observers and need not be elaborated upon here. By contrast, Catholicism has stressed community

responsibility and morality. In general, the Catholic Church is
the only empirical example in Europe which approximates the
sociological definition of an <u>ecclesia</u> which conceives of itself
as being God-ordained, possessing an institutionalized hierarchy
independent of and superior to any secular political institution,
and which claims the allegiance of all people who are believed
to belong to it <u>by its own criteria</u>, irrespective of their
actual religious beliefs and behaviour.

Within the Protestant and Orthodox religious areas, only the
Netherlands and Britain among the Protestant countries, and
Greece among the Orthodox states have not had a meaningful
agrarian party. In the Netherlands the Protestant churches
joined Catholics and working class movements in opposition to
the burgher-dominated political system. In rural Protestant
areas - Groningen, Friesland, Noord-Holland - political
discrimination and agricultural depression led to mobilization
by Protestant parties or by the Radical and Socialist parties.[67]
The only agrarian party to emerge in Britain was the short-lived
Crofters' Party in the Scottish Highlands. In England the
original Conservative-Liberal cleavage changed from an urban-
rural conflict in the late nineteenth century because of a
merger of rural, urban and suburban interests.[68] This is not to
say that agrarian parties ought to emerge in Protestant or
Orthodox countries, only that they are more likely to do so.
Without suggesting any kind of causal relationship, it is
interesting to note that such parties developed in Lutheran
rather than Calvinist or other Protestant societies. We have
already seen that Protestant Germany did not produce a large
agrarian party. However, the Prussian Conservatives and their
Weimar successor were in large measure agrarian parties, as were
most of the numerous regional rural parties after 1918.

Significant agrarian parties generally failed to establish
themselves in the Western areas of Catholicism. In Belgium the
most influential agrarian organization was the <u>Boerenbond</u>,
modelled upon the associations developed by the German <u>Zentrum</u>.
Founded in Flanders in 1890 by parish priests, it concerned
itself for two decades mainly with cooperative activity. Each
local guild was directed by a priest, and it rapidly became an
important political pillar of the Belgian Catholic Party. It

merged with the Catholic-directed Alliance Agricole in Wallonia. But by the 1930 the Boerenbond held almost two-thirds of Flemish farmers, while only about ten percent of Walloon farmers belonged to the Francophone equivalent.[69] In Ireland neither the Farmers' Party of the 1920s nor Clann na Talmhan succeeded in surviving. The Farmers' Party grew out of the Irish Farmers' Union which had supported the 1923 Treaty and had decided to take advantage of the lower representation threshold offered by proportional representation to form a political party. The land reforms of the late nineteenth century had strengthened the economic position of the Church. This, plus its already overwhelming cultural and moral strength, permitted it to become the dominant influence in the educational and socialization processes of the Republic. Cleavages in Irish politics revolved around issues of nationalism and relationships with Britain, within the cultural consensus of Catholicism: the break with Britain represented a secession by a fairly cohesive and agrarian periphery to form its own state.[70]

The relationship between religion and the small French and Spanish agrarian parties has already been discussed in some detail. The failure of strong religious or agrarian parties in France is interesting, but it should be contrasted with the persistent strength of many specialized agricultural associations, though it was only after 1945 that serious attempts, not entirely successful, were made to form a single all-embracing association. One of the most active and influential groups has been the Centre national des jeunes agriculteurs (CNJA). Its predecessor, the Jeunesse Agricole Catholique, was founded in 1929 by priests (with a membership of only 27), primarily to prevent further secularization. By 1939 it had consolidated its position in staunchly Catholic regions with a membership of 20,000: by the 1950s it had expanded to become a major force in rural France, changing its leadership in the process from priests to farmers and peasants. Reliance in France seems to have been placed upon professional organization and direct action rather than parliamentary activity.[71] In Italy the most effective rural mobilization was also undertaken by Catholic groups. The Catholic Congresses, created after Pope Pius IX sponsored the establishment of effective lay organizations, set up rural banks and cooperatives and, especially in Northern Italy, laid the foundations for a Catholic mass party, despite the 1874 papal interdict (Non Expedit) on Catholic electoral and governmental participation. By 1920 and their absorption by the Popular Party (PPI), Catholic unions and cooperative organizations had 1,800,000 members: 935,000 of these were in agriculture.[72]

In the religiously mixed belt of West-Central Europe agrarian parties tended to be confined to Protestant areas. This is true of the pan-German Landbund of the First Austrian Republic, which gained its support from wealthier cultivators in Carinthia and Styria. In Carinthia it was strongly supported by Protestant farmers who had left those East Prussian territories ceded to Poland after 1918, and who had been given land expropriated from Carinthian Slovenes. A further small agrarian party appeared in Styria in 1920. Clerically-oriented, it failed to survive against the powerful Bauernbund association strongly influenced by the Catholic Church.[73] After 1945 the Protestant Landbund was voluntarily absorbed by the Bauernbund which continued as the backbone of the People's Party (ÖVP): in elections to the Chamber of Agriculture the ÖVP-directed Bauernbund has regularly won more than 80 per cent of the votes. Similarly, the several cantonal parties of Switzerland were limited to Protestant regions: the strength of the Catholic-Conservative party rested with the Catholic peasants. The institutional structure of Switzerland meant that many of these movements resisted centralization and electoral cooperation with the Farmers', Traders' and Citizens' Party (BGB), at least at the cantonal level: indeed, many of them were also opposed by the farmers' union (Bauernverband) which feared a reduction of its own political influence. An all-Swiss agrarian political organization did not occur until 1937. But where fundamentalist religion was significant, as in Graubünden, the farmers preferred to remain within a party which emphasized their spiritual concerns. In other Protestant cantons such as Vaud, the farmers continued to support the Radicals. Religion, language, fundamentalism, and institutional structure all inhibited the emergence of a national Swiss agrarian party.[74] In Germany most rural movements after 1870 emerged in Protestant regions over dissatisfaction with central policies and because the national conservative parties were closely identified with large estate owners. But in East Prussia after 1920 the small farmers joined the estate owners in voicing "separatist" discontent through the DNVP. In the Catholic South and West, by contrast, rural political mobilization was dominated by religious organizations.[75]

Significant agrarian parties appeared in Catholic areas of Eastern Europe, such as Czechoslovakia and Croatia. Therefore, the assertion by Lipset and Rokkan concerning the unlikelihood of agrarian parties in Catholic countries appears to be in need of further examination. In the first instance, Slovenia and Slovakia do not seem to present many problems. While Slovakia was essentially rural (61 per cent dependent upon agriculture compared to the overall Czech figure of 33 per cent), the national agrarian party, the Republicans, found it difficult to compete against the particularistic clerical-led Slovak Populists. The Republican strength in Slovakia was due to the 1920 amalgamation with the Slovak National and Farmers' Party, which drew its support primarily from the Protestant minority (18 per cent of the Slovak population): the Slovak leadership of the Republicans was almost exclusively Protestant. Among the Magyar minority, the ethnic agrarian party was almost entirely Calvinist.[76] The Slovenian Populist party was similar to Western Christian Democrat parties. Indeed, it is an outstanding example of the force of earlier institutionalization. Founded in 1890 by Catholic priests, the only prominent indigenous elite, it became the focus of Slovene objections to arbitrary Vienna rule. But until 1918 it owed much to the fact that the extension of its organization was inspired by its assimilation by the powerful Christian Socialist movement in the Austrian provinces. After 1918 it reigned supreme in the province, winning more than 60 per cent of the Slovenian vote in all elections bar that of 1920, and possessing a network of viable organizations and socialization programmes, all directed by Catholic priests. It was able to resist the challenge of a Slovene peasantist party in 1920 (which it rapidly assimilated) and a later Republican Peasant Party which, under the direction of the Croat Peasant Party, won 11 per cent of the Slovene vote in 1925 before disappearing abruptly.[77]

The Latvian case mixed "western" and "eastern" characteristics, with a regionally concentrated Catholic minority and a regional party system. During the crucial period of the Reformation the province of Latgale was under Polish jurisdiction while the other provinces were part of the Swedish empire: the province had also been administered separately under the Russian empire. The "national" party system, including the agrarian Peasant Union and New Settlers, could not compete against a sturdy Latgalian party system, prominent in which was a Christian Farmers' and a smaller Progressive Farmers' Party. Despite relative ethnic homogenity, the Latvian party system was similar to those states with large ethnic minorities. In neighbouring Catholic Lithuania the existence of a Peasants' Union presents no difficulties, for it was little more than the rural pillar of the dominant Christian Democrats who were organized along "federal-social" lines much like the Austrian or Belgian Christian Socialists. But as distinct from their Western counterparts, the Lithuanian Peasants contested elections separately. The Christian Democrats were strongly Catholic, but also firmly anti-Polish and anti-Russian: for a while they were alienated from the Vatican which in 1926 recognized Vilnius - the historic Lithuanian capital seized by the new Polish state after 1918 - as part of the ecclesiastical province of Poland instead of that of Lithuania. The Catholic Church was able to consolidate its hold upon the countryside both because of previous foreign domination, and because of the neighbouring presence of the Soviet Union which had "sovietized" Lithuania briefly in 1917, primarily through the support of the predominantly urban Jewish population.[78]

No Christian Democrat party developed in Hungary. This is not surprising when one considers that the social and political climate favoured the continuation of close relationships between the Catholic Church and the traditional elites - even though many of the latter were Protestant - after the brief interlude of Bela Kun's short-lived Communist regime. The continuation of the traditional structures may have held out little hope for the peasantry, yet Communism and peasantism were both identified with Russian expansionism. Mitrany notes that "Kun did not let the peasants take the land, intending to apply to it the Marxist program and nationalize the land and collectivize agriculture.

The upshot was that he neither won the support of the peasant nor checked the power of the landed class. Reaction came more quickly and strongly in Hungary than anywhere else".[79] Under the reconstruction of the Horthy regime, the creation of religious parties was unlikely and perhaps unnecessary: most factions in fact attached the prefix "Christian" to their name. Indeed, the social and political climate discouraged the formation and growth of organized parties in general. Until at least 1933 Hungarian politics was almost exclusively a conflict between the landed magnates on the one hand and the smaller gentry and officialdom on the other. The country was dominated by the Government Party (which frequently changed its name), the sole purpose of which was to retain power:

In all its history, the Party never committed itself to any principle except only that of being counter-revolutionary, and even that it interpreted with extreme elasticity, invoking it sometimes to justify measures of extreme reaction, sometimes of radical change ... Thus a person holding any opinion could without violence to his conscience join the Party in the hope of getting it to adopt his favoured policy from inside. In a way, this inclusiveness within the Party compensated for the exclusiveness of the system towards any other party: the will of the Government Party was the substitute for the will of the electorate.[80]

A Smallholders Party did appear after World War I and enjoyed a brief electoral success, but in July 1920 it was absorbed by the Government Party: in any case a "smallholder" in Hungary was defined as a proprietor who owned less than about 60 hectares of land. An Independent Smallholders faction later broke from the Government Party in 1931. However, it was led by an opportunist politician, appealed to the gentry, and until its demise all its parliamentary representatives came from the urban middle class. Hungarian developments (or their lack) are easily understood in the light of the rudimentary level of organized political activity.

More difficult to explain perhaps are two prominent agrarian parties in Catholic Czechoslovakia and Croatia which in their formative years were at least non-religious if not anticlerical in their outlook. In the Czech case the particular historical circumstances of the Czech provinces offer perhaps the best explanation. The most prominent nationalist agitation in the closing decades of the Hapsburg Empire occurred in Bohemia and Moravia. Nationalism became identified to some extent with anticlericalism as a reaction against the Catholic Hapsburgs and the destruction of the old Bohemian state. Unlike similar sentiments in France or Belgium it even led to an attempt to establish an independent Czech Catholic Church. This move never succeeded, and the overwhelming majority of Czechs remained at least nominal Roman Catholics. There is a strong historical link between the Protestant Hussite kingdom destroyed by the Hapsburgs at the Battle of the White Mountain in 1620 and the resurgence of Czech nationalism in the late nineteenth century. The Hapsburgs may have reconverted the provinces, but Bohemia at least remained in spirit very much a Protestant country: in addition, the small number of Protestants wielded disproportionate influence in political life. It was in Bohemia that the Czech Republicans enjoyed their greatest support. The Czech Populists (the Catholic party), under clerical leadership, had their main base among the small farmers and agricultural workers of Moravia-Silesia, while the intensity of religion coupled with autonomous sentiments in the more rural province of Slovakia hindered the development there of a strong agrarian political movement. The Czech Agrarians were fortunate under the Hapsburg regime in that nationalist resurgence, with which they were strongly identified, coincided with deteriorating agricultural conditions. Moreover, they were led by talented politicians who were able to capture intact a substantial part of the organization of the Young Czech party, which they had formerly helped to victory over the Old Czechs. By 1906 the party dominated the agricultural districts. Thereafter its major rivals were the Catholics and Socialists. The latter suffered from their urban origins, while the Czech Populists displayed Austrophil tendencies until at least 1914. Moreover, the Republicans proved to be the most successfully organized party in rural areas with a solid foundation of effective and efficient cooperatives, mutual benefit associations, and credit and savings banks.[81] Similarly, nationalism played an influential role in Croatia. Before 1918 the development of the Croat Peasant Party took place under Magyar rule. Like its Czech counterpart the Croat party was anticlerical, as well as developing, along with the Bulgarian Agrarian Union, the most comprehensive peasantist ideology. After 1918 Croat hostility to what was seen as a Greater Serbia enabled the party to accept a <u>rapprochement</u> with the Church and to claim to represent not just agrarian interests, but also broad national aspirations among all social groups.[82]

Poland is an interesting case with both numerically significant, but politically weak Catholic and agrarian parties. Throughout the decades of imperial rule, a sense of national identity and values had been preserved across the Polish regions, a bond which facilitated political reintegration in 1918. The intelligentsia had been the main carriers of this national style, and in the new state their reward was to dominate the central bureaucracy and the parties.[83] Yet the different levels and characteristics of institutionalization under the various imperial regimes was an important determinant of the postwar Polish party system. Quite apart from the distinctive Ukrainian and Jewish party systems, different kinds of party competition existed in the regions previously ruled from Berlin, Vienna and St. Petersburg. These different regions had undergone different experiences which to a considerable extent determined their later political characteristics and party competition. Catholic parties were strong only in ex-German Poland. Nationalist policies had been enforced extremely rigorously in the Polish regions of the <u>Reich</u>: for example, the Polish language was prohibited in the state administration and educational system.[84] As a consequence, the regions were reinforced in their Catholicism and nationalism. In Poznan the National Democrats were the major party. Led by the wealthier landlords, they had collaborated before 1918 with the German Free Conservatives.[85] The Christian Democrats were largely confined to the industrial population of Silesia, who had originally been mobilized by the German <u>Zentrum</u>. Agrarian parties made little headway in Western Poland, a high yield agricultural region that had suffered economically from the severance with Germany, yet displayed little sympathy for the more backward south and east. The largest agrarian party, the Piast Populists, had been formed before 1914 in Austrian Galicia. The region contained a large number of medium-sized peasant proprietors who were moderate

with regard to further land reform, and also susceptible to
Catholic influence. Here the Poles had been a privileged group
in Austrian politics, favoured by the regime over a large,
poorer Ukrainian peasantry linked by race and language to the
Tsarist Empire. Piast remained strong in this area after 1918,
receiving 40 per cent of the vote in Galicia in 1919, but
failing to achieve much success elsewhere, despite the absorption
of smaller groups in Poznan and ex-Congress regions.[86] By
contrast, Congress Poland and the poverty-stricken Kresy were
the home of a more radical agrarian movement, Wyzwolenie,
founded in 1915 by urban intellectuals: it was somewhat anticlerical, in favour of radical land reform within a framework
of private property, and rather peasantist in its pronouncements.[87]

7. Conditions for the Formation of Agrarian Parties

This survey of the emergence of European agrarian parties should
enable us to evaluate the relative importance of the various
conditions stipulated as necessary for the formation of parties
for agrarian defence. What we have is a set of circumstances in
which all countries have witnessed attempts to build agrarian
parties or parties based on a farming vote, yet only in a few
instances have these succeeded on a durable and organized basis.
In considering this question, we must bear in mind the assets
and liabilities of agricultural populations, assets such as their
large numbers and spatial concentrations and liabilities such as
their late mobilization, low levels of education and socialization,
spatial isolation, and what seems to be an ingrained impatience
with regularized and institutionalized procedures and structures.

It seems clear that two major conditions arise from two
themes constant throughout European agrarian history: the
structure of land tenure and the market relationship between
town and countryside. The key phrase is "defence": agrarian
parties were typically conceived to defend both a particular
structure of farm occupation, and the countryside from urban
contamination. In terms of farm structure the crucial point is
the characterization of a region by small or medium-sized owner-
operators highly involved in market operations. While such
parties in Eastern Europe frequently appeared to demand the end

of large estates and land redistribution under the principle of private property, land reform was usually carried out without the application of any significant pressure by the parties. Moreover, the greatest impetus for their consolidation came only after land redistribution and after the lowering of the threshold of political representation. The second major consideration is the existence of hostility towards the towns, buttressed by cultural difference between city and countryside. It would seem that the numerical weakness of the cities at the time of the decisive extensions of the suffrage is more significant than their political weight in a country, since the existence of a strongly entrenched rural stratification system enabled several landed elites who were not religiously, ethnically or linguistically distinct from the rural masses to mobilize the latter behind various political banners.

The principal distinctions between Eastern and Western Europe lie in the level of organization and institutionalization of rural life, and in the degree of market penetration into the countryside. What may be called Western-type agrarian parties were concerned more with defending agrarian economic interests within a market economy, even where the degree of penetration was weak. We should not, for example, confuse the intensity of the urban-rural conflict in Scandinavia in the nineteenth century with the fact that the agrarian parties there were not established until after 1900 when these countries were already in the throes of industrialization, with the concomitant rapid spread of a money economy. By contrast, agrarian parties in Eastern Europe were more prone to espouse at least superficially peasantist doctrines, and appeared more concerned with preventing the contamination of rural areas by the market economy. Similarly, Western parties had a firmer institutional base in established agricultural associations and cooperatives, whether national or regional. Cooperative movements in Eastern Europe were more likely to be formed simultaneously with agrarian parties or later by political parties. Their economic importance for the peasantry was more limited than in the West. Moreover, a greater premium seemed to be placed upon their desirability as a politically partisan rather than an economic force.

The importance of the Catholic Church seems to be more

limited. To understand this question we must consider why religious parties were formed. In the first instance, conflict arose only where the Church was not prepared to accept a passive role in politics. Typically the Catholic Church faced two challenges in the nineteenth century. It faced a <u>political</u> challenge from governments in a struggle between the mobilizing nation-states and the corporate claims of the churches: this struggle was most acute in Catholic regions because of the distinctive hierarchial structure, theology and self-image of Roman Catholicism. However, the Church also faced a <u>social</u> challenge in the shape of industrialization, urbanization and concomitant secularization. To focus only on the first challenge, as Lipset and Rokkan tend to do, is perhaps to concentrate upon a feature which may have generated a deep social cleavage, but one which did not lead immediately and automatically to the formation of religious parties: witness the examples of France and Italy. The earliest formation of Catholic political organizations came perhaps in Germany where the political attack upon the Church came from governments backed by a Protestant majority.[88] Moreover, the initial Catholic political response came not only in the rural areas, but also among the growing Catholic industrial population. Again, Belgian Catholic associations were explicitly modelled upon the German experience. It is a moot point whether later Catholic mobilization elsewhere - of both urban and rural populations - arose primarily from the country's contemporary political situation, the church-state cleavage, increased urbanization, or an attempt to replicate the successful mobilization and institutionalization of Catholics in Germany and elsewhere. If the social challenge was important for party formation, then it is perhaps less surprising that Catholic formations were less successful in Eastern Europe, or that Catholicism did not constitute so significant a barrier to the formation of agrarian parties, except where, as in Ireland and Western Poland, the Church became the main indigeneous source of authority under foreign rule: the necessary level of urbanization did not exist. Moreover, the proto-typical Catholic developments are not so apparent or important in regions displaying an intense and idiosyncratic nationalism, whether they be within the

Catholic heartland as in Catalonia or among the Basques, or out along the Catholic periphery as typified by Ireland and Poland.

Finally, it should be noted that institutional arrangements at the time of the crucial expansion of the suffrage or of the formation of agrarian parties are very important. A federal structure can affect the way in which parties emerge, or whether or not national parties appear, as in Switzerland. In particular, the introduction of proportional representation is a powerful stimulus for an increase in the number of parties, among them agrarian parties. In Scandinavia proportional representation was a major guarantee for the survival of the agrarian secessions from the old Left coalitions. On the other hand, it should be remembered that agrarian parties tend to be favoured electorally even without proportional representation, because of the territorial concentration of farmers. Above all, the various experiences of earlier institutionalization under previous regimes of its component regions is extremely significant for a new political system: the post-1918 experiences of Poland, Czechoslovakia and Yugoslavia bear eloquent witness to this point.

When we examine parties, political systems and societies, we should be concerned not with a unilinear flow of influence or causation, but with a complex interaction of influence which may not have any straightforward pattern. Parties and party systems are key variables, but they can be simultaneously dependent, intervening and independent variables. As Sartori has emphasized, we can acquire a complete picture only when we assess jointly "to what extent parties are dependent variables reflecting social stratification and cleavages and, vice versa, to what extent these cleavages reflect the channelling imprint of a structured party system".[89] Parties and party systems inevitably reflect, to a greater or lesser extent, the conditions of the regime within which they operate.[90] The different character of regimes and societies in Europe significantly affected the type of party which emerged in the formative period of competitive party politics.

CHAPTER 7   The Social Cohesion and Support of Agrarian Parties

If political parties are formed by social groups, then it might be expected that parties would receive a very high degree of electoral support from those who collectively are imputed to give them birth: similarly, these groups should constitute the overwhelming majority of a party's electorate. The intention here is to explore in more detail the social support of agrarian parties, since the functioning of any political party is inevitably affected by the nature of its support. The social cohesion of political parties has been the subject of many studies, using various approaches such as survey data and electoral geography, from the empirical study of the West of France by André Siegfried onwards.[1] Unfortunately, both adequate survey and aggregate data are lacking for any kind of systematic diachronic analysis. Primarily, therefore, the discussion here is based on more fragmentary and impressionistic evidence: nevertheless, it should be possible to draw certain conclusions about the social cohesion of agrarian parties which could provide the basis of more intensive research in the future.

1. The Agrarian Basis of Party Support
Survey data provide the most adequate means of studying this question, but of course such data are available only for the competitive party systems of Western Europe over the past two decades or so. Let us then begin with these party systems: the amount of agrarian support obtained by contemporary parties, measured as a percentage of their total support, can serve as an

entry point for a broader discussion of the problem of agrarian political cohesion. Table 7.1 refers to the proportion of party support that comes from agrarian groups. Clearly, the potential for large agrarian-based parties after 1945 is extremely circumscribed by the low numbers of cultivators in any one society. Each of the Scandinavian countries provides an example of a party based on rural support: until recently these parties in Norway, Sweden and Finland contained the word "Agrarian" in their title. The Danish Venstre is regarded as occupationally an agrarian party because of its history, its expressed intentions, its heavily non-urban support, and its highly distinctive backing from farmers. By contrast, one nominally agricultural party, the Dutch Boerenpartij, has not been primarily dependent upon farmers for its support. Founded in 1958, the Boerenpartij received its highest vote in the 1966 municipal elections. Its average vote was almost nine per cent, but it received more than this in cities like Amsterdam and the Hague. Outside Scandinavia the only permanent party which is clearly a rural party is the Swiss Bauern-, Gewerbe- und Bürgerpartei (BGB). The BGB has been a regional party with a core strength in the cantons of Zürich, Aargau and Bern. While the data here refer only to the canton of Zürich, limited data from the other cantons suggest that there too it is very much a rural party. Like its Scandinavian equivalents, this party has changed its name (to the Schweizerische Volkspartei) by merging with the small Democrat party in order to widen its appeal.[2] If we consider those Western party systems for which no data are available, the list would be expanded very little: only the Icelandic Progressive Party would be admissable as a distinctively agrarian party. There have also been in the post-1945 period smaller ephemeral parties in Ireland and elsewhere which have been distinctively rural.

The ranking of parties in Table 7.1 is based on an examination of data relating to 65 parties. Yet only three gain more than one-half of their support from farmers, while only 20 obtain more than 20 per cent of their support from agrarian groups. Aggregate election results, superficially at least, suggest that these distinctions in the cohesion of political parties in Western Europe have changed very little since the introduction

Table 7.1: Levels of Agrarian Support of Political Parties

Percentage of Party Support coming from Agrarian Groups

over 60%	50-59%	40-49%	30-39%	20-29%
Finland: Centre (Agrarian)	Denmark: Venstre	France: Radical Christian Democrat Conservative	France: Socialist	Austria: People's
Norway: Centre (Agrarian)		Finland: Swedish People's		Denmark: Radical
Switzerland: Farmers (BGB)		Germany: Bavarian		France: Communist Gaullist
		Sweden: Centre (Agrarian)		Italy: Christian Democrat Monarchist
				Netherlands: Farmers'
				Norway: Liberal
				Switzerland: Radical

Sources: Rose and Urwin, "Social Cohesion"; J.J. De Jong, Overheid en Onderdaan (Wageningen, 1956), pp. 80, 85, 120; Hill, "Belgium", p. 48; A.H. Thomas, Parliamentary Parties in Denmark, 1945-1972 (Strathclyde Survey Research Centre, Occasional Paper Nr. 13, Glasgow, 1973), p. 61; Linz, "Cleavage and Consensus in West German Politics", p. 288; H. Gruijters et al, Experimenten en Democratie (Amsterdam, 1967), pp. 111-117.

of mass politics. In Sweden, for example, the Agrarian Party obtained no votes at all from urban districts in 1928. Similarly, the very low rural support of the German Social Democrats has increased only slightly over time: during the Second Reich it gained hardly any votes in most rural electoral districts. Not all of the parties ranked in Table 7.1 are unambiguous agrarian parties. They include the Christian Democrat and Conservative parties from the Fourth French Republic, the Swedish People's Party in Finland, and the Italian Christian Democrats. Many of these parties with more than one-fifth of their support coming from agrarian groups cannot be exactly classified as rural parties: it is possible for parties to make a strong appeal in the countryside as well as in the cities, but on religious or linguistic rather than agricultural economic grounds. The fact that the Christian Democrat parties of France, Austria and Italy have gained a substantial rural following is not surprising, as they are simply religious parties which cannot ignore farmers. The general failure of farmers to give rise to their own enduring class parties is theoretically very significant, for farmers have been at least as distinctive occupationally, in lifestyle, and in spatial segregation as industrial workers.

It is clear from even a cursory comparison of electoral and occupational data in our universe that in no instance has an agrarian party succeeded in mobilizing the entire agricultural population. Parties such as the <u>Parti Paysan</u>, the Spanish <u>Agrarios</u> and the several German parties can be dismissed immediately because of their inability or unwillingness to transcend regional boundaries: even within these regional constraints they frequently failed to achieve a very high degree of support. At its peak success in 1951, two-thirds of the <u>Parti Paysan's</u> deputies came from south of the Loire, with the core from the old <u>Parti Agraire</u> heartlands in the Massif Central where it did have the appearance of a mass movement. Among the Scandinavian parties only the Danish <u>Venstre</u> is distinguished by winning at times an electoral support equal to or greater than the number of people engaged in agriculture - though, not of course, the entire agrarian population. But the <u>Venstre</u> differs from the other Nordic agrarian parties in that it was not formed specifically as an agrarian party. Originally an urban-rural alliance against absolutism and the central bureaucracy, it succeeded in holding its urban and rural wings in harness. However, the two sides have not always found it easy to reach agreement on strategy and policy. Hence the party has always suffered from factionalism: for example, some rural elements broke away in 1935 to form a short-lived Free People's (Peasant) Party, while in 1965 an urban faction seceded over taxation policy to form a Liberal Centre party. While the <u>Venstre</u> started out life as a rural party, the level of its agrarian support has been steadily contracting ever since. Now, few of its candidates are farmers.[3]

The same strictures apply with even greater force in the more agrarian East. Two examples will stress the point. The two most agricultural countries in our universe were Bulgaria and Yugoslavia, if we set aside Albania, where perhaps even a rudimentary party system failed to develop in the 1920s.[4] In both countries 75 per cent of the population was dependent upon agriculture around 1930.

The failure to achieve a high level of national integration in Yugoslavia effectively prevented any party from mobilizing the electorate cross-regionally.[5] Even within the various linguistic regions it proved very difficult for an agrarian party to mobilize all the peasantry. And given the political weight of the intelligentsia it is not surprising, for example, that in 1927 only one-tenth of the parliamentary deputies in the <u>Skupshtina</u> were peasants or agricultural workers. In each linguistic-ethnic region a hegemonic party, built around the personality of a strong leader, tended to emerge as the defender of its specific cultural-linguistic features. In the core kingdom of Serbia this was the Serbian Radical Party under Nikola Pasić, against which the Serbian Union of Peasants failed to achieve any notable electoral success. Similarly, Catholic Slovenia gave overwhelming support to the regional clerically-led Popular Party, while the dominant party in Bosnia and Hercegovina was the Yugoslav Muslim Organization. The only regional agrarian party to enjoy majority status within its own region was the Croat Peasant Party. After the seizure of power by the king in 1931 it was claimed that it held the allegiance of more than 90 per cent of all Croats. Moreover, this success, even if exaggerated, was probably due less to its agrarian nature than to its negative attitude towards Belgrade and its uncompromising position on constitutional reform in favour of federalism and substantial regional autonomy. In gaining considerable urban support in Croatia the party shed much of its original peasantist ideology. Moreover, after 1918 it largely abandoned its vociferous anticlericalism. Hence, non-agrarian elements capitalized on its success: other Croatian parties, unable to compete with it electorally, simply joined it, so enabling it to emerge as the symbol of Croat opposition to Serbian dominance in the new Yugoslav state. The retention of rural support was buttressed by the slow build-up throughout the 1920s and 1930s of its cooperative movement, the <u>Gospodarska</u>

Sloga, originally established to publish and distribute textbooks in Croatia and generally improve the level of rural education. Even so, by 1940 the cooperative membership consisted of only one-third of all peasant holdings in Croatia. After the party finally entered the government in August 1939, it supervised the creation of a quasifederal structure. In the new Banovina of Croatia the Croat Peasants were in a virtually dictatorial position, and the Gospodarska Sloga functioned as the government agency which handled all matters relating to agricultural production.[6]

Conditions in Bulgaria appeared to be more favourable for the establishment of a large agrarian party: it possessed a highly egalitarian structure, and was homogeneous in terms of both religion and race. Yet politics became the same as elsewhere - a factional struggle to share in the spoils. The powerful sense of Slavic identity led to the strong influence in Bulgaria of narodnik thinking. The Agrarian Union had reached significant electoral proportions before 1914. But under the leadership of Aleksandŭr Stamboliski it dominated Bulgarian politics for a few years after 1918, with a membership of over 120,000 by 1922. Strongly Slavic and anti-German, it had rebelled against the political elite's war miscalculations with a great march on Sofia in 1919: the insurgence was quelled only with the help of German troops. More than any other agrarian party, it attempted to put into practice the principles of agrarian populism. It even insisted that only peasants or bona fide sons of peasants could be members of the party, and that only peasants were spiritually and morally qualified to take on the leadership of the nation. While it was the only agrarian party ever to achieve an electoral majority without overly blatant electoral manipulation, its radicalism cannot be explained only by this victory, which in any case was extremely short-lived. Stamboliski's authoritarianism extended not only to open hatred of city life, but also to intolerance of his party confrères. But political conditions were not conducive to the appearance of organized competitive political parties. The urban-rural gap was perhaps wider than anywhere else: certainly it was exacerbated by the radical and extremely anti-urban politics of Stamboliski who, probably with some justification, was believed to be intent upon establishing a rural dictatorship and eliminating urban society entirely. Stamboliski argued that mechanization was not the most satisfactory or rational way of reorganizing agriculture, that Bulgaria should possess only secondary industries of direct value to the countryside, and that industrial workers should be placed under the direct political control of the Agrarian Union and its para-military arm, the Orange Guard: in 1920 he had without hesitation ordered troops into action to end a strike by railway workers. Fearing for their survival, the urban bourgeoisie were galvanized into forging a counter-revolutionary alliance. The final choice was made after the huge Agrarian success in 1923, under an electoral law introduced by the party and aided by the intimidatory tactics of the Orange Guard. The commercial classes, bureaucracy and intelligentsia joined forces with the monarchy and the army, as well as - paradoxically - two revolutionary movements, the large Communist party and the Macedonian terrorists of IMRO, to destroy the Agrarian Union and purge it of its leadership. All had previously crossed swords with Stamboliski and had suffered from his policies. By driving city and countryside into total opposition to each other, Stamboliski had perhaps sealed his own fate. At the height of electoral success, he had allowed an apocalyptic fervour to obscure the fact that "political power does not automatically grow out of demographic statistics".[7] Thereafter, with Stamboliski dead, and hindered by official obstruction, the Union fragmented into several personal and competing factions. Never again did it enjoy such significant success. To ensure their own survival, later generations of leaders were either willing to collaborate with the bureaucratic regime or sought in vain to collaborate with industrial workers to construct a socialist state.[8]

2. The Failure to Gain Urban Support

These examples illustrate some of the problems attendant upon the agrarian parties' attempts to mobilize their potential electorate in different social contexts. On the other hand, very few agrarian parties have been successful in attracting urban support. Excluding the <u>Venstre</u>, the Swedish Agrarians have been most successful of the contemporary Scandinavian parties in this respect. But their expansion into the towns is only of recent vintage, arising from the contraction of the agricultural population and the party's will for survival. A Swedish study showed that in 1950 the percentage of support for the Agrarians in communities with 50 per cent of the work force employed in agriculture was 29 per cent; in other rural areas, 10 per cent; in smaller cities and towns, 2 per cent; and in Stockholm, Göteborg and Malmö, only one per cent. The same data indicate that 75 per cent of Agrarian support came from agricultural communities, 21 per cent from other rural areas, while only 3 per cent came from smaller cities and towns, and one per cent from the three major cities.[9] Similarly, the Finnish Agrarians have been confined within a one per cent barrier in the two major cities of Helsinki and Tampere.[10]

The number of agrarian parties which have been able to appeal to urban groups is very limited. Agrarian parties seem able to win urban votes in significant numbers only where special historical circumstances exist, or where nationalist or ethnic-linguistic cleavages are of overriding importance. We have already discussed the Danish and Croat cases. They seem to be typical. In Denmark the <u>Venstre</u> began as an urban-rural alliance against the central bureaucracy, and succeeded in maintaining this coalition. Croat national hostility against Serbian dominance in the new Yugoslav state enabled the party to reign supreme in the region: ethnic and religious cleavages similarly prevented it from expanding beyond Croatia. In terms of political and governmental influence, the most successful agrarian party in the interwar period was the Czech Republican Party. The party attracted urban votes in the first instance because of nationalist sentiments and the party's prominence in the struggle for independence. Later, it almost certainly won an urban vote because of its perpetual presence in government and the patronage it could dispense.

Their failure to mobilize the whole rural population and their inability to secure substantial numbers of urban voters are two major problems which have confronted European agrarian parties in the twentieth century. To understand the conditions determining this situation, we need to explore more fully those factors which persuade rural voters to support other parties. We need to know which kind of non-agrarian party is electorally successful in the countryside. Further, it is necessary to consider whether the failure of agrarian parties to secure their potential electorate is due to lower rates of political mobilization, participation and institutionalization in rural areas. It is also essential to consider which rural groups are more likely to support agrarian parties. In order to answer some of these questions, it seems profitable to offer first a review of the circumstances of particular parties. Unfortunately, most data are not sufficiently detailed to explore internal differentiation among the rural population.

The Swedish Agrarian Party has primarily been a party of small farmers. It receives little support from agricultural labourers. Regionally, it has been slightly stronger in southern than in northern districts. On the other hand, Ingulfson and Hagman indicate that while the support gained by all other parties in the countryside varied with income levels, the Agrarians' electoral base was constant in all income groups. The limits of Agrarian support to some extent were determined by the timing of rural mobilization, which occurred before the relatively late formation of the party. Certain agrarian groups were successfully organized by other parties before the Agrarians came on the scene as an independent force: the 1930s were the intensive years of mobilization and organization building for the party. Above all, the party is closely connected with the Swedish Farmers' Union (<u>Riksförbundet Landsbygdens Folk</u>) founded in 1929. Most union leaders belong to the party, and the union is stronger among the farmer-capitalist enterprises of the south.[11]

The Norwegian Agrarians are similarly almost exclusively a rural party. On the other hand, they have never been able to secure more than one-half of the farming vote. Survey evidence suggests that the party gains more support among wealthier than among smaller farmers. The best predictor seems to be simply the proportion of the population in the area actively engaged in agriculture, coupled with the size of holdings: the larger average farm size in the commune, the greater the Agrarian vote. Moreover, its support is regionally distinctive, being concentrated more in the East Inland and Trondelag regions and, to a lesser extent, in the cultural periphery of the South-West, where it is associated with the language dimension of Norwegian politics. In the South-West the party reflects the historical rural cultural opposition to the centre, being stronger in the least accessible communes. In the East and Trondelag regions such a clear gradation does not occur. Again, therefore, a mixture of historical circumstances, the size of enterprise, and the extent of involvement in commercial farming seems to shape the limits of agrarian support.[12]

Larger, wealthier farmers were also more prominent in the Baltic agrarian parties. In Estonia the larger rural party, the Agrarian League, appears to have appealed in particular to those farmers who had ownership of land or security of tenure before the widespread redistribution of land in 1919. These reforms gave land to many peasants, but holdings tended to be smaller and poorer. The new proprietors, seeking more government aid, became dissatisfied with the moderate, even conservative policies and attitudes of the Agrarian League, and in 1923 provided the core of the New Farmers' or Settlers' Party. Unlike the Agrarians they were willing in 1928 to enter a coalition government with the Socialists, the Lutheran Christian Democrats, and a moderately radical middle class Labour Party. A similar differentiation occurred in Latvia. More secure, wealthier farmers provided an electoral base for the conservative Peasant Union while those who became proprietors after the redistribution of land veered to the more radical New Farmers' Party: the Catholic province of Latgale produced its own rural party, the Latgalian Christian Farmers' Party. In Lithuania the various functional offshoots of the Christian Democrats obtained rural support according to the economic position of the voter. Wealthier farmers supported the Peasant Union, while the less prosperous preferred the Federation of Labour.[13] In all these countries a substantial ethnic minority settled in rural areas voted for ethnic parties, hence reducing the potential electorate for the major agrarian parties. The more conservative stance of the latter can perhaps be explained by the proximity of the Soviet Union and the early prominence of Socialist parties which in 1917 and 1918 attempted to mobilize the countryside. These considerations might also apply to Finland after 1918.

The considerable regional differences that existed in Rumania are not surprising when we recall that the National Peasants were the result of a merger in 1926 between the Peasant Party of the Old Kingdom (itself a merger of the peasant parties of the Regat and Bessarabia) and the Transylvanian Nationalists. The two wings of the party were never entirely fused. The Nationalists tended more towards pragmatism, while the peasantist wing remained more virulently anti-urban and anti-bourgeois à la Stamboliski. The different effects of land reforms in the regions, plus the distribution of ethnic minorities and the feeling in the more advanced regions of Transylvania and the Banat that they were little more than colonies of the Regat, also probably affected its electoral base. Any indication of the party's true support is difficult to find, considering the violent electoral fluctuations that occurred in the 1920s and 1930s. However, in line with other Eastern agrarian parties, it seems that more prosperous cultivators played a more prominent role within the party. This is especially true in Transylvania where the Nationalist movement had been formed before 1914 to fight Magyar domination of the land and its administration. The party did have a peasant base but few of its leaders were peasants. It enjoyed significant urban support and before the merger had also absorbed some remnants of the old Conservatives, who had represented the landlord class.[14]

Undoubtedly the agrarian party that proved the most successful in mobilizing its potential electorate was the Czech Republican Party, as long as we remember its regional base in Bohemia and Moravia, and the multiethnic nature of the country. In its origins it resembled many other parties. Between its inception in 1896 and the expansion of the suffrage in Cis-Leithania in 1906 it was specifically a party of landowners and large farmers. After 1918 the necessity to present a united national front led it initially to cooperate with the strong Social Democrats. This, plus the land reforms, gave it a more progressive image which it never entirely lost throughout the interwar period. Attempts were made in 1925 by dissident elements to lead a conservative secession but these all failed. But by the 1930s the party had become a protagonist of numerous agricultural industries, state monopolies, financial interests, and huge cartels in several industrial fields, all of which inevitably pushed it in a conservative direction. While remaining loyal to the Czech cultivator, it attracted significant urban support: for example, in 1925 it won 17 per cent of the vote in Prague, second only to the National Socialists. The more commercially oriented character of Czech agriculture, more prosperous farmers, high rural levels of education, all enabled the party to discard a peasantist orientation. Moreover, its dominant position in all interwar coalition governments helped to consolidate its core rural support and its wide network of cooperative and marketing institutions: its permanent occupation of the Ministry of Agriculture permitted it great influence in the distribution of farm machinery, price-fixing, the purchasing of grain, and on the Peasant Bank which the vast majority of farmers had at one time or another to approach for loans. In its behaviour, therefore, the party became in many ways a broker party which appealed to several groups: in turn this diversified its electoral clientele (although diversification was not a necessary consequence of a change in the party's appeal). Its own bank (originally established as a credit cooperative to aid wealthier peasants and village craftsmen) rapidly grew to become the largest credit body in the country. Controlling over 35 per cent of Czech industry, it was able to play an active role in all aspects of the financial and economic life of the country. The party's penetration of industry and finance also made it somewhat attractive to employees and workers.[15]

While the party's policies favoured an integration of urban and rural support, they also hindered it in its attempts to reach the whole rural population, especially outside its regional strongholds. Within the more economically viable western provinces its original anticlerical or agnostic tendencies forfeited the party some support in the more strongly Catholic areas of Moravia-Silesia, where it faced stern competition from the Catholic Populists. On the other hand, the political relevance of economic distinctions among rural groups also applied here. The Republicans attracted more support among the wealthier cultivators, while the Populists were more favoured by smallholders and agricultural labourers.[16] The party also failed to surmount the country's ethnic cleavages. The large German and the small Magyar and Jewish minorities developed autonomous party systems, in which an agrarian party was prominent. The <u>Bund der Landwirte</u> was particularly successful in mobilizing the German farmers of the Sudetenland: from 1924 it cooperated closely in government with the Czech Republicans.[17] The latter did attract some support in the small province of Ruthenia, so backward in 1919 as to be described as little more than a Hungarian deer park. But even here a minority party system developed, and the most successful Czech party proved to be the Communists. Czech Republican support in Ruthenia came primarily from the numerous Czech administrators there, and through an electoral alliance with one of the Ruthenian parties.[18] Similarly, the party could not overcome the Czech-Slovak cleavage. It remained oriented to the more prosperous commercial farmers of the west than to the more rural east. In Slovakia the Republicans' main support came from the wealthier Protestant minority through its absorption of the Slovak National and Farmers' party. Slovak antagonism to Czech dominance arose from several causes. Even in Slovakia the administrative service was dominated by Czechs. In the absence of qualified Slovaks, Czech bureaucrats had had to take over from the departing Hungarians in 1918. Yet despite an extensive educational and training programme and Slovak claims that they now possessed a sufficient reservoir of qualified personnel, Czech predominance did not entirely disappear over the next decade. In 1930 Czechs occupied 41.3 per cent of administrative posts in Slovakia, compared to 47.5 per cent filled by Slovaks. Resentment was felt against the somewhat pronounced agnosticism, or even anti-clericalism of the Czechs. Moreover, the Catholic hierarchy in Slovakia still contained several Hungarians and overall was Magyarphil. It is perhaps doubtful whether there was in 1918 an overwhelming desire for separation from Hungary or, if so, whether union with the Czechs was preferred over independence. Certainly, union was embraced only in expectation of an autonomous political status. The particular economic problems of Slovakia also weakened the appeal of Czech parties. The major trade before 1918 had been in forestry and had been

directed towards Hungary, while Budapest subsidies and
protectionist policies had encouraged a nascent industrialization.
All this had changed abruptly. The new state boundaries and
Czech-Magyar hostility throughout the interwar period virtually
eliminated the timber trade, while the embryonic Slovak industry
could not compete with its highly developed Czech counterpart.
Similarly, both the industrial and agricultural policies of the
Czech Republicans consistently favoured the western provinces.[19]

3. Factors Influencing The Support of Agrarian Parties

After this review of several agrarian parties, we can turn to
propose some generalizations about their social support. To
state the obvious, agrarian parties have been unable to secure
the total vote of their potential rural electorates. Several
factors seem to account for this. First, apart from exceptional
circumstances, internal economic differentiation within agricultural society has oriented cultivators in different political
directions. For example, all 68 candidates of the Irish Farmers'
Party in 1922 were fairly large farmers and all stood only in
constituencies containing large farms.[20] In areas of small
proprietors distinctions in income levels and production
orientation, often associated with the geographical proximity to
a market centre, seem to have been effective in limiting rural
integration behind a single agrarian party. In political terms
this posed problems of organization and unity similar to those
typically experienced by religiously-based parties; that is,
internal tension between sections of the party along economic
lines. The political expression of this tension took one of two
forms. An articulate dissident group sometimes remained within
the party, as was the case of radical elements within the Croat
Peasants or the Pladne group within the Bulgarian Agrarian Union.
Alternatively, these differences may lead to the formation of
more than one agrarian party, as in Poland and the Baltic
states.[21] Some of the smaller factions were more willing than
the larger agrarian parties to enter electoral or governmental
coalitions with urban radical parties. Again, landless
labourers, who were quite often radicalized because of their
failure to benefit from any previous land reform, and rural

workers engaged in more isolated and economically hazardous occupations such as forestry were less susceptible to agrarian appeals. Hence, despite the claims made by peasantist apologists, considerable internal social and economic diversification within rural society led also to political and electoral diversity. The potential of economic stratification to disrupt even a long-established and well-organized agrarian party is well illustrated by the rapid rise in the 1960s in Finland of the Smallholders Party which made severe inroads into the Centre (Agrarian) vote in the northern and eastern provinces at a time when the latter party was seeking to widen its electoral base beyond the farming world.[22]

Rural electorates were often mobilized by political forces arising from or appealing to other social cleavages. Religious divisions and loyalties in Catholic countries generally proved effective in hindering or preventing the formation of an agrarian party, or attempts by one to expand its electoral base. This is especially true in states where the Catholic Church had to face the social challenge of industrialization and secularization: there the likelihood of an effectively organized religious party was greater. Moreover, the countryside was usually much more strongly committed to and influenced by the Church. Ethnic and linguistic loyalties frequently had the same effect, for ethnic minorities were more often to be found in the countryside than in the towns. In Finland for instance, the Swedish farmers have voted largely for the Swedish People's Party rather than the Agrarians: typically, perhaps, for a multi-cultural society, the Finnish Agrarians had alienated the Swedish farmers by articulating strong anti-Swedish views on the language question.[23] Where there were large ethnic minorities, there developed a separate ethnic-based party system. Where an ethnic agrarian party appeared as part of a subcultural party system, it rarely cooperated more than minimally with the major agrarian party. The outstanding exception, perhaps, was the <u>Bund der Landwirte</u> which more than any other German party played a positive role in Czechoslovak politics from the mid-1920s onwards, despite strong opposition from its local leaders and voters in the rural Egerland, claimed to have been the most pan-Germanic area in Europe.[24]

Earlier mobilization of cultivators by an urban-based party could effectively block agrarian electoral expansion. This was clearly the situation in Greece. In Serbia the Agrarians found their way barred by the Radicals. The latter had (for the Balkans) an effective organization in both town and countryside through which, together with the great prestige of Pasić and the utilization of patronage and credit as political tools, they were able to appeal successfully to the peasantry. At least until the end of the 1920s the Radicals were identified by the peasants as the party most suitably expressing their prejudices against the other nationalities in Yugoslavia, especially the Croats.[25] In the previous chapter we emphasized the significance of earlier historical experiences for later political mobilization and institutionalization. Quite apart from its ethnic problems, Poland, like many other Eastern European countries, was imperfectly integrated. In 1918, for example, both Galicia and Cracow strenuously opposed the establishment of a centralized governmental system directed from Warsaw. Despite their desire to secede from Germany, the Poles in Poznan held serious reservations about joining Poland and for a short while even erected a tariff barrier between it and other Polish provinces. This kind of action, springing from earlier institutionalization, seriously inhibited the ability of the Polish agrarian parties to expand beyond their original geographical bases: they failed to win any significant support in the western provinces.[26] Distinctive historical development could also affect relatively small regions. In Finland the Agrarians' weakest rural support has come from the western province of Vaasa, where historically there had been an egalitarian stratification system with a congruent pattern of agricultural enterprises, as well as a profound fundamentalist movement within the Lutheran Church. Moreover, Vaasa had been the original centre of White opposition to the Reds in the 1918 civil war: later it was a rallying ground for the extreme nationalist Lapuan movement. The vast majority of Vaasa farmers have persistently supported the conservative National Coalition, while the Agrarian deputies from the province have consistently been among the most conservative in the parliamentary party.[27]

Agrarian parties basically represent a very distinctive

occupational group. The more such a party identifies itself with that group, the less the appeal it can have for other social groups. The dilemma is a familiar one for party leaders. Parties, through actively seeking to institutionalize existing social divisions, determine to what extent they will penetrate different sectors of the society. They may seek electoral support and intensive organization among several groups, or they may deliberately content themselves with the formation and consolidation of a <u>Ghettopartei</u>. Since the relative size of social groups varies cross-nationally, and since parties vary in their definition of their optimal support, the problem of reconciling internal solidarity with electoral expansion will be faced differently by different types of parties. Institutionalization becomes an intervening variable between a party's behaviour and its socially cohesive following. However, it is not a necessary function of parties. Not all leaders will attempt to institutionalize their actual or potential electoral reservoir, and some may do so with no social basis of cohesion.[28]

Where an agrarian party laid claim to some kind of peasantism, only if it abandoned or drastically modified its ideological base and its political tactics could it hope to attract non-agrarian support. The Czech Republicans are a good example, occupying the moderate and constitutional pole of a continuum that ranged across to the radical Bulgarian Agrarian Union. The relative failure of agrarian parties to attract other groups contrasts strongly with the situation of other parties: urban-based parties have proved electorally successful in the countryside. Apart from the special circumstances of the Danish <u>Venstre</u>, even the moderate (that is, less ideological) Scandinavian parties failed to expand outside the increasingly limited agricultural sector: instead, they had to behave more like interest groups. In the Baltic states, the more powerful agrarian parties seem in some ways to have behaved similarly.

The strongest contrast to this more pragmatic approach, was found in the Balkans, where agrarian parties possessed at least the trappings of a peasantist ideology. Although the rural sector of the population was larger here than anywhere else in Europe - hence making urban support less essential for majority-oriented parties - many of these agrarian parties did succeed in attracting relatively more urban support than the Scandinavian parties. Ironically, in most instances the leadership of the Balkan agrarian parties was overwhelmingly urban, mainly professional men and intelligentsia.[29] A 1936 publication contained a list of prominent Rumanian politicians with their party affiliation and occupation. Of the 195 individuals who belonged to the National Peasants, 85 (43.6 per cent) were lawyers and 70 (35.9 per cent) belonged to other urban groups, mainly the educational intelligentsia, while only 11 (5.6 per cent) were employed in agriculture.[30]

The Balkan parties were perhaps less immutable than most. Their emphasis upon peasant integralism rapidly disappeared: originally founded to oppose the urban middle class, they soon cooperated closely with some urban party, and even more so acquired a leadership dominated by the intelligentsia. While some individuals were no doubt attracted by the *narodnik* sentiments within peasantism, most perhaps saw party politics as a means of advancing their own carrier in societies where job competition within the professional occupations was exceptionally severe. Many would be first generation city dwellers who frequently rejected totally their peasant origins.[31] On the whole, urban groups, especially the working classes, were hostile to peasantist culture. While this prevented the agrarian parties achieving a mass urban base, it did not inhibit the cities from utilizing the agrarian electorate for their own interests: as Roberts succintly comments, "politics .... was the art of taking advantage of the amorphous character of the peasantry".[32]

The major Balkan exception to these comments was the Bulgarian Agrarian Union during its heyday in the early 1920s. It vigorously pursued a policy of denying membership to all but peasants: however, people who could prove that they were direct descendants of peasants were permitted membership.[33] This attitude is found elsewhere only among certain extreme anarchist and syndicalist groups towards non-working class groups. In Bulgaria it was a specific anti-intelligentsia move by the most radical and far-reaching peasantist movement. However, the fate of the Agrarian Union illustrates what may happen if an agrarian party moves too far in the opposite direction. In provoking all other political groups to form an unholy alliance in 1923, the uncompromising stance of Stamboliski sowed the seeds of the party's destruction.

By contrast, agrarian parties have been able to win significant non-rural support where they became identified with the political expression of other social cleavages. This usually meant that an agrarian party became the spokesman for a geographic or social ethnic periphery opposed to the cultural and economic policies of a centralizing government. This was specifically the case of Croatia and, to a lesser extent, of ethnic minorities in some of the other multilingual states of Eastern Europe. The Rumanian National Peasants are a dubious case in that no ethnic conflict was involved. Instead, it is necessary to make a distinction between the Regat and Bessarabia where the Peasant wing won hardly any urban votes, and Transylvania where the old urban-rural alliance, originally forged against the Magyar landlords and administrators, survived after 1918, not only because severance from Hungary had damaged the region's economy, but also as a protest against the centralist economic policies of the governments and financiers in Bucharest.

The identification of an agrarian movement with regional religious interests was much less likely to occur. Latgale is the only European example of a religious periphery, which was not also ethnically distinctive, generating its own party system. The major instance in Western Europe of an agrarian party receiving support from a cultural periphery is the South-West of Norway, where language and religious issues have tended to reinforce each other: however, the Agrarians have been more cohesive here on linguistic grounds (70 per cent of its support are Nynorsk speakers) than because of religious activity or the temperance issue.[34] Clearly, where an agrarian party also became the standard bearer of some other cleavage, the change affected not only the party's social base, but also its policy orientation and behaviour: in short, in its strategy and behaviour tha party became less the defender of farmers and more a protagonist of other cultural interests.[35]

Two further, more general political factors, discussed previously in a wider context, may also affect the ability of an agrarian party to reach its potential electorate. Paradoxically, the social and economic isolation of the small cultivator makes it easier for official pressure to be brought to bear upon him, while simultaneously making it more difficult to organize him in any institutionalized political movement. Hence, the political and economic power holders in the twentieth century found, just as their predecessors had, that in general the peasantry were more amenable than most groups to political persuasion and pressure: "Universal suffrage did not protect the peasant masses from the intimidation or manipulation of (the) political class of bureaucrats and intelligentsia, and election results generally reflected its overall priorities if not always its particular preferences."[36] Governmental and urban control of credit became a major economic and political lever against the countryside. The most extreme situations existed in Hungary and Rumania. In Hungary the retention of open voting in rural areas until 1938 made it easier for the elites to bring all kinds of legal and illegal pressures to bear upon the agricultural population. The violent fluctuations of the Rumanian electorate - always in favour of the government of the day - reflected the widespread corruption and administrative pressure that prevailed in the countryside. On the other hand, the social and geographical isolation of the cultivator has always posed problems for political movements seeking to mobilize and institutionalize the rural vote. The more "peasantist" the society, the greater these difficulties become. It is a dilemma which has never been satisfactorily resolved.

4. Party Survival and a Declining Agrarian Population

It will be appropriate to conclude this discussion of the social support of agrarian parties with an examination of the greatest challenge to their survival that the parties have had to face: the continuing decline of the agricultural population to negligible proportions. We shall end therefore as we began, by looking at the agrarian parties of Western Europe after 1945 and the impact of an accelerated rate of agricultural decline. The overwhelmingly agricultural milieu of most of the agrarian parties in Eastern and Central Europe in the interwar period means that the inclusion of these decades would be largely irrelevant.

An empirical study of the dynamic properties of political parties in 19 countries, using the aggregate vote for each party in each election to the major national legislative assembly, included seven agrarian parties in the analysis: the Agrarians in Finland, Norway and Sweden, the Danish Venstre, the Icelandic Progressives, the Swiss BGB, and Clann na Talmhan in Ireland. Whatever index of changed used, a measure of trends or any of several measures of fluctuation over time, the position was the same: the electoral support of most parties in Western nations since 1945 has changed very little from election to election, from decade to decade, or within the lifespan of a single generation. This was equally true of the agrarian parties: only the Icelandic Progressives showed a marked upward trend, while only Clann na Talmhan (which eventually became extinct) plotted a marked downward course. Indices of variability and of persistence showed that here too the votes of the agrarian parties, with the exception of the Icelandic Progressives, were skewed towards steadiness and persistence. A similar analysis of the same party systems in the interwar period indicated that in fact very little had changed between 1918 and the 1970s. Between the wars the Venstre, the Irish Farmers' Party and, to a lesser extent, the Icelandic Progressives showed marked downward trends: the other four parties displayed nil trend. The fluctuation in the parties' support was equally as persistent in the interwar period, although more variable: this last difference, however, is probably due to the generally greater volatility of Western European party systems during these two decades.[37] These empirical studies indicate that despite the continuing decline in agriculture since 1918, specifically agrarian parties in Western Europe have held their position exceptionally well. Since 1918 there have been inter-election variations in electoral support, but these have been in response to short-term influence upon electoral behaviour. For example, the immediate post-1945 decline of the Norwegian Agrarian Party is often attributed to a popular belief that during the war its leaders had leaned in the direction of collaboration with the Nazi occupation forces.

The failure to confirm some of the commonplace assumptions of sociologists about political change suggests that more attention might be directed to some of the conventional assumptions of political scientists about the electoral role of parties and party leaders. Parties are independent as well as dependent variables. As such, they also have consequences for the societies in which they operate: Schattschneider, for example, has demonstrated very lucidly how the dynamics of a party system can be understood in terms of attempts of disadvantaged parties to change the dimensions along which voters divide to ones more favourable to themselves.[38] The Scandinavian agrarian parties have been well aware of the possible threat posed by a declining agricultural population. In the late 1950s and early 1960s those in Sweden, Norway and Finland changed their name to that of Centre Party. In 1971 the Swiss BGB merged on the national level with the Democrats to become the Swiss People's Party, though the old names have been retained at the cantonal level. The change of name symbolizes the change of emphasis in these parties' programmes and their attempts to mobilize voters in non-agrarian occupations. In Norway the party gradually abandoned its activist agricultural and rather conservative position on many issues. A new generation and a new leadership was more conciliatory towards other parties and more anxious to occupy the key position in the centre of the party spectrum. Even the Danish <u>Venstre</u> has sought to play down its agrarian heritage. The new leader of the party elected in 1964 was the first who did not possess an agricultural background, while in recent years few farmers have emerged as party candidates. Perhaps the most successful transition has been made by the Swedish Agrarians, who have emphasized decentralization and the rights of the small man. The proportion of its support that comes from farmers has steadily declined, and in the 1964 national election it won a seat in Stockholm for the first time.[39]

Clearly, the amount of change that has occurred is limited. In Denmark, for example, the distribution of the <u>Venstre</u> vote between Copenhagen, larger towns and cities, smaller towns and rural areas changed only slightly between the early 1950s and the late 1960s. Are, then, agrarian parties doomed to extinction? Such a question would seem at first glance to depend upon the likelihood of the agricultural population becoming miniscule, the probability that agrarian parties will more likely fail in their attempts to broaden their electoral base, or indeed that by seeking such a base the parties would alienate their agrarian following without gaining compensatory support elsewhere. But a change of name or even of programme may be insufficient without accompanying political socialization. Even where efforts at political socialization are made, there will be an inevitable time lag between changes in the rationale of a party and in its electoral support. Moreover, it is imperative that we should not overlook the significance of organization and institutionalization. Institutions such as parties may over time endure without change, be abruptly destroyed, sink into obsolescence, or evolve into new forms.[40] In fact, even when the original raison d'être for their formation has become obsolescent, parties have rarely withered away without the aid of some traumatic shock inflicted upon the society and the political system. The ability of parties, including agrarian parties, to survive such regime shocks as the two world wars and the economic and political disruptions of the 1930s suggests that agrarian parties may well be able to endure and perhaps succeed in broadening their electoral base. Of course, such developments are invariably long-term. Since the deliberate attempt by the agrarian leaderships to widen their electoral appeal was initiated less than two decades ago, it may be as yet to assess the success or failure of the strategy. But the key to the success of any party in such an endeavour rests primarily in the strength of its organization and the degree of institutionalization in the party system. In any case, the ability of an established party to survive has empirically always been considerably greater than the chances of a new party consolidating itself in an already institutionalized party system.

CHAPTER 8   The Behaviour of Agrarian Parties

The structure of a party system can be assumed to make a considerable difference both in the style of party activity and in the behaviour of party leaders. Party strategy will vary according to how near the party system is to straightforward majority dominance by one party, and with the opportunity and degree of responsibility each party has for central governmental decision-making. In other words, parties must also be considered as independent variables. Political parties can activate or institutionalize sub-cultural divisions by deciding to what extent they desire to penetrate different social or geographic sectors of the society. Through their internal nominating and electoral processes, parties can also advance the political influence and prestige of social groups. By selecting candidates who are connected and identified with specific social groups, parties can hope to reach these groups more easily and allocate their scarce resources elsewhere. Above all, parties play a vital role in regime maintenance. However, parties are not only significant elements of representation and national integration: they can also formulate less benign demands that may threaten the maintenance or existence of the regime.[1]

1. The Strategy of Parties

The important aspect of the significance of parties for regime maintenance is their involvement with government. Parties form governments, either by themselves or in coalition with other parties. The degree of security of those forming the government, and their propensity to cooperate with other parties (<u>Koalitionsfähigkeit</u>) will have consequences both for the political system and the society. Moreover, parties in government seek to carry through legislation. Governmental output can be an indication of the attitude, competence and popularity of parties. However, party policy-making is conditioned by several possible obstacles. Not only can it be affected by external influences from, for example, socio-economic or bureaucratic sources: coalition governments may themselves prove to be obstacles to a party's policy objectives. It would be advisable to examine this aspect of party life diachronically: as a pure opposition group, first outside and then inside the legislature, then as a participant in a coalition government, and finally as the only governing party. Within each set of circumstances the freedom of the party to manoeuvre is constrained by the institutional rules of the game: their strategy, moreover, can be understood only if we bear in mind the development of cleavage structures and partisan organization in each country. Further restraints may be imposed by the character of the party itself. A party that is unable to adapt itself to changes in its legislative and social circumstances may be more immature and less pragmatic than one that can.

The concern with coalition formation refers here to the propensity of agrarian parties to cooperate with other parties: in particular, it refers to the inclination to participate in coalition governments. Perhaps the most important question is who will be their allies, the urban middle class or the working class. It is less necessary to discuss agrarian parties as forces of pure opposition. Their role as a parliamentary opposition can be related to their coalition capacity, while few have existed as opposition forces outside the legislature after mass political mobilization and the granting of universal suffrage: moreover their role in nineteenth century politics has already been discussed. At the other extreme, there have been only two instances of an agrarian party forming a single-party majority government: the Bulgarian Agrarian Union in the early 1920s and the Rumanian National Peasants in 1928. As we saw, the Bulgarian experiment lasted for only a few turbulent years. The Rumanian National Peasant government was more durable, but equally unsuccessful. It would seem more appropriate to discuss these cases in the context of coalition governments.

Parties enter coalition governments to obtain certain goals and to seek certain benefits. Equally, they will almost certainly be aware that participation in coalitions involves costs as well as benefits. The major pioneering theoretical work on party behaviour by Anthony Downs is limited by its assumption of a bipolar party system.[2] Gunnar Sjöblom has more recently made a significant contribution to the literature of political science by his theoretical discussion of party behaviour in a multi-party context. As a guide to subsequent discussion it would seem to be most convenient here simply to extrapolate from Sjöblom's list of the costs and benefits of coalition participation.[3] The benefits claimed are as follows: i) within a majority coalition, the realization of programmes for which the coalition was formed, ii) prevention of alternative programmes that are less favourable; iii) an opportunity to influence the views of the coalition partners on other questions; iv) the possibility of influencing more easily the views of parties outside the coalition (that is, make them modify their position); v) making possible a desired change in the party's own programme (that is, if the party adhered to a policy which is later modified or abandoned, entering the coalition can be advanced as an excuse for the change); vi) aiding the electoral collaboration of the coalition partners - parties in coalition may subsequently find it difficult to oppose each other electorally; vii) the party gains increased parliamentary resources; it improves the party's efficacy-image; viii) it reduces the costs of communicating the party's policy to its members and voters; ix) it makes possible a breakthrough into communication networks that were not available earlier, for example, by appealing to the supporters of its coalition partners; x) it increases the opportunities for new initiatives in the parliamentary arena; xi) it increases the stability of the regime. By contrast, Sjöblom suggests that the possible costs are i) participation may force the party to modify or abandon its own evaluation system, for example, through the necessity to compromise upon policy and legislative details; ii) it may have negative effects upon the evaluation of the party and its image by both its members and voters; iii) it may have negative effects upon the ability of the party's members and voters to make predictions about the party and its position on various issues; iv) it may reduce the possibilities of politicization (for example, constraints may be imposed upon the party's ability to make electoral capital by commenting critically upon those questions for which the coalition was formed); v) it may increase the costs of communication: if the party does modify or abandon its original standpoint or image, the move must be explained.

The coalition propensity and behaviour of parties is limited by internal institutional, developmental, and social structure constraints. The analysis of the history of agrarian politics in Europe suggests that two major influences have been the structure and size of the agricultural population, and the market-urban-rural nexus. To conform with the analysis of the formation and support of agrarian parties, it will be most simple to begin with a consideration of the relative size of the agricultural sector. Two very general kinds of situation exist. The first consists of countries where both agrarian parties and the proportion of the population engaged in agriculture are a clear minority. Different problems will be raised where agrarian parties exist in predominantly agricultural societies.

2. Interest Group Politics

In the first instance, an agrarian party must accomodate itself within a set of political alignments created and maintained by urban, industrial society, in which the rural-urban dimension of political differences may be relatively insignificant or irrelevant. In a sense, therefore, an agrarian party must fit into the traditional "left-right" cleavage determined by urban economic differences. The possibility of an agrarian party being part of an urban society and party system dominated by a religious or linguistic-ethnic cleavage, while theoretically possible, has in practice been a remote possibility. The apogee of party strategy is to enter a government coalition. In a multiparty system the agrarian party has a choice of potential targets or partners in its efforts to secure greater influence upon the policy-formation process. The agrarian parties faced with this situation over the whole period under consideration would seem to be those in Scandinavia, Switzerland and Czechoslovakia. Finland is included because of the exceptionally rapid decline in the size of its agricultural population in the twentieth century, and because the Agrarian Party has had strong links with the powerful and commercially-oriented Agricultural Producers Association, making it similar to its Nordic brethren.[4]

The behaviour of the Swedish Agrarians reflected the economic interests of the wealthier farmers who predominated in the party organization. For two decades after the party's birth they cooperated closely with the middle class parties without, however, becoming a formal member of governments. The critical period was the great depression of the early 1930s and the 1932 election. The election result produced a <u>Riksdag</u> majority for a possible coalition of Social Democrats and Agrarians. Rural discontent over the proposed policies of the middle class parties to solve the economic crisis led to an internal rebellion within the Agrarian Party. The party leadership, which had originally supported the bourgeois anti-depression policies of severe limitation of public expenditure, was overtaken by members prepared to align the party with the Social Democrats' expansionist strategy in return for reflation in the agricultural sector. While the Agrarians may have hoped to occupy a future pivotal position in the system, they were denied this by the continued electoral success of the Social Democrats to a position of almost uninterrupted hegemony. Nevertheless, they cooperated in two coalitions with the Social Democrats, helped sustain several Social Democrat governments, and remained the most "radical" of the non-socialist parties.[5]

However, the party always sought to establish itself as the fulcrum of the party system. It refused an invitation to enter a coalition with the Social Democrats in 1948 because the latter did not command an overall majority in the lower chamber. Towards the end of its second long spell as the junior partner in a Socialist government between 1951 and 1957, many of its supporters became restive over government policies, although an equally influential reason for the unhappiness may have been the continued decline in its electoral support. In 1957 the

Agrarians withdrew from the government over the Social Democrats' controversial pensions legislation. After 1960 the strength of the Social Democrats and all the other parties have been more evenly balanced. The more tenuous nature of government stability created a more delicate situation in which behind-the-scenes bargaining increased in importance. Hence, the Agrarians have been able to persist in asserting a centralist position. The change of name to that of Centre Party did not overly affect strategy. Its policies still indicated a preference for maintaining close links with all other parties in order to extract the maximum advantage from being the pivot of the party system. The attempt to spread its electoral appeal has not been at the expense of its traditional policy outlook: it claims to be the protector of small farmers, small businessmen and local interests against the impersonal threat of central bureaucracy. It is reasonable, then, to suggest that the behaviour of the Swedish Agrarians since 1932 has been flexible and essentially opportunistic. The major concern has been to wrest from governments the maximum advantage for farmers and to prevent governments from damaging agrarian interests. The Agrarians' behaviour has been essentially that of interest-group politics, as befits a party which is closely associated with farming organizations: one condition of its participation in government has always been that it should control the Ministry of Agriculture, while as early as 1940 the powerful farming associations and cooperatives linked to or directed by the party had been charged with administering some of the most important policies in the agricultural sector passed by Social Democrat governments.[6]

A similar pattern of strategic developments occurred in Norway. In the 1933 election the Labour Party increased its Storting representation to 69 of the 150 seats: the Labour electoral advance had been preceded by the internal defeat of the party's revolutionary element by moderates who reaffirmed their commitment to parliamentary democracy and announced their willingness to form a government. The economic consequences of the depression upon Norwegian agriculture and the refusal of the middle class parties to increase government aid to agriculture caused the Agrarians to revise their strategy and consider the possibility of entering a coalition government with the Labour Party. In 1935 they eventually agreed to support a Labour government in return for a guarantee of financial support for agriculture. More so than in Sweden the electoral expansion of the Labour Party prevented the Norwegian Agrarians from occupying a pivotal position in the party system. In addition, the party has been more conservative than its Swedish counterpart. After 1945 it has on the whole aligned itself with the bourgeois parties. However, its concern with the politics of agrarian defence means that it too has to a considerable extent pursued an essentially opportunistic strategy determined by its close ties with farmers' association. This is directly in the tradition of the antecedent Norsk Landmannsforbund of 1896. Moreover, as in Sweden, there was early established the principle of the performance of public tasks by private organizations: farming associations have administered a variety of government-initiated agricultural programmes.[7]

Circumstances in Denmark, Finland, Switzerland and Czechoslovakia have been rather different because of differing constellations of party strength and attitudes. The Danish Venstre has always been conservatively inclined, due primarily to its historical development and social base. While the era of direct competition with the old Right (Conservatives) lingered on into the 1920s, the Conservatives have nevertheless been the closest partners of the Venstre among the traditional parties. Since 1918 Danish politics has generally witnessed a quasi-duality with the Venstre associating with the Conservatives, while the fraction which seceded in 1905, the Radical Venstre, has usually consorted with the Social Democrats. The greater strength of the Venstre and the weaker position of the Social Democrats meant that there was no reassessment of coalition strategy in the 1930s as in Norway and Sweden. However, one major consequence of the depression of the 1930s was a pattern similar to that of its Scandinavian neighbours: farming organizations became involved in administering government policies relating to and affecting their sphere of interest. Despite its broad social base, the Venstre has continued to stress its agricultural interest: between 1953 and 1970, while in opposition, it nevertheless participated in 87 per cent of agricultural bill coalitions.[8]

The Agrarian Party of Finland stood in a more rural country: until the 1930s a majority of the population was dependent upon agriculture. The party also occupied the central position in a more complex party system. Its original attitude was somewhat radical because of a concern with nationalism and land reform: its sponsorship of land reform in 1922 was supported by the Social Democrats and opposed by the leading middle class party, the conservative National Coalition. In general, the constellation and range of party forces in Finland have entailed multiparty governments, in which the Agrarians have occupied the pivotal position. Hence, the party has cooperated with both Marxist and middle class parties, and Red-Green coalitions have not been exceptional. However, the scars left by the civil war and the proximity of the Soviet Union led the Agrarians to succumb somewhat to the nationalist fervour which pervaded interwar Finland. Reconciliation between Social Democrats and Agrarians, at least in the shape of formal governmental coalition, did not come about until after World War II. Even so, the strains upon a red-green alliance have continued to be intense, and the 1950s were dominated by the attempts to construct a stable Agrarian-Social Democrat coalition. Several governments collapsed between 1951 and 1957 because of incompatability between the Agrarian concern for rural interests, as for example demands for wage controls or for increased prices for farm produce, and the socialist and trade union insistence upon preventing rises in the cost of living. In short, the cooperation blossomed under good economic conditions and withered under adverse climates. The Finnish pattern also deviates slightly from that of its Nordic neighbours because of the existence of a large Communist party. This competitor for the left-wing vote has limited the strategic options and flexibility available to the Social Democrats. At the same time, the fact that a substantial Communist vote comes from the poorer rural areas of the north and east means that on occasions Agrarians and Communists have come together to pursue common agricultural interests. But overall the Agrarians have been the dominant government party, willing to look for allies from all quarters if this aids its own predilections with farming interests: between 1945 and 1969 it served in 20 of the 21 governments, supplying the premier on twelve occasions. The party's behaviour until the 1930s was sufficiently distinctive from that of several agrarian parties in the other successor states to be placed in a separate category, and increasingly it came to resemble its Scandinavian counterparts.[9]

Rather different forms of government structure emerged in Switzerland and Czechoslovakia. In both countries elite behaviour tended to fit into the category which Arend Lijphart has described as consociationalism.[10] Government was by coalition on the widest possible basis. Parties which represent or claim to represent significant social groups become more or less permanent members of the government, or at least they have to concur voluntarily with government proposals before the latter can be implemented: generally, these have been the largest parties in the system. The unique collegial system that is the Swiss government, which stipulates that there must be executive representation for major parties, the various linguistic communities, and the major cantons, is sufficiently well-known not to receive further elaboration here. The BGB was admitted to the government in 1929 by the Radicals and Catholic-Conservatives, only eight years after its secession from the former. Since then it has been a permanent member of the Federal Council, although it had to yield one of its two seats to the Social Democrats when they became the fourth government party in 1943. The BGB has been the largest party in the canton of Bern, a canton which because of its size has always had a strong claim to executive representation: in practice the Bern seat in the Federal Council has been occupied by the BGB. The party is in a sense the junior member of the government with only one seat compared to the two held by each of the other three parties. Nevertheless, its permanent presence has guaranteed it a certain influence upon federal policies. Its importance is further enhanced by its persistent presence on a similar basis in several cantonal governments.[11]

Allowing for the complex multiethnic pattern of Czech society and politics, the strategic possibilities of the Czech Republicans were similar to those in Finland. As in Finland the post-1918 land reform was sponsored by a Red-Green coalition.

With internal dissension among the Socialists and the emergence
of a strong Communist movement, the Republicans were forced to
turn elsewhere to secure a government majority. The party led
all governments after 1922, freely looking to the Socialists on
the left (but not the Communists) and to the Czech Populists
and middle class parties for possible partners. After the mid-
1920s the moderate German parties - Social Democrats, Christian
Socialists and <u>Bund der Landwirte</u>, the latter supporting Czech
Republican arguments for a protective tariff - were also regarded
as potential government material. The involvement of the
Republicans in industry and finance through its own banks meant
that the party was equally as interested in industrialization as
in agriculture and cooperatives. Indeed, the Republicans
developed a system of direct exchanges between agricultural
cooperatives and the Social Democrat-directed consumer
cooperatives in the towns.

Government membership was important, for the parties were
job-providers on a large scale, not only in the bureaucracy, but
also in industry, the banks, unions and associations which
mushroomed around each party. Governmental stability was high
despite the succession of seventeen cabinets between 1918 and
1938. No government was dissolved because of a vote of censure,
and government-sponsored bills were invariably accepted.
Government changes, in fact, were usually little more than a
reshuffling of personnel. Ministries tended to remain in the
hands of one party from government to government. Within the
bureaucracy, ministries tended to be staffed almost entirely by
officials belonging to one party: for example, most of the
higher officials in the Ministry of the Interior were members of
the Republican Party. Within this patronage system the
Republicans were predominant, for after 1920 they usually held
the premiership as well as the Ministries of the Interior,
Defence and Agriculture. A contemporary observer, commenting
upon the political acumen of the Republican leader, Antonín
Svehla, stated that he "regarded the spirit of opposition as
something in the nature of sin".[12] While membership of
government coalitions was politically significant for a party,
perhaps a more important qualification was for it to be accepted
as a member of the <u>Petka</u>: because of the existence of the <u>Petka</u>

cabinet membership was not necessarily seen by the established parties as a margin between electoral defeat or victory. The Petka originated as an informal consultative committee where the leaders of the five major Czech parties in 1919 - Social Democrats, National Socialists, Republicans, Populists, and National Democrats - met to resolve differences over policy, especially in foreign affairs. Over the years the Petka acquired permanency and a legitimacy at least equal to that of the cabinet. At the same time, its ranks were extended to include other Czech and minority parties which had agreed to accept and support the regime. Government participation was not a prerequisite for Petka participation.[13]

What this brief survey illustrates is that, within the context of the institutional structure of the country and the nature of the party system, agrarian parties in urbanizing and industrializing societies must decide upon which strategy to pursue, since their relative divorce from the economic issues arising out of industrial society gives them a certain degree of freedom in considering potential electoral and governmental partners. The fact that these agrarian parties at one time or another entered or were willing to enter coalitions with most kinds of other parties indicates an overall concern with agricultural economic problems. In other words, the agrarian parties consistently emphasized these interests over questions arising from other social cleavages with which the parties may have been linked, or involved. Perhaps the most outstanding example is the German Bund der Landwirte in Czechoslovakia, which abandoned all commitment to any kind of Deutschtum to seek accomodation within the Czech system in order to protect the interests of German farmers.[14]

The activity of these agrarian parties, irrespective of how long they remained in or how often they entered government coalition, has been essentially that of an interest group. This view is reinforced if we consider the timing when and the issues over which the agrarian parties switched from one set of coalition partners to another. In nearly every instance a change of partner was occasioned by a reconsideration of what benefits other parties were prepared to offer the farming community. Several other factors clearly contributed to this kind of

behaviour: the minority position of agriculture, a deep
involvement with capitalist agriculture, a multiparty system,
and the relatively non-ideological style of the party system.
These agrarian parties were never in a position to hope for a
majority in the legislature. To the extent that their desire to
influence policy outputs could best be achieved in government,
the parties were concerned with gaining power. However, it might
be more appropriate to conclude that, with the possible
exception of the Czech Republicans, solidly entrenched in the
country's economic and social institutions and appealing to a
wide social base, these agrarian parties were concerned less
with gaining power than with influencing policy outputs, no
matter which parties formed the government, for the benefit of
their constituents.

3. Peasantist Politics

Agrarian parties in the predominantly rural countries of Eastern
Europe were confronted with very different problems. Since most
of these states achieved national independence only in 1918 (or
at the very earliest two or three decades before), two general
phases of development can be detected. For the new states the
first phase involved political mobilization and the consolidation
of national independence and integration: for the parties it
entailed political mobilization and the consolidation of at
least a substantial part of their potential electorate. During
this first phase the issue of independence and related questions
such as land reforms ensured a relatively high degree of
political participation. Unfortunately, the concern for
independence and integration, and the interests of social groups
in more specific issues did not run in tandem. In most states
which have been instituted within the last one hundred years the
greater mobilization of individuals behind the banner of
independence brought about a plethora of demands upon the nascent
political systems which the latter were by and large incapable
of satisfying: moreover, support for independence did not
necessarily lead to a corresponding high level of support for
the new political systems and regimes.[15] These divergent
tendencies worked to prevent or decrease stability in the new

regimes. Moreover, political parties frequently had only the appearance of a modern organizational structure: underneath, most were merely personal coteries jostling for power. Stability could result only if one elite was securely in control of all or most positions of influence.

It is within the context of the institutional instability of these states that party strategies must be examined. Between 1919 and 1940 dictatorial or authoritarian regimes, reflecting the shadow of the recent past, were imposed sooner or later upon all the states of Eastern Europe. However, there were considerable variations in the kind of regime established. Most frequent was the seizure of power by the new monarchies with the aid of the army and bourgeois groups, as in Yugoslavia, Bulgaria and Rumania. Poland accepted a monarchial surrogate in the charismatic leadership of Pilsudski. In Latvia and Estonia it was the leading agrarian party - or rather some of their urban leaders - which seized control of the state. After the defeat of Bela Kun, the Horthy-Bethlen regime in Hungary rejected even the limited democratic ideas introduced in 1919 by the victorious Entente, and imposed a paternalistic authoritarian structure more reminiscent of the country's own past than of twentieth century Europe.[16] In most countries party activity and elections continued after the abrogation of unhindered political life: however, politics essentially involved a confrontation between two blocs of parties, one supporting and the other opposed to the new authoritarian structure. In most instances where electoral competition was permitted, the agrarian parties were lined up with the opposition forces. Because of the difficulties impeding party activity and the severely limited "market" situation for strategy formulation and coalition formation, the authoritarian period will not be considered here.

The activity of agrarian parties during the first phase of national independence focused primarily upon securing land reform. Generally this was only part of a wider notion that the political influence of non-peasant elements ought to be reduced significantly or eliminated altogether. Hence, the parties were hostile not just to the earlier landlords, who were usually of a different ethnic stock, but also to all urban groups. To a greater or lesser extent the parties adopted the ideology of peasantism which, in seeking to preserve what were perceived to be traditional virtues and ways of life, was essentially a conservative doctrine - although paradoxically also implicitly revolutionary. However, only the Bulgarian Agrarian Union persisted with a revolutionary course.

The general lack of institutionalization of party support was paralleled by the inchoate nature of party strategy. Previous inexperience, the absence of political education, and the inability to formulate coherent doctrines all limited the ability of the agrarian leadership to develop positive strategies. One contemporary observer noted that "peasant ideologies and peasant movements in countries of peasant farming show very little knowledge indeed of the real conditions of peasant property and of the peasants. These ideologies and movements are based on irrational elements - the past, religion, nationality - and take little into account of the economic facts of life".[17] The pursuance of an unambiguous policy emerged only when a party sought to assert unequivocal peasant dominance, as the Bulgarian Agrarian Union did before 1923, or where the party stood in uncompromising opposition to the regime, which was the case of the Croat Peasants. But even in such instances the party's commitment was fundamentally to some vague ideal, and its position on specific issues was often unclear. For example, one writer claims that Stjepan Radić, the leader of the Croat Peasants, possessed "an astonishing capacity for changing his mind, an inability to formulate clear demands or to stick to them, and a willingness to obstruct rather than construct".[18] Yet his sterile policy of non-cooperation was never seriously questioned inside Croatia because of its frustration in the new Yugoslavia. In a similar vein, the leader of the Polish <u>Wyzwolenie</u> bitterly commented in 1924 that "in Poland everyone wants to be in opposition: on no account will anyone accept responsibility".[19]

The second phase of development began after the redistribution of land and its consolidation, and when elections had demonstrated the popular strength and limitations of the various parties. In each instance, general elections showed that a populist ideology was not sufficient to garner votes for the agrarian parties: only the Bulgarian Agrarian Union was able to achieve a single-party government. Coalition governments were normally necessary. Because these agrarian parties had to formulate strategies and policies with regard to potential coalition allies, it ought to be possible to examine them in the same way as those in more industrialized countries.

In fact, such a procedure is relatively difficult because of the more unstructured, non-institutionalized nature of the political system. Governments tended to be highly fragile creations, not least because the support of several parties was often required for a government to be assured of a nominal parliamentary majority. The major exception was Rumania which, until the assumption of direct control by King Carol in 1938, had a tradition of single-party governments. Until 1938 the party which was the government at the time of the election (not necessarily the one which had won the previous election) was able, through the electoral system, corruption and administrative pressures, to achieve a numerically unassailable parliamentary majority.[20] The National Peasants formed the government only once, between 1928 and 1930. Invited by the king to form a government in 1928 they followed precedent by calling a general election in order to gain a hegemonic parliamentary position. However, once in power, their policies proved to be little different from those of all other governments: the real power continued to remain with the National Liberals who controlled the country's financial system, and with the army, essentially a tool of the monarchy. Although the National Peasant government repudiated the liberal stress on economic self-sufficiency and asserted the primary of agriculture, its efforts were negated by world depression and its own uninspired policies. By the end of the 1920s the party had moved far away from the doctrines of peasantism.[21]

The linguistic and regional cleavages of Yugoslavia were equally dominant an influence upon governments. All governments were Serbian-oriented, and all tended to be directed by the Serbian Radicals: despite this orientation, however, the small Serbian Agrarian Party never participated in government. The Croat Peasants were normally in opposition, a stance which most suited their political style. They did enter a government with the Serbian Radicals on three occasions in 1925 and 1926, but their tenure of office was exceptionally brief on each occasion, respectively 16 months, 8 months and one month. Despite pressing agricultural problems, the increasingly urban and intellectual leadership of the party seemed to ignore everything in their quest for independence or autonomy.[22]

Between January 1919 and Pilsudski's coup d'état in May 1926, Poland endured no less than 19 governments. The *Piast* agrarian party participated in 15 of these. While this makes it appear as an "Establishment" party, its governmental presence in the first instance has a simpler explanation. The great number of parties, the small size of all, and the not inconsiderable parliamentary strength of the ethnic minorities meant that many parties had to be drawn into the governmental orbit if a majority was to be assured. Nevertheless, the *Piast* leadership was essentially non-doctrinaire, and clearly not averse to this situation. *Piast* "preferred to gratify the expectations of its constituency through such devices as patronage, public works, and other state favors. This required it to strive to be always a government party".[23] While the party normally participated in centrist-right governments, it did not refuse to consider cooperation with the Socialists on three occasions. Yet the party's constituency was less the Polish and more the Galician cultivator. While the party's major concern meant that it failed to become strongly identified with either nationalism or the Catholic Church, the concern with agrarian defence was frequently relegated below the major fears of Polish politics: the proximity of Germany and Russia, and the large ethnic minorities. It opposed more land reform because this would benefit the Byelorussian and Ukrainian minorities in the east. *Piast* joined the conservative and nationalist parties in demanding that all governments should have a Polish majority in the *Sejm*. The move of *Piast* to the right led to a fresh splintering of the party. The more radical *Wyzwolenie* agrarian faction participated in nine governments: strangely, it shared government office with the Socialists only once. Indeed, in mid-1925 *Wyzwolenie* decided to go into opposition when the Socialists entered a centrist coalition. Moreover, different regional bases of strength, different policies, and personal antagonisms all made it extremely difficult for the agrarian parties to cooperate with each other. From his Czech exile in 1938, the <u>Piast</u> leader, Witos, wrote bitterly of Wyzwolenie, that it "comprised the rural branch of socialism, sometimes competing with then in demagogy. Dominated by semiintellectuals and socialist shool-teachers, directed, moreover, by an unseen hand (Pilsudski), it pursued a policy remote from the interests and desires of the peasantry while appearing to have great concern for them".[24]

A somewhat similar pattern emerged in the Baltic states. The various agrarian parties in both Latvia and Estonia participated in most of the coalition governments during the period of competitive party politics.[25] In Estonia the Agrarians participated in 17 of the 20 coalitions between 1919 and 1934: they held the premiership in ten governments. Similarly, the Latvian Peasant Union served in all but two of the 18 coalition governments between 1919 and 1934, leading 13 of them. In both instances the parties pursued conservative policies and preferred to accept conservative and middle class coalition partners. In Estonia the urban-oriented middle class parties entered 16 cabinets: the Socialists participated in only six governments, acquiring the premiership once. Despite the fact that the "left" bloc was numerically stronger than the "agrarian" bloc in the Latvian <u>Saeima</u>, the Social Democrats entered only three governments: two centre-left and one agrarian-centre-left. Most governments were therefore coalitions of conservative agrarian and middle class parties. The smaller agrarian parties - the New Settlers in Estonia and the New Farmers in Latvia - participated much less in government. Both were more willing to seek alliances with more "left" parties, although the former resolved the dilemma by merging (albeit briefly) with the Agrarian League. Typically, the small Latgalian agrarian parties participated in most governments. Agrarian dictatorship brought both regimes to an end in 1934.[26]

The greater conservative orientation of the leading Baltic agrarian parties may perhaps be partly explained in terms of the proximity of the Soviet Union and its claims upon the ex-Tsarist provinces. Estonia experienced a dangerous, but abortive Communist insurrection in 1924. In addition, the Socialist parties here were more articulate and stronger than in South-East

Europe. The Polish Socialist Party was one of the most prominent in Eastern Europe, while Riga, the Latvian capital, had been before 1924 one of the most industrialized cities in the Russian Empire and remained the home of a vigorous Social Democrat movement. It is perhaps no accident that in these regions where the Marxist presence was felt more strongly, the agrarian parties adopted a more consistent and more conservative attitude and political strategy.

Conservatism also arose from the traditionalism inherent in peasantist thought and from the acquisition of an urban leadership. Peasantist ideologies hankered for some kind of golden age in either the past or the future, in which mysticism took precedence over economic reality: "disliking the present and the immediate future, it seeks to mould the further future in accordance with its visions of the past".[24] All those agrarian parties which acclaimed the virtues of peasantism were fundamentally conservative in their orientation. This basic sentiment helped to structure what strategy and policies they possessed. Despite the less institutionalized nature of politics, these parties paradoxically were seemingly more consistent in their behaviour than the interest-oriented agrarian parties in Western Europe. Regime instability, little institutionalization in the political system, the individualistic and generational nature of party leadership all constituted parameters determining party behaviour. One further distinction was the acquisition by the eastern parties of an urban leadership. This further distracted them from agricultural problems: more and more, the parties were manipulated by and became the agents of leaderships which frequently appeared to use them to further different economic interests and their own political careers. If any priority was given to the economic betterment of the peasantry and improvements of agricultural production, it was very low indeed.

4. Political and Economic Bases of Party Behaviour

Two prime determinants of agrarian politics are first the nature of the urban-rural relationship, and second the degree of involvement in the market economy. Despite the originally sharp urban-rural cleavage which helped to generate distinctive agrarian political movements in Western Europe, the agrarian parties here quickly came to terms with urban society and their own limited strength in the political system. In short, they attempted to utilize to their own advantage the political divisions which emerged from urban society. The particular strategies and behaviour varied from country to country, being dependent, as for example in the contrast between Scandinavia and Czechoslovakia, upon the particular political circumstances and constellations in individual countries. In essence, however, the basic problems were perceived to be the same: how to capitalize upon urban differences to gain benefits for the agricultural population. Nothing was to be gained, and everything to be lost, in a straightforward urban-rural confrontation. This strategy contrasts directly with the situation in Eastern Europe where the urban-rural dimension of politics remained overwhelmingly important. Whereas the pre-1914 populist movements had been reluctant to identify with specific class interests, many of the new agrarian parties made the representation and social elevation of the peasant class their sole ideological raison d'être. The urban leadership of these agrarian parties did nothing to diminish the salience of this political dimension, while simultaneously weakening both the likelihood of a specific urban-rural confrontation and the chances of an agrarian victory.

Marked differences also emerge when we examine attitudes towards the market economy. The penetration of the money economy into rural areas produced a sudden and violent agrarian response throughout Europe. Again, however, the cultivators in Western Europe more readily came to terms with commercial farming, accepting that the benefits might well outweigh the costs. The western agrarian parties were concerned with defending the commercial interests of the farmer from the worst dangers of a capitalist market. Various economic strategies and policies existed, advocated by various parties. But the basic choice of the agrarian parties was seen as supporting those parties whose economic policies were beneficial to, or, at the worst, least detrimental to the farmer. The ability of the agrarian parties to assess economic consequences and to act as effective interest groups within the legislature was aided by their close ties with efficient and well-organized farming associations. By contrast, the fundamental attitude of the "peasantist" parties was almost total opposition to or at the least indifference to the market economy. They failed to realize that it would not disappear if ignored, and that inaction simply worsened the lot of the peasantry. Alternatively, the middle class leadership may have acknowledged the existence of the market, but were disinterested in its effects upon the peasants. Party options were further foreclosed by these countries' weak standing in the world economy and their chronic political instability.

Where cultivators did not organize their own party, several alternative options were available. First, they could advance their interests through their own organizational structures of unions and cooperatives. Most Western countries developed strong and effective farming organizations which worked, for example, for the injection of capital into rural areas and price supports for farmers. In the case of Scandinavia this did not preclude the existence of associated agrarian parties. Alternatively, the farmers could choose to operate as a faction with a larger political party, as has often been the case in France and is the situation of the small western farmers of Ireland within Fianna Fail. The peasantry of Eastern Europe rarely reached the same degree of effectiveness even when these options were utilized.

The distinction drawn earlier between land reform and agricultural reform also seems to apply to the agrarian parties. In the last resort, both types of party - interest group and peasantist - were interested in and concerned with the politics of agrarian defence. However, interest group politics meant that the parties were concerned with the economic position of the farmer. They wanted to secure higher farm incomes and economic betterment. By contrast, peasantist notions meant that the parties were concerned more with the social and political position of the cultivator. What they were defending was the idea of property, of a society of small owner-occupied farms populated by people possessing some vaguely conceived moral virtues. Their general failure when in government to introduce or press for measures to alleviate the economic burden of the peasantry indicates the relatively low priority placed upon or their inability to appreciate the economics of farming within an international capitalist order.

CONCLUSION   Agrarian Political Movements

Agrarian politics can be appreciated only within the context of
the political and economic structure of the whole society.
Agrarian political involvement in Europe has sprung either from
the nature of agrarian structure or the impact of the money
economy upon agriculture. In each instance political activity
has been a reaction against what the agricultural population has
regarded as injustices in the society, most specifically against
economic hardships or the low political and social status of the
farming population. We have attempted to review the various
social, political and economic stimuli of agrarian movements:
for example, attempts to increase the work load of the labour
force without a corresponding remunerative increase, a turnover
of landlords, changes in the marketing system for agricultural
produce or for those urban products required by the farming
population. Any one has been likely to increase the political
activity of cultivators. Hence, agrarian political behaviour
cannot be understood without reference to the total political
and economic configuration of the society.
   Moreover, an appreciation of agrarian politics can be
achieved only if political, economic and social structures are
analyzed diachronically. Clearly, no society is entirely static,
and change of some kind has invariably been the catalyst of
agrarian political activity. Change has been of two kinds: a
transformation of the situation of those engaged in agricultural
production, and developments outside the primary economy which
have had major consequences for agriculture. Historically, for
instance, agrarian upsurges have occurred when new elites or

groups have appeared to challenge the pre-eminence of traditional, established elites. Again, they may be a consequence of objective political events such as war, or because of a transformation in the structure and importance of agriculture. Technological developments, new styles in crop production, and the growth of international trade may have consequences for the agricultural population not only directly, but also indirectly through their effect upon both urban and rural masses. These patterns can be seen quite clearly in pre-industrial Europe, as for example in England in 1381 or Germany in 1525. Alternatively, agrarian political interest may be stimulated by increased economic aspirations and a sense of deprivation relative to urban prosperity, a motivation which grew in importance after the Industrial Revolution.

In the complex social structure of a modernized society, it has become more difficult for farmers to equate their security and prosperity with changes in the objective conditions and status of any other single social group. How far the contagion of new radical philosophies and ideas emerging from the cities affects the countryside depends upon the structure of land tenure. The linkage of egalitarian radicalism with rising expectations became politically significant only where the majority of the agrarian population did not possess land. This helps to explain why, for example, narodnik sentiments were more attractive to Eastern European peasants in the late nineteenth century, while failing to secure any firm foothold in Western Europe. Similarly, it goes some way towards explaining why politics in the latifundia areas of Italy and Iberia have been so distinctive.

1. The Aims of Agrarian Politics

The aims of agrarian movements can be compared in terms of their structure and contents. Fundamentally, the content of agrarian demands hinges upon economic defence. For the domestic-oriented cultivator, this involves defence of his land and labour commitments: for the capitalist farmer, it involves protection of his financial and economic position in the market economy. The content of agrarian demands has been a major theme in this analysis and need not be elaborated further here.

The structuring of these goals may vary considerably. In the first instance, agrarian aims may be viewed in terms of their intensity and extensiveness. For example, a single limited demand such as a reduction in rent cannot be considered to be extensive. The more demands accumulate - for example, easier credit facilities or protective tariffs - the more extensive agrarian demands become. The intensity of agrarian demands may be assessed in terms of the consequence that their achievement has upon the society. The greater the number of institutional and structural changes wrought by the attainment of agrarian goals, the more revolutionary these goals are. This is an extremely complex question. For example, the yearning for owner-occupancy may be revolutionary in its effects upon the structure of landownership and, indirectly, upon the distribution of political influence among various social groups. Yet, depending on the value system and orientation of the agrarian population, it can simultaneously be a highly conservative and stabilizing force. The granting of the suffrage is usually regarded as a revolutionary step forward in the process of political mobilization and modernization. But if the cultivators vote according to the directives of the landlords, as in Hungary, or of government officials, as in Rumania, it can hardly be termed a revolutionary advance.

In general, it would seem that the aims of European agrarian political movements became both more extensive and more intensive with the increase in the number of non-agrarian groups involved. Alternatively, their breadth and intensity became greater with an increase in the number of essentially non-economic institutions that became interlocked with the economic sector. The most diffuse and intense agrarian responses appeared in traditional, highly stratified societies where institutions such as churches and governments were also land-owners, and where landowners also performed non-economic functions such as political and judicial decision-making. Again, therefore, the structuring of agrarian demands cannot be entirely divorced from the surrounding institutional milieu. The latter has simply been concealed by the apparently "spontaneous" nature of many agrarian upsurges. This diffuse kind of movement typically appeared within more traditional, pre-industrial societies with congruent vertical status differences, and where the differences between the various strata were ultimately based upon the relationship of each to the structure of landownership. The central concerns of agrarian movements in such situations were not only economic in nature. They were drawn equally from the political aspects of the actual and the desired structure of landownership: the expropriation, confiscation, redistribution or renting of land. In many ways, these considerations provided the driving motive of nearly all peasant movements in Europe from the English rebellion of 1381 through to those in Russia throughout the nineteenth century. The land reforms of the early twentieth century were in a sense the final expression of this genre of movement in so far as they were imbued, no matter how faintly, with the spirit of populism.

By contrast, in industrialized countries with highly complex societies, the relationship between cause and affect, between complaint and remedy, becomes, paradoxically, both more difficult to detect and more precise. When a society's institutions became more complex, specialized and differentiated, the aims of the agrarian movement tended to become more narrow and specific. The effect of agrarian organizations such as cooperatives, and of involvement in commercialized agriculture was to switch attention and concern away from the political question of the structure of landownership toward the economic problems of farming. Where capitalist farming developed within a "modernized" society, agricultural demands contracted to become more limited in scope and more specialized. Subsidies, price support schemes, protective tariffs, financial compensation, and aid from government for technical and mechanical improvements, became the package of goods that cultivators desired.

Admittedly, in most instances where farming organizations consolidated their position, the question of landownership had already been settled. While it may be true that agrarian attention cannot be focused upon the economics of capitalist farming until the issue of landownership has been resolved, the one does not automatically follow from the other. The experience of Eastern Europe after 1918 suggests that a satisfactory resolution of the landownership question is by itself not sufficient to induce a concern for economic improvements and agricultural efficiency. Nor does the European experience suggest that there is any causal relationship between land reform and political stability. After testing the hypothesis that chronic political instability is the result of the concentration of landownership on a global scale, Bruce Russett concludes that "There are many instances where relative equality of land is not associated with stable democracy; it is no <u>guarantee</u> of democratic developments. Land reform may provide the soil to nourish free institutions, but the seed must first be planted".[1] A few centuries ago, it was possible, under certain conditions, for a peasant uprising in a small region to spread like an epidemic across the countryside to challenge governments and the fabric of societies. Today, direct action by farmers may be politically embarrassing, but rarely does it have political ramifications beyond the immediate locality. In any case, such behaviour is a secondary form of activity. No matter how substantial the agrarian economic demand, both institutionalized and anomic agrarian activity are unlikely to have such serious consequences as previously upon other sectors of society. Of course, this is not to say that this kind of agrarian protest can be ignored. But the "spillover" effect is hindered by the complexity and specialization of a modernized society. Pattern maintenance institutions such as the churches have few direct links with the economy. The political institutions of the state are, if not less directly involved in the economy, at least involved in a different way from the past. At the same time, both the political centre and the cities have at their disposal greater resources with which they can blunt or suppress the agrarian challenge.

Agrarian movements also vary in the degree of precision with which they express their goals. The degree of clarity of purpose may be placed along a continuous ranging from no aims whatsoever to a list of highly precise, well-formulated goals. Cathartic movements with no goals other than the act of destruction were most likely to occur in highly traditional societies where the absence of institutionalization, organization, education and communication prevented the peasant from perceiving any other solution or alternative channels of action. The _jacquerie_ constituted a typical form of agrarian protest from the disintegration of feudal structures through to the consolidation of industrialization. Moreover, the cultivator frequently saw that the hierarchical structure of society rested upon the control of force: the subjection of the peasant to violence led him in turn to espouse violent action. However, without a knowledge of the interrelationships of society, the cultivator was frequently unable to see how he could achieve his ends beyond the simple destruction of the symbols of his oppression. Hence, the formulation of precise goals is related to the general educational and organizational levels of the cultivators and their spokesmen. Only then can they perceive societal relationships and the alternative channels of action that are available. In turn, institutionalization serves as a mould for agrarian activity. Institutionalization in effect becomes a reference point by which agrarian groups can relate their problems and goals to institutions, and assess the likelihood of success. By making farmers aware of their vulnerability, the market economy forced them to form organizations and to formulate precise goals.

The aims of agrarian movements may also vary both over time and because of internal differentiation. Since the relationship to the land has been an important influence upon agrarian politics, the distinction between domestic-consumptive and farmer-capitalist enterprises is valuable in drawing attention to the differing emphasis upon the political and economic aspects of farming. In Europe the changing patterns combined with capitalist involvement to shape the aims of agrarian movements. Large capitalist farmers, smaller owner-occupiers, tenant farmers, and agricultural labourers displayed different attitudes towards the question of landownership and on the economics of farming: the numeral mix of these various groups in any one movement, especially in terms of office-holding, determined to a considerable extent which goals it opted to pursue. Likewise, variations in crop production produced different economic problems and different perceived solutions.

Variations can also occur within the hierarchy of an agrarian movement. Rank and file members tend to see an organization as a means of attaining solutions to their own problems. By contrast, the leadership may be more concerned with ensuring the maintenance of the organization and their own position within it.[2] This organizational predicament appeared in many of the interwar agrarian parties in Eastern Europe: their leadership was often relatively uninterested in peasant problems, seemingly utilizing the organization primarily to advance their own policies and often also their own social and political careers.

Agrarian goals may also change over time. The analysis of European developments suggests that two main changes have occurred. In general, agrarian demands became more specific over time with the increasing commercialization of agriculture and the greater political institutionalization of society. The narrowing of goals again reflected a switch of emphasis from political and social to economic problems. However, where the original demands were rejected or frustrated, agrarian politics became radicalized, with a concomitant increase in the breadth of the goals sought. Moreover, the degree of radicalism inherent in agrarian aims reflected the general social atmosphere. Agrarian goals were radical not only within rigid societies which turned a deaf ear to agrarian requests, but also where other social groups had been radicalized. Thus, for example, agrarian discontent increased in intensity and became more radical in the nineteenth century with the growth of an industrial working class, and as nationalist elements in the urban middle classes sought to secure rural political support for their dreams of independence.

2. The Ideology of Agrarian Politics

An ideology may be defined as a pattern of beliefs and values about society, embracing perceptions of what society used to be like and the direction in which it is moving: most important is the evaluation of these states of the past, present and future, and of the role of different social institutions.[3] While hypotheses relating behaviour to ideology may be useful in analysing the actions of political elites, they are not particularly valuable in analyses of mass politics for, as Converse has demonstrated empirically, most people do not think of politics in anything approaching explicit ideological terms.[4]

At the very most, they hold implicit and diffuse assumptions which they find difficult to verbalize precisely.

It would be surprising therefore to find mass movements that possessed an explicit ideology. We have already discussed the ideological trappings of agrarian politics in some detail, and have demonstrated that by and large the ideological connotations of agrarian movements have been diffuse. Ideologies, along with goals, may be placed on continua of degree of clarity, intensity and extensiveness. To a considerable extent the ideology possessed by an agrarian movement derived from its leadership. Frequently, the most ideologically motivated leaders did not belong to the agrarian population. This was particularly true of more radical ideologies that were less rooted in the cultural experience and mores of the extant society. Peasantism as an ideology was elaborated not by peasants, but by the urban intelligentsia. Indeed, cultivators have been less likely than most social groups to think in ideological terms and to act on the basis of ideological motivations and assumptions. On the whole, agrarian ideologies, while organic, have been imprecise, shallow and parochial, if not unsystematic and contradictory. Moreover, they have been essentially negative. While peasantism, like other populist ideologies, ostensibly worshipped the common people, its basic characteristic was that it was against something. All forces and groups outside the familiar world of the local communities were unknown and feared. Agrarian ideologies have been essentially anti-urban, anti-capitalist and anti-labour, a negative posture that was strengthened by xenophobic and sometimes antisemitic attitudes. Perhaps peasantism would be better described as a mentality rather than as an ideology.

One can detect a sequential movement in European agrarian history from little or no ideological awareness, through the attempt to formulate a peasantist ideology, to the relegation of ideological shibboleths below the formulation of more precise and pragmatic economic demands. Before extensive industrialization most agrarian movements reflected only local conditions: the general level of education did not permit an awareness of society as a whole. The only movements in this phase which possessed distinctive ideological overtones were the numerous chiliastic upsurges – but religion rather than agricultural life provided the ideological stimulus. An agrarian ideology as such appeared only in the nineteenth century, in part as a response to the challenges of capitalism, industrialization and nationalism. Even so, peasantist and <u>narodnik</u> sentiments excited more comment among the intelligentsia of Eastern Europe than among the peasantry: in using the terms "populist" and "peasantist" we must be wary of overestimating both the strength of the mass articulation of their tenets, and the extent of mass involvement in such movements.

Peasantism saw the problems and situation of individual and society as being intimately related, but it never developed strong roots in the agrarian parties, either among voters or leaders: it remained little more than a collection of vague notions to which people paid lip-service. By contrast, in countries which became industrialized societies, the commercialization and numerical decline of agriculture did not spawn an ideologically motivated politics of agrarian defence. Once the question of land tenure had been settled, there developed a pragmatic style of politics which fundamentally treated each issue on its own merits.

3. The Methods of Agrarian Politics

Methods refer to the means by which agrarian movements seek to achieve their goals. These too may be assessed in terms of clarity, extensiveness, and intensity. Again, the means employed reflected the general structure of the society. Under highly repressive regimes in which violence was a key method of control by the elites, agrarian political activity also tended to be violent. The degree of coherence varied with the educational and cultural level of the society, but overall insurrection and revolution rather than legitimate channels of action were perceived as the only possible paths. Similarly, institutionalization becomes an intervening variable. Political institutionalization was more successful in stable societies with a high level of education and legitimacy. Thus, before the wholehearted entry of the cultivator into the national political system and the capitalist market, the lack of institutionalization and the low level of education inhibited the development of legitimate, standardized practices.

However, the post-1918 experiences of Europe demonstrate that political involvement defined, for example, in terms of the right to vote did not automatically generate support for the regime or for legitimate actions or protests. As Huntington has argued, "Modernization in practice always involves change in and usually the disintegration of a traditional political system, but it does not necessarily involve significant movement toward a modern political system".[5] In those societies of Eastern Europe where political institutionalization remained weak, violent and anomic forms of activity persisted as a latent threat to the regime. By contrast, legitimate and formalized means became accepted by farmers in those European countries which enjoyed high educational levels and where a significant degree of political institutionalization had materialized.

Finally, we may note that the methods employed by agrarian movements may be influenced by their goals and ideologies. Furthermore, all tend to be affected by the level of organization. In movements which in essence sought nothing more than some kind of cathartic absolution, the resort to violence and insurrection were stronger historically among followers than among leaders. The more goal-oriented the movement, the more likely it was to enjoy a high level of organization, hence, the more likely that leaders were able to restrain their followers, or channel their actions along acceptable paths. However, irrespective of the kind of mass support, a leadership, being more politically motivated, may nevertheless be willing to utilize violence as a secondary but important element of strategy, either to sustain their own position, to maintain a united movement, or to seek concessions from the government and society.

4. The Support of Agrarian Movements

No agrarian movement has enjoyed the support of the whole farming population. Nor have the participants in such movements done so with equal intensity. Agrarian uprisings in Europe were often confined to limited geographical areas, even within the same state. Even where a peasant revolt spread from area to area, it had often passed its zenith or had died in some regions before the flames were fanned in others. Similarly, the discussion of agrarian political parties and voting behaviour emphasized wide variations in partisan support, and in the level of support for agrarian parties, both between regions and between various agricultural groups.

These distinctions are significant in that they determined not only the likelihood of success, but also the quality of political activity. In other words, the kind of mass base that a movement possessed determined to a considerable extent its goals, ideology, and methods. The various points can be discussed under four broad heading: psychological traits and values, economic conditions, demographic and community factors, and indicators of modernization.

The most important psychological trait is the individual's attitude towards the land. The domestic orientation of the landed peasant enables (or forces) him to endure situations which both commercial farmers and landless peasants might well find intolerable. The latter groups may, for different reasons, react more readily to a wider variety of political and economic stimuli. While levels of education, community awareness, and organization can offset the barriers hindering political mobilization implicit in a structure of domestic consumptive enterprises, they can be further negated by the subordinate position of most peasants in the local and national status hierarchy. In particular, poor peasants and landless labourers have few resources of their own to take political initiatives. Their mobilization, especially into revolutionary movements, becomes more likely only when they can depend upon support from other social groups.[6] By contrast, the wealthier peasant may be more easily politically activated, but of course is more unlikely to endorse revolutionary movements. Those who may more easily be mobilized under revolutionary banners constitute the middle range: their land commitment is reasonably secure, they can generate some economic surplus, and they are less subject to intense landlord control. These are major themes in the literature of political anthropology: yet, while the relationship to the land may have been of considerable importance in traditional societies, one tentative conclusion of this study is that few meaningful differences appeared to exist in Europe after the granting of universal male suffrage.

The structure of landownership affected participation rates and partisanship. In general, it was the wealthier elements within the farming community which were more susceptible to organization. Both in the numerous agrarian revolts throughout European history and in the several agrarian parties that emerged after suffrage extension, that part of the leadership drawn from agricultural circles was usually recruited from better-off, more secure cultivators. The corollary is that poorer cultivators and labourers furnished proportionally less of the mass basis of these movements, and were always under-represented among the leaders and activists. Evidence from countries as disparate in their development as Norway and Italy suggests that low status groups were frequently ignored by the high status group: Indeed, the latter were often hostile to the former, who then were more openly available for mobilization by a different political party or group. Overall, different styles of politics and varying rates of participation were manifested by domestic-oriented peasants and capitalist farmers, by wealthy and poor farmers, large and small farmers, and by owner-occupiers, tenant farmers and agricultural labourers.

From a political perspective agrarian movements are interest groups, whether they are anomic uprisings or well-established parties and cooperatives. From an administrative and sociological perspective, however, they are organizations. To a greater or lesser extent they possess institutions of planning and coordination of activities, and organs for internal channels of communication. The degree of organizational cohesion affects political participation. As Slicher van Bath has argued, the ability of farmers or peasants to adhere together in concerted action depends to a considerable extent upon whether they have developed a marked sense of community awareness and of the value of cooperation.[7] The general life of a community may have provided it with past cooperative experiences that could serve as a basis for united political action and a sense of community responsibility. More vital and successful peasant movements in Europe appeared in those areas where daily life and work had already provided a setting for cooperative endeavour. Similarly, under universal suffrage the most successful agrarian political movements were those which had behind them a solid level of effective organization in the form of cooperatives and farmers' associations.

Several other observations may be made in this context. First, it is clear that the traditional value system and culture of rural communities frequently constituted a constraint upon agrarian movements. Other constraints often appeared because of the particular relationship of the rural community to its own elites - landlords, priests, teachers. For example, one simple but important consideration was whether a landlord lived among his tenants and workers. Relationships with other social groups became significant because the latter could support or oppose agrarian action. One final constraint was the demographic structure of the agrarian population. The level of agricultural expertise and mechanization, and the kind of agricultural techniques employed both exerted an indirect constraint in that they could influence the degree of concentration or dispersal of the population. The spatial dispersion of the rural population has been a major barrier thwarting effective communication and organization, and so has been a major determinant of the mass basis of agrarian movements.

Finally, we can consider those factors which may be called indicators of political modernization: these raise the question of whether the "peasantry" can be a force for modernization, or whether on the contrary they are a force resisting modernization.[8] Here we simply wish to stress their role in making the cultivator aware of the society outside his own parochial limits. The most significant critical juncture was the penetration of the rural community by the national economic and political systems. In all its facets penetration remoulded the agrarian environment and individual personalities, and introduced new skills and indeed an awareness of relative deprivation. "Active" participation in agrarian capitalism increased the likelihood of political participation on a persisting and regularized basis. The factors that transformed agrarian environments and values have been discussed in some detail. Here we may simply reiterate that those individuals who were more prominent in agrarian uprisings, or as supporters and leaders of agrarian parties were those whose traditional values had, as it were, undergone a metamorphosis because of direct exposure to the national society, political regime, and economy. Overall, education was important in the processes of national integration and political socialization. In certain instances, the compulsory movement of peasants away from the land through military conscription may, as for example in France, provide the rural masses with wider perspectives. Furthermore, the historical evidence and the analysis of agrarian parties suggest that a solid framework of social organization, which provide a basis for political action, becomes more likely with a full commitment to capitalist farming and where the urban-rural gap was bridged by the proximity of towns and/or effective communication and transportation networks.

5. Agrarian Organizations

So far we have tended to avoid the term "organization", preferring to describe agrarian activity as "movement". As pointed out earlier, certain institutionalized manifestations such as planning, coordination and channels of internal communication are necessary for an organization to exist. It is clear that many agrarian movements were not organizations in any sense of the word: rather, they were expressive anomic uprisings which looked for and achieved little more than some cathartic purging. Similarly, it is dubious whether some of the European parties could be called organizations.

Agrarian movements can again be placed upon a continuum from those which possess no organization, being nothing more than an aggregation of isolated individual actions, to those which possess a complex organization with a clearly defined internal hierarchy and explicit internal functional differentiation. The degree to which an agrarian movement possesses an organizational structure is determined by the factors discussed earlier. An agrarian movement which pursues extensive goals within a broad ideological framework would ideally require a strong organization to propagate its intentions. Similarly, a movement which seeks to achieve its goals by violent or revolutionary means should ideally possess a tightly disciplined paramilitary organization enjoying well-structured channels of communication for the rapid transmission of information and commands.

The analysis suggests that the quality and level of organization in Europe was deeply influenced by the existing pattern of social, economic and community relationships. The nature of agricultural economic activity and geographical isolation were major barriers hindering both the spatial extension and temporal durability of agrarian organizations. Similarly, the psychological traits of the peasantry constituted obstacles to the structuring of a regularized administrative and communications system.[9] The development of agrarian organizations came only with the mass entry into national politics and the market economy. If political mobilization led to a lowering of the suffrage threshold or if it followed upon suffrage extension, the chances of establishing a mass-based agrarian organization were increased. As distinct from earlier uprisings, political activity meant minimally only joining a party and voting, actions which did not entail disrupting the cycle of cultivation. Similarly, entry into the wider capitalist market obliged a cultivator to defend his economic position against the economic demands of other social groups. In organizational terms the most successful agrarian parties in Europe, such as those in Scandinavia and Czechoslovakia, were those which were related to or appeared where there was already in existence a well-structured network of efficient and effective economic cooperatives.

Finally, the quality of organizational structures depends upon the quality, effectiveness, and internal cohesiveness of their leadership.[10] In less modernized societies with poor national integration and weak or localized market economies, the leadership was less able to build and direct an effective agrarian organization. In most cases, the leadership that existed was recruited from external sources: the urban middle class, especially the intelligentsia, or the local bourgeoisie and artisans. This was true of most agrarian uprisings before industrialization, and of the interwar peasant parties of Eastern Europe. The critical variables of social and political development that permit the leadership to be drawn from the agricultural community seem to include capitalist farming, a highly developed social system of communication, a limited agricultural work force (which implies a more industrialized society), a social structure free from intense cleavages along non-agrarian dimensions, and a high level of education among the agrarian community.

At this point we may add that similar organizational problems beset the attempts to establish after 1918 an International of agrarian parties. The most vocal advocate of a European Peasant Union was Stamboliski. The Bulgarian Agrarian Union was prominent in setting up the Agrarian (Green) International in 1927, supported by the Czech, Serbian and Polish parties. By 1929 it had 17 national or regional parties as members, and for a while its expansion worried the Comintern. The International very quickly was taken over by the Czech Republicans who tended to give it a Slavic flavour: for this reason Western parties, and even more so non-Slavic parties from Eastern Europe such as the Rumanian National Peasants, were suspicious of it. In any event the elaborate edifice of offices, congresses and bulletins was built upon extremely precarious foundations: the Green International slowly but relentlessly became moribund during the economic crisis of the early 1930s.[11]

6. Agrarian Movements and other Social Groups

We have argued that agrarian problems cannot be understood in isolation. Similarly, agrarian movements cannot be appreciated without reference to other social groups. The resources which other groups offer, either in support of or in opposition to agrarian movements, significantly affect the probability of the latter successfully achieving their goals. Several social groups have been allies or opponents of agrarian movements. While external support will not guarantee agrarian success, it may greatly increase the prospects of victory. In a straightforward agrarian-urban confrontation, the agrarian community invariably emerged as the loser. This pattern is even true where the cities were numerically weak. The greater organizational ability of the latter and their control of greater economic and technological resources almost invariably gave them a superior strength.[12]

Opponents were obviously those groups which stood to lose power, status or income if the agrarian movement achieved its goals: the most common enemy historically was the landlord class, but under certain circumstances churches, politicians and bureaucrats also moved into opposition. The discussion has demonstrated that European agrarian movements could expect only three kinds of major allies, each of which was prepared to cooperate under certain circumstances and at specific points in time: an expanding, upwardly mobile and ambitious urban bourgeoisie seeking to challenge the supremacy of traditional landholding, aristocratic and bureaucratic elites; churches that sought to defend traditional moral and ethical values against the challenge of secularization which invariably expanded outwards from the cities; and nationalist-oriented groups, usually from the urban middle class, which looked for support for their quest to win independence or autonomy for a region. However, all of these groups were basically disinterested either in the economics of farming and/or the agrarian concern with the ownership of land. Their main aim was to mobilize the agrarian population in order to achieve their own goals. Once these were attained, the alliance with the agrarian movement frequently disintegrated: indeed, the two sides often moved into opposition and conflict. Hence, the alliance formed by agrarian movements with other social groups tended to be temporary rather than permanent.

7. The Success of Agrarian Movements

An assessment of the success or failure of agrarian movements can take one of two forms: it may consider the survival of the movements in terms of the establishment and maintainance of an organization, or it can consider the attainment of goals. Logically, either one is possible without the other. European experiences, however, suggest that agrarian movements have rarely been successful in achieving either, at least until the twentieth century.

In traditional societies with wide ranges of vertical status, poor institutionalization, and where rural communities were characterized by insecurity of tenure, agrarian movements were mainly revolutionary in character. Their anomic nature was not conducive to permanent or effective organization. But these movements failed to attain their goals except where the society was already experiencing a similar process of significant change. In such instances the agrarian contribution may have assisted in the transformation of society, but it was rarely the prime agent of change. Thus rural political mobilization greatly aided the nationalist cause in nineteenth century Europe, but it was not the major cause of the downfall of the old empires.

Greater possibilities of success emerged in modernized European societies. By modernization we mean those societies which possessed widespread functional specialization and a high degree of institutionalization, and in which status differences were reduced. Such societies were also more industrial and urban: the agrarian population was relatively small, diminishing in size, and more or less fully integrated in national politics and a market economy. In this respect it is pertinent to point to Neubauer's thesis that "political development, to the extent that it represents democratic political developments, is a threshold phenomenon. Certain levels of 'basic' socio-economic development appear to be necessary to elevate countries to a level at which they can begin to support complex, nation-wide patterns of political interaction, one of which may be democracy."[13] Success became more likely because of a greater realism by agrarian groups in presenting more limited demands. The combination of more restricted, specific demands, and of a better knowledge of political processes and tactics increased the chances of accommodation. In turn, this reduced the likelihood of frustration and a resort to violent means.

Overall, the degree of organization depended indirectly upon the societal levels of education, economic development, and political institutionalization. The general level of social progress and mobilization affected the quality of organization through determining the milieu in which agrarian movements operated. It is these features which help to distinguish what we have called interest group politics from peasantist politics. By contrast to Western societies, the political evolution of Eastern Europe after 1900 was characterized by increasing conflicts along several dimensions of social cleavage. The lack of institutionalization was reflected in the unstable nature of the regimes and in the presence of unstable and individualistic leaderships. In an atmosphere marked by unimaginative and often stupid social and economic policies, widespread corruption and declining standards of efficiency and impartiality among politicians and bureaucrats, and the alienation of significant social groups, it is not surprising that structured agrarian organizations failed to emerge, nor that the performance of the various agrarian parties must be measured in terms of failure rather than success. In other words, the agrarian parties here were victims of the fragile political system. Moreover, the low level of political education and the weak interior articulation among the masses prevented the development of effective political participation and political and economic organization.

A major explanation of the variations in European developments therefore rests with the congruence or incongruence in the rate and nature of political, social and economic developments. In Western Europe change in each of these three fields was generally more in tune with the change in the others. By contrast, Eastern Europe after 1900 experienced rapid social change and political mobilization, but only slow economic progress, or even stagnation and decline, all within a framework marked by an absence of a sense of political responsibility, political education, and political institutionalization.[14]

In effect, what we are saying is that agrarian movements succeeded in attaining their economic and political goals, and in raising the social status of their followers only when events and processes were moving the society in this direction. Peasant rebellions in Europe, for example, were repressed more often than victorious. The chances of agrarian success were strong only where the social status of the farming population was rising, and where other social groups were prepared to become allies of the movement or to concede the justness of the agrarian case. Moreover, the success of agrarian movements tended to be negative, particularly where they sought their ends by revolutionary means. As Barrington Moore has stated, "The peasants have provided the dynamite to bring down the old building. To the subsequent work of reconstruction they have brought nothing: instead they have been its first victims".[15]

Hence, in the long term the feeling that farming groups have enjoyed a political influence disproportionate to their share of the total population may be rather misleading. From European experiences we can see that from the English revolution of 1381 and the French <u>jacquerie</u> of 1358 to the several parties, cooperatives and farming associations of the twentieth century, agrarian groups have fought on the whole a successful rearguard action, but it has been a <u>rearguard</u> action.

8. The Analysis of Agrarian Politics

This exploration of agrarian politics in Europe has drawn upon several academic disciplines, especially those of history and political sociology. The traditional historical approach has been to illuminate the specific event without necessarily referring to the generalization of which it is an example. By contrast, modern political sociology, which is more theoretically oriented, has been more interested in formulating the general rule. The combination of the two disciplines hopefully serves to explain more specific events and to permit the formulation of more adequate general rules.

We have not offered a theory of agrarian politics: the lack of data prohibits any attempt to construct an empirically based theory. The emphasis has been upon the comparative, upon the synchronic and diachronic uniformities and differences between political systems and between similar aspects of different political systems. The analysis has tried to demonstrate how many political activities of agrarian groups are related to some of their fundamental aims, and that there has been a high degree of uniformity in the political behaviour of European cultivators. Agrarian political behaviour in Europe has derived from two basic conflicts: an opposition in the commodity market between landed and urban interests, and a conflict arising from internal differentiation, primarily from the structure of landownership and the style of farming.

The discussion suggests that there are three dimensions of agrarian politics. First, the agrarian reaction may be individualistic or it may take collective, cooperative forms. Second, it may be distinguished in terms of the explicitness of

its goals. And finally, it may be distinguished in terms of
how far its aims, ideology and methods uphold or challenge the
status quo. These dimensions of agrarian politics, when taken
in conjunction with the developmental aspects derived from
political integration and degree of involvement with the
capitalist economy, hopefully offer a systematic basis which can
serve as a means by which further research could lead to a
systematic and integrated theory of the political behaviour of
farming groups.

No matter which aspect of the problem is selected for study,
a developmental approach seems to be the most appropriate.
Above all, agrarian politics must be studied within its own
terms of reference. Numerous analogies can and have been drawn
between peasants and industrial workers, or between farmers and
urban entrepreneurs. To equate urban and rural society
completely is to miss some of the significant aspects of agrarian
life. The absorption of the operators of domestic consumptive
enterprises with their immediate social conditions is similar to
the concerns of industrial workers. With the penetration of
centralizing forces and the consolidation of national political
systems, communities and economic markets, both groups were
essentially newcomers in the polity and economy. The conflict
between worker and employer in the labour market revolved around
the workers' attempts to organize collectively in order to demand
a share of their product, and over how the latter was actually
distributed between owner, worker and consumer. Where the two
sides were amenable to bargaining, the difference could be
resolved amicably by collective bargaining. In effect, a non-
zero sum situation can develop. Essentially, contemporary class
conflicts are over the distribution of money: the latter is a
variable capable of infinite division. This cannot usually be
said of other conflicts.[16]

By contrast, where the cultivator's major concern involves a
relationship with a landlord, the situation is exactly the
opposite of that in industrial society. In the cities economic
growth and the use of money as the basic measurement of wealth
and livelihood make possible a more equitable distribution of
income. In the countryside, economic growth presupposes
commercial agriculture: by and large, without an equitable

distribution of landownership and usage, agrarian capitalism seemingly is not conducive to political stability and economic satisfaction. The operators of both domestic consumptive and farmer capitalist enterprises are analogous to a mixture of entrepreneur and worker. But to attempt to understand the agrarian world in these urban terms is perhaps to miss the peculiar aspects of that world which derive from the land, the origin of its basic resources and equipment. In addition, there is the question of value conflicts which, whatever the economic similarities between town and countryside, suggest that farmers and rural society possess a way of life which at least to some extent is quite distinctive from that of the cities, and that these aspects of agriculture and rural life have important political consequences. The land is the basic factor of economic production in the countryside. It is simultaneously, in its extent and quality, the measurement of economic prosperity and social status. The limited supply of land, the varying relationships to it of different groups and the general inability of urban groups to appreciate the central position it occupies in farming life are the factors which give rise to the basic conflicts of agrarian political behaviour: cleavages arising from differences between town and countryside, from capitalist involvement, and from the structure of landownership.

NOTES

Introduction

1. M. Dogan & R. Rose (eds), <u>European Politics</u>. Boston, 1971, p. xi.

2. T.G. Jordan, <u>The European Culture Area</u>. New York, 1973, pp. 6-7. The geographical criterion effectively excludes European fragment or plantation societies elsewhere, such as the Anglo-American and Latin American settlements. Their historical and agrarian experiences are to some extent quite different from those of the European continent.

3. R. Rose (ed), <u>Electoral Behavior</u>. New York, 1974, p. 14.

4. In general this period, especially the interwar decades, has been neglected by contemporary political scientists. For a fuller discussion of this and other lacunae in the literature of comparative European politics, see D.W. Urwin, "Political Parties, Societies and Regimes in Europe: Some Reflections on the Literature". <u>European Journal of Political Research</u> 1 (1973), pp. 179-204.

5. S.M. Lipset & S. Rokkan (eds), <u>Party Systems and Voter Alignments</u>. New York, 1967.

6. An "Iron Curtain" syndrome afflicts much of the literature on Europe: see the comments in Urwin, "Political Parties, Societies and Regimes", pp. 183-184.

7. E.R. Wolf, Introduction to special issue, "Peasants and Political Mobilization", <u>Comparative Studies in Society and History</u> 17 (1975). The literature on peasantry is vast. A list of the more significant commentaries would include A.D. Chayanov, <u>The Theory of Peasant Economy</u>. Homewood, 1966; F.M. Foster, <u>Tzintzuntzan: Mexican Peasants in a Changing World</u>. Boston, 1967; S.H. Franklin, <u>The European Peasantry</u>. London, 1969; S.H. Franklin, <u>Rural Societies</u>. London, 1971; B. Galeski,

Basic Concepts in Rural Sociology. Manchester, 1971; M. Lipton, "The Theory of the Optimising Peasant". Journal of Development Studies 4 (1968), pp. 327-351; M. Nash, Primitive and Peasant Economic Systems. San Francisco, 1966; M.F. Nimkoff & R. Middleton, "Types of Family and Types of Economy", American Journal of Sociology 66 (1960), pp. 215-225; R. Redfield, Peasant Society and Culture. Chicago, 1960; T. Shanin (ed), Peasants and Peasant Societies. London, 1971; E.R. Wolf, Peasants. Englewood Cliffs, 1966.

8. B.H. Slicher van Bath, The Agrarian History of Western Europe, AD 500-1850. London, 1963, p. 24.

9. The more interesting typologies include E.R. Wolf, "Types of Latin American Peasantry: A Preliminary Discussion". American Anthropologist 57 (1955), pp. 452-471; B. Galeski, "Social Organization and Rural Social Change". Sociologia Ruralis 8 (1968), pp. 258-281; A.L. Stinchcombe, "Agricultural Enterprise and Rural Class Relations". American Journal of Sociology 67 (1961), pp. 165-176. On Latin America see inter alia H.A. Landsberger (ed), Latin American Peasant Movements. Ithaca, 1969; R. Stavenhagen (ed), Agrarian Problems and Peasant Movements in Latin America New York, 1970 ; H.A. Landsberger (ed), Rural Protest: Peasant Movements and Social Change. New York, 1973.

10. J.M. Paige, Agrarian Revolution: Social Movements and Export Agriculture in the Underdeveloped World. New York, 1975.

11. J.J. Linz, "Patterns of Land Tenure, Division of Labor, and Voting Behavior in Europe". Comparative Politics 8 (1976), p. 366.

12. Linz, "Patterns of Land Tenure". His categories are derived from a lengthy list originally constructed by P.A. Sorokin et al, A Systematic Source Book in Rural Sociology. Minneapolis, 1930, I pp. 362-370.

13. Lipset & Rokkan, Party Systems.

Chapter 1

1. Slicher van Bath, Agrarian History, p. 24.

2. See A.R. Lewis, "The Closing of the European Frontier". Speculum 33 (1958), pp. 475-483.

3. I. Wallerstein, The Modern World System: Capitalist Agriculture and the Origins of the European World-Economy in the Sixteenth Century. New York, 1974.

4. For a discussion of these cities and their significance for later political developments, see the interesting analyses by S. Rokkan, "Cities, States and Nations: A Dimensional Model for the Study of Contrasts in Development", in S.N. Eisenstadt & S. Rokkan (eds), Building States and Nations. London/Beverly Hills, 1973, I, pp. 73-97; and "Dimensions of State Formation and Nation Building: A Possible Paradigm for Research on Variations within Europe", in C. Tilly (ed), The Formation of National States in Western Europe. Princeton, 1975, pp. 562-600. See also B. Moore, Social Origins of Dictatorship and Democracy. Boston, 1966; O. Brunner, Neue Wege der Sozialgeschichte. Göttingen, 1956, pp. 80-115; P. Dollinger, The German Hansa. Stanford, 1970.

5. H. Koeningsberger, Estates and Revolutions. Ithaca, 1971, pp. 23-28.

6. A.R. Bridberg, Economic Growth: England in the Later Middle Ages. London, 1962; D.A. Holmes, The Estates of the Higher Nobility in Fourteenth Century England. Cambridge, 1957; J. Thirsk (ed), The Agrarian History of England and Wales, IV. 1500-1640. Cambridge, 1967. For the international context see Wallerstein, The Modern World System, Ch. 1.

7. See the seminal article by L. White, "Technology and Invention in the Middle Ages". Speculum 15 (1940), pp. 141-159: also Slicher van Bath, Agrarian History; M.M. Postan (ed), The Cambridge Economic History of Europe, I. The Agrarian Life of the Middle Ages. Cambridge, 1966; W. Abel, Agrarkrisen und Agrarkonjunktur. Eine Geschichte der Land- und Ernährungswirtschaft Mitteleuropas seit dem hohen Mittelalter. Hamburg, 1966; W. Abel, Geschichte des deutschen Landwirtschaft vom frühen Mittelalters bis zum 19. Jahrhundert. Stuttgart, 1967; G. Duby, Rural Economy and Country Life in the Medieval West. Columbia, SC, 1968; D. Herlihy, "The Agrarian Revolution in Southern France and Italy, 801-1150". Speculum 33 (1958), pp. 23-41. The distinction between technical improvement and organizational improvement is drawn by W.H. Becket, "The Development of Peasant Agriculture", in P. Ruopp (ed), Approaches to Community Development. Hague, 1953, pp. 138-143.

8. The authoritative account of agricultural developments associated with the Industrial Revolution in Britain by J.D. Chambers & G.E. Mingay, The Agricultural Revolution 1750-1850. London, 1966, stresses that the increase in agricultural production in eighteenth century England was due less to higher yields than to an increase in the area of cultivated land and to improved rotation systems. This follows on from Chambers' earlier argument that quantitative data (albeit limited) suggest that the enclosures did not, as conventionally interpreted, lead to depopulated vilages, a reduction in the rural labour force, and increased yields through a simple consolidation of holdings: J.D. Chambers, "Enclosure and Labour Supply in the Industrial Revolution". Economic History Review, 2 series, 5 (1953), pp.319-343. A stepwise progression in technical transformation is outlined by F.M.L. Thompson, "The

Second Agricultural Revolution, 1815-1880". *Economic History Review*, 2 series, 21 (1968), pp. 62-77. See also H.J. Habbakuk, "English Landownership, 1680-1740". *Economic History Review* 10 (1940), pp. 2-17; G.E. Mingay, "The Size of Farms in the Eighteenth Century". *Economic History Review*, 2 series, 14 (1962), pp. 469-488.

9. For a review of agriculture and the European economy in the late eighteenth century, see A. Milward & S.B. Saul, *The Economic Development of Continental Europe 1780-1870*. London, 1973, pp. 40-83.

10. H. Daalder, "Parties, Elites, and Political Developments in Western Europe", in J. LaPalombara & M. Weiner (eds), *Political Parties and Political Development*. Princeton, 1966, pp. 45-52.

11. See Wolf, *Peasants*, pp. 50-59; R. Bendix, *Nation-Building and Citizenship*. New York, 1964, pp. 43-44; S.N. Eisenstadt, *The Political Systems of Empires*. New York, 1963, Chs. 5, 7-8; G.C. Homans, *English Villagers of the Thirteenth Century*. New York, 1960, pp. 269ff.

12. For example, while patrimonialism was the typical form in medieval Western Europe, prebendal ownership could frequently, and mercantilism sometimes, be found. See for instance S.L. Thrupp, "Economy and Society in Medieval England". *Journal of British Studies* 2 (1962), pp. 5-8.

13. See, for example, the comparative analysis of England, France and Germany in F.L. Ganshof, *Feudalism*. New York, 1961, pp. 160-166. Comprehensive analyses of feudal characteristics can be found in O. Brunner, *Land und Herrschaft*. Vienna, 1959; M. Bloch, *Feudal Society*. Chicago, 1961.

14. Koenigsberger, *Estates and Revolutions*, pp. 27-34. One may also consult the intensive study by J. Larner, *The Lords of Romagna: Romagnal Society and the Origins of the Signorie*. Ithaca, 1965. On sharecropping as a risk-sharing exercise see S.N.S. Cheung, *The Theory of Share Tenancy*. Chicago, 1969.

15. E.F. Heckscher, *An Economic History of Sweden*. Cambridge, Mass., 1963, pp. 67ff; I. Semmingen, "The Dissolution of Estate Society in Norway". *Scandinavian Economic History Review* 2 (1954), pp. 166-203; H. Björvik, "The Farm Territories". *Ibid*. 4 (1956), pp. 33-61; R. Frimannslund, "Farm Community and Neighbourhood Community". *Ibid*. 4 (1956), pp. 62-81; A. Holmesen, "Landowners and Tenants in Norway". *Ibid*. 6 (1958), pp. 121-131. A good comparative review of Scandinavian agricultural structures is Ö. Österud, "Agrarian Structure and Peasant Politics in Scandinavia". Doctoral dissertation, University of London, 1974, pp. 82-142.

16. P. Stearns, *European Society in Upheaval*. New York, 1967, pp. 27-30. Collectivist practices are described in Slicher van

Bath, Agrarian History; R.H. Hilton, Bond Men Made Free. New York, 1973. See also the careful study of the linkages between socio-economic structures and the distribution of land by G. Lefebvre, Les paysans du Nord pendant la Révolution française. Bari, 1959. Here and there a few villages even attempted to impose some obligatory economic equality upon all their residents.

17. Milward & Saul, Economic Development, p. 43.

18. See for example R. Koselleek, Preussen zwischen Reform und Revolution: Allgemeines Landrecht, Verwaltung, und soziale Bewegung von 1791 bis 1848. Stuttgart, 1967. This was also the case in Austria: see J. Blum, Noble Landowners and Agriculture in Austria, 1815-1848. Baltimore, 1948, pp. 68-87; and also the study (primarily of Bohemia) by W.E. Wright, Serf, Seigneur and Sovereign. Minneapolis, 1966.

19. N. Salomon, La campagne de nouvelle Castile à la fin du XVIe siècle, d'après les Relaciones Topográficas. Paris, 1964.

20. J. Lopreato, Peasants No More. San Francisco, 1967, pp. 12-14.

21. C.E. Black, "Eastern Europe in Historical Perspective", in C.E. Black (ed), Challenge in Eastern Europe. New Brunswick, 1954, p. 19; Eisenstadt, Political Systems of Empires, pp. 22-24.

22. It is important to remember that these three enclosure phases were not strictly confined everywhere to a distinct time period, nor are they clearly separable from each other. On the later period see Chambers & Mingay, The Agricultural Revolution; C.S. Orwin, A History of English Farming. London, 1949, pp. 35-74. An early study of the commutations which remains of interest is E.P. Cheyney, "The Disappearance of English Serfdom". English Historical Review 15 (1900), pp. 20-37. On the importance for the future of the elimination of a more "traditional" peasantry, see F.M.L. Thompson, "The Social Distribution of Landed Property in England since the Sixteenth Century". Economic History Review, 2 series, 19 (1966), pp. 505-517.

23. Moore, Social Origins, p. 419; also Bendix, Nation-Building, pp. 50-57.

24. Generally, see R.R. Palmer, The Age of the Democratic Revolution: The Challenge. Princeton, 1959, pp. 100-107. On the Hats and Caps see G. Olsson, Hattar och Mössor. Studiet över partiväsendet i Sverige 1751-1762. Gothenberg, 1963. The Swedish curial system is analyzed in detail in S. Carlsson, Standsamhälle och Standspersoner 1700-1865. Lund, 1949. Its success may be compared to the fate of that in Finland, established in 1772 and 1789, which on passing from Sweden to Russia retained its peasant estate. However, absolute authority now rested with the Tsar, who rarely invoked the Diet: its first

summons did not occur until 1863.

25. The "screening" effect of a church is emphasized in S.P. Dunn & E. Dunn, The Peasants of Central Russia. New York, 1967, pp. 29-30; T. Stoianovich, "The Social Foundations of Balkan Politics 1750-1941", in C. Jelavich & B. Jelavich (eds), The Balkans in Transition. Berkeley/Los Angeles, 1963. p. 313. More generally, see M. Weber, The Sociology of Religion. Boston, 1963, pp. 80-84.

26. C. Tilly, The Vendée. Cambridge, Mass., 1964, pp. 103-110; P. Bois, Paysans de l'Ouest. Le Mans, 1960, pp. 614-615.

27. Eisenstadt, Political Systems of Empires, pp. 208-209.

28. On the economic virtues of métayage see Duby, Rural Economy, p. 280.

29. R. Mousnier, Peasant Uprisings in Seventeenth Century France, Russia and China. London, 1970. The broad view is taken by G. Lefebvre, Études sur la Révolution française. Paris, 1954; see also P. Sagnac, La formation de la société française moderne. Paris, 1945, I pp. 139-143; A. Cobban, The Social Interpretation of the French Revolution. Cambridge, 1964, pp. 112-117.

30. See Duby, Rural Economy, p. 331; E. LeRoy Ladurie, Les Paysans de Languedoc. Paris, 1966, I pp. 326-328; Abel, Geschichte der deutschen Landwirtschaft, pp. 186-189.

31. D. Sabean, Landbesitz und Gesellschaft am Vorabend des Bauernkriegs. Stuttgart, 1972; G. Franz, Der Deutsche Bauernkrieg. Darmstadt, 1956.

32. D. Sabean, "The Communal Basis of pre-1800 Peasant Uprisings in Western Europe". Comparative Politics 8 (1976), pp. 355-364. The account by A.J. Peacock, Bread or Blood: A Study of the Agrarian Riots in East Anglia in 1816. London, 1965, is a perfect illustration of this "territorial ripple" effect.

33. Mousnier, Peasant Uprisings, Chs. 7-10. The increasingly polarized nature of Russian society contributed to the persisting peasant unrest (and even revolutionary sentiments) of subsequent centuries.

34. L. Stavrianos, The Balkans Since 1453. New York, 1963, p. 144, on the decline of the Ottomans: also Eisenstadt, Political Systems of Empires, pp. 169-172, 269, 291, 347-349.

35. Palmer, Age of the Democratic Revolution; G. Rudé, Revolutionary Europe 1783-1815. New York, 1964; R.W. Greenlaw (ed), The Economic Origins of the French Revolution: Poverty or Prosperity?.Boston, 1958. Indeed, Palmer argues that the

revolutions were victorious only in France and the United States, where there was an alliance between middle class leaders and agrarian masses: elsewhere revolutionary ardour was quenched partly because of the political weakness of disinterest of the agrarian population.

36. The literature on millenarianism and its implications is extensive and informative: see <u>inter alia</u> E.J. Hobsbaum, <u>Primitive Rebels</u>. Manchester, 1959; N. Cohn, <u>The Pursuit of the Millenium</u>. New York, 1961; W.E. Mühlmann (ed), <u>Chiliasmus und Nativismus</u>. Berlin, 1961; S.L. Thrupp (ed), <u>Millenial Dreams in Action</u>. Hague, 1961. The most comprehensive discussion of the relationship between religion and legitimate secular authority remains H. Frankfort, <u>Kingship and the Gods</u>. Chicago, 1948.

37. Cohn, <u>Pursuit of the Millenium</u>, pp. 25-29, 317.

38. Franz, <u>Der Deutsche Bauernkrieg</u>, p. 291.

39. F.L. Carsten, <u>The Origins of Prussia</u>. London, 1954, Part I; C.A. Macartney, <u>The Hapsburg Empire 1790-1918</u>. London, 1968, pp. 37-38; F.L. Carsten, "Der Bauernkrieg in Ostpreussen 1525". <u>International Review for Social History</u> 3 (1938), pp. 398-409. It is worth noting that the economic problems of a similar shortage in eighteenth century Denmark led to the introduction of agrarian bondage (<u>Stavnsbaand</u>) to prevent the migration of rural labourers, while by contrast a relative labour shortage had earlier assisted the emancipation of the serfs in England.

40. Franz, <u>Der Deutsche Bauernkrieg</u>, p. 287: more generally, see Cohn, <u>Pursuit of the Millenium</u>; and G. Rudé, <u>The Crowd in History</u>. New York, 1964, who suggests that by the eighteenth century the most direct peasant response to capitalist pressures was to seek to block the export of grain from the locality.

41. Moore, <u>Social Origins</u>, p. xvii.

42. Moore, <u>Social Origins</u>, especially pp. 63-64, 418-420.

43. In the seventeenth century the Hohenzollerns also gained supremacy over the aristocracy. Most Prussian provinces were occupied by Swedish or Hapsburg troops during the Thirty Years War, while the monarchy survived unscathed in remote East Prussia. Upon their return the Hohenzollerns demanded the political submission of a weakened aristocracy as their price for the further consolidation of serfdom and subjugation of the cities. See Carsten, <u>Origins of Prussia</u>, especially Ch. 12; Koselleek, <u>Preussen zwischen Reform und Revolution</u>; H. Rosenberg, <u>Bureaucracy, Aristocracy and Autocracy: The Prussian Experience</u>. Cambridge, Mass., 1958.

44. There is a vast romantic literature on the Russian collective unit, the <u>mir</u>, praising the virtues of peasant communalism:

reality was rather different. Because he could not sell, mortgage or inherit land, or plan his agricultural production without the approval of the collectivity, the individual peasant was virtually imprisoned within the community. The Russian state recognized the integrity of the community until 1906, for example by making it collectively responsible for such things as payment of taxes or the conformity of its members to state laws. See the comments in L. Volin, "The Peasant Household under the Mir and the Kolkhoz in Modern Russian History", in C. Ware (ed), The Cultural Approach to History. New York, 1940, pp. 125-139; T. Shanin, The Awkward Class. Oxford, 1971; G.T. Robinson, Rural Russia under the Old Regime, New York, 1949; J. Blum, Lord and Peasant in Russia from the Ninth to the Nineteenth Century. Princeton, 1961. On the Balkan equivalent, the zadruga (meaning cooperative), see D. Tomasič, Personality and Culture in Eastern European Politics. New York, 1948, pp. 148-205; J. Tomasevich, Peasants, Politics, and Economic Change in Yugoslavia. Stanford, 1955, pp. 178-202.

45. Wallerstein, The Modern World System, Ch. 6; Blum, Lord and Peasant in Russia, Chs. 8-14; P.I. Lyashchenko, History of the National Economy of Russia to the 1917 Revolution. New York, 1949 pp. 311ff.

46. Abel, Geschichte der deutschen Landwirtschaft, pp. 187-193; F. Wunderlich, Farm Labor in Germany 1810-1945. Princeton, 1961, p. 10; W. Conze, "Die Wirkungen der liberalen Agrarreformen auf die Volksordnung in Mitteleuropa im 19. Jahrhundert", Vierteljahresschrift für Sozial- und Wirtschaftsgeschichte 38 (1951), pp. 2-43; K. Borchardt, "The Industrial Revolution in Germany 1700-1914", in C.M. Cipolla (ed), The Emergence of Industrial Societies. London, 1973, I p. 98.

47. See M.W. Graham, New Governments of Eastern Europe. New York, 1927, pp. 246-249; J.H. Jackson, Estonia. London, 1948, Ch. 4; S.W. Page, The Formation of the Baltic States. Cambridge, Mass., 1959, pp. 10-22; A. Rūsis, "Land and Peasant: Latvia", in V. Gsovski & K. Grzybowski (eds), Government, Law and Courts in the Soviet Union and Eastern Europe. New York, 1960, II pp. 1676-1677; B.V. Maciuika, "Agriculture in Soviet Latvia", in G.B. Carson Jr. (ed), Latvia: An Area Study. New Haven, 1956, p. 504. The language structure of the Baltic provinces is interesting. The Balt overlords refused to allow their Lettish and Estonian serfs to learn German. Instead they took pains to learn the difficult local languages: C.A. Macartney, National States and National Minorities. London, 1934, p. 60.

48. J.R. Western, The End of European Primacy. London, 1965, p. 47. Compensation was paid to the lord by the state, which then reclaimed it from the peasant in annual instalments. By 1880 arrears were already 27 per cent of the annual payment. Each village had been made collectively responsible for collecting these payments. In practice it meant that a peasant was unable to sell his land unless he could offer the village a substantial sum towards the outstanding debt. For a good discussion of the power of the lords, see W.E. Mosse, Alexander

II and the Modernization of Russia. London, 1958, pp. 47-75.

49. See J. Blum, Noble Landowners and Agriculture in Austria, pp. 192-202.

50. D. Mitrany, Marx Against The Peasant. Chapel Hill, 1951, p. 27. See also his more detailed analysis, The Land and the Peasant in Rumania. London, 1930, pp. 228-283.

51. Lyashchenko, History of the National Economy of Russia, p. 370; Blum, Lord and Peasant in Russia, p. 554. Soviet historians have tended to equate peasant uprisings with Cossack revolts. However, the Cossacks were reacting against the growing centralization of the state. No Cossack revolt was directed against the institution of serfdom itself: see the discussion in L. Yaresh, "The 'Peasant Wars' in Soviet Historiography". American Slavic and East European Review 16 (1957), pp. 241-259.

52. Stavrianos, The Balkans, Ch. 9. Under the old timar system the powers of the landlords were regulated by the central bureaucracy, and the peasants possessed a number of important rights such as the hereditary right to land. Under the proposed chiflik system peasant rights and central control were to be removed.

53. S. Bolin, "Medieval Agrarian Society in its Prime: Scandinavia", in Postan, Agrarian Life, pp. 633-659; G. Olsen, Hovedgård og Bondegård. Studier over stordriftens udvikling i Danmark i tiden 1525-1774. Copenhagen, 1957, pp. 76ff.

54. Daalder, "Parties, Elites, and Political Development", p. 55.

55. Bendix, Nation-Building, p. 107. A review of the history of education can be found in R. Ulich, The Education of Nations. Cambridge, Mass., 1961.

56. Franz, Der Deutsche Bauernkrieg; B.H. Slicher van Bath, "The Economic and Social Conditions in the Frisian Districts 900-1500". Afdeling Agrarische Geschiedenis Bijdragen 13 (1965), pp. 97-133. S.F. Silverman, "Agricultural Organization, Social Structure, and Values in Italy: Amoral Familism Reconsidered". American Anthropologist 70 (1968), pp. 1-20, also suggests that the sharecropping tenure system in Tuscany encouraged neighbourhood cooperation. See also Slicher van Bath, Agrarian History, pp. 189-194; Homans, English Villagers. M. Beqiraj, Peasantry in Revolution. Ithaca, 1966; and Paige, Agrarian Revolution, both develop hypotheses that seek to relate contemporary peasant rebellions to the structure and practices of local communities.

57. J. Blum, "The Rise of Serfdom in Eastern Europe". American Historical Review 62 (1957), pp. 807-836.

58. Rokkan, "Cities, States and Nations"; and "Dimensions of State Formation".

59. See C. Tilly, "Food Supply and Public Order in Modern Europe", in Tilly, The Formation of National States, pp. 380-455.

60. An outstanding analysis of the growth of European cities and of the distinctions that emerged between east and west is Brunner, Neue Wege der Sozialgeschichte, pp. 80-115. The peasantry in the manorial areas of the Mediterranean littoral were placed in circumstances similar to those in Eastern Europe. In some ways their condition may have been even more depressed since absenteeism was a common phenomenon among the landlords. At least in many manorial areas like Prussia the landlords tended to reside on their estates. See the comments on Sardinia in D.M. Smith, Victor Emanuel, Cavour, and the Risorgimento. London, 1971, p. 250.

61. This process is discussed with acumen in S.P. Huntington, Political Order in Changing Societies. New Haven, 1968, pp. 291-300.

Chapter 2

1. See the classic study by D. Landes, The Unbound Prometheus. Cambridge, 1969.

2. K.F. Helleiner, "The Population of Europe from the Black Death to the Eve of the Vital Revolution", in E.E. Rich & C.H. Wilson (eds), The Cambridge Economic History of Europe. London, 1967, IV, pp. 58-94; E.L. Jones, "Agricultural Origins of Industry", Past and Present 40 (1968), pp. 58-71; also the authoritative study of agricultural developments associated with the Industrial Revolution in Britain, Chambers & Mingay, The Agricultural Revolution.

3. Basic references are E.F. Heckscher, Mercantilism. London, 1955; Wallerstein, The Modern World System. On how the isolation of rural communities in France and their ability to live off themselves was decisively penetrated by the expansion of the railway and road networks after 1850, see C. Fohlen, "The Industrial Revolution in France 1700-1914", in Cipolla, The Emergence of Industrial Societies, I pp. 27-28; E. Weber, Peasants into Frenchmen: The Modernization of Rural France 1870-1914. Stanford, 1976, Ch. 12.

4. Subsequent economic developments in France, with their seemingly implicit acceptance of a kind of Malthusian doctrine of only a fixed amount of economic expansion and profit being available in a country, lead one to suggest that the "transitional" period lasted for more than a century. A review of the various arguments and hypotheses can be found in Fohlen, "The Industrial Revolution in France", pp. 71-75.

5. See inter alia Slicher van Bath, Agrarian History; E.L. Jones & S.J. Woolf (eds), Agrarian Change and Economic Development. London, 1969. For the market penetration of and economic change in German and Swedish agriculture, see the good quantitative studies by H.W. Graf Finck zu Finckenstein, Die Entwicklung der Landwirtschaft in Preussen und Deutschland 1800-1930. Würzburg, 1960; J. Kuuse, Från redskap til maskiner. Mekaniseringsspridning och kommersialisering inom svensk jordbruk. Gothenberg, 1970.

6. See the fascinating analysis of the decline of local community customs in nineteenth century France in Weber, Peasants into Frenchmen, Chs. 21-22. The rapid growth in associational life has been traced in some detail for Wissous, a village in Seine-et-Oise, in R.T. Anderson & B.G. Anderson, Bus Stop for Paris: The Transformation of a French Village. New York, 1965.

7. K.D. Jacobsen, Teknisk hjelp og politisk struktur. Oslo, 1964; F. Valen-Sendstad, Norske landbrukeredskaper, 1800-1850-årene. Lillehammer, 1964.

8. E.N. Anderson & P.R. Anderson, Political Institutions and Social Change in Continental Europe in The Nineteenth Century. Berkeley/Los Angeles, 1967, pp. 85-86.

9. Lyashchenko, History of the National Economy of Russia, pp. 323-324. Good contributions on landlord-peasant relations include Robinson, Rural Russia; W.S. Vucinich (ed), The Peasant in Nineteenth-Century Russia. Stanford, 1968, especially T. Emmons, "The Peasant and the Emancipation"; Blum, Lord and Peasant in Russia. The consequences of the Great Reform are more specifically the theme of Mosse, Alexander II; and A. Gerschenkron, "Agrarian Policies and Industrialization 1861-1917", in H.J. Habbakuk & M.M. Postan (eds), The Cambridge Economic History of Europe. Cambridge, 1965, VI, pp. 706-800. For Prussia see Finckenstein, Die Entwicklung der Landwirtschaft; W. Görlitz, Die Junker, Adel und Bauer im deutschen Ost. Glücksburg, 1956; Koselleek, Preussen zwischen Reform und Revolution.

10. Stavrianos, The Balkans Since 1453, p. 354; also more generally, M. Emerit, Les paysans roumains depuis le Traité d'Andrinople jusqu'à la libération des terres, 1829-1864. Paris, 1937. Serfdom was late in arriving in Rumania: Of the law abolishing serfdom, it has been said that it was "hastily conceived, imperfectly prepared and frequently badly applied": I.L. Evans, The Agrarian Revolution in Rumania. Cambridge, 1924, p. 41.

11. Palmer, Age of the Democratic Revolution, p. 482.

12. H. Rosenberg, "Der Pseudodemokratisierung der Rittergutsbesitzerklasse", in H.U. Wehler (ed), Moderne deutsche Sozialgeschichte. Cologne, 1966, pp. 287-308.

13. Robinson, *Rural Russia*, pp. 56-57; also M. Raeff, *Origins of the Russian Intelligentsia*. New York, 1966, pp. 106-109.

14. On Italy, see L. Gallino, "Italy", in M.S. Archer & S. Giner (eds), *Contemporary Europe*. London, 1971, p. 98; Lopreato, *Peasants No More*, p. 12; L. Graziano, "Patron-Client Relationships in Southern Italy", *European Journal of Political Research* 1 (1973), pp. 6-7. The changed conditions were far more severe on those peasants who previously worked for the Catholic Church, which had been less repressive than the secular landlords. On Spain, see J. Nordal, "The Failure of the Industrial Revolution in Spain 1830-1914", in Cipolla, *Emergence of Industrial Societies*, II pp. 553-567; E.E. Malefakis, *Agrarian Reform and Peasant Revolution in Spain*. New Haven, 1970, p. 4.

15. Milward & Saul, *Economic Development of Continental Europe*, p. 452.

16. See for example Malefakis, *Agrarian Reform*, pp. 82-85; Lopreato, *Peasants No More*, Ch. 2; F. Vöchting, *La Questione Meridionale*. Naples, 1955, pp. 46-47.

17. Vochting, *La Questione Meridionale*, pp. 55-56. An excellent portrait is drawn by C. Levi, *Christ Stopped at Eboli*. New York, 1947: by the 1920s three large proprietors owned almost everything in Eboli.

18. France also experienced this phenomenon: the dramatic decrease in the French birth rate did not begin until about 1850. It is interesting to note that similar low birth rates also appeared in French-speaking regions of Belgium and Switzerland - but not in Germanic speaking Alsace. Britain (even excluding Ireland) was unique in that the continued increase in the agricultural population that typified other industrializing countries was unusually weak: see F. Dovring, *Land and Labor in Europe 1900-1950*. Hague, 1960, pp. 61-79.

19. H.J. Habbakuk, "La disparition du paysan anglais". *Annales* 20 (1965), pp. 649-663.

20. Wallerstein, *The Modern World-System*.

21. F.M.L. Thompson, *English Landed Society in the Nineteenth Century*. London, 1963, pp. 308-318; H. Rosenberg, "Political and Social Consequences of the Great Depression of 1873-1896 in Central Europe". *Economic History Review* 13 (1943), pp. 58-73.

22. Agricultural protectionism, of course, was not a new phenomenon: for example, tariffs had existed in France long before the Méline laws of the 1890s, while Spanish agriculture was protected against foreign competition throughout most of the nineteenth century.

23. Jacobsen, <u>Teknisk hjelp</u>, pp. 172-196; T. Aasland, <u>Fra Landmannsorganisasjon til Bondeparti</u>. Oslo, 1974, pp. 104-111; S. Rokkan, Electoral Mobilization, Party Competition and National Integration", in LaPalombara & Weiner, <u>Political Parties</u>, p. 254.

24. Huntington, <u>Political Order</u>, pp. 297-298. The best single nation study is on France: Weber, <u>Peasants into Frenchmen</u>.

25. See the discussion in E.R. Wolf, <u>Peasant Wars of the Twentieth Century</u>. New York, 1969, pp. 286-287. On how, before suffrage expansion, the landlords in a small Umbrian village acted as mediators on behalf of their sharecroppers with the outside world, see S.F. Silverman, "Patronage and Community-Nation Relationships in Central Italy". <u>Ethnology</u> 4 (1965), pp. 172-189.

26. See Palmer, <u>Age of the Democratic Revolution</u>, Ch. 2.

27. A point stressed by G. Kitson Clark, <u>The Making of Victorian England</u>. London, 1962; and Thompson, <u>English Landed Society</u>.

28. See <u>inter alia</u> the discussion of grain and tariff reform issues in A. Gerschenkron, <u>Bread and Democracy in Germany</u>. Berkeley/Los Angeles, 1943; F. Lütge, <u>Deutsche Sozial- und Wirtschaftsgeschichte</u>. Berlin, 1966, pp. 504-518; Rosenberg, "Political and Social Consequences"; H. Rosenberg, <u>Grosse Depression und Bismarckzeit</u>. Berlin, 1967, pp. 38-51; B. Nedelmann, "Zur Parteientstehung in Schweden (1866-1907): Historische-soziologische Aspekte der Institutionalisierung politische Organisationen". Doctoral dissertation, University of Mannheim, 1970, pp. 209-236.

29. Anderson & Anderson, <u>Political Institutions</u>, p. 9; also K.J. Newman, <u>European Democracy Between The Wars</u>. London, 1970, pp. 35-59.

30. See H. Kohn, <u>The Idea of Nationalism</u>. New York, 1951, pp. 329-330; L. Snyder, <u>The Meaning of Nationalism</u>. New Brunswick, 1954, pp. 118-120. A good summary of the problems raised by the various meanings of nationalism is B.C. Schafer, <u>Faces of Nationalism</u>. New York, 1972, pp. 3-22. See also A. Cobban, <u>The Nation State and National Self-Determination</u>. New York, 1969; H.M. Chadwick, <u>The Nationalities of Europe and the Growth of National Ideologies</u>. London, 1945. On the distribution of European languages see J.S. Dugdale, <u>The Linguistic Map of Europe</u>. London, 1969; J. Geipel, <u>The Europeans: An Ethnohistorical Survey</u>. London, 1969. On the dramatic increases in mass literacy in the late nineteenth century see C.M. Cipolla, <u>Literacy and Development in the West</u>. London, 1969; P. Flora, "Historische Prozesse sozialer Mobilisierung: Urbanisierung und Alphabetisierung, 1850-1965". <u>Zeitschrift für Soziologie</u> 1 (1972), pp. 85-117; L. Stone, "Literacy and Education in England 1640-1900", <u>Past and Present</u> 42 (1969), pp. 69-139. Literacy rates have generally been regarded as important indicators of political development: for example K.W. Deutsch, "Social

Mobilization and Political Development", <u>American Political Science Review</u> 55 (1961), pp. 493-514, suggests their utility in this field, while S.M. Lipset, <u>Political Man</u>. London, 1960, pp. 55-60, sees a positive correlation between literacy and democracy.

31. Weber, <u>Peasants into Frenchmen</u>.

32. D. Thornley, <u>Isaac Butt and Home Rule</u>. London, 1964, p. 13.

33. See the argument in T.B. Bottomore, <u>Elites and Society</u>. London, 1966, pp. 99-100.

34. Anderson & Anderson, <u>Political Institutions</u>, p. 100: they typify such activity as "the adjustment of limited means to specific ends".

35. Norwegian voting rights are reviewed in U. Torgersen, <u>Norsk politiske institusjoner</u>. Oslo, 1964, Chs. 2, 5. Estimates of the proportions qualified are given in S. Kuhnle, "Stemmeretten i 1814: beregninger over antall stemmerettskvalifiserte etter Grunnloven". <u>Historisk Tidsskrift</u> 51 (1972), pp. 373-390; S. Rokkan, "Geography, Religion, and Social Class: Cross-cutting Cleavages in Norwegian Politics", in Lipset & Rokkan, <u>Party Systems</u>, pp. 378-386. On the political participation of Swedish cultivators in the nineteenth century see G. Wallin, <u>Valrörelser och valresultat: Andrakammarvalen i Sverige 1866-1884</u>. Stockholm, 1961.

36. An interesting attempt to pursue this concept in some detail is K.W. Deutsch, <u>Nationalism and Social Communication</u>. New York, 1953, pp. 100-101: it is also a major theme of the important studies by Palmer, <u>Age of the Democratic Revolution</u>; and Bendix, <u>Nation-Building</u>.

37. On the Assembly, peasant opposition, and an attempt to form a rival landless assembly, see M.W. Graham, <u>The Diplomatic Recognition of the Border States</u>. Berkeley/Los Angeles, 1941, p. 401; Page, <u>Formation of the Baltic States</u>, pp. 62-68; U. Germanis, "The Idea of Independent Latvia and Its Development in 1917", in A. Sprudzs & A. Rūsis (eds), <u>Res Baltica</u>. Leiden, 1968, pp. 41-55. The role of the Latvian battalions is discussed by D. Federoff-White, <u>The Growth of the Red Army</u>. Princeton, 1944, pp. 25-28. German attitudes and policies are discussed by F. Fischer, <u>Griff nach der Weltmacht. Die Kriegszielpolitik des Kaiserlichen Deutschlands, 1914-1918</u>. Düsseldorf, 1961; G. Linde, <u>Die deutsche Politik in Litauen im ersten Weltkrieg</u>. Wiesbaden, 1965.

38. <u>Milward & Saul, Economic Development of Continental Europe</u>, p. 43; C.A. Gulick, <u>Austria from Hapsburg to Hitler</u>. Berkeley/Los Angeles, 1948, I p. 171.

39. Mitrany, <u>Marx Against The Peasant</u>, pp. 87-88. On Bela Kun and agriculture see R.L. Tökés, <u>Bela Kun and the Hungarian Soviet Republic</u>. New York, 1967, pp. 156-157; I. Deak, "Budapest and the Hungarian Revolution of 1918-1919". <u>Slavonic and East European Review</u> 46 (1968), p. 135.

40. See P. Jousse, <u>Les tendances des réformes agraires dans l'Europe centrale, l'Europe orientale, et l'Europe méridionale, 1918-1924</u>. Niort, 1925, p. 48; Tomasevich, <u>Peasants, Politics, and Economic Change</u>, p. 371; M.Ts. Bouroff, <u>La réforme agraire en Bulgarie, 1921-1924</u>. Paris, 1925, p. 90; <u>Agrarian Reform in Czechoslovakia</u>. Prague, 1923, p. 12. Apart from Bulgaria, the successor states preferred to give priority to veterans (especially wounded ones) of the national liberation armies and to widows of veterans: Jousse, <u>Les tendances des réformes agraires</u>, pp. 37-48; Tomasevich, <u>Peasants, Politics, and Economic Change</u>, pp. 340-348.

41. E. Allardt & P. Pesonen, "Cleavages in Finnish Politics", in Lipset & Rokkan, <u>Party Systems</u>, p. 331; P. Pesonen, "Finland: Party Support in a Fragmented System", in Rose, <u>Electoral Behavior</u>, p. 291; C.E. Knoellinger, <u>Labor in Finland</u>. Cambridge, Mass., 1960, pp. 20-22.

42. Maciuika, "Agriculture in Soviet Latvia", pp. 508-512; Graham, <u>New Governments of Eastern Europe</u>, pp. 265-277, 334-335; Jackson, <u>Estonia</u>, pp. 156-161; Royal Institute for International Affairs (hereafter cited as RIIA), <u>The Baltic States</u>. London, 1938, p. 29; T. Parming, <u>The Collapse of Liberal Democracy and the Rise of Authoritarianism in Estonia</u>. Sage Professional Papers in Contemporary Political Sociology 06-010. London/Beverly Hills, 1975, pp. 23-25.

43. Graham, <u>New Governments of Eastern Europe</u>, pp. 512-515; R. Buell, <u>Poland: Key to Europe</u>. New York, 1939, Ch. 7; A. Polonsky, <u>Politics in Independent Poland</u>. Oxford, 1972, pp. 10-16, 104-120.

44. See J.S. Roucek, "Economic Geography of Bulgaria". <u>Economic Geography</u> 11 (1935), pp. 307-323.

45. Mitrany, <u>The Land and the Peasant in Rumania</u>; J.S. Roucek, <u>Contemporary Roumania and Her Problems</u>. Stanford, 1932, pp. 293-306; H.L. Roberts, <u>Rumania: Political Problems of an Agrarian State</u>. New Haven, 1951, pp. 22-39; M. Constantinesco, <u>L'évolution de la propriété rurale et la réforme agraire en Roumanie</u>. Bucharest, 1925; Evans, <u>The Agrarian Revolution in Rumania</u>.

46. Mitrany, <u>Marx Against The Peasant</u>, p. 90. The literature on the Eastern land reforms is extensive. In addition to the references cited <u>supra</u>, see: on Lithuania, Graham, <u>New Governments of Eastern Europe</u>, pp. 350-354, 383-385; A. Gerutis, "Independent Lithuania", in A. Gerutis (ed), <u>Lithuania 700 Years</u>.

New York, 1969, p. 199; E.J. Harrison, Lithuania, <u>Past and Present</u>. New York, 1922, pp. 93-96; on Yugoslavia, Tomasevich, <u>Peasants, Politics, and Economic Change</u>, pp. 344-382; R.M. Brašič, <u>Land Reform and Ownership in Yugoslavia 1919-1953</u>. New York, 1954; on Czechoslovakia, L.E. Textor, <u>Land Reform in Czechoslovakia</u>. London, 1923; and more generally, W.E. Moore, <u>Economic Demography of Eastern and Southern Europe</u>. Geneva, 1945.

47. G.D. Jackson, <u>The Comintern and Peasant in Eastern Europe</u>. New York, 1966, p. 9; RIIA, <u>World Agriculture, An International Survey</u>. London, 1932, p. 149.

48. Mitrany, <u>Marx Against The Peasant</u>, p. 89. Similar ideas were included and as strongly resisted in the first draft of the abortive legislation for land reform in the Spanish <u>latifundia</u> regions by the Provisional Republican Government in 1931. Many experts in Spain favoured collective cultivation after the economic failure of the individualistic solution adopted in Eastern Europe: see Malefakis, <u>Agrarian Reform</u>, pp. 173-195.

49. Tomasevich, <u>Peasants, Politics, and Economic Change</u>, pp. 350, 364, 378.

50. L. Stavrianos, "The Influence of the West upon the Balkans", in Jelavich & Jelavich, <u>The Balkans in Transition</u>, p. 200. The same theme is stressed by all analyses of the period: see S. Zagoroff <u>et al</u>, <u>The Agricultural Economy of the Danubian Countries, 1935-1945</u>. Stanford, 1955; Moore, <u>Economic Demography</u>, especially pp. 61-75. Moore's work is the most detailed analysis of rural overpopulation. On the basis of the total agricultural production in crops and livestock, he compares the resulting <u>per capita</u> level with the average value of production in Europe as a whole. This method is challenged by Tomasevich, <u>Peasants, Politics, and Economic Change</u>, pp. 309-314, who simply relates the agricultural population to land resources. However, all these figures can only be a general guide, as there is little reliable statistical information.

51. See for example A. Gerschenkron, <u>Economic Backwardness in Historical Perspective</u>. Cambridge, Mass., 1962, p. 229; J.S. Mollov (ed), <u>Die sozialökonomische Struktur der bulgarischen Landwirtschaft</u>. Berlin, 1936, pp. 48-49.

52. F. Zweig, <u>Poland Between Two Wars</u>. London, 1944, pp. 87-88.

53. J.H. Kautsky (ed), <u>Political Change in Underdeveloped Countries</u>. New York, 1962, p. 47.

54. One problem of many of the successor states was that they could inherit very little liquid wealth from the Hapsburg Empire which had failed to build up capital to the same extent as Western European states: see A. Vodopivec, <u>Die Balkanisierung Österreichs</u>. Vienna, 1966, pp. 22-23. A survey of governmental economic policies in the 1920s is L. Pasvolsky, <u>Economic</u>

Nationalism of the Danubian States. New York, 1928. The 1930s are covered by A. Basch, The Danube Basin and the German Economic Sphere. New York, 1943. Moore, Economic Demography, surveys the entire interwar period: see also Newman, European Democracy, pp. 174-181; M. Matossian, "Ideologies of Delayed Industrialization: Some Tensions and Ambiguities". Economic Development and Cultural Change 6 (1958), pp. 217-228.

55. For example, although Bulgaria was already essentially a country of small owner-occupiers, a further 81,652 hectares of land had been confiscated by 1923. But there were 79,527 families eligible to partake in its redistribution: Bouroff, La réforme agraire, pp. 89-116.

56. Paradoxically, the survival of large estates reduced the likelihood of agricultural unemployment by their greater ability to act as capitalist enterprises, and so employ substantial numbers of labourers: see Moore, Economic Demography, p. 224; Buell, Poland, p. 205.

57. Eastern Poland, however, was a sparsely populated region which made population transfer easier, even though both soil fertility and agricultural productivity were poor: W. Markert (ed), Polen. Cologne, 1959, pp. 37-42, 74.

58. See B. Seebohm Rowntree, Land and Labour: Lessons from Belgium. London, 1910.

59. Dovring, Land and Labor in Europe, pp. 104-105.

60. H. Raupach, "Der interregionale Wohlfahrtsausgleich als Problem der Politik des Deutschen Reiches", in W. Conze & H. Raupach (eds), Die Staats- und Wirtschaftskrise des Deutschen Reiches 1929-33. Stuttgart, 1967, pp. 13-34.

61. J. LaPalombara, Italy: The Politics of Planning. Syracuse, 1966, p. 5. Serious attempts to introduce land reform came only after World War II. Land reform laws were initiated in 1950 with the expropriation of especially unproductive estates. But this reform, even with the implementation of the Fund for the South of the same year and the Green Plan of 1961 to pump investments and subsidies into the South, failed to solve the problems of land-hunger. Many of the new farms were too small to be viable, and peasants have been forced to rely upon, and also have tended to expect, aid from the government.

62. See E.R. Hooker, Readjustments of Agricultural Tenure in Ireland. Chapel Hill, 1938; J.E. Pomfret, The Struggle for the Land in Ireland, 1800-1923. Princeton, 1930; L.P. Curtis, Coercion and Conciliation in Ireland, 1880-1892. Princeton, 1963; also C.M. Arensberg & S.T. Kimball, Family and Community in Ireland. Cambridge, Mass., 1940; K.H. Connell, Irish Peasant Society. London, 1969. The Tenants' Defence Associations of 1878 were the first organized movements of Irish peasants

seeking changes in the pattern of land tenure: E.R. Norman, <u>A History of Modern Ireland</u>. London, 1971, pp. 203ff.

63. Farms of less than five hectares constituted 63.1 per cent of holdings and 30 per cent of the farm area in Bulgaria. The figures for Rumania were 75 per cent and 28 per cent, and for Yugoslavia 67.8 per cent and 28 per cent, despite the minimum size set in each of these countries of five hectares: Jackson, <u>Comintern and Peasant</u>, p. 9. The associated problems are discussed in some detail in RIIA, <u>Agrarian Problems from the Baltic to the Aegean</u>. London, 1943; Political and Economic Planning, <u>Economic Developments in South-Eastern Europe</u>. London, 1945.

64. The "classic" north-south distinction began to appear in the early nineteenth century with increasing productivity in the north. Peasant unrest came more from the south and west, and it was the shortage of manpower and the demand for food during World War I that forced the small French peasant firmly into the orbit of the market for almost the first time. See Lefebvre, <u>Études sur la Révolution française</u>, pp. 256ff; Weber, <u>Peasants into Frenchmen</u>; G. Wright, <u>Rural Revolution in France</u>. Stanford, 1964; J. Pautard, <u>Les disparités régionales dans la croissance de l'agriculture française</u>. Paris, 1965; Fondation Nationale des Sciences Politiques (FNSP), <u>L'Univers politique des paysans</u>. Paris, 1972.

65. Carson, <u>Latvia</u>, I pp. 117-118.

66. The variety of contractual arrangements was great: small renters (<u>affitti</u>), share tenants on permanent farmhouse units (mezzadri), share tenants not provided with either buildings or equipment (coloni), and sharecroppers (compartecipnati). This is a reminder of the complexities of structure that can exist in any one country. In Italy there are several Norths and many Souths: see S.G. Tarrow, <u>Peasant Communism in Southern Italy</u>. New Haven, 1967, pp. 31-32, 291-292, and the review of this book by N. Kogan in <u>American Political Science Review</u> 62 (1968), pp. 1282-1283; also V. Lutz, <u>Italy: A Study in Economic Development</u>. London, 1962, Ch. 5; G.H. Hildebrande, <u>Growth and Structure of the Economy of Modern Italy</u>. Cambridge, Mass., 1965; G. Schacter, <u>The Italian South: Economic Development in Southern Europe</u>. New York, 1965; Silverman, "Patronage and Community-Nation Relationships"; P.A. Allum, <u>Politics and Society in Post-War Naples</u>. Cambridge, 1973, pp. 19-32, 42-58.

67. Malefakis, <u>Agrarian Reform</u>, Chs. 2-3.

68. Warriner, <u>The Economics of Peasant Farming</u>, p. 50; I.T. Sanders, <u>Balkan Village</u>. Lexington, Ky, 1949, pp. 105-106.

69. See <u>Technical and Economic Changes in Danish Farming. 40 Years of Farm Records, 1917-1957</u>. Copenhagen 1959.

70. See A. Herz, "The Case of an East European Intelligentsia". Journal of Central European Affairs 11 (1951), pp. 10-26.

71. Moreover, the landless left at a greater rate. In industrialized countries with large estates, such as Germany, this ironically created a labour shortage. On the steady decline of agricultural workers, see P. Quante, Die Abwanderung aus der Landwirtschaft. Kiel, 1958; also C. van Deenen, Materialen auf Arbeitwirtschaft. Bonn, 1964; Wunderlich, Farm Labor in Germany, pp. 41-46.

72. Mitrany, Marx Against The Peasant, p. 115.

73. Stoianovich, "The Social Foundations of Balkan Politics", pp. 330-331.

74. See Gerschenkron, Economic Backwardness, p. 9. Bulgaria also had to cope with heavy reparations payments as a consequence of supporting the losing side in World War I: L. Pasvolsky, Bulgaria's Economic Position. Washington, 1930, p. 116.

75. The same is true of Spain and Southern Italy: see for example J. Costadoat-Lamargue, La Question agraire en Andalousie. Paris, 1922, pp. 103-119.

76. Zweig, Poland Between Two Wars, p. 126.

77. Even though after 1945 Finland attempted to accommodate the influx of Karelian refugees by pioneering new farmsteads in the northern forests: see W.R. Mead, "The Cold Farm in Finland, Resettlement of Finland's Displaced Farmers". Geographical Review 41 (1951), pp. 529-543.

78. See, for instance, R.E. Dickinson, "The Geography of Commuting in Western Germany", Annals of the Association of American Geographers 49 (1959), pp. 443-456; H. Seidal et al, Die regionale Dynamik der österreichischen Wirtschaft. Vienna, 1966, pp. 27ff.

79. The argument has many supporters: see H. Kötter, Landbevölkerung im soziale Wandel. Düsseldorf, 1958; J. Saville, Rural Depopulation in England and Wales, 1851-1951. London, 1957; M. Gervais et al, Une France sans paysans. Paris, 1965; H. Mendras, La fin des paysans. Paris, 1968. A useful general survey of modern agricultural developments can be found in M. Tracey, Agriculture in Western Europe: Crisis and Adaptation since 1880. London, 1964.

Chapter 3

1. D. Thornley, "Historical Introduction", in B. Chubb, The Government and Politics of Ireland. Stanford, 1970, p. 13.

2. For völkish-national antisemitism in the late nineteenth century German countryside, and within the agrarian party (Bund der Landwirte) of the period, see H.R. Puhle, <u>Agrarische Interessenpolitik und preussischer Konservatismus im Wilhelmischen Reich</u>. Berlin, 1967, pp. 125-140.

3. Stearns, <u>European Society in Upheaval</u>, p. 103. In particular, they lacked the ability to focus their resentment. The importance of such awareness for the crystallization of revolutionary sentiments is suggested by J.S. Macdonald, "Agricultural Organization, Migration and Labour Militancy in Rural Italy". <u>Economic History Review</u> 2 series, 16 (1963), pp. 61-75. By contrast, it is worth noting that when O'Connell first induced a sense of political consciousness into the Irish peasantry in the nineteenth century, their major concern was with political issues such as Catholic emancipation and repeal of the Union, neither of which was calculated directly or immediately to ameliorate land and labour conditions in rural Ireland: see Norman, <u>History of Modern Ireland</u>, p. 18.

4. A most apt comment on the failure of subsequent French revolutions to generate much rural support was made by G. Chaffard, <u>Les Orages de mai</u>. Paris, 1968, p. 10, who points out that the unrest of 1968 failed completely to penetrate deeply the "leathery tissue" of rural France. Smith, <u>Victor Emanuel</u>, Ch. 10, illustrates this point quite clearly in his analysis of the parallel but unrelated peasant revolts and political revolution in Sicily during Garibaldi's conquest of the island: see also K.R. Greenfield, <u>Economics and Liberalism in the Risorgimento</u>. Baltimore, 1965, pp. 263-267, 285-287; R. Grew, <u>A Sterner Plan for Italian Unity</u>. Princeton, 1963, pp. 233-234, 442-464.

5. The Fasci Siciliani were spontaneous groups of peasants and workers who attempted both to withhold their labour and to occupy the common lands. They were quickly repressed by the proprietors who were strongly supported by the government under Crispi: see D.M. Smith, <u>Italy: A Modern History</u>. Ann Arbor, 1959, p. 173. Andalusia is discussed by G. Brenan, <u>The Spanish Labyrinth</u>. Cambridge, 1943, pp. 140-162. See also Hobsbaum, <u>Primitive Rebels</u>, Chs 5-6. J.S. Macdonald & L. Madconald, "Institutional Economics and Rural Development: Two Italian Types". <u>Human Organization</u> 23 (1964), pp. 113-118, suggestively attempt to explain the militancy of the Southern Italian peasantry during this period by analyzing separately the various status sub-dimensions of the society.

6. The populist beliefs of the narodnichestvo simply involved a hegemony of the masses over the privileged elites. See the useful semantic summary in A. Walicki, "Russia", in G. Ionescu & E. Gellner (eds), <u>Populism: Its National Characteristics</u>. London, 1969, pp. 62-96; also the general definition offered by P. Wiles, "A Syndrome, Not A Doctrine: Some Elementary Theses on Populism", in <u>ibid</u>, p. 166 - populism is any creed or movement based on the major premiss that "virtue resides in the simple people, who are the overwhelming majority, and in their

collective traditions". See also the major study by F. Venturi, Roots of Revolution: A History of the Populist and Socialist Movements in Nineteenth-Century Russia. London, 1960; also Mitrany, Marx Against The Peasant, Ch. 4; B.M. Pešelj, "Peasantism: Its Ideology and Achievements", in Black, Challenge in Eastern Europe, pp. 109-131.

7. C.A. Macartney, October 15th, A History of Hungary 1929-1945. New York, 1956, I p. 12; Macartney, The Hapsburg Empire, p. 671; Seton-Watson, Eastern Europe Between The Wars, p. 42.

8. G.G. Arnakis, "The Role of Religion in the Development of Balkan Nationalism", in Jelavich & Jelavich, The Balkans in Transition, pp. 115-144; R.L. Wolff, The Balkans in Our Time. Cambridge, Mass., 1956, pp. 71-74; R.R. Florescu, "The Uniate Church: Catalyst of Rumanian National Consciousness". Slavonic and East European Review 45 (1967), pp. 334-337. The role of the Orthodox priests here contrasts markedly to the hierarchy's attitude in Greece itself, especially in the early nineteenth century: see N. Mouzalis & M. Attalides, "Greece", in Archer & Giner, Contemporary Europe, pp. 168-169. The role of the Catholic Church in nineteenth century Ireland offers striking parallels.

9. Except perhaps where protest evolved into "organized" banditry: see Hobsbaum, Primitive Rebels; A. Blok, "On brigandage with special reference to peasant mobilization". Sociologia neerlandica 8 (1972), pp. 1-13.

10. E. Rumpf. Nationalismus und Sozialismus in Ireland. Meisenheim, 1959, pp. 68-71. The same is true of the earlier anti-tithe movement of the 1830s, which was dominated by the wealthier Catholic tenant farmers, who may be described as the rural middle class of the period: see Norman, History of Modern Ireland, pp. 94-95.

11. Rokkan, "Geography, Religion, and Social Class", p. 371. For a critique of Rokkan's centre-periphery model of Norway by a Norwegian historian see J.A. Seip, "Modellens Tyranni: Analyse av Stein Rokkans anvendelse av en sentrum-periferi modell på norsk historie". Paper at the Nordic Conference on Methodology in History, Röros, 1974. On peasant protests see also P.A. Munch, "The Peasant Movement in Norway: A Study in Class and Culture". British Journal of Sociology 5 (1954), pp. 173-210; Österud, "Agrarian Structure and Peasant Politics".

12. The Vendée has been well-documented. See the excellent historical and sociological studies by Tilly, The Vendée, especially pp. 67-79, 114-125; and Bois, Paysans de l'Ouest, especially pp. 610-617. More generally, see Moore, Social Origins, pp. 70-92.

13. See M. Bloch, Les caractères originaux de l'histoire rurale française. Paris, 1955, I pp. 120-154; Lefebvre, Études sur la

Révolution française, pp. 232-242; and Lefebvre, Les paysans du Nord, pp. 911-916.

14. Hobsbaum, Primitive Rebels, p. 68; C. Seton-Watson, Italy from Liberalism to Fascism 1870-1925. London, 1969, p. 189; Tarrow, Peasant Communism, p. 277.

15. See A. Mayer (ed), Hundert Jahre Österreichischer Wirtschaftsentwicklung. Vienna, 1949.

16. Brenan, The Spanish Labyrinth, pp. 140-162; Malefakis, Agrarian Reform, pp. 137-139.

17. Roberts, Rumania, Ch. 1; Mitrany, The Land and the Peasant. An intensification of antisemitic sentiments in the countryside was a widespread phenomenon.

18. Malefakis, Agrarian Reform, p. 5.

19. An excellent summary of the cumulation of problems and grievances in Russia, one of the more backward regions of Europe, is B. Brutzkus, "The Historical Peculiarities of the Social and Economic Development of Russia", in R. Bendix & S.M. Lipset (eds), Class, Status, and Power. Glencoe, 1953, pp. 517-540.

20. K.R. Cox & G.J. Demko, "Conflict Behavior in a Spatio-Temporal Context". Sociological Focus 1 (1968), pp. 55-67; M. Perrie, "The Russian Peasant Movement of 1905-1907: Its Social Composition and Revolutionary Significance". Past and Present 57 (1972), pp. 123-155.

21. H. Böker & F. von Bölow, Die Landpfluchte in der Tchechoslowakei. Geneva, 1935, p. 177.

22. Dovring, Land and Labor in Europe, pp. 61-79.

23. A point emphasized by F.W. Riggs, "Agraria vs Industria: Toward a Typology of Comparative Administration", in W.J. Sifflin (ed), Towards a Comparative Study of Public Administration. Bloomington, 1959, p. 37.

24. An excellent overview of the problems involved is Linz, "Patterns of Land Tenure", pp. 412-423.

25. The history of the Bund der Landwirte is described in Puhle, Agrarische Interessenpolitik; see pp. 37-45 for its membership, pp. 72-110 for its programme, and pp. 165-212 for its political activity. See also S.R. Tirrell, German Agrarian Politics after Bismarck's Fall. New York, 1951; Rosenberg, "Die Pseudo-demokratisierung der Rittergutsbesitzerklasse", pp. 287-308; K.E. Born, "Der sozial und wirtschaftliche Strukturwandel Deutschlands am Ende des 19. Jahrhundert", in Wehler, Moderne

deutsche Sozialgeschichte, pp. 277ff; Borchardt, "The Industrial Revolution in Germany", pp. 125-128; H. Booms, Die Deutschkonservative Partei: Preussischer Charakter, Reichsauffassung, Nationalbegriff. Düsseldorf, 1954.

26. See the outstanding analysis of G. Carlsson, Lantmannapolitiken och industrialismen. Partigruppering och oppinionsförskytningar i svensk politik 1890-1902. Stockholm, 1953; also Wallin, Valrörelser och valresultat; T. Vallender, I kamp för demokratien. Rösträttsrörelsen i Sverige 1886-1890. Stockholm, 1962; J. Svensson, Jordbruk och depression 1870-1900. Lund, 1965; Nedelmann, "Zur Parteientstehung in Schweden", pp. 209-236.

27. See A. Gerschenkron, "Notes on the Rate of Industrial Growth in Italy, 1881-1913". Journal of Economic History 15 (1955), p. 368; A. Kahan, "Nineteenth-Century European Experience with Policies of Economic Nationalism", in H.G. Johnson (ed), Economic Nationalism in Old and New States. Chicago, 1967, pp. 17-30.

28. Good accounts of the Prussian electoral system and its effects are T. Nipperdey, Die Organisation der deutschen Parteien vor 1918. Düsseldorf, 1961; H. Boberach, Wahlrechtsfrage im Vormärz. Die Wahlrechtsanschauung im Rheinland 1815-1849 und die Entstehung des Dreiklassenwahlrechts. Düsseldorf, 1959.

29. Stoianovich, "The Social Foundations of Balkan Politics", p. 322.

30. K.E. Miller, The Government and Politics of Denmark. Boston, 1968, pp. 32-33.

31. D.W. Crowley, "The Crofters' Party, 1885-1892". Scottish Historical Review 35 (1956), pp. 110-126.

32. Weber, Peasants into Frenchmen, Ch. 15; Annuaire statistique de la République française 1910, p. 11; P. Barral, Les agrariens français de Méline à Pisani. Paris, 1958, p. 81. On an earlier period, A. Tudesq, Les conseilleurs généraux en France au Temps de Guizot 1840-1848. Paris, 1967, shows the little effect manhood suffrage had upon the control of these public offices by small town notables. A great influx of working peasants into either politics or cooperatives did not occur until the 1930s: see the careful histories in Barral, Les agrariens français; Wright, Rural Revolution in France.

33. Annuaire statistique de la République Polonaise 1924, p. 199.

34. On the spread of agricultural machinery 1875-1900, see Milward & Saul, Economic Development of Continental Europe, pp. 212-213.

35. L. Jörberg, "The Nordic Countries 1850-1914", in Cipolla, The Emergence of Industrial Societies, II pp. 393-406; K. Bjerke

& N. Ussing, Studier over Danmarks nationalprodukt 1870-1950. Copenhagen, 1958, p. 52; also E. Jensen, Danish Agriculture: Its Economic Development. Copenhagen, 1937.

36. C.K. Warner, The Winegrowers of France and the Government since 1875. New York, 1960.

37. E. Jutikkala, Bonden i Finland genom tiderna. Helsinki, 1963, pp. 386ff.

38. Stoianovich, "The Social Foundations of Balkan Politics", p. 329. Furthermore, agriculture on the eastern estates was usually more dependent upon the production of grain, which by its nature needed huge armies of ploughmen and harvesters for only limited periods of the year.

39. G.A. Almond & S. Verba, The Civic Culture. Princeton, 1963.

40. Dovring, Land and Labor in Europe, Ch. 5.

41. Some basic works on French agriculture are M. Augé-Laribé, La politique agricole de la France de 1880 à 1940. Paris, 1950; Barral, Les agrariens français; Wright, Rural Revolution in France. Some of Barral's theses have been recently criticized by P. Gratton, Les Luttes de classes dans les campagnes. Paris, 1971. See also J. Fauvet & H. Mendras (eds), Les paysans et la politique. Paris, 1958. A recent important case study of Finistère is S. Berger, Peasants Against Politics. Cambridge, Mass., 1972.

42. Seton-Watson, Italy from Liberalism to Fascism, p. 88. In the Po valley syndicalism was beginning to appeal to agricultural workers: see also Silverman, "Agricultural Organization"; Linz, "Patterns of Land Tenure", pp. 412-423.

43. See F. Skrubbeltrang & K. Hansen, Det danske landbruges historie. Copenhagen, 1945; H. Faber, Cooperation in Danish Agriculture. London, 1931.

44. Norman, History of Modern Ireland, p. 226.

45. Jörberg, "The Nordic Countries", p. 471.

46. Some approximate figures on the number of cooperatives and the size of their membership over time are given in Dovring, Land and Labor in Europe, pp. 201-210. These data, however, are incomplete.

47. Wright, Rural Revolution in France, p. 21.

48. See Wright, Rural Revolution in France, Ch. 2; M. Augé-Laribé,

Syndicats et coopératives agricoles. Paris, 1938. G. Hunter, Peasantry and Crisis in France. London, 1938, claims membership of one million families for the Right associations by 1914, and 600,000 for the Left. But Augé-Laribé, La politique agricole de la France, p. 136, argues that there were no more than half a million in toto. The Church was also prominent in establishing cooperatives, especially in Brittany after 1900: Wright, Rural Revolution in France, pp. 24-25, 37-39. One writer found that even recently in Brittany the cooperative movement worked best at the local level if it consisted of young, committed Catholics or of members of a single extended family: E. Morin, Une commune en France. Paris, 1967, pp. 116-120.

49. See H. Goldberg, The Life of Jean Jaurès. Madison, 1961, pp. 179-194; C. Landauer, "The Guesdists and the Small Farmer: Early Erosion of French Marxism". International Review of Social History 6 (1961), pp. 212-225; G. Dupeux, Le Front Populaire et les élections de 1936. Paris, 1959, pp. 103-117, 149-171; Stearns, European Society in Upheaval, p. 335; Linz, Patterns of Land Tenure", pp. 418-421.

50. Mitrany, Marx Against The Peasant, p. 113; L. Feirabend, "Land Reform and Agricultural Improvement", in Black, Challenge in Eastern Europe, p. 97; Zweig, Poland Between Two Wars, pp. 124-129, 155-157.

51. Dovring, Land and Labor in Europe, p. 198.

52. Feirabend, "Land Reform", p. 96.

53. See for instance, Wolff, The Balkans in Our Time, p. 173.

54. Wolff, The Balkans in Our Time, pp. 170-176.

55. M. Pernot, Balkans nouveaux. Paris, 1929, p. 232; J. Lefarge, Martyrdom of Slovenia. New York, 1942, pp. 13-14.

56. On Poland, Buell, Poland, p. 215; Zweig, Poland Between Two Wars, pp. 124-129, 155-157. See also Lopreato, Peasants No More, p. 28, on Italy; Maciuika, "Agriculture in Soviet Latvia", pp. 504-519, on Latvia; and more generally, Feirabend, "Land Reform"; Warriner, The Economics of Peasant Farming.

57. R.L. Heilbroner, The Making of Economic Society. Englewood Cliffs, 1962, pp. 63-64.

58. J.P. Nettl, Political Mobilization. London, 1967, p. 70.

Chapter 4

1. L.W. Milbrath, *Political Participation*. Chicago, 1965, p. 18. On the meaning of participation see also M. Weiner, "Political Participation: Crisis of the Political Process", in L. Binder *et al*, *Crises and Sequences in Political Development*. Princeton, 1971, pp. 159-204. The question of thresholds is discussed in Lipset & Rokkan, *Party Systems*, pp. 26-33; S. Rokkan, *Citizens, Elections, Parties*. New York, Chs. 1, 3.

2. K. Marx, *The Eighteenth Brumaire of Louis Napoleon*. New York, 1957, p. 109.

3. J.G. Thompson, *Urbanization*. New York, 1927, pp. 322-340; W. Woytinsky, *Die Welt in Zahlen*. Berlin, 1926.

4. See for example, two "classics": Lipset, *Political Man*, Ch. 6; B. Berelson *et al*, *Voting*. Chicago, 1954, especially pp. 336-337.

5. See especially Rokkan, "Electoral Mobilization", pp. 241-265; S. Rokkan & H. Valen, "The Mobilization of the Periphery", in S. Rokkan (ed), *Approaches to the Study of Political Participation*. Bergen, 1962, pp. 111-159; also T. Hjellum, "The Politicization of Local Government: Rates of Change, Conditioning Factors, Effects on Political Culture". *Scandinavian Political Studies* 2 (1967), pp. 69-93.

6. Thompson, *Urbanization*, p. 332.

7. Rokkan & Valen, "The Mobilization of the Periphery, pp. 114-119, 134-141; Rokkan, "Geography, Religion, and Social Class", pp. 378-386; *Forbudsavstemingen av 18 oktober 1926*. Oslo, 1927.

8. See H. Tingsten, *Political Behaviour*. London, 1937, pp. 10-12; Rokkan, "Electoral Mobilization", p. 261; B. Särlvik, "Sweden: The Social Bases of the Parties in a Developmental Perspective", in Rose, *Electoral Behavior*, pp. 390-391.

9. E. Högh, *Vaelgeradferd i Danmark 1849-1901: en politisk og sociologisk analyse*. Copenhagen, 1972; also J. Jeppesen & P. Meyer, *Sofavaelgerne: Valgdeltagelsen ved danske folketings-valg*. Aarhus, 1964.

10. Tingsten, *Political Behaviour*, pp. 19-21.

11. Tingsten, *Political Behaviour*, pp. 21-24; also E. Allardt & K. Bruun, "Characteristics of the Finnish Non-voter", *Transactions of the Westermarck Society* 3 (1956), pp. 55-76.

12. *Élections à la Saeima de la République Lettonie en 1925*. Riga, 1926, p. 3.

13. Eesti statistika. Tallinn, 1923; Eesti statistika. Tallinn, 1933.

14. Statistique des élections effectuée le 5 et le 12 novembre 1922. Warsaw, 1923, p. viii; Statistique des élections effectuée le 4 et le 11 mars 1926. Warsaw, 1928, p. xxxviii.

15. Chubb, The Government and Politics of Ireland, p. 332.

16. Calculated from the mass of data in R. Steifbold et al, Wahlen und Parteien in Österreich. Vienna, 1966, vol. III.

17. Annuaire statistique de la Belgique 1924-1925, p. 72. In the contemporary period there has been no decisive pattern of urban-rural differences: see Annuaire statistique de la Belgique 1967. But in the Netherlands the highest turnouts now tend to be in the rural districts, and the lowest in the largest cities: see Statistiek der Verkiezingen 1967. Hague, 1967, p. 14.

18. G. Di Palma, Apathy and Participation: Mass Politics in Western Society. New York, 1970, pp. 132-133.

19. See S.G. Tarrow, "The Urban-Rural Cleavage in Political Involvement: The Case of France". American Political Science Review 65 (1971), pp. 341-357; J. Meynaud & A. Lancelot, La participation des français à la politique. Paris, 1965.

20. H. Gosnell, Why Europe Votes. Chicago, 1930, pp. 140-141.

21. There is no good general study of electoral trends in Germany. A pertinent discussion can be found in E. Faul, Wahlen und Wähler in Westdeutschland. Villingen, 1960, pp. 156-161; also Tingsten, Political Behaviour, pp. 88, 137-138; K.D. Bracher, Die Auflösung der Weimarer Republik. Villingen, 1960. The Federal Republic of Germany after 1949 has evidenced no unambiguous differences between urban and rural turnout levels.

22. Calculated from the data in F.W.S. Craig (ed), British Parliamentary Election Results 1918-1949. Glasgow, 1969.

23. See H. Abraham, Compulsory Voting. Washington, 1955.

24. See Rokkan & Valen, "The Mobilization of the Periphery"; Tingsten, Political Behaviour, pp. 18-20, 88.

25. Calculated from the data in Stiefbold et al, Wahlen und Parteien in Österreich.

26. Lipset, Political Man, p. 184.

27. See for example, W. Mattes, Die bayerischen Bauernrate.

Eine soziologische und historische Untersuchung über bauerliche Politik. Stuttgart, 1921; E. Banfield, The Moral Basis of a Backward Society. Glencoe, 1958; Högh, Vaelgeradferd i Danmark.

28. Jeppesen & Meyer, Sofavaelgerne, p. 51.

29. E. Reigrotzki, Soziale Verflechtungen in der Bundesrepublik. Tübingen, 1956, pp. 63-68; J.J. Linz, "The Social Bases of West German Politics". Doctoral dissertation, Columbia University, 1959, p. 747.

30. See the outstanding analysis of political developments in Schleswig-Holstein by R. Heberle, From Democracy to Nazism. Baton Rouge, 1945; also on Lower Saxony by G. Franz, Die politische Wahlen in Niedersachsen, 1867 bis 1949. Bremen, 1957; on Bavaria by Mattes, Die bayerischen Bauernrate; and the more localized analysis of E.M. Wallner, Die Reichstags- und Bundestagswahlen im Landkreis Freiburg seit der Jahrhundertwende. Buhl, 1965.

31. See the comments in Rokkan, Citizens, Elections, Parties, p. 91.

Chapter 5

1. R.R. Alford, Party and Society. Chicago, 1963, pp. 79-80.

2. Tarrow, Peasant Communism, pp. 67-68. A forceful argument on the great variations within the South is the review of Tarrow's book by N. Kogan in American Political Science Review 62 (1968), pp. 1282-1283. See also G. Wright, "Agrarian Syndicalism in Postwar France". American Political Science Review 47 (1953), p. 415.

3. A. Campbell et al, The American Voter. New York, 1960, p.403.

4. Examples of the first approach are Alford, Party and Society; Lipset, Political Man; Rose, Electoral Behavior: of the second, R. Rose & D.W. Urwin, "Social Cohesion, Political Parties and Strains in Regimes". Comparative Political Studies 2 (1969), pp. 7-67.

5. This chapter was prepared before the publication of the extensive article by Juan Linz, "Patterns of Land Tenure". It seemed pointless to pursue the subject at any greater length because of the wealth of detail in Linz's study: those who wish to consider agrarian political behaviour in more depth, especially in South-West Europe, should refer to this excellent article.

6. See FNSP, Tradition et Changement en Toscane. Paris, 1970,

especially R. Nouat, "La société paysanne", pp. 59-83, and
J. Besson, "Comportements électoraux et politique", pp. 331-401;
G. Braga, Sociologia elettorale della Toscana. Rome, 1963;
Seton-Watson, Italy from Liberalism to Fascism, pp. 303ff;
G. Galli & A. Prandi, Patterns of Political Participation in
Italy. New Haven, 1970, pp. 58-64; Linz, "Patterns of Land
Tenure", pp. 402-412.

7. Tarrow, Peasant Communism, p. 187.

8. Paige, Agrarian Revolution.

9. G. Mammarella, Italy After Fascism. South Bend, 1966,
pp. 37-41; C.F. Delzell, Mussolini's Enemies: The Italian Anti-
Fascist Resistance. Princeton, 1961, pp. 219-220; M. Grindrod,
The Rebuilding of Italy. London, 1955, p. 18.

10. Tarrow, Peasant Communism, pp. 205-208, 221-225; M. Dogan,
"Political Cleavages and Social Stratification in France and
Italy", in Lipset & Rokkan, Party Systems, pp. 129-195.

11. See H.W. Ehrmann, "The French Peasant and Communism".
American Political Science Review 56 (1952), pp. 19-43;
J. Fauvet, La France déchirée. Paris, 1957, pp. 86-89;
S. Derruau-Boniol, "Le Département de la Creuse, structure
sociale et évolution". Revue française de science politique 7
(1957), pp. 38-66; also Y. Tavernier, "Le mouvement de
coordination et de défence des exploitations agricoles
familiales". Revue française de science politique 18 (1968),
pp. 542-563; FNSP, L'Univers politique des paysans, especially
D. Derivry, "Analyse écologique du vote paysan", pp. 131-162,
and P. Gaborit, "Le Parti communiste français et les paysans",
pp. 197-222.

12. Noted by B.M.E. Leger, Les opinions politiques des provinces
françaises. Paris, 1934.

13. S.R. Schram, Protestantism and Politics in France. Alençon,
1954, pp. 172-218; also G. Wright, "Catholics and the Peasantry
in France", Political Science Quarterly 68 (1953), pp. 526-551.
L. Wylie, Village in the Vaucluse. Cambridge, Mass., 1964,
pp. 218-220, found a similar orientation among the Communist
voters in his small village.

14. Lipset, Political Man, pp. 231-234. Evidence from several
countries seems to suggest that this is a general cross-national
phenomenon.

15. S. Rydenfelt, Kommunismen i Sverige. Lund, 1954.

16. E. Allardt, "Social Sources of Finnish Communism:
Traditional and Emerging Radicalism". International Journal of
Comparative Sociology 5 (1964), pp. 47-70; and his "Patterns of

Class Conflict and Working Class Consciousness in Finnish Politics", in E. Allardt & Y. Littunen (eds), <u>Cleavages, Ideologies and Party Systems</u>. Helsinki, 1964, pp. 97-131.

17. See O.H. Radkey, <u>The Election to the Russian Constituent Assembly of 1917</u>. Cambridge, Mass., 1950.

18. See Page, <u>Formation of the Baltic States</u>; also U. Germanis, "The Idea of Independent Latvia", pp. 58ff; W.S. Hanchett, "The Communists and the Latvian Countryside, 1919-1949", in Sprudzs & Rūsis, <u>Res Baltica</u>, pp. 88-90.

19. R.V. Burks, <u>The Dynamics of Communism</u>. Princeton, 1961, pp. 54-78, 131-149.

20. See Mattes, <u>Die bayerischen Bauernraten</u>, pp. 66-113, 191-192; F.L. Carsten, <u>Revolution in Central Europe 1918-1919</u>. London, 1972, pp. 178-209; A. Mitchell, <u>Revolution in Bavaria 1918-1919</u>. Princeton, 1965.

21. These developments are described in detail in Rokkan, "Geography, Religion, and Social Class"; S. Rokkan, "Norway: Numerical Democracy and Corporate Pluralism", in Dahl, <u>Political Oppositions</u>, pp. 70-115; S. Rokkan & H. Valen, "Regional Contrasts in Norwegian Politics", in Allardt & Littunen, <u>Cleavages, Ideologies and Party Systems</u>, pp. 162-238.

22. S.S. Nilson, "Wahlsoziologische Probleme des National-sozialismus". <u>Zeitschrift für die gesamte Staatswissenschaft</u> 110 (1954), pp. 279-311.

23. See the synthesis in Linz, "Patterns of Land Tenure", pp. 396-398.

24. A. Siegfried, <u>Tableau Politique de la France de l'Ouest sous la Troisième République</u>. Paris, 1913, pp. 243-247.

25. Linz, "Patterns of Land Tenure", pp. 416-417.

26. Booms, <u>Die Deutsch-Konservative Partei</u>; Puhle, <u>Agrarische Interessenpolitik</u>.

27. E. Krehbiel, "Geographic Influences in British Elections", <u>Geographical Review</u> 2 (1961), pp. 419-432.

28. D.W. Urwin, "The Development of the Conservative Party Organisation in Scotland until 1912". <u>Scottish Historical Review</u> 44 (1965), pp. 89-111.

29. Siegfried, <u>Tableau Politique</u>, p. 374.

30. Tarrow, Peasant Communism, p. 187. On the structure of these large settlements, see A. Blok, "The South Italian Agro-Town". Comparative Studies in Society and History 11 (1969), pp. 121-135.

31. Macdonald, "Agricultural Organization"; Tarrow, Peasant Communism; G.F. Ciaurro, "Movimento migratori e scelte politiche", in M. Dogan & O.M. Petracca (eds), Partiti politiche e strutture sociali in Italia. Milan, 1968, pp. 275-351; S.F. Silverman, "'Exploitation' in Rural Central Italy: Structure and Ideology in Stratification Study". Comparative Studies in Society and History 12 (1970), pp. 327-339; Malefakis, Agrarian Reform; Brenan, Spanish Labyrinth pp. 114-123, 140-160.

32. Radkey, Election to the Russian Constituent Assembly.

33. Heberle, From Democracy to Nazism, pp. 90-120.

34. Siegfried, Tableau Politique, p. 378; A. Szymanski, "Fascism, Industrialism and Socialism: The Case of Italy". Comparative Studies in Society and History 15 (1975), pp. 395-404.

35. Heberle, From Democracy to Nazism; F.M. Snowden, "On the Social Origins of Agrarian Fascism in Italy". European Journal of Sociology 13 (1972), pp. 268-295.

36. V. Capecchi et al, Il comportamento elettorale in Italia. Bologna, 1968, pp. 119-130. Other data suggest an increasing polarization in the 1950s, with both the Christian Democrats and Communists increasing in strength in the most agricultural communes: C. Barberis & G. Corazziari, "Strutture economiche e dinamica elettorale", in Dogan & Petracca, Partiti politiche, pp. 423-425.

37. Linz, "Patterns of Land Tenure", p. 413.

38. Siegfried, Tableau Politique.

39. Heberle, From Democracy to Nazism, p. 101.

40. See Wright, Rural Revolution; Y. Tavernier, La F.N.S.E.A.. Paris, 1965.

41. Whyte, "Ireland", pp. 632-633.

42. J. LaPalombara, Interest Groups in Italian Politics. Princeton, 1964, pp. 235-246; R. Zariski, Italy: The Politics of Uneven Development. Hinsdale, 1972, pp. 206-207; J.P. Chasseriaud, Le parti democrat chrétien en Italie. Paris, 1965, p. 262.

43. H.W. Ehrmann, Le Mouvement Poujade. Paris, 1956, pp. 194-201, 333-341.

44. Rokkan, "Electoral Mobilization", p. 249.

45. Tingsten, Political Behaviour, Ch. 1; H. Cantril, Public Opinion, 1935-1946. Princeton, 1951, pp. 688-689; D.A. Rustow, The Politics of Compromise. Princeton, 1955, pp. 91-101. The two wings of the Liberals were reunited in 1934. On Estonia see R.C. Heffner (ed), The Estonians. New Haven, 1954.

46. The past and continuing importance of the religion-temperance-language nexus in rural Norway is demonstrated in Valen & Rokkan, "Norway"; F.H. Aarebrot & D.W. Urwin, "The Politics of Cultural Dissent: Religion, Language and Demonstrative Action in Norway". Scandinavian Political Studies, new series 2 (1979), pp. 75-98.

47. Siegfried, Tableau Politique, pp. 181-194; Wright, "Catholics and the Peasantry"; also J. Klatzman, "Géographie électoral de l'agriculture française", pp. 39-67, and J. Labbens, "L'Église Catholique et l'expression politique du monde rurale", pp. 327-343, in Fauvet & Mendras, Les paysans et la politique.

48. Hill, "Belgium", p. 85.

49. Burks, Dynamics of Communism, pp. 42, 54-57, 74-76. See also the analysis of the various Communist strategies and attempts through the Krestintern to mobilize the East European peasantry in the 1920s in Jackson, Comintern and Peasant.

50. R.V. Burks, "Catholic Parties in Latin Europe". Journal of Modern History 24 (1952), p. 279.

51. See M. Anderson, Conservative Politics in France. London, 1974, pp. 100-110.

52. Rumpf, Nationalismus und Sozialismus, pp. 48-92; also Chubb, Government and Politics of Ireland, pp. 78-85.

53. See S.A. Rice, Farmers and Workers in American Politics. New York, 1924; J.O. Hicks, The Populist Revolt. Minneapolis, 1931; C.B. Macpherson, Democracy in Alberta. Toronto, 1953; S.M. Lipset, Agrarian Socialism. Berkeley/Los Angeles, 1950.

54. J. Fauvet, "La répresentation politique du monde paysan", in M. Duverger (ed), Partis politiques et classes sociales en France. Paris, 1955, pp. 155-157.

55. P. Bernard, Économie et sociologie de la Seine-et-Marne 1850-1950. Paris, 1953, pp. 181-184; also P. George, Géographie économique et sociale de la France. Paris, 1946, pp. 71-72.

56. See C.T. Schmidt, The Plough and the Sword: Labor, Land and Property in Fascist Italy. New York, 1938, p. 7.

57. Gosnell, *Why Europe Votes*, pp. 134-135.

58. Linz, "Patterns of Land Tenure", p. 427.

59. Heberle, *From Democracy to Nazism*, pp. 46-47.

60. Quoted in Mitrany, *Marx Against The Peasant*, p. 18.

61. Quoted in Carsten, *Revolution in Central Europe*, p. 180.

62. Galli & Prandi, *Patterns of Political Participation*, pp. 183-188.

63. R. Hofstadter, *The Age of Reform: From Bryan to FDR*. New York, 1955, p. 58.

Chapter 6

1. Huntington, *Political Order*, p. 394.

2. R.A. Dahl, *Preface to Democratic Theory*. Chicago, 1956, pp. 90-123.

3. M. Duverger, *Political Parties*. London, 1954, p. 294.

4. On parties as modern organizations see LaPalombara & Weiner, *Political Parties*, pp. 3-4.

5. Lipset & Rokkan, *Party Systems*, pp. 41-46. Many commentators have noted the strong urban-rural links in English society and have drawn similar inferences.

6. See A.D. Rees, *Life in a Welsh Countryside*. Cardiff, 1950; K.O. Morgan, *Wales in British Politics*. Cardiff, 1963; K. Cox, "Geography, Social Contexts and Voting Behavior in Wales, 1861-1951", in E. Allardt & S. Rokkan (eds), *Mass Politics*. New York, 1970, pp. 127-143.

7. The politics of interwar Eastern Europe has been largely neglected in comparative political studies. A good general survey is J. Rothschild, *East Central Europe between the Two World Wars*. Seattle, 1974: also valuable is the older work of Seton-Watson, *Eastern Europe*.

8. A good review is LaPalombara & Weiner, *Political Parties*, pp. 8-21. The model developed by Lipset & Rokkan is an interesting attempt to link these three approaches.

9. However, we should note the brief (and successful) appearance of the Crofters' Party in Scotland: Crowley, "The

Crofters' Party".

10. On the BP see A.T.J. Nooij, "Political Radicalism among Dutch Farmers". <u>Sociologia Ruralis</u> 9 (1969), pp. 43-61, and "Radical Dutch Farmers", <u>Sociologia neerlandica</u> 7 (1971), pp. 28-41. During the 1967-1971 Parliament the BP split into four factions: the three "secessionist" groups lost all their seats in 1971.

11. On the Bund der Landwirte see Puhle, <u>Agrarische Interessenpolitik</u>; Tirrell, <u>Agrarian Politics</u>; Gerschenkron, <u>Bread and Democracy</u>. On post-1918 Germany see Mattes, <u>Die bayerischen Bauernraten</u>, pp. 36-50, 66-93; Mitchell, <u>Revolution in Bavaria</u>; L. Hertzman, <u>DNVP: Right Wing Opposition in the Weimar Republic</u>. Lincoln, 1963; Heberle, <u>From Democracy to Nazism</u>.

12. See Wright, <u>Rural Revolution</u>, pp. 49-55, 116-117; Barral, <u>Les agrariens français</u>, pp. 237-240.

13. Lopreato, <u>Peasants No More</u>, p. 28.

14. See A. Antenen, <u>Die Agrarpolitik des schweizerischen landwirtschaftlichen Verbände und ihre Stellung in Staat und Wirtschaft</u>. Winterthur, 1959; B. Junker, <u>Die Bauern auf dem Wege zur Politik</u>. Bern, 1968.

15. The Agrarians have been described as a "parliamentary amalgam, improvised from disparate political forces": R.A.H. Robinson, "The Parties of the Right and the Republic", in R. Carr (ed), <u>The Republic and the Civil War in Spain</u>. London, 1971, p. 53.

16. See S.Skendi, <u>The Albanian National Awakening</u>. Princeton, 1967.

17. Compare, for example, the account of I.T. Sanders, <u>Rainbow in the Rock</u>, Cambridge, Mass, 1962, with that of J. Pitt-Rivers, <u>The People of the Sierra</u>. New York, 1955.

18. See J.K. Campbell, <u>Honour, Family and Patronage</u>. Oxford, 1964; E. Friedl, "The Role of Kinship in the Transmission of National Culture to Rural Villages in Mainland Greece". <u>American Anthropologist</u> 61 (1959), pp. 30-38; Mouzalis & Attalides, "Greece", pp. 172-175.

19. This is a basic theme of all Stein Rokkan's research on Norway. But it should be reiterated that important cultural divisions in Scandinavia between town and countryside reinforced the peasantry's economic protests. See also Thompson, <u>English Landed Society</u>; Nipperdey, <u>Die Organisation der deutschen Parteien</u>; Siegfried, <u>Tableau Politique</u>.

20. Peselj, "Peasantism", p. 109.

21. The nationalist role of the Polish aristocracy is discussed in R.F. Leslie, <u>Polish Politics and the Revolution of November 1830</u>. London, 1956; and his <u>Reform and Insurrection in Russian Poland 1856-1865</u>. London, 1963. Hungarian efforts are covered in Macartney, <u>The Hapsburg Empire</u>. It should be noted that the aristocracy had been permitted to consolidate their position by being given many privileges in their own territories. The Hungarian landed magnates won autonomy in 1867, while in Galicia the Poles were favourably treated by the Hapsburgs who regarded their support as vital against the large Ukrainian population and a possible Russian threat. In Congress Poland however, the Russians proceeded to destroy almost all Polish autonomy after the abortive 1863 uprising.

22. I. Deak, "Hungary", in H. Rogger & E. Weber (eds), <u>The European Right</u>. Berkeley/Los Angeles, 1965, pp. 367-368: see also Stoianovich, "The Social Foundations of Balkan Politics", pp. 326-330.

23. Buell, <u>Poland</u>, p. 239; Polonsky, <u>Politics in Independent Poland</u>, p. 41; Rothschild, <u>East Central Europe</u>, p. 35.

24. Rothschild, <u>East Central Europe</u>, p. 10.

25. Wolff, <u>The Balkans in Our Time</u>, pp. 103-105. More than most this party was originally inspired by the writings of the narodni, as filtered through the ideas of Constantin Stere, a Bessarabian nobleman who argued that it was too late for a Rumanian state to industrialize: instead, it should aim for a rural democracy in which there would only be a "craft industry" located in the villages and peasant households. A good summary of Stere's philosophy can be found in Roberts, <u>Rumania</u>.

26. Stoianovich, "The Social Foundations of Balkan Politics", p. 336.

27. Mitrany, <u>Marx Against The Peasant</u>, p. 103: see also Tomasevich, <u>Peasants, Politics, and Economic Change</u>; E. Shils, "The Intellectuals in the Political Development of the New States", in Kautsky, <u>Political Change</u>, pp. 195-234; H. Seton-Watson, <u>Neither War Nor Peace</u>. New York, 1962.

28. J.S. Roucek, <u>Balkan Politics</u>. Stanford, 1948, pp. 49-54.

29. F.W. Riggs, "Bureaucrats and Political Development: A Paradoxical View", in J. LaPalombara (ed), <u>Bureaucracy and Political Development</u>. Princeton, 1963, pp. 120-167.

30. Roucek, <u>Contemporary Roumania</u>, pp. 78-79; Roberts, <u>Rumania</u>, p. 20. French influences had been strong in the Regat (the Old Kingdom of Moldavia and Wallachia) since 1798. The nineteenth-century nationalists were often described as "the French party".

31. See the major study by Venturi, Roots of Revolution: also Ionescu & Gellner, Populism; Mitrany, Marx Against The Peasant; Jackson, Comintern and Peasant, especially pp. 40-48.

32. J. Rothschild, The Communist Party of Bulgaria. New York, 1959, pp. 165-168; K. Todorov, Balkan Firebrand. New York, 1943, pp. 218-222. Radić's application had in any case imposed "impossible" conditions upon Moscow: that his party did not endorse revolution; that the peasantry, not the proletariat, were "the chosen people" in Yugoslavia; that Croatia would be a peasant republic; and that the Krestintern would be independent of the Comintern.

33. Rudolf Herceg, a leader of the party, argued in Marxist terms that history had been a story of minority usurpation of majority rights. For him, however, the peasantry were the chosen people: even in the Soviet Union their revolution would follow that of the workers. See R. Herceg, Die Ideologie der Kroatischen Bauernbewegung. Zagreb, 1923; also Tomasevich, Peasants, Politics, and Economic Change, pp. 254-260; D. Tomašić, "Ideologies and the Structure of Eastern European Society". American Journal of Sociology 53 (1947-48), pp. 367-375.

34. See the analysis of speeches and manifestos in Roberts, Rumania, pp. 142-156. A failure to recognise (or at least stress) this change of emphasis mars the two important reviews of peasantism by Pešelj, "Peasantism"; and Mitrany, Marx Against The Peasant.

35. O.H. Radkey, The Agrarian Foes of Bolshevism. New York, 1958, p. 3; also J.S. Roucek, The Politics of the Balkans. New York, 1939, p. 124. Another author has suggested that peasantism appealed most in those areas marked by an egalitarian agrarian structure: Tomašić, Personality and Culture, pp. 209-213.

36. Roberts, Rumania, p. 165; Tomasevich, Peasants, Politics, and Economic Change, p. 258.

37. Roberts, Rumania, p. 147.

38. Heberle, From Democracy to Nazism; also G. Stoltenberg, Politische Strömungen im schleswig-holsteinischen Landvolk 1918-1933. Düsseldorf, 1962; Franz, Die politische Wahlen in Niedersachsen; M. Hagman, Der Weg ins Verhängnis. Reichstagswahlergebnisse 1919 bis 1933, besonders aus Bayern. Munich, 1946, pp. 27-88; C.P. Loomis & J.A. Beegle, "The Spread of German Nazism in Rural Areas". American Sociological Review 11 (1946), pp. 726-727; E. Schmahl, Entwicklung der völkischen Bewegung. Giessen, 1933; Bracher, Die Auflösung der Weimarer Republik; J.K. Pollock, "An Areal Study of the German Electorate, 1930-1933". American Political Science Review 38 (1944), pp. 89-95; C.J. Friedrich, "The Agricultural Basis of Emotional Nationalism". Public Opinion Quarterly 1 (1937), pp. 50-61.

39. Schmidt, The Plough and the Sword, pp. 34-38; also Snowden, "Social Origins of Agrarian Fascism", which analyzes fascist support before the March on Rome; and Szymanski, "Fascism, Industrialism and Socialism", for an ecological analysis of the relationship between fascist violence and rural Socialist strength.

40. See S.B. Clough, A History of the Flemish Movement in Belgium. New York, 1930; A. Willemsen, Het Vlaamse Nationalisme 1914-40. Groningen, 1958; R. Pfeiffer & J. Ladrière, L'aventure Rexiste. Brussels, 1966; J-M. Étienne, Le mouvement Rexiste jusqu'en 1940. Paris, 1968; F.L. Carsten, The Rise of Fascism. Berkeley/Los Angeles, 1967, pp. 206-216; J. Stengers, "Belgium", in Rogger & Weber, The European Right, pp. 152-157.

41. See K. Fröland, Krise og kamp. Oslo, 1962.

42. See Wright, Rural Revolution; L. Gabriel-Robinet, Dorgères et le Front Paysan. Paris, 1937; Anderson, Conservative Politics in France, Ch. 4; Hunter, Peasantry and Crisis, pp. 245-248. One observer claimed that the Front Paysan drew its support primarily from wealthier farmers: W.R. Sharp, The Government of the Third Republic. New York, 1938, p. 333. Similarly, in the 1950s many peasants supported the Poujadists: Hoffman, Le Movement Poujade, pp. 58-60.

43. See L. Jedlicka, "The Austrian Heimwehr". Journal of Contemporary History 1 (1966), pp. 127-144; D. Strong, Austria (October 1918-March 1919): Transition from Empire to Republic. New York, 1939; M. Macdonald, The Republic of Austria 1918-1934. London, 1946; E. Hoor, Österreich, 1918-1938: Staat ohne Nation, Republik ohne Republikaner. Vienna, 1966; H. Anders, Der Staat den Keiner wollte. Vienna, 1962. The relationship between the army and politics is explored by L. Jedlicka, Ein Heer im Schatten der Parteien. Graz, 1955, especially Ch. 3.

44. E. Weber, "Romania", in Rogger & Weber, The European Right, p. 545. An English translation of its programme is in S. Fischer-Galati (ed), Twentieth-Century Europe: A Documentary History. Philadelphia, 1956, pp. 137-140.

45. RIIA, The Baltic States, pp. 48-55; Jackson, Estonia, pp. 188-196; G. von Knorring, "Krisenjahr in Estland", Baltische Hefte 8 (1962), pp. 86-95; J. von Hehn, Lettland zwischen Demokratie und Diktatur. Munich, 1957; Parming, The Collapse of Liberal Democracy.

46. For the origins of the Ustashe, its policies and actions, and later control of a puppet regime in Croatia, see L. Hory & M. Broszat, Der Kroatische Ustasche-Staat 1941-1945. Stuttgart, 1964. The statement on Czechoslovakia clearly does not include the German minority and also perhaps Slovakia: see E. Wiskemann, Czechs and Germans. London, 1938; J.W. Bruegel, Czechoslovakia Before Munich. London, 1973, pp. 110-146.

47. International Reference Library, Politics and Political Parties in Rumania. London, 1936, pp. 147-148.

48. Wolff, The Balkans in Our Time, p. 102: see also the biographical study by C. Jelavich, "Nikola P. Pašić: Greater Serbia or Yugoslavia?". Journal of Central European Affairs 16 (1956), pp. 133-151.

49. A.C. Janos, "The One-Party State and Social Mobilization: East Europe Between The Wars", in S.P. Huntington & C.H. Moore (eds), Authoritarian Politics in Modern Society. New York, 1970, pp. 204-236.

50. Stoianovich, "The Social Foundations of Balkan Politics", p. 318.

51. See Tarrow, Peasant Communism, pp. 322-332; Chasseriaud, Le parti democrat chrétien, pp. 325-343.

52. "The sharp separation between town and country, the inability of burghers and agricultural people to enter into each other's interests and points of view ... was one of the fundamental differences between Eastern Europe on the one hand, and Western Europe and North America on the other": Palmer, Age of the Democratic Revolution, p. 414.

53. The foro was a common form of lease in Galicia which became the subject of centuries of litigation and conflict among the titular owners, the foreros (tenants) and subforados (subtenants). The rabassaires were medium peasants who sharecropped land on what had been rabassa morta (dead vine) leases: Malefakis, Agrarian Reform, pp. 108-126.

54. A good introduction to the historical background of social divisions in Spain is R.M. Pidal, The Spaniards in Their History. New York, 1966. Malefakis, Agrarian Reform, is indispensable for politics and agriculture. The religious factor is traced in J.C. Ullman, The Tragic Week: A Study of Anticlericalism in Spain 1875-1912. Cambridge, Mass., 1968; J.M. Sańchez, The Politico-Religious Background of the Spanish Civil War. Chapel Hill, 1962. For the movement of centres of economic growth to the peripheries see J. Gentil da Silva, En Espagne, développement économique, subsistence, déclin. Paris, 1965. For peripheral nationalisms, see S.G. Payne, "Catalan and Basque Nationalism". Journal of Contemporary History 6 (1971), pp. 15-51; J.J. Linz, "Early State-Building and Late Peripheral Nationalisms against the State. The Case of Spain", in Eisenstadt & Rokkan, Building States and Nations, II pp. 32-116; P. Gonzalez Blasco, "Modern Nationalism in Old Nations as a Consequence of Earlier State-Building: The Case of Basque Spain", in W. Bell & W.E. Freeman (eds), Ethnicity and Nation-Building. London/Beverly Hills, 1974, pp. 341-373; J.J. Linz & A. de Miguel, "Within-Nation Differences and Comparisons: The Eight Spains", in R.L. Merritt & S. Rokkan (eds), Comparing Nations. New Haven, 1966, pp. 267-319. Mention

must also be made of the massive and brilliant study of
Catalonia by P. Vilar, La Catalogne dans l'Espagne moderne.
Paris, 1962. On Andalusia and anarchism see Brenan, Spanish
Labyrinth; H. Thomas, "Anarchist Agrarian Collectives in the
Spanish Civil War", in Carr, The Republic and the Civil War,
pp. 239-256. On the First Republic see C.A.M. Hennessy, The
Federal Republic in Spain: Pi y Margall and the Federal
Republican Movement, 1968-1874. Oxford, 1962, especially
pp. 200-206.

55. Malefakis, Agrarian Reform, Chs. 7, 10; J.J. Linz, "The
Party System of Spain: Past and Future", in Lipset & Rokkan,
Party Systems; R.A.H. Robinson, The Origins of Franco's Spain.
Newton Abbot, 1970, pp. 25, 46-57, 155-156, 373. In addition to
a concern with wheat prices, many Agrarian representatives could
be described as ex-Monarchist Catholics. The cooperatives in
these Agrarian strongholds were established between 1910 and
1930 by Catholic priests.

56. See D.W. Urwin, "Germany: Continuity and Change in Electoral
Politics", in Rose, Electoral Behavior, pp. 109-170.

57. These developments have been most succinctly summarized for
Norway by Rokkan, "Norway", pp. 74-79, and his "Geography,
Religion, and Social Class". The most comprehensive study of
language in Norway is E. Haugen, Language Conflict and Language
Planning: The Case of Modern Norwegian. Cambridge, Mass., 1966.

58. A good comparative study of the folk high schools is
E. Simon, Réveil national et culture populaire en Scandinavie.
Paris, 1960: see also A.J. Youngson, Overhead Capital.
Edinburgh, 1967; K.A. Eliassen & M. Pedersen, "Political
Mobilization, Democratization and the Transformation of Political
Elites in Norway and Denmark". Paper at the European Consortium
for Political Research workshop on Recruitment, Careers and
Attitudes of Legislators, Mannheim, 1973.

59. For Sweden, see Wallin, Valrörelser och valresultat;
Vallender, I kamp för demokratie; E. Thermaenius, Lantmanna-
partiet. Dess uppkomst, organisation och tidigare utveckling.
Uppsala, 1928; Carlsson, Lantmannapolitiken och industrialismen;
Nedelmann, "Zur Parteientstehung in Schweden"; D. Verney,
Parliamentary Reform in Sweden 1866-1921. Oxford, 1957. On
Denmark, see P. Salomonsen, Den politiske magtkamp 1866-1901.
Copenhagen, 1968; V. Dybdahl, Partier og erhverv, 1880-1893.
Aarhus, 1969. On Norway see A. Kaartvedt, Kampen mot
parlamentarisme. Oslo, 1967; L. Svåsand, "Stortingsvalget i 1882:
en analyse av geografiske og ökonomiske konfliktlinjer".
Dissertation, University of Bergen, 1972, Ch. 4; Aasland, Fra
Landmannsorganisasjon til Bondeparti, Chs. 10-13; Rokkan,
"Geography, Religion, and Social Class".

60. Cox, "Geography, Social Contexts and Voting Behavior": also
Morgan, Wales in British Politics, pp. 245-255.

61. Aasland, Fra Landmannsorganisasjon til Bondeparti, Chs. 8,13.

62. See Junker, Die Bauern auf dem Wege zur Politik, pp. 9-32, 60-120; also Antenen, Die Agrarpolitik; H. Brugger, Schweizerischer landwirtschaftlicher Verein 1863-1963. Zürich, 1963; B. Junker & R. Maurer, Kampf und Verantwortung: Bernische Bauern-, Gewerbe- und Bürgerpartei 1918-1968. Bern, 1968. The BGB was originally the result of a Radical split in Bern, and at first was active only in that canton.

63. R. Melson & H. Wolpe, "Modernization and the Politics of Communalism: A Theoretical Perspective". American Political Science Review 64 (1970), p. 1119.

64. As outlined for example in A. Rabushka & K.A. Shepsle, Politics in Plural Societies: A Theory of Democratic Instability. Columbus, 1972, p. 66.

65. Roucek, Contemporary Roumania, pp. 61-65. This was also true of the Rumanians and Ukrainians who adopted the Uniate religion after the sixteenth century: see J. Mirtshuk, "The Ukrainian Uniate Church". Slavonic Review 10 (1931-32), pp. 377-385. See also Clough, History of the Flemish Movement, pp. 103-107, 251-252; Brenan, Spanish Labyrinth, pp. 206-211.

66. A. Ramos Oliviera, Politics, Economics and Men of Modern Spain. London, 1946, p. 420. See also G. Jackson, The Spanish Republic and the Civil War. Princeton, 1965, pp. 141-142; S.G. Payne, "Spain", in Rogger & Weber, The European Right, p. 174; Linz, "Early State-Building". See also the comments on Bavaria in K. Schwend, Bayern zwischen Monarchie und Diktatur. Munich, 1954; and on Alsace-Lorraine in D.P. Silverman, Reluctant Union. University Park, Pa, 1972; F.G. Dreyfus, La vie politique en Alsace 1919-1936. Paris, 1969; S. Bonnet, Sociologie politique et religieuse de la Lorraine. Paris, 1972; Anderson, Conservative Politics in France, pp. 110-116.

67. H. Daalder, "The Netherlands: Opposition in a Segmented Society", in Dahl, Political Oppositions, p. 208.

68. J. Cornford, "The Transformation of Conservatism in the Late Nineteenth Century". Victorian Studies 7 (1963), pp. 35-66.

69. See A. Lugan, Une oeuvre belge: Origine et organisation du Boerenbond. Paris, 1925; A. Melot, Le parti catholique en Belgique. Louvain, 1933; A. Varzim, Le Boerenbond Belge. Paris, 1934; C.A. Simon, Le parti Catholique Belge 1830-1945. Brussels, 1958.

70. See D. Miller, Church, State and Nation in Ireland 1898-1921. Dublin, 1974; J.H. Whyte, Church and State in Modern Ireland, 1923-1970. Dublin, 1971; E. Larkin, "Economic Growth, Capital Investment and the Catholic Church in Nineteenth Century Ireland".

American Historical Review 72 (1967), pp. 852-884; J. Blanchard, The Church in Contemporary Ireland. Dublin, 1963; W. Moss, Political Parties in the Irish Free State. New York, 1933; T. Garvin, "Political Cleavages, Party Politics and Urbanization in Ireland: the Case of the Periphery-Dominated Centre". European Journal of Political Research 2 (1974), pp. 307-328.

71. On specialized groups, see Warner, The Winegrowers of France; B. Brown, "Alcohol and Politics in France". American Political Science Review 61 (1957), pp. 976-990; Wright, Rural Revolution; Tavernier, La F.N.S.E.A.. On the JAC see the account of its secretary-general, M. Debatisse, La révolution silencieuse: le combat des paysans. Paris, 1963; also J. Meynaud, Les groupes de pression. Paris, 1958, pp. 672-697.

72. R.A. Webster, The Cross and the Fasces. Stanford, 1960, pp. 3-23.

73. M.W. Graham, New Governments of Central Europe. London, 1924, p. 186. The Slovenes were forced to emigrate to Yugoslavia. Anton Rinelen, Land governor and leader of the Christian Socialists in Styria, said that the Landbund provided severe competition for his party: A. Diamant, Austrian Catholics and the First Republic. Princeton, 1960, p. 76; E. Wienzierl, "Das österreichische Staatsbewusstsein", in E. Wienzierl (ed), Der Österreichischer und Sein Staat. Vienna, 1965, pp. 15-16. With its entry into a close association with the Heimwehr after 1927, the Landbund split into competing factions over the issue of cooperation in 1929.

74. Gosnell, Why Europe Votes, pp. 134-135; E. Gruner, Die Parteien in der Schweiz. Bern, 1969, pp. 151-154.

75. See Booms, Die Deutsch-Konservative Partei; Hertzman, DNVP, pp. 8-31; D. Hertz-Eicherode, Politik und Landwirtschaft in Ostpreussen 1919-1930. Opladen, 1969; Mattes, Die bayerischen Bauernraten; Mitchell, Revolution in Bavaria.

76. On the Slovak Populists see J.K. Hoensch, Die Slowakei und Hitlers Ostpolitik. Cologne, 1965, pp. 1-77; R. Morrock, "The Rich Peasant in Politics: A Comparative Study of the Slovak People's Party and the Akali Dal". Social Theory and Practice 1 (1971), pp. 11-21; C. Hoch, The Political Parties in Czechoslovakia. Prague, 1936, pp. 28-29.

77. See J.A. Arnez, Slovenia in European Affairs. New York, 1958, pp. 140-155; Macartney, The Hapsburg Empire, p. 645; Pernot, Balkans nouveaux, pp. 232, 321; Wolff, The Balkans in Our Time, p. 120; Tomasevich, Peasants, Politics, and Economic Change, pp. 253-254.

78. Gerutis, "Independent Lithuania", pp. 194-216; Graham, New Governments of Eastern Europe, pp. 376-377; Page, Formation of the Baltic States, pp. 130-134; M. Hellman, "Litauen zwischen

Demokratie und autoritäter Staatsform", in H-E. Volkmann (ed), Die Krise des Parlamentarismus in Ostmitteleuropa zwischen den beiden Weltkrigen. Marburg, 1967, pp. 156-167; also A.E. Senn, The Great Powers, Lithuania and the Vilna Question 1920-1928. Leiden, 1966; J. Stukas, Awakening Lithuania. Madison, 1966. Vilnius was claimed by both Poland and Lithuania on ethnic grounds, though its population was mainly Jewish. The complex fluidity of East European politics are also vividly protrayed by Lithuania. The Farmers' Party (1926) was really a liberal urban faction, while the Peasant Populist Union was a so-called reformist socialist group with an urban base which in practice preached a kind of nineteenth century laissez-faire doctrine. Lithuania was also deprived of Klaipeda (Memel) from 1918 to 1923. The mainly German population of Memel developed its own autonomist party system which included a Memelländische Landwirtschaftspartei and a smaller Lithuanian Peasant Party: Gerutis, "Independent Lithuania", pp. 203-213, 234-238; S. Dauksa, Le Régime d'Autonome du Territoire de Klaipeda. Paris, 1937.

79. Mitrany, Marx Against The Peasant, p. 88; also Tökés, Bela Kun and the Hungarian Soviet Republic, pp. 156-157; Deak, "Budapest and the Hungarian Revolution", p. 135.

80. Macartney, October 15th, I pp. 46-47. On the system of open voting in the countryside after 1920, Deak, "Hungary, pp. 375-376, drily comments: "when necessary, the dead were made to vote in the open ballot areas, and the living were kept away from the polls by gendarmes". See also R. Horvath, "Sociologie Électorale: une Synthèse du Droit Électoral Bourgeois en Hongrie (1848-1939), Essai de Statistique Histoire". L'Année Sociologique 3 (1962), pp. 280-292.

81. Hoch, Political Parties, pp. 17-20; J.S. Roucek, "The Czechoslovak Party System". Journal of Central European Affairs 1 (1942), pp. 428-445.

82. The party was careful to distinguish between anticlericalism and the peasantry's religious commitment. Its leader, Stjepan Radić, sometimes opened his meeting with the declamation, "Praise be to Jesus, down with the clergy!": quoted by Tomasevich, Peasants, Politics, and Economic Change, p. 255; see also pp. 237, 241-242, 258. In the 15 Yugoslav governments between 1929 and 1941, 73 of the 121 ministers were Serbs. In 1938 there were 165 army generals, of whom 161 were Serbs: W.S. Vucinich (ed), Contemporary Yugoslavia. Berkeley/Los Angeles, 1969, pp. 10-11. See also G. Schopflin, "The Ideology of Croat Nationalism". Survey 19 (1973), pp. 123-146; and the memoirs of the peasant leader, V. Maček, In the Struggle for Freedom. New York, 1957.

83. Rothschild, East Central Europe, pp. 28-29.

84. See R.W. Tims, Germanizing Prussian Poland: The H-K-T Society and the Struggle for the Eastern Marches in the German

Empire, 1894-1919. New York, 1941.

85. The National Democrat vote in 1922 was 29.1 per cent, and by region: Eastern Kresy 5.4 per cent; Congress 33.2 per cent; Galicia 18.5 per cent - but in the western areas it was, Silesia 36.5 per cent, Poznan 48.9 per cent, and Pomerania 55.7 per cent. On elections generally, see A. Groth, "Proportional Representation in Prewar Poland". Slavic Review 23 (1964), pp. 103-114.

86. P. Brock, "The Early Years of the Polish Peasant Party, 1895-1907". Journal of Central European Affairs 14 (1954), pp. 219-235; and "Boleslaw Wyslouch, Founder of the Polish Peasant Party". Slavonic and East European Review 30 (1951), pp. 139-163; Graham, New Governments of Eastern Europe, pp. 423-439, 460; G.W. Strobel, "Die parlamentarische Idee und die polnischen Parteien", in Volkmann, Die Krise des Parlamentarismus, pp. 36-63. Voting figures for Piast in 1922 were: nationally 13.2 per cent; west 5.1 per cent; Congress 10.1 per cent; Galicia 32.6 per cent.

87. Polonsky, Politics in Independent Poland, pp. 81-82. Voting figures in 1922 were: nationally 11 per cent; Congress 16 per cent; Kresy 19.3 per cent; Galicia 2.9 per cent; west 0.1 per cent. There were numerous other peasant groups in the 1920s ranging from a right-wing Catholic Peasant Party through ethnic parties to a few Communist groups: all were generally insignificant in support and influence.

88. See for example the comments by A. Diamant, Austrian Catholics, pp. 21-23; Silverman, Reluctant Union, Chs. 5-6. The distinction between the social and political challenges is not new, and was often recognized by Catholic writers, who seemed to be more concerned with the problems arising from the expansion of financial capitalism and the market economy.

89. G. Sartori, "The Sociology of Parties: A Critical Review", in O. Stammer (ed), Party Systems, Party Organization, and the Politics of New Masses. Berlin, 1968, p. 22.

90. The most brilliant analysis of this theme is the study of the SPD during the Second Reich by G. Roth, The Social Democrats in Imperial Germany. Totowa, 1963, who demonstrates that in a political system with a powerful and expanding bureaucracy, other organizations which opposed the bureaucracy were nevertheless forced to copy it and organize themselves in a similar manner.

Chapter 7

1. Siegfried, Tableau Politique. The most thorough empirical analysis is Rose & Urwin, "Social Cohesion".

2. In the canton of Bern The BGB has frequently been the only active party in many small rural communities: see J. Steiner, Die Beziehungen zwischen den Stimmberechtigen und den Gewählten in ländlichem und städtlichem Milieu. Bern, 1959.

3. Thomas, Parliamentary Parties in Denmark, pp. 61-63.

4. Albania experienced turbulent political activity after independence, but the general absence of party competition on a more or less regularized basis means that its politics are excluded here: see Skendi, The Albanian National Awakening; J. Swire, The Rise of a Kingdom. London, 1929; J.S. Roucek, "Characteristics of Albanian Politics". Social Science 10 (1935), pp. 71-79.

5. The various facets and meanings of integration are discussed in M. Weiner, "Political Integration and Political Development", in J.L. Finkle & R.W. Gabel (eds), Political Development and Social Change. New York, 1971, pp. 643-654; Urwin, "Political Parties".

6. Tomasevich, Peasants, Politics, and Economic Change, pp. 237,252; Roucek, The Politics of the Balkans, p. 69; Jelavich, "Nikola P. Pašić"; Wølff, The Balkans in Our Time, p. 106; Mitrany, Marx Against The Peasant, pp. 239-240. An outstanding literary portrayal of the nature and identity of Serb-Croat antagonisms is R. West, Black Lamb and Grey Falcon. New York, 1940.

7. Rothschild, East Central Europe, p. 341.

8. Wolff, The Balkans in Our Time, p. 132; Rothschild, The Communist Party of Bulgaria, pp. 8-9; Jackson, The Comintern and Peasant, pp. 42-43, 59-66, 165-171; Jousse, Les Tendances des réformes agraires, p. 55; Bouroff, La réforme agraire en Bulgarie, p. 106; Seton-Watson, Eastern Europe, pp. 242-256. One follower said of Stamboliski, "He is a prophet. He leads us to Canaan, but we have to clear the way ourselves": quoted by Todorov, Balkan Firebrand, p. 155. A journalistic account which captures something of the flavour of the turbulence of Bulgarian politics is J. Swire, Bulgarian Conspiracy. London, 1939. See also E. Barker, Macedonia: Its Place in Balkan Power Politics. London, 1950.

9. H. Ingulfson & R. Hagman, "De Svenska Partiernas Sociala och Andra Grundvaler", in E. Håstad (ed), 'Gallup' och den Svenska Väljarkåren. Uppsala, 1950, p. 156. L. Lewin et al, The Swedish Electorate, 1887-1968. Stockholm, 1972, point to the dominance of vertical mobilization (each party having its own "class"), with horizontal mobilization being almost non-existent.

10. The Agrarians established an organization in Tampere only in 1939: P. Pesonen, An Election in Finland. New Haven, 1969, pp. 36,46.

11. Lewin et al, The Swedish Electorate, pp. 149-156, 171-172, 189-204; Ingulfson & Hagman, "De Svenska Partiernas Sociala och Andra Grundvaler", p. 174; N. Andren, Modern Swedish Government. Stockholm, 1961, pp. 28-29; also G. Hellström, Föreningsdemokrati och förtroendemannakår. Halmstad, 1964; N. Elvander, Intresseorganisationerna i dagens Sverige. Lund, 1966.

12. Aasland, Fra Landmannsorganisasjon til Bondeparti, pp. 63-69, 87-89; Rokkan & Valen, "Regional Contrasts in Norwegian Politics"; Valen & Rokkan, "Norway", pp. 341, 351-353; Rokkan, "Geography, Religion, and Social Class", pp. 396-412.

13. RIIA, The Baltic States, pp. 45-58; Jackson, Estonia, pp. 123-124, 156, 179; Page, The Formation of the Baltic States, p. 9; Parming, The Collapse of Liberal Democracy. The Latvian Peasant Union was much more conservative than its Estonian counterpart, and even displayed fascist tendencies.

14. Roberts, Rumania, pp. 67-68, 141; Wolff, The Balkans in Our Time, pp. 103-105; Roucek, Contemporary Roumania, pp. 91-96; C.A. Macartney, Hungary and Her Successors. London, 1937, pp. 269-275, 331-334. Here too the ethnic minorities formed their own parties.

15. J. Chmelar, Political Parties in Czechoslovakia. Prague, 1926, pp. 31-38; Rapport de l'Office de la République Tchechoslovaque 1925, pp. 539-542; K. Witt, Wirtschaftskräfte und Wirtschaftspolitik der Tchechoslowakei. Leipzig, 1936; Hoch, Political Parties, pp. 17-20; P.E. Zinner, Communist Strategy and Tactics in Czechoslovakia, 1918-1948. New York, 1963, p. 139; L.E. Textor, "Agriculture and Agrarian Reform", in R.J. Kerner (ed), Czechoslovakia. Berkeley/Los Angeles, 1945, p. 230; S. Grant Duff, Europe and the Czechs. London, 1938, p. 114.

16. Chmelar, Political Parties, p. 54.

17. On the Sudetenland see Wiskemann, Czechs and Germans; also R. Luža, The Transfer of the Sudeten Germans: A Study of Czech-German Relations 1933-1962. London, 1964.

18. In the central administration of Ruthenia in 1935, 696 of the 967 positions were occupied by Czechs, and only 133 by Ruthenes: Macartney, Hungary, p. 225; H. Wanklyn, Czechoslovakia. New York, 1954, p. 412; also Hoch, Political Parties, pp. 51-57, on the complex party system of Ruthenia and the shifting nature of alliances with the Czech parties.

19. Macartney, Hungary, pp. 94, 133-134; R.W. Seton-Watson (ed), Slovakia Then and Now. London, 1931, p. 30; J. Hajda (ed), Czechoslovakia. New Haven, 1955, p. 69; W. Kolarz, Myths and Realities in Eastern Europe. London, 1946, p. 145. A positive history of Slovakia is J. Lettrich, History of Modern Slovakia. New York, 1955: more negative are J.A. Mikuš, Slovakia, A Political History: 1918-1950. Milwaukee, 1963; J.M. Kirschbaum

(ed), Slovakia in the Nineteenth and Twentieth Centuries. Toronto, 1973.

20. Moss, Political Parties, pp. 39-40; Chubb, Government and Politics of Ireland, pp. 83-87.

21. Polonsky, Politics in Independent Poland, p. 102. Poorer cultivators, especially in ex-German Poland, were more susceptible to religious and nationalist influences.

22. On the decline in agrarian support for the Centre, see the data in Pesonen, "Finland", p. 295.

23. Allardt & Pesonen, "Cleavages in Finnish Politics", pp. 342-343; Pesonen, "Finland", p. 307; O. Rantala, "The Political Regions of Finland". Scandinavian Political Studies, 2 (1967), p. 126.

24. Wiskemann, Czechs and Germans, pp. 131-132, 160.

24. Tomasevich, Peasants, Politics, and Economic Change, p. 252; Stoianovich, "The Social Foundations of Balkan Politics", p. 317. It is interesting to note that the Radical Party, formed in the 1870s by disciples of Russian utopian socialism, had by the close of the 1880s become a militant peasantist movement: but it very quickly became urban-dominated, and identified with Serbian nationalism: see H. Seton-Watson, The East European Revolution. New York, 1956, p. 27.

26. Buell, Poland, pp. 245-248; Polonsky, Politics in Independent Poland, p. 7; S. Horak, Poland and Her National Minorities 1919-1939. New York, 1961, p. 35; W.J. Rose, The Drama of Upper Silesia. London, 1936, pp. 180-181.

27. Allardt & Pesonen, "Cleavages in Finnish Politics", pp. 343-344; Knoellinger, Labor in Finland, p. 65. This was also a characteristic feature of the two French agrarian parties: D. MacRae, Parliament, Parties, and Society in France 1946-1958. London, 1967, p. 135.

28. Huntington, Political Order, pp. 427ff; S. Verba, Small Groups and Political Behavior. Princeton, 1961, Chs. 6-7; Urwin, "Political Parties", pp. 194-197. In his discussion of American parties, conventionally regarded as the best examples of parties drawing support from numerous social groups, T. Lowi, "Party, Policy and Constitution in America", in W.N. Chambers & W.D. Burnham (eds), The American Party Systems. New York, 1967, p. 258, stresses that party behaviour determines the political saliency of social characteristics at any one time.

29. Mitrany, Marx Against The Peasant, pp. 131-133; Seton-Watson, The East European Revolution, p. 35; Wolff, The Balkans in Our Time, p. 105.

30. Calculated from data in International Political Reference Library, Politics and Political Parties in Rumania, pp. 395ff.

31. They displayed many of the characteristics suggested as typical of the intelligentsia of developing countries in Shils, "Intellectuals in Political Development".

32. Roberts, Rumania, pp. 90-91.

33. A. Omelianov, "A Bulgarian Experiment", in Sorokin et al, A Systematic Source Book in Rural Sociology, II p. 641.

34. See the data in Rokkan "Geography, Religion, and Social Class", p. 426; Valen & Rokkan, "Norway", pp. 351-353.

35. See Tomasevich, Peasants, Politics, and Economic Change, pp. 256-257, on how such developments affected the Croat Peasants.

36. Rothschild, East Central Europe, pp. 19-20.

37. R. Rose & D.W. Urwin, "Persistence and Change in Western Party Systems since 1945". Political Studies 18 (1970), pp. 287-319, which also includes a detailed discussion of the measures employed; D.W. Urwin & R. Rose, "Persistence and Disruption in Western Party Systems Between The Wars". Paper at the World Congress of the International Sociological Association, Varna, 1970.

38. E.E. Schattschneider, The Semi-Sovereign People, New York, 1960, Ch. 4.

39. U. Torgersen, "The Trend Towards Political Consensus: The Case of Norway", in Allardt & Rokkan, Mass Politics, pp. 95-96; Miller, Government and Politics of Denmark, pp. 70-79; Thomas, Parliamentary Parties in Denmark, p. 61; H. Wislander (ed), De politiska partiernas program. Stockholm, 1964, p. 39; Särlvik, "Sweden", pp. 373, 393.

40. See the excellent theoretical discussion in P.E. Converse, "Of Time and Partisan Stability". Comparative Political Studies 2 (1969), pp. 139-171; E.A. Nordlinger, "Political Development: Time Sequences and Rates of Change", in E.A. Nordlinger (ed), Politics and Society. Englewood Cliffs, 1970, pp. 329-347.

Chapter 8
1. For a discussion of these points and a review of the literature, see Urwin, "Political Parties".

2. A. Downs, An Economic Theory of Democracy. New York, 1957.

3. G. Sjöblom, Party Strategies in a Multiparty System. Lund, 1968, especially pp. 267-268; also Dahl, Political Oppositions, Chs. 11-13.

4. Knoellinger, Labor in Finland, pp. 22-27.

5. See O. Nyman, Svensk parlamentarism 1932-1936. Från minoritetsparlamentarism till majoritetskoalition. Uppsala, 1947; also Rustow, The Politics of Compromise, pp. 104-109.

6. The best analysis of governments and coalitions after 1945 is O. Ruin, Mellan samlingsregering och tvåpartisystem. Stockholm, 1968. See also Elvander, Intresseorganisationerna; Rustow, The Politics of Compromise, pp. 144-152; Stjernquist, "Sweden", pp. 124-141; M.D. Hancock, Sweden: The Politics of Postindustrial Change. Hinsdale, 1972, pp. 132-137.

7. J. Björgum, Venstre og kriseforliket. Landbrukspolitikk og parlamentarisk spill 1934-1935. Oslo, 1970; K.D. Jacobsen, "Public Administration under Pressure: The Role of the Expert in the Modernization of Traditional Agriculture". Scandinavian Political Studies 1 (1966), pp. 59-93; Landbruketssentralforbund, Norwegian Agriculture and its Organizations. Oslo, 1966; Aasland, Fra Landmannsorganisasjon til Bondeparti, Ch. 8; also S. Rokkan & A. Campbell, "Factors in the Recruitment of Active Participants in Politics: A Comparative Analysis of Survey Data for Norway and the United States". International Social Science Bulletin 12 (1960), pp. 69-99; H. Valen & D. Katz, Political Parties in Norway. Oslo, 1964.

8. E. Damgaard, "Party Coalitions in Danish Law-Making 1953-1970". European Journal of Political Research 1 (1973), pp. 35-66; also RIIA, The Scandinavian States and Finland. London, 1951, pp. 28-30; Miller, Government and Politics of Denmark, p. 50.

9. Knoellinger, Labor in Finland, Chs. 5-6; J. Nousiainen, The Finnish Political System. Cambridge, Mass., 1971, Chs. 2, 6; P. Nyholm, "Parliament, Government and Multi-Dimensional Party Relations in Finland", Commentationes Scientiarum Socialium 2 (1972), pp. 21-31; P. Pesonen, "Dimensions of Political Cleavage in Multi-Party Systems". European Journal of Political Research 1 (1973), pp. 109-132; also A. Mazour, Finland Between East and West. New York, 1956. The land reform law (Lex Kallio) was named after the Agrarian leader.

10. A. Lijphart, "Typologies of Democratic Systems". Comparative Political Studies 1 (1968), pp. 3-44; also his The Politics of Accommodation. There is now a wide literature on the subject: see the review in H. Daalder, "The Consociational Democracy Theme". World Politics 26 (1974), pp. 604-621.

11. Such as Bern, Basel-Land, Aargau, Thurgau, Schaffhausen, Zürich, Freiburg and Vaud. See Gruner, Die Parteien in der Schweiz; G. Lehmbruch, Proporzdemokratie. Tübingen, 1967; Junker, Die Bauern auf dem Wege zur Politik; R. Girod, "Le système des partis en Suisse". Revue française de science politique 14 (1964), pp. 1114-1133. The BGB may in many ways be described as the party of Bern. In addition to always supplying the party's member of the Federal Council, the general secretary has always been the general secretary of the cantonal party: even so, it has tended to win less than one-third of the Bern vote, and over one-half of the party's members come from other cantons.

12. J. Borovička, Ten Years of Czechoslovak Politics. Prague, 1929, p. 108.

13. J.S. Roucek, "The Working of Czechoslovak Constitutional Democracy". World Affairs Interpreter 8 (1937), pp. 157-167; M.W. Graham, "Parties and Politics", in Kerner, Czechoslovakia, pp. 137-170; Chmelar, Political Parties; Borovička, Ten Years of Czechoslovak Politics; Hoch, Political Parties; E. Taborsky, Czechoslovak Democracy At Work. London, 1945; Grant Duff, Europe and the Czechs; Zinner, Communist Strategy, Ch. 1; Bruegel, Czechoslovakia Before Munich, pp. 74-85.

14. As early as May 1919, a party conference resolved "to take up contacts with the peasantry of the other nation": quoted in Bruegel, Czechoslovakia Before Munich, p. 35. This was the first expression by a German party of a wish to cooperate actively in the new state.

15. See Weiner, "Political Integration". Deutsch, Nationalism and Social Communication, pp. 18-21, draws attention to the importance of the dependence of the integration of a society upon the degree of homogeneity or differentiation in the recruitment of elites. Alternatively, the process may be described as empire-building rather than nation-building, according to G. Roth, "Personal Leadership, Patrimonialism and Empire-Building in the New States". Paper at the World Congress of the International Sociological Association. Evian, 1966.

16. See Janos, "The One-Party State and Social Mobilization"; Polonsky, Politics in Independent Poland; von Hehn, Lettland zwischen Demokratie und Diktatur; von Knorring, "Krisenjahr in Estland"; Parming, The Collapse of Liberal Democracy; J. Rothschild, Pilsudski's Coup d'État. New York, 1966.

17. M. Mirković, Održanje Seljačkog Posjeda. Zagreb, 1937, p. 106, quoted in Tomasevich, Peasants, Politics, and Economic Change, p. 259.

18. Wolff, The Balkans in Our Time, p. 105.

19. Quoted in Polonsky, Politics in Independent Poland, p. 53.

20. The party that won an election usually had previously agreed upon an electoral alliance with some small parties. These normally did not enter the government, but were content with enjoying some of the ensuing patronage. The small German party, for instance, was almost always allied with the victorious party.

21. An analysis of the policies of the various National Liberal, People's and National Peasant governments between 1920 and 1930 demonstrates a basic continuity: F.E. Manoliou, La Réconstruction économique et financière de la Roumanie et les partis politiques. Paris, 1931: also Roberts, Rumania, pp. 155-161. Similarly, foreign banks possessed a virtual monopoly of commercial and industrial credit in Bulgaria: Pasvolsky, Bulgaria's Economic Position.

22. J.S. Roucek (ed), Slavonic Encyclopaedia. New York, 1949, pp. 505-510; Maček, In the Struggle for Freedom, pp. 80-81.

23. Rothschild, East Central Europe, p. 32. The Piast leader, Witos, regarded himself as a realist. Like the Czechoslovak leader, Svehla, he saw compromise as the only way of achieving objectives: Markert, Polen, pp. 37-42, 74; also Polonsky, Politics in Independent Poland; P. Brock, "The Politics of the Polish Peasant". International Review of Social History 1 (1956), pp. 210-222; Graham, New Governments of Eastern Europe, p. 500; R. Machray, Poland 1914-1931. London, 1932, pp. 185, 251-253.

24. Quoted in Polonsky, Politics in Independent Poland, p. 81.

25. The Lithuanian Peasant Union may be discounted since it was a functional adjunct of the Christian Democrats. As such, it was represented in all governments until 1926.

26. Graham, New Governments of Eastern Europe, pp. 306, 344; RIIA, The Baltic States, pp. 45-56; Parming, The Collapse of Liberal Democracy, pp. 13-17.

27. Wiles, "A Syndrome, Not A Doctrine", p. 170.

Conclusion

1. B.M. Russett, "Inequality and Instability: The Relation of Land Tenure to Politics". World Politics 16 (1964), p. 453: italics in the original.

2. See G. Di Palma, "Disaffection and Participation in Western Democracies: The Role of Political Oppositions". Journal of Politics 31 (1969), p. 1008.

3. See N.J. Smelser, Theory of Collective Behavior. New York, 1962, pp. 319-381.

4. P.E. Converse, "The Nature of Belief Systems in Mass Publics", in D.E. Apter (ed), *Ideology and Discontent*. New York, 1964, pp. 206-261.

5. Huntington, *Political Order*, p. 35: see also R. Emerson, *From Empire to Nation*. Cambridge, Mass., 1960, Ch. 5.

6. Wolf, *Peasant Wars*, Ch. 1.

7. Slicher van Bath, *Agrarian History*, pp. 189-194.

8. See Moore, *Social Origins*, pp. 479-480.

9. Rothschild, *The Communist Party of Bulgaria*, p. 86, describes the peasant as a "natural anarchosyndicalist".

10. See H.D. Lasswell & A. Kaplan, *Power and Society*. New Haven, 1950, p. 200.

11. This complex subject is adequately covered in Jackson, *The Comintern and Peasant*.

12. We are referring here to mass agrarian movements. Hence, we are disregarding those cases, such as the defeat of the cities by the Prussian *Junker* and *Gutsbesitzer* classes, where the rural elites emerged victorious in an urban-rural confrontation.

13. D.E. Neubauer, "Some Conditions of Democracy". *American Political Science Review* 61 (1967), p. 1007. The article is a critique and partial reanalysis of the data and article by P. Cutright, "National Political Development: Its Measurement and Social Correlates", in N.W. Polsby et al, *Politics and Social Life*. Boston, 1963, pp. 569-582.

14. See Huntington, *Political Order*, pp. 12-24.

15. Moore, *Social Origins*, p. 480.

16. For a discussion of how class conflicts may be distinguished along these lines from political conflicts generated by other social cleavages, see Rose & Urwin, "Social Cohesion", pp. 31-45.

Bibliography

Aarebrot, F.H. & Urwin, D.W., "The Politics of Cultural Dissent: Religion, Language and Demonstrative Action in Norway", *Scandinavian Political Studies*, new series 2 (1979), pp. 75-98.
Aasland, T., *Fra Landmannsorganisasjon til Bondeparti*. Oslo, 1974.
Abel, W., *Geschichte der Deutschen Landwirtschaft*. Stuttgart, 1967.
Abel, W., *Agrarkrisen und Agrarkonjunktur. Eine Geschichte der Land- und Ernährungswirtschaft Mitteleuropas seit dem hohen Mittelalter*. Hamburg, 1966.
Abraham, H., *Compulsory Voting*. Washington, 1955.
Alford, R.R., *Party and Society*. Chicago, 1963.
Allardt, E., "Social Sources of Finnish Communism: Traditional and Emerging Radicalism", *International Journal of Comparative Sociology* 5 (1964), 47-70.
Allardt, E., "Patterns of Class Conflict and Working Class Consciousness in Finnish Politics", in E. Allardt & Y. Littunen (eds), *Cleavages, Ideologies and Party Systems*. Helsinki, 1964, pp. 97-131.
Allardt, E. & Bruun, K., "Characteristics of the Finnish Non-Voter". *Transactions of the Westermarck Society* 3 (1956), pp. 55-76.
Allardt, E. & Pesonen, P., "Cleavages in Finnish Politics", in S.M. Lipset & S. Rokkan (eds), *Party Systems and Voter Alignments*. New York, 1967, pp. 325-366.
Allen, W.S., *The Nazi Seizure of Power*. London, 1966.
Allum, P.A., *Politics and Society in Post-War Naples*. Cambridge, 1973.
Almond, G.A., & Powell, G.B., *Comparative Politics*. Boston, 1966.
Almond, G.A., & Verba, S., *The Civic Culture*. Princeton, 1963.
Anders, H., *Der Staat den Keiner Wollte*. Vienna, 1962.
Anderson, E.N., *The Social and Political Conflict in Prussia, 1858-1864*. Lincoln, 1954.
Anderson, E.N. & Anderson, P.R., *Political Institutions and Social Change in Continental Europe in the Nineteenth Century*. Berkeley/Los Angeles, 1967.
Anderson, M., *Conservative Politics in France*. London, 1974.
Anderson, M.S., *Europe in the Eighteenth Century*. New York, 1962.
Anderson, R.T., & Anderson, B.G., *Bus Stop for Paris: The Transformation of a French Village*. New York, 1965.
Andren, N., *Modern Swedish Government*. Stockholm, 1961.
Annuaire Statistique de la Belgique. Brussels.

Annuaire Statistique de la France. Paris.
Annuaire Statistique de la Lettonie. Riga.
Annuaire Statistique de la République Polonaise. Warsaw.
Annuaire Statistique de la République Tchécoslovaque. Prague.
Annuaire Statistique de Royaume de Bulgarie. Sofia.
Annuario Statistico Italiano. Rome.
Antenen, A., Die Agrarpolitik der schweizerischen landwirt-
   schaftlichen Verbände und ihre Stellung in Staat und
   Wirtschaft. Winterthur, 1959.
Apter, D.E., The Politics of Modernization. Chicago, 1965.
Arensberg, C.M., & Kimball, S.T., Family and Community in
   Ireland. Cambridge, Mass., 1940.
Arnakis, G.G., "The Role of Religion in the Development of Balkan
   Nationalism", in C. Jelavich & B. Jelavich (eds), The
   Balkans in Transition. Berkeley/Los Angeles, 1963,
   pp. 115-144.
Armstrong, J.A., "Collaborationism in World War II: The Integral
   Nationalist Variant in Eastern Europe". Journal of Modern
   History 40 (1968), pp. 396-410.
Arnez, J.A., Slovenia in European Affairs. New York/Washington,
   1958.
Ashby, A.W., & Evans, I.L., The Agriculture of Wales and
   Monmouthshire. Cardiff, 1944.
Ashton, T.S., An Economic History of England: The Eighteenth
   Century. London, 1955.
Augé-Laribé, M., La politique agricole de la France de 1880 à
   1940. Paris, 1950.
Augé-Laribé, M., Syndicats et cooperatives agricoles. Paris, 1938.

Balodis, F., "Latvia and the Latvians",. Journal of Central
   European Affairs 6 (1946), pp. 241-282.
Banfield, E., The Moral Basis of a Backward Society. Glencoe,1958.
Barberis, C., & Corazziari, G., "Strutture economiche e dinamica
   elettorale", in M. Dogan & O. Pettraca (eds), Partito
   politici e strutture sociali in Italia. Milan, 1968,
   pp. 411-464.
Barker, E., Macedonia: Its Place in Balkan Power Politics.
   London, 1950.
Barnes, J.A., "Class and Committees in a Norwegian Island
   Parish". Human Relations 7 (1954), pp. 39-58.
Barral, P., Le département de l'Isère sous le IIIe République.
   Paris, 1962.
Barral, P., Les agrariens français de Méline à Pisani.
   Paris, 1958.
Barrillon, R., "Les Modérés: Paysans et Indépendents-Paysans",
   in J. Fauvet & H. Mendras (eds), Les Paysans et la politique.
   Paris, 1958, pp. 131-147.
Barton, A., "Sociological and Psychological Implications of
   Economic Planning in Norway", doctoral dissertation,
   Columbia Univ., 1954.
Basch, A., The Danube Basin and the German Economic Sphere.
   New York, 1943.
Batilliat, R., Origins et développement des institutions
   politique en Lithuanie. Lille, 1932.
Beard, C.A. & Radin, G., The Balkan Pivot: Yugoslavia.
   New York, 1929.
Becarud, J., La deuxième République espagnole, 1931-1936.
   Paris, 1962.

Becket, W.H., "The Development of Peasant Agriculture", in P. Ruopp (ed), Approaches to Community Development. Hague, 1953.
Bendix, R., Nation-Building and Citizenship. New York, 1964.
Benjamin, G.G., "German and French Socialists and the Agrarian Movement". Journal of Political Economy 34 (1926), pp. 349-376.
Beqiraj, M., Peasantry in Revolution. Ithaca, 1966.
Berelson, B., Lazarsfeld, P.F. & McPhee, W., Voting. Chicago, 1954.
Beresford, M., The Lost Villages of England. London, 1954.
Berger, S., Peasants Against Politics. Cambridge, Mass., 1972.
Bernard, P., Économie et Sociologie de la Seine-et-Marne. Paris, 1953.
Bitton, J.D., The French Nobility in Crisis. Stanford, 1969.
Bizzell, W.B., The Green Uprising. New York, 1926.
Bjerke, K., & Ussing, N., Studier over Danmarks nationalprodukt 1870-1950. Copenhagen, 1958.
Björgum, J., Venstre og kriseforliket. Landbrukspolitikk og parlamentarisk spill 1934-1935. Oslo, 1970.
Björvik, H., "The Farm Territories", Scandinavian Economic History Review 4 (1956), pp. 33-61.
Black, C.E., The Dynamics of Modernization. New York, 1966.
Black, C.E., (ed), Challenge in Eastern Europe. New Brunswick, 1954.
Blanchard, J., The Church in Contemporary Ireland. Dublin, 1963.
Bloch, M., Feudal Society. Chicago, 1961.
Bloch, M., Les caractères originaux de l'histoire rurale française. Paris, 1955-56. 2 vols.
Blok, A., "On brigandage with special reference to peasant mobilization". Sociologia neerlandica 8 (1972), pp. 1-13.
Blok, A., "The South Italian Agro-Town". Comparative Studies in Society and History 11 (1969), pp. 121-135.
Blondel, J., "Party Systems and Patterns of Government in Western Democracies". Canadian Journal of Political Science 1 (1968), pp. 180-203.
Blum, J., Lord and Peasant in Russia from the Ninth to the Nineteenth Century. Princeton, 1961.
Blum, J., "The Rise of Serfdom in Eastern Europe". American Historical Review 62 (1957), pp. 807-836.
Blum, J., Noble Landowners and Agriculture in Austria, 1815-1848. Baltimore, 1948.
Boberach, H., Wahlrechtsfrage im Vormärz. Die Wahlrechtsanschauung im Rheinland 1815-1849 und die Entstehung des Dreiklassenwahlrechts. Düsseldorf, 1959.
Bodzenta, E., Die Katholiken in Österreich: Ein religionssoziologischer Überblick. Vienna, 1962.
Bois, P., Paysans de l'Oest. Le Mans 1960.
Boisseau, P., "La participation des agriculteurs français aux programmes de développement économique". Sociologia Ruralis 14 (1974), pp. 108-119.
Böker, H.& von Bölow, F., Die Landplucht in der Tchechoslowakei. Geneva, 1935.
Bolin, S., "Medieval Agrarian Society in its Prime: Scandinavia", in M.M. Postan (ed), The Cambridge Economic History of Europe, I. The Agrarian Life of the Middle Ages. Cambridge, 1966.
Bonnet, S., Sociologie politique et religieuse de la Lorraine. Paris, 1972.

Booms, H., Die Deutsch-Konservative Partei: Preussischer Charakter Reichsauffassung, Nationalbegriff. Düsseldorf,1954.
Borchardt, K., "The Industrial Revolution in Germany 1700-1914", in C.M. Cipolla (ed), The Emergence of Industrial Societies. London, 1973. I, pp. 76-160.
Born, K.E., "Der sozial und wirtschaftliche Strukturwandel Deutschlands am Ende des 19. Jahrhundert", in H.U. Wehler (ed), Moderne deutsche Sozialgeschichte. Cologne, 1966.
Borovička, J., Ten Years of Czechoslovak Politics. Prague, 1929.
Bosworth, W., Catholicism and Crisis in Modern France. Princeton, 1962.
Bottomore, T.B., Elites and Society. London, 1966.
Bouroff, M.Ts., La réforme agraire en Bulgarie, 1921-1924. Paris, 1925.
Bowden, P.J., The Wool Trade in Tudor and Stuart England. London, 1962.
Bracher, K.D., Die Auflösung der Weimarer Republik. Villingen,1960.
Braga, G., Sociologia elettorale della Toscana. Rome, 1963.
Brašič, R.M., Land Reform and Ownership in Yugoslavia 1919-1953. New York, 1954.
Braun, A., "Die Reichstagswahlen von 1898 und 1903", Archiv für Sozialgesetzgebung und Statistik 18 (1903), pp. 538-563.
Brenan, G., The Spanish Labyrinth. Cambridge, 1943.
Bridberg, A.R., Economic Growth: England in the Later Middle Ages. London, 1962.
Brock, P., "The Politics of the Polish Peasant", International Review of Social History 1 (1956), pp. 210-222.
Brock, P., "The Early Years of the Polish Peasant Party, 1895-1907", Journal of Central European Affairs 14 (1954), pp. 219-235.
Brock, P., "Boleslaw Wyslouch, Founder of the Polish Peasant Party", Slavonic and East European Review 30 (1951), pp. 139-163.
Brown, B., "Alcohol and Politics in France", American Political Science Review 51 (1957), pp. 976-990.
Bruegel, J.W., Czechoslovakia Before Munich. London, 1973.
Brugger, H., Schweizerischer landwirtschaftlicher Verein 1863-1963. Zürich, 1963.
Brunner, O., Land und Herrschaft. Vienna, 1959.
Brunner, O., Neue Wege der Sozialgeschichte. Göttingen, 1956.
Brutzkus, B., "The Historical Peculiarities of the Social and Economic Development of Russia", in R. Bendix & S.M. Lipset (eds), Class, Status, and Power. Glencoe, 1953, pp. 517-540.
Buell, R., Poland: Key to Europe. New York, 1939.
Bullock, M., Austria 1918-1919. A Study in Failure. London, 1939.
Burks, R.V., The Dynamics of Communism. Princeton, 1961.
Burks, R.V., "Catholic Parties in Latin Europe", Journal of Modern History 24 (1952), pp. 269-286.

Cam, H.M., "The Decline and Fall of English Feudalism", History N.S. 25 (1946), pp. 216-233.
Campbell, A., Converse, P., Miller, W. & Stokes, D., The American Voter. New York, 1960.
Campbell, J.K., Honour, Family and Patronage. Oxford, 1964.
Cantril, H., Public Opinion, 1935-1946. Princeton, 1951.
Capecchi, V., Cioni Polacchini, V., Galli, G. & Sivino, G., Il comportamento elettorale in Italia. Bologna, 1968.

Carlsson, G., Lantmannapolitiken och industrialismen. Partigruppering och oppinionsförskytningar i svensk politik 1890-1902. Stockholm, 1953.
Carlsson, S., Standsamhälle och Standspersoner 1700-1865. Lund, 1949.
Carr, R. (ed), The Republic and the Civil War in Spain. London, 1971.
Carson, G.B. (ed), Latvia: An Area Study. New Haven, 1956. 2 vols.
Carsten, F.L., Revolution in Central Europe 1918-1919. London, 1972.
Carsten, F.L., The Rise of Fascism. Berkeley/Los Angeles, 1967.
Carsten, F.L., The Origins of Prussia. London, 1954.
Carsten, F.L., "Der Bauernkrieg in Ostpreussen 1525", International Review for Social History 3 (1938), pp. 398-409.
Chadwick, H.M., The Nationalities of Europe and the Growth of National Ideologies. London, 1945.
Chaffard, G., Les Orages de mai. Paris, 1968.
Chambers, J.D., "Enclosure and Labour Supply in the Industrial Revolution". Economic History Review, 2 series, 5 (1953), pp. 319-343.
Chambers, J.D. & Mingay, G.E., The Agricultural Revolution 1750-1850. London, 1966.
Chase, T.G., The Story of Lithuania. New York, 1946.
Chasseriaud, J.P., Le parti democrat chrétien en Italie. Paris, 1965.
Chayanov, A.D., The Theory of Peasant Economy. Homewood, 1966.
Cheung, S.N.S., The Theory of Share Tenancy. Chicago, 1969.
Cheyney, E.P., "The Disappearance of English Serfdom", English Historical Review 15 (1900), pp. 20-37.
Chmelar, J., Political Parties in Czechoslovakia. Prague, 1926.
Chubb, B., The Government and Politics of Ireland. Stanford, 1970.
Cipolla, C.M., Literacy and Development in the West. London, 1969.
Clough, S.B., A History of the Flemish Movement in Belgium. New York, 1930.
Cobban, A., The Nation State and National Self-Determination. New York, 1969.
Cobban, A., The Social Interpretation of the French Revolution. Cambridge, 1964.
Codding, G.A., The Federal Government of Switzerland. Boston, 1961.
Cohn, N., The Pursuit of the Millenium. New York, 1961.
Coleman, J.S. (ed), Education and Political Development. Princeton, 1965.
Connell, K.H., Irish Peasant Society. London, 1969.
Constantinesco, M., L'évolution de la propriété rurale et la réforme agraire en Roumanie. Bucharest, 1925.
Converse, P.E., "Of Time and Partisan Stability", Comparative Political Studies 2 (1969), pp. 139-171.
Converse, P.E., "The Nature of Belief Systems in Mass Publics", in D.E. Apter (ed), Ideology and Discontent. New York, 1964, pp. 206-261.
Conze, W., "Die Wirkungen der liberalen Agrarreformen auf die Volksordnung in Mitteleuropa im 19. Jahrhundert", Vierteljahresschrift für Sozial- und Wirtschaftsgeschichte 38 (1951), pp. 2-43.
Conze, W., Agrarverfassung und Bevölkerung in Litauen und Weissrussland. Leipzig, 1940.
Cooper, J.P., "The Social Distribution of Land and Men in England, 1436-1700", Economic History Review, 2 series, 20 (1967), pp. 419-440.

Cornford, J., "The Transformation of Conservatism in the Late Nineteenth Century". *Victorian Studies* 7 (1963), pp. 35-66.
Costedoat-Lamargue, J., *La Question agraire en Andalousie*. Paris, 1922.
Cox, K.R., "Geography, Social Contexts and Voting Behavior in Wales, 1861-1951", in E. Allardt & S. Rokkan (eds), *Mass Politics*. New York, 1970, pp. 117-159.
Cox, K.R. & Demko, G.J., "Conflict Behavior in a Spatio-Temporal Context", *Sociological Focus* 1 (1968), pp. 55-67.
Craig, F.W.S. (ed), *British Parliamentary Election Results 1918-1949*. Glasgow, 1969.
Crowley, D.W., "The Crofters' Party 1885-1892". *Scottish Historical Review* 35 (1956), pp. 110-126.
Curtis, L.P., *Coercion and Conciliation in Ireland, 1880-1892*. Princeton, 1963.
Cutright, P., "National Political Development: Its Measurement and Social Correlates", in N.W. Polsby, R.A. Dentler & P.A. Smith (eds), *Politics and Social Life*. Boston, 1963, pp. 569-582.

Daalder, H., "The Consociational Democracy Theme", *World Politics* 26 (1974), pp. 604-621.
Daalder, H., "Parties, Elites, and Political Developments in Western Europe", in J. LaPalombara & M. Weiner (eds), *Political Parties and Political Development*. Princeton, 1966, pp. 43-77.
Dahl, R.A. (ed), *Political Oppositions in Western Democracies*. New Haven, 1966.
Dahl, R.A., *Preface to Democratic Theory*. Chicago, 1956.
Damgaard, E., "Party Coalitions in Danish Law-Making 1953-1970", *European Journal of Political Research* 1 (1973), pp. 35-66.
Dauksa, S., *Le Régime d'autonomie du territoire de Klaipeda*. Paris, 1937.
Davies, J.C., "Toward a Theory of Revolution", *American Sociological Review* 27 (1962), pp. 5-19.
Deak, I., "Budapest and the Hungarian Revolution of 1918-1919". *Slavonic and East European Review* 46 (1968).
Deane, P., & Cole, W.A. (ed), *British Economic Growth 1688-1959: Trends and Structure*. Cambridge, 1962.
Debatisse, M., *La révolution silencieuse: le combat des paysans*. Paris, 1963.
De Jong, J.J., *Overheid en Onderdaan*. Wageningen, 1956.
Delzell, C.F., *Mussolini's Enemies: The Italian Anti-Fascist Resistance*. Princeton, 1961.
Derruau-Boniol, S., "Le Département de la Creuse, structure social et évolution". *Revue francaise de science politique* 7 (1957), pp. 38-66.
Der Schweizer Wähler. Basel, 1963.
De Tocqueville, A., *The Old Regime and the French Revolution*. New York, 1955.
Deutsch, K.W., "Social Mobilization and Political Development". *American Political Science Review* 55 (1961), pp. 493-514.
Deutsch, K.W., *Nationalism and Social Communication*. New York, 1953.
Diamant, A., *Austrian Catholics and the First Republic*. Princeton, 1960.
Dickinson, R., "The Geography of Commuting in Western Germany". *Annals of the Association of American Geographers* 49 (1959) pp. 443-456.

Di Palma, G., *Apathy and Participation: Mass Politics in Western Society*. New York, 1970.
Di Palma, G., "Disaffection and Participation in Western Democracies: The Role of Political Oppositions", *Journal of Politics* 31 (1969).
Dobson, R.B. (ed), *The Peasants' Revolt of 1381*. London 1970.
Dogan, M. & Petracca (eds), *Partiti politiche e strutture sociali in Italia*. Milan, 1968.
Dogan, M. & Rose, R (eds), *European Politics*. Boston, 1971.
Dollinger, P., *The German Hansa*. Stanford, 1970.
Dovring, F., *Land and Labor in Europe 1900-1950*. Hague, 1960. 2 ed.
Downs, A., *An Economic Theory of Democracy*. New York, 1957.
Dreyfus, F.G., *La vie politique en Alsace 1919-1936*. Paris, 1969.
Duby, G., *Rural Economy and Country Life in the Medieval West*. Columbia, SC, 1968.
Dugdale, J.S., *The Linguistic Map of Europe*. London, 1969.
Dunn, S.P. & Dunn, E., *The Peasants of Central Russia*. New York, 1967.
Dupeux, G., *Aspects de l'histoire sociale et politique du Loir-et-Cher, 1848-1914*. Paris, 1962.
Dupeux, G., *Le Front Populaire et les élections de 1936*. Paris, 1959.
Duverger, M., *Political Parties*. London, 1954.
Dybdahl, V., *Partier og erhverv, 1880-1893*. Aarhus, 1969.

Eesti Statistika. Tallinn.
Ehrmann, H.W., *Le Mouvement Poujade*. Paris, 1956.
Ehrmann, H.W., "The French Peasant and Communism". *American Political Science Review* 56 (1952), pp. 19-43.
Eisenstadt, S.N., *Modernization: Protest and Change*. Englewood Cliffs, 1966.
Eisenstadt, S.N., *The Political Systems of Empires*. New York, 1963.
Eisenstadt, S.N. & Rokkan, S. (eds), *Building States and Nations*. London/Beverly Hills, 1973. 2 vols.
Élections à la Saeima de la République Lettonie. Riga.
Élections à parlement, (1923-1932). Tallinn.
Eliassen, K.A., & Pedersen, M., "Political Mobilization, Democratization and the Transformation of Political Elites in Norway and Denmark". Paper at the European Consortium for Political Research Workshop on Recruitment, Careers and Attitudes of Legislators. Mannheim, 1973.
Elvander, N., *Intresseorganisationerna i dagens Sverige*. Lund, 1966.
Emerit, M., *Les paysans roumains depuis le Traité d'Andrinople jusqu'à la libération des terres, 1829-1864*. Paris, 1937.
Emerson, R., *From Empire to Nation*. Cambridge, Mass., 1960.
Engels, F., *The Peasant War in Germany*. New York, 1926.
Essen, W., *Die ländlichen Siedlungen in Litauen*. Leipzig, 1931.
Étienne, J-M., *Le mouvement Rexiste jusqu'en 1940*. Paris, 1968.
Evans, I.L., *The Agrarian Revolution in Rumania*. Cambridge, 1924.

Faber, H., *Cooperation in Danish Agriculture*. London, 1931.
Faul, E., *Wahlen und Wähler in Westdeutschland*. Villingen, 1960.
Fauvet, J., *La France déchirée*. Paris, 1957.
Fauvet, J., "La répresentation politique du monde paysan", in M. Duverger (ed), *Partis politiques et classes sociales en France*. Paris, 1955.
Fauvet, J. & Mendras, H. (eds), *Les paysans et la politique*. Paris, 1958.

Federoff-White, D., The Growth of the Red Army. Princeton, 1944.
Feirabend, L., Agricultural Cooperatives in Czechoslovakia. New York, 1952.
Finck zu Finckenstein, H.W. Graf, Die Entwicklung der Landwirtschaft in Preussen und Deutschland 1800-1930. Würzburg, 1960.
Firth, R., Elements of Social Organization. London, 1951.
Fischer, F., Griff nach der Weltmacht. Die Kriegszielpolitik des Kaiserlichen Deutschlands 1914-1918. Düsseldorf, 1961.
Fischer-Galati, S. (ed), Twentieth-Century Europe: A Documentary History. Philadelphia, 1956.
Flora, P., "Historische Prozesse sozialer Mobilisierung: Urbanisierung und Alphabetisierung, 1850-1965". Zeitschrift für Soziologie, 1 (1972), pp. 85-117.
Florescu, R.R., "The Uniate Church: Catalyst of Rumanian National Consciousness", Slavonic and East European Review 45 (1967).
Fohlen, C., "The Industrial Revolution in France 1700-1914", in C.M. Cipolla (ed), The Emergence of Industrial Societies. London, 1973. I, pp. 7-75.
Fondation National des Sciences Politiques (FNSP), L'Univers politique des paysans. Paris, 1972.
FNSP, Tradition et changement en Toscane. Paris, 1970.
Forbudsavstemingen 18 oktober 1926. Oslo, 1927.
Forster, R., The Nobility of Toulouse in the Eighteenth Century. Baltimore, 1960.
Foster, G.M., Tzintzuntzan: Mexican Peasants in a Changing World. Boston, 1967.
Frankel, H., Poland: The Struggle for Power, 1772-1939. London, 1946.
Frankfort, H., Kingship and the Gods. Chicago, 1948.
Franklin, S.H., Rural Societies. London, 1971.
Franklin, S.H., The European Peasantry. London, 1969.
Franklin, S.H., "Systems of Production: Systems of Appropriation". Pacific Viewpoint 6 (1965), pp. 145-166.
Franz, G., Die politische Wahlen in Niedersachsen, 1867 bis 1949. Bremen, 1957. 3 ed.
Franz, G., Der Deutsche Bauernkrieg. Darmstadt, 1956.
Friedl, E., "The Role of Kinship in the Transmission of National Culture to Rural Villages in Mainland Greece". American Anthropologist 61 (1959), pp. 30-38.
Friedrich, C.J., "The Agricultural Basis of Emotional Nationalism". Public Opinion Quarterly 1 (1937), pp. 50-61.
Frimannslund, R., "Farm Community and Neighbourhood Community". Scandinavian Economic History Review 4 (1956), pp. 62-81.
Fröland, K., Krise og kamp. Oslo, 1962.

Gabriel-Robinet, L., Dorgères et le Front Paysan. Paris, 1937.
Galeski, B., Basic Concepts in Rural Sociology. Manchester, 1971.
Galeski, B., "Social Organization and Rural Social Change". Sociologia Ruralis 8 (1968), pp. 258-281.
Galli, G. & Prandi, A., Patterns of Political Participation in Italy. New Haven, 1970.
Gallino, L., "Italy", in M.S. Archer & S. Giner (eds), Contemporary Europe. London, 1971, pp. 90-124.
Ganshof, F.L., Feudalism. New York, 1961.
Garvin, T., "Political Cleavages, Party Politics and Urbanization in Ireland: The Case of the Periphery-Dominated Centre". European Journal of Political Research 2 (1974), pp. 307-328.

Geertz, C., "The Integrative Revolution", in C. Geertz (ed),
   Old Societies and New States. New York, 1963, pp. 105-157.
Geipel, J., The Europeans: An Ethnohistorical Survey.
   London, 1969.
Gentil da Silva, J., En Espagne, développement économique,
   subsistence, déclin. Paris, 1965.
George, P., Géographie économique et sociale de la France.
   Paris, 1946.
Gĕrmanis, U., "The Idea of Independent Latvia and Its Development
   in 1917", in A. Sprudzs & A. Rūsis (eds), Res Baltica.
   Leiden, 1968, pp. 27-87.
Gerschenkron, A., "Agrarian Policies and Industrialization
   1861-1917", in H.J. Habbakuk & M.M. Postan (eds), The
   Cambridge Economic History of Europe. Cambridge, 1965. VI,
   pp. 706-800.
Gerschenkron, A., Economic Backwardness in Historical Perspective.
   Cambridge, Mass., 1962.
Gerschenkron, A., "Notes on the Rate of Industrial Growth in
   Italy, 1881-1913". Journal of Economic History 15 (1955).
Gerschenkron, A., Bread and Democracy in Germany. Berkeley/
   Los Angeles, 1943.
Gerutis, A., "Independent Lithuania", in A. Gerutis (ed),
   Lithuania 700 Years. New York, 1969, pp. 145-312.
Gervais, M., Servolin, C. & Weil, J., Une France sans paysans.
   Paris, 1965.
Girod, M., "Milieux politiques et classes sociales en Suisse".
   Cahiers internationaux de sociologie (1965), pp. 29-54.
Girod, R., "Le système des partis en Suisse". Revue française
   de science politique 14 (1964), pp. 1114-1133.
Goguel, F., Géographie des élections françaises. Paris, 1951.
Goldberg, H., The Life of Jean Jaurès. Madison NJ, 1961.
Gonzalez Blasco, P., "Modern Nationalism in Old Nations as a
   Consequence of Earlier State-Building: The Case of Basque
   Spain", in W. Bell & W.E. Freeman (eds), Ethnicity and
   Nation-Building. London/Beverly Hills, 1974, pp. 341-373.
Görlitz, W., Die Junker, Adel und Bauer im deutschen Ost.
   Glücksburg, 1956.
Gosnell, H., Why Europe Votes. Chicago, 1930.
Graham, M.W., The Diplomatic Recognition of the Border States.
   Berkeley/Los Angeles, 1941.
Graham, M.W., New Governments of Eastern Europe. New York, 1927.
Graham, M.W., New Governments of Central Europe. London, 1924.
Grant Duff, S., Europe and the Czechs. London, 1938.
Gratton, P., Les luttes de classes dans les campagnes.
   Paris, 1971.
Graziano, L., "Patron-Client Relationships in Southern Italy".
   European Journal of Political Research 1 (1973), pp. 3-34.
Greenfield, K.R., Economics and Liberalism in the Risorgimento.
   Baltimore, 1965.
Greenlaw, R.W. (ed), The Economic Origins of the French
   Revolution: Poverty or Prosperity?. Boston, 1958.
Grew, R., A Sterner Plan for Italian Unity. Princeton, 1963.
Grindrod, M., The Rebuilding of Italy. London, 1955.
Groth, A., "Proportional Representation in Prewar Poland".
   Slavic Review 23 (1964), pp. 103-114.
Gruijters, H., Schermer, K. & Slootman, K., Experimenten en
   Democratie. Amsterdam, 1967.
Gruner, E., Die Parteien in der Schweiz. Bern, 1969.

Gulick, C.A., *Austria from Hapsburg to Hitler*. Berkeley/ Los Angeles, 1948. 2 vols.
Gusfield, J.R., "Tradition and Modernity: Misplaced Polarities in the Study of Social Change". *American Journal of Sociology* 72 (1967), pp. 351-362.

Habbakuk, H.J., "La disparition du paysan anglais". *Annales* 20 (1965), pp. 649-663.
Habbakuk, H.J., "English Landownership, 1680-1740". *Economic History Review* 10 (1940), pp. 2-17.
Hagman, M., *Der Weg ins Verhängnis. Reichstagswahlergebnisse 1919 bis 1933, besonders aus Bayern*. Munich, 1946.
Hajda, J. (ed), *Czechoslovakia*. New Haven, 1955.
Halpern, M., *A Serbian Village*. New York, 1958.
Hanchett, W.S., "The Communists and the Latvian Countryside, 1919-1949", in A. Sprudzs & A. Rūsis (eds), *Res Baltica*. Leiden, 1968, pp. 88-116.
Hancock, M.D., *Sweden: The Politics of Postindustrial Change*. Hinsdale, 1972.
Harrison, E.J., *Lithuania 1928*. London, 1928.
Harrison, E.J., *Lithuania, Past and Present*. New York, 1922.
Haugen, E., *Language Conflict and Language Planning: The Case of Modern Norwegian*. Cambridge, Mass., 1966.
Heberle, R., *From Democracy to Nazism*. Baton Rouge, 1945.
Heckscher, E.F., *An Economic History of Sweden*. Cambridge, Mass., 1963.
Heckscher, E.F., *Mercantilism*. London, 1955.
Heffner, R.C. (ed), *The Estonians*. New Haven, 1954.
Heike, O., *Das Deutschtum in Polen, 1918-1939*. Bonn, 1955.
Heilbroner, R.L., *The Making of Economic Society*. Englewood Cliffs, 1962.
Helleiner, K.F., "The Population of Europe from the Black Death to the eve of the Vital Revolution", in E.E. Rich & C.H. Wilson (eds), *The Cambridge Economic History of Europe*. Cambridge, 1967. IV, pp. 1-95.
Hellström, G., *Föreningsdemokrati och förtroendemannakår*. Halmstad, 1964.
Hennessy, C.A.M., *The Federal Republic in Spain: Pi y Margall and the Federal Republican Movement, 1868-1874*. Oxford, 1962.
Herceg, R., *Die Ideologie der Kroatischen Bauernbewegung*. Zagreb, 1923.
Herlihy, D., "The Agrarian Revolution in Southern France and Italy, 801-1150". *Speculum* 33 (1958), pp. 23-41.
Hertzman, L., *DNVP: Right-Wing Opposition in the Weimar Republic*. Lincoln, 1963.
Herz, A., "The Social Background of the Prewar Polish Political Structure". *Journal of Central European Affairs* 2 (1942), pp. 145-161.
Herz, A., "The Case of an East European Intelligentsia". *Journal of Central European Affairs* 11 (1951), pp. 10-26.
Herz-Eicherode, D., *Politik und Landwirtschaft in Ostpreussen 1919-1930*. Opladen, 1969.
Hicks, J.O., *The Populist Revolt*. Minneapolis, 1931.
Hildebrande, G.H., *Growth and Structure in the Economy of Modern Italy*. Cambridge, Mass., 1965.
Hill, K., "Belgium: Political Change in a Segmented Society", in R. Rose (ed), *Electoral Behavior*. New York, 1974, pp. 29-207.

Hillgruber, A., *Hitler, König Carol und Marshall Antonescu: Die deutsch-rümanischen Beziehungen 1938-1944*. Wiesbaden, 1965.
Hilton, R.H., *Bond Men Made Free*. New York, 1973.
Hindley, D., "Political Conflict Potential, Politicisation, and the Peasantry in Underdeveloped Countries". *Asian Studies* 3 (1965), pp. 470-489.
Hjellum, T., "The Politicization of Local Government: Rates of Change, Conditioning Factors, Effects on Political Culture". *Scandinavian Political Studies* 2 (1967), pp. 69-93.
Hobsbaum, E.J., *Primitive Rebels*. Manchester, 1959.
Hoch, C., *The Political Parties in Czechoslovakia*. Prague, 1936.
Hoensch, J.K., *Geschichte der tschechoslowakischen Republik*. Stuttgart, 1966.
Hoensch, J.K., *Die Slowakei und Hitlers Ostpolitik*. Cologne, 1965.
Hofstadter, R., *The Age of Reform: From Bryan to FDR*. New York, 1955.
Högh, E., *Vaelgeradferd i Danmark 1849-1901: en politisk og sociologisk analyse*. Copenhagen, 1972.
Holmes, D.A., *The Estates of the Higher Nobility in Fourteenth Century England*. Cambridge, 1957.
Holmesen, A., "Landowners and Tenants in Norway". *Scandinavian Economic History Review* 6 (1958), pp. 121-131.
Homans, G.C., *English Villagers of the Thirteenth Century*. New York, 1960.
Hooker, E.R., *Readjustments of Agricultural Tenure in Ireland*. Chapel Hill, 1938.
Hoor, E., *Österreich, 1918-1938. Staat ohne Nation, Republik ohne Republikaner*. Vienna, 1966.
Hopfner, H., *Die ländlichen Siedlungen der altkastilischen Meseta*. Hamburg. 1939.
Horak, S., *Poland and Her National Minorities 1919-1939*. New York, 1961.
Horvath, R., "Sociologie Électorale: une synthèse du Droit Électoral Bourgeois en Hongrie (1848-1939), Essai de Statistique Historique". *L'Année Sociologique* 3 (1962), pp. 280-292.
Hory, L. & Broszat, M., *Der Kroatische Ustascha-Staat 1941-1945*. Stuttgart, 1964.
Hoskins, W.G., *The Midland Peasant*. London, 1957.
Hovde, B.J., *The Scandinavian Countries*, 1720-1865. Boston, 1943. 2 vols.
Hunter, G., *Peasantry and Crisis in France*. London, 1938.
Huntington, S.J., *Political Order in Changing Societies*. New Haven, 1968.

Information Statistique de la République Polonaise. Warsaw, 1930.
Ingulfson, H. & Hagman, R., "De Svenska Partiernas Sociala och Andra Grundvaler", in E. Håstad (ed), *"Gallup" och den Svenska Väljarkåren*. Uppsala, 1950, pp. 123-181.
International Reference Library, *Politics and Political Parties in Rumania*. London, 1936.
Ionescu, G. & Gellner, E., (eds), *Populism: Its National Characteristics*. London, 1969.
Irving, R.E.M., *Christian Democracy in France*. London, 1973.

Jaacijfers voor Nederland. Hague.
Jackson, G., *The Spanish Republic and the Civil War*. Princeton, 1965.

Jackson, G.D., Comintern and Peasant in Eastern Europe 1919-1930. New York, 1966.
Jackson, J.H., Estonia. London, 1948.
Jacobsen, K.D., "Public Administration under Pressure: The Role of the Expert in the Modernization of Traditional Agriculture". Scandinavian Political Studies 1 (1966), pp. 59-93.
Jacobsen, K.D., Teknisk hjelp og politisk struktur. Oslo, 1964.
James, M., Social Problems and Policy during the Puritan Revolution 1640-1660. London, 1930.
Janos, A.C., "The One-Party State and Social Mobilization: East Europe Between the Wars", in S.P. Huntington & C.H. Moore (eds), Authoritarian Politics in Modern Society. New York, 1970, pp. 204-236.
Jedlicka, L., "The Austrian Heimwehr", Journal of Contemporary History 1 (1966), pp. 127-144.
Jedlicka, L., Ein Heer im Schatten der Parteien. Graz, 1955.
Jelavich, C., "Nikola P. Pašić: Greater Serbia or Yugoslavia?". Journal of Central European Affairs 11 (1954), pp. 133-151.
Jenks, W.A., The Austrian Electoral Reform of 1907. New York, 1950.
Jensen, E., Danish Agriculture: Its Economic Development. Copenhagen, 1937.
Jeppesen, J.& Meyer, P., Sofavaelgerne: Valgdeltagelsen ved danske folketingsvalg. Aarhus, 1964.
Jones, E.L., "Agricultural Origins of Industry", Past and Present 40 (1968), pp. 58-71.
Jones, E.L. & Woolf, S.J. (eds), Agrarian Change and Economic Development. London, 1969.
Jörberg, L., "The Nordic Countries 1850-1914", in C.M. Cipolla (ed), The Emergence of Industrial Societies. London, 1973. II pp. 375-485.
Jordan, T.G., The European Culture Area. New York, 1973.
Jousse, P., Les tendances des réformes agraires dans l'Europe centrale, l'Europe orientale, et l'Europe méridionale, 1918-1924. Niort, 1925.
Junker, B., Die Bauern auf dem Wege zur Politik. Die Entstehung der Bernischen Bauern-, Gewerbe- und Bürgerpartei. Bern, 1968.
Junker, B. & Maurer, R., Kampf und Verantwortung: Bernische Bauern-, Gewerbe- und Bürgerpartei 1918-1968. Bern, 1968.
Jutikkala, E., Bonden i Finland genom tiderna. Helsinki, 1963.

Kaartvedt, A., Kampen mot parlamentarisme. Oslo, 1967.
Kagan, G., "The Agrarian Regime of Pre-War Poland". Journal of Central European Affairs 3 (1943), pp. 241-269.
Kahan, A., "Nineteenth-Century European Experience with Policies of Economic Nationalism", in H.G. Johnson (ed), Economic Nationalism in Old and New States. Chicago, 1967, pp. 17-30.
Kahler, W., Das Agrarproblem in den Industrieländern. Göttingen, 1958.
Karisch, H., Staat, Parteien und Verbände in Österreichs Wirtschaftsordnung. Vienna, 1965.
Katona, G., Psychological Analysis of Economic Behavior. New York, 1963.
Kauer, U., Wirtschaftsstruktur und Wirtschaftspolitik des Freistaates Estland, 1918-1940. Bonn, 1962.
Kautsky, J.H. (ed), Political Change in Underdeveloped Countries. New York, 1962.
Kerner, R.J. (ed), Czechoslovakia. Berkeley/Los Angeles. 1945.

Kirschbaum, J.M. (ed), Slovakia in the Nineteenth and Twentieth Centuries. Toronto, 1973.
Kitson Clark, G., The Making of Victorian England. London, 1962.
Klöverkorn, M., Die sprachliche Struktur Finlands 1880-1950. Helsinki, 1960.
Knoellinger, C.E., Labor in Finland. Cambridge, Mass., 1960.
Koenigsberger, H., Estates and Revolutions. Ithaca, 1971.
Kogan, A.G., "The Social Democrats and the Conflict of Nationalities in the Hapsburg Monarchy". Journal of Modern History 21 (1949), pp. 204-217.
Kohn, H., Pan-Slavism: Its History and Ideology. South Bend,1953.
Kohn, H., The Idea of Nationalism. New York, 1951.
Kolarz, W., Myths and Realities in Eastern Europe. London, 1946.
Komarnicki, T., Rebirth of the Polish Republic. London, 1957.
Koselleek, R., Preussen zwischen Reform und Revolution. Allgemeines Landrecht. Verwaltung und soziale Bewegung von 1791 bis 1848. Stuttgart, 1967.
Kötter, H., Landbevölkerung im sozialen Wandel. Düsseldorf, 1958.
Krader, L., "The Transition from Serf to Peasant in Eastern Europe". Anthropological Quarterly 33 (1960), pp. 76-90.
Krehbiel, E., "Geographic Influences in British Elections". Geographical Review 2 (1961), pp. 419-432.
Kuhnle, S., "Stemmeretten i 1814: beregninger over antall stemmerettskvalifiserte etter Grunnloven". Historisk Tidsskrift 51 (1972), pp. 373-390.
Kuuse, J., Från redskap til maskinar. Mekaniseringsspridning och kommersialisering inom svensk jordbruk. Gotenberg, 1970.

Lafferty, W.L., Economic Development and the Response of Labor in Scandinavia. Oslo, 1971.
Landauer, C., "The Guesdists and the Small Farmer: Early Erosion of French Marxism". International Review of Social History 6 (1961), pp. 212-225.
Landbruketssentralforbund, Norwegian Agriculture and its Organizations. Oslo, 1966.
Landes, D., The Unbound Prometheus. Cambridge, 1969.
Landsberger, H.A. (ed), Rural Protest: Peasant Movements and Social Change. New York, 1973.
Landsberger, H.A. (ed) Latin American Peasant Movements. Ithaca, 1969.
LaPalombara, J., Italy: The Politics of Planning. Syracuse, 1966.
LaPalombara, J., Interest Groups in Italian Politics. Princeton, 1964.
LaPalombara, J. & Weiner, M. (eds), Political Parties and Political Development. Princeton, 1966.
Larkin, E., "Economic Growth, Capital Investment and the Catholic Church in Nineteenth Century Ireland". American Historical Review 72 (1967), pp. 852-884.
Larner, J., The Lords of Romagna: Romagnal Society and the Origins of the Signorie. Ithaca, 1965.
Lasswell, H.D. & Kaplan, A., Power and Society. New Haven, 1950.
Lederer, I.J., Yugoslavia at the Paris Peace Conference. New Haven, 1963.
LeFarge, J., Martyrdom of Slovenia. New York, 1942.
Lefebvre, G., Les Paysans du Nord pendant la Révolution française. Bari, 1959.
Lefebvre, G., Études sur la Révolution française. Paris, 1954.
Léger, B.M.E., Les opinions politiques des provinces françaises.

Lehmbruch, G., *Proporzdemokratie*. Tübingen, 1967.
Le Roy Ladurie, E., *Les Paysans de Languedoc*. Paris, 1966. 2 vols.
Leslie, R.F., *Reform and Insurrection in Russian Poland 1856-1865*. London, 1963.
Leslie, R.F., *Polish Politics and the Revolution of November 1830*. London, 1956.
Lettrich, J., *History of Modern Slovakia*. New York, 1955.
Levi, C., *Christ Stopped at Eboli*. New York, 1947.
Lewin, L., Jansson, B. & Sörbom, D., *The Swedish Electorate 1887-1968*. Stockholm, 1972.
Lewis, A.R., "The Closing of the European Frontier". *Speculum* 33 (1958), pp. 475-483.
Lijphart, A., *Class Voting and Religious Voting in the European Democracies*. Glasgow, Survey Research Centre Occasional Paper 8, 1971.
Lijphart, A., "Typologies of Democratic Systems". *Comparative Political Studies* 1 (1968), pp. 3-44.
Lijphart, A., *The Politics of Accommodation*. Berkeley/ Los Angeles, 1968.
Linde, G., *Die deutsche Politik in Litauen im ersten Weltkrieg*. Wiesbaden, 1965.
Linz, J.J., "Patterns of Land Tenure, Division of Labor, and Voting Behavior in Europe". *Comparative Politics* 8 (1976), pp. 365-430.
Linz, J.J., "Early State-Building and Late Peripheral Nationalisms against the State: The Case of Spain", in S.N. Eisenstadt & S. Rokkan (eds), *Building States and Nations*. London/ Beverly Hills, 1973. II, pp. 32-116.
Linz, J.J., "Cleavage and Consensus in West German Politics: The Early Fifties", in S.M. Lipset & S. Rokkan (eds), *Party Systems and Voter Alignments*. New York, 1967.
Linz, J.J., "The Party System of Spain", in S.M. Lipset & S. Rokkan (eds), *Party Systems and Voter Alignments*. New York, 1967.
Linz, J.J., "The Social Bases of West German Politics". Doctoral dissertation, Columbia University, 1959.
Linz, J.J. & de Miguel, A., "Within-Nation Differences and Comparisons: The Eight Spains", in R.L. Merritt & S. Rokkan (eds), *Comparing Nations*. New Haven, 1966, pp. 267-319.
Lipset, S.M., *Political Man*. London, 1960.
Lipset, S.M., *Agrarian Socialism*. Berkeley/Los Angeles, 1950.
Lipset, S.M. & Rokkan, S. (eds), *Party Systems and Voter Alignments*. New York, 1967.
Lipton, M., "The Theory of the Optimising Peasant". *Journal of Development Studies* 4 (1968), pp. 327-351.
Loomis, C.P. & Beagle, J.A., "The Spread of German Nacism in Rural Areas". *American Sociological Review* 11 (1946), pp. 724-734.
Lopreato, J., *Peasants No More*. San Francisco, 1967.
Lowi, T., "Party, Policy and Constitution in America", in W.N. Chambers & W.D. Burnham (eds), *The American Party Systems*. New York, 1967, pp. 238-276.
Lugan, A., *Une Oeuvre belge: Origins et organisation du Boerenbond*. Paris, 1925.
Lupri, E., "The Rural-Urban Variable Reconsidered". *Sociologia Ruralis* 7 (1967), pp. 1-20.

Lütge, F., *Deutsche Sozial- und Wirtschaftsgeschichte.* Berlin, 1966.
Lutz, V., *Italy: A Study in Economic Development.* London, 1962.
Luza, R., *The Transfer of the Sudeten Germans: A Study of Czech-German Relations 1933-1962.* London, 1964.
Lyashchenko, P.I., *History of the National Economy of Russia to the 1917 Revolution.* New York, 1949.

Macartney, C.A., *The Hapsburg Empire 1790-1918.* London, 1968.
Macartney, C.A., *October 15th, A History of Hungary 1929-1945.* New York, 1956. 2 vols.
Macartney, C.A., *Hungary and Her Successors.* London, 1937.
Macartney, C.A., *National States and National Minorities.* London, 1934.
Macartney, C.A. & Palmer, A.W., *Independent Eastern Europe.* London, 1962.
MacDonald, J.S., "Agricultural Organization, Migration and Labour Militancy in Rural Italy". *Economic History Review,* 2 series, 15 (1963), pp. 61-75.
MacDonald, J.S. & MacDonald, L., "Institutional Economics and Rural Development: Two Italian Types". *Human Organization* 23 (1964), pp. 113-118.
Macdonald, M., *The Republic of Austria 1918-1934.* London, 1946.
Macek, V., *In the Struggle for Freedom.* New York, 1957.
Machray, R., *Poland 1914-1931.* London, 1932.
Maciuika, B.V., "Agriculture in Soviet Latvia", in G.B. Carson (ed), *Latvia: An Area Study.* New Haven, 1956.
Mackie, T.T. & Rose, R. (eds), *The International Almanac of Electoral History.* London, 1974.
Macpherson, C.B., *Democracy in Alberta.* Toronto, 1953.
MacRae, D., *Parliament, Parties, and Society in France 1946-1958.* London, 1967.
Malefakis, E.E., *Agrarian Reform and Peasant Revolution in Spain.* New Haven, 1970.
Mallet, S., *Les paysans contre le passé.* Paris, 1962.
Malowist, M., "The Problem of the Inequality of Economic Development in Europe in the later Middle Ages". *Economic History Review* 19 (1966), pp. 115-128.
Mammarella, G., *Italy After Fascism.* South Bend, 1966.
Manning, M., *Irish Political Parties.* Dublin, 1972.
Manoliou, F.E., *La Réconstruction économique et financière de la Roumanie et les partis politiques.* Paris, 1931.
Markert, W. (ed), *Polen.* Cologne, 1959.
Marshall, T.H., *Citizenship and Social Class.* Cambridge, 1950.
Marx, K., *The Eighteenth Brumaire of Louis Bonaparte.* New York, 1957.
Mattes, W., *Die Bayerischen Bauernraten. Eine Soziologische und Historische Untersuchung über bauerliche Politik.* Stuttgart, 1921.
May, A.J., *The Hapsburg Monarchy 1867-1914.* Cambridge, Mass., 1960.
Mayer, H. (ed), *Hundert Jahre Österreichischer Wirtschafts-entwicklung.* Vienna, 1949.
Mazour, A., *Finland Between East and West.* New York, 1956.
Mead, W.R., "The Cold Farm in Finland, Resettlement of Finland's Dislocated Farmers". *Geographical Review* 41 (1951), pp. 529-543.
Medici, G., *Land Property and Land Tenure in Italy.* Bologna, 1952.
Melot, A., *Le parti catholique en Belgique.* Louvain, 1933.

Melson, R. & Wolpe, H., "Modernization and the Politics of Communalism: A Theoretical Perspective". *American Political Science Review* 64 (1970), pp. 1112-1130.
Mendras, H., *La fin des paysans*. Paris, 1968.
Meynaud, J., *Les groupes de pression*. Paris, 1958.
Meynaud, J. & Lancelot, A., *La participation des français à la politique*. Paris, 1965.
Mikus, J.A., *Slovakia, A Political History: 1918-1950*. Milwaukee, 1963.
Milbrath, L.W., *Political Participation*. Chicago, 1965.
Miller, D., *Church, State and Nation in Ireland 1898-1921*. Dublin, 1974.
Miller, K.E., *The Government and Politics of Denmark*. Boston, 1968.
Milward, A. & Saul, S.B., *The Economic Development of Continental Europe 1780-1870*. London, 1973.
Mingay, G.E., *English Landed Society in the Eighteenth Century*. London, 1963.
Mirkine-Guetzevitch, B. & Tibal, A., *La Pologne*. Paris, 1930.
Mirtshuk, J., "The Ukrainian Uniate Church". *Slavonic Review* 10 (1931-2), pp. 377-385.
Mitchell, A., *Revolution in Bavaria 1918-1919*. Princeton, 1965.
Mitrany, D., *Marx Against The Peasant*. Chapel Hill, 1951.
Mitrany, D., *The Land and the Peasant in Rumania*. London, 1930.
Mogey, J.M., *Rural Life in Northern Ireland*. London, 1947.
Mollov, J.S. (ed), *Die sozialökonomische Struktur der bulgarischen Landwirtschaft*. Berlin, 1936.
Moore, B., *Social Origins of Dictatorship and Democracy*. Boston, 1966.
Moore, W.E., *Industrialization and Labor*. Ithaca, 1951.
Moore, W.E., *Economic Demography of Eastern and Southern Europe*. Geneva, 1945.
Morgan, K.O., *Wales in British Politics*. Cardiff, 1963.
Morin, E., *Une Commune en France*. Paris, 1967.
Morrock, R., "The Rich Peasant in Politics: A Comparative Study of the Slovakian People's Party and the Akali Dal". *Social Theory and Practice* 1 (1971), pp. 11-21.
Moss, W., *Political Parties in the Irish Free State*. New York, 1933.
Mosse, W.E., *Alexander II and the Modernization of Russia*. London, 1958.
Mousnier, R., *Peasant Uprisings in Seventeenth-Century France, Russia and China*. London, 1971.
Mouzalis, N. & Attalides, M., "Greece", in M.S. Archer & S. Giner (eds), *Contemporary Europe*. London, 1971, pp. 162-197.
Mühlmann, W.E. (ed), *Chiliasmus und Nativismus*. Berlin, 1961.
Munch, P.A., "The Peasant Movement in Norway: A Study in Class and Culture". *British Journal of Sociology* 5 (1954), pp. 173-210.

Nagy, F., *The Struggle Behind the Iron Curtain*. New York, 1948.
Nagy-Talavera, N.M., *The Green Shirts and the Others*. Stanford, 1970.
Nash, M., *Primitive and Peasant Economic Systems*. San Francisco, 1966.
Nedelmann, B., "Zur Parteientstehung in Schweden (1866-1907): Historische-soziologische Aspekte der Institutionalisierung politische Organisationen". Doctoral dissertation, University of Mannheim, 1970.

Nettl, J.P., Political Mobilization. London, 1967.
Neubauer, D.E., "Some Conditions of Democracy". American Political Science Review 61 (1967), pp. 1002-1009.
Newman, K.J., European Democracy Between The Wars. London, 1970.
Nilson, S.S., "Wahlsoziologische Probleme des Nationalsozialismus". Zeitschrift für die gesamte Staatswissenschaft. 110 (1954), pp. 279-311.
Nimkoff, M.F. & Middleton, R., "Types of Family and Types of Economy". American Journal of Sociology. 66 (1960), pp. 215-225.
Nipperdey, T., Die Organisation der deutschen Parteien vor 1918. Düsseldorf, 1961.
Nodel, E., Estonia: Nation on the Anvil. New York, 1963.
Nooij, A.T.J., "Radical Dutch Farmers". Sociologia neerlandica 7 (1971), pp. 28-41.
Nooij, A.T.J., "Political Radicalism among Dutch Farmers". Sociologia Ruralis 9 (1969), pp. 43-61.
Nordal, J., "The Failure of the Industrial Revolution in Spain 1830-1914", in C.M. Cipolla (ed), The Emergence of Industrial Societies. London, 1973. II, pp. 532-626.
Nordlinger, E.A., "Political Development: Time Sequences and Rates of Change", in E.A. Nordlinger (ed), Politics and Society. Englewood Cliffs, 1970, ppl 329-347.
Norman, E.R., A History of Modern Ireland. London, 1971.
Nousiainen, J., The Finnish Political System. Cambridge, Mass., 1971.
Nyholm, P., "Parliament, Government and Multi-Dimensional Party Relations in Finland". Commentationes Scientiarum Socialium 2 (1972).
Nyman, O., Svensk parlamentarism 1932-1936. Från minoritetsparlamentarism till majoritetskoalition. Uppsala, 1947.

Olsen, G., Hovedgård og Bondegård. Studier over stordriftens udvikling i Danmark i tiden 1525-1774. Copenhagen, 1957.
Olsson, G., Hattar och Mössor. Studiet över partiväsendet i Sverige 1751-1762. Gothenberg, 1963.
Omelianov, A., "A Bulgarian Experiment", in P.A. Sorokin, C.C. Zimmerman & C.J. Galpin (eds), A Systematic Source Book in Rural Sociology. Minneapolis, 1931. II, pp. 638-647.
Orwin, C.S., A History of English Farming. London, 1949.
Österud, Ö., "Agrarian Structure and Peasant Politics in Scandinavia". Doctoral dissertation, University of London, 1974.

Page, S.W., The Formation of the Baltic States. Cambridge, Mass., 1959.
Paige, J.M., Agrarian Revolution: Social Movements and Export Agriculture in the Underdeveloped World. New York, 1975.
Palmer, R.R., The Age of the Democratic Revolution: The Challenge. Princeton, 1959.
Paprocki, J., La Pologne et le Problème des Minorités. Warsaw, 1935.
Parming, T., The Collapse of Liberal Democracy and the Rise of Authoritarianism in Estonia. Sage Professional Papers in Contemporary Political Sociology 06-010. London/Beverly Hills, 1975.
Pasvolsky, L., Bulgaria's Economic Position. Washington, 1930.

Pasvolsky, L., Economic Nationalism of the Danubian States. New York, 1928.
Pautard, J., Les disparités régionales dans la croissance de l'agriculture française. Paris, 1965.
Payne, S.G., "Catalan and Basque Nationalism". Journal of Contemporary History 6 (1971), pp. 15-51.
Peacock, A.J., Bread or Blood: A Study of the Agrarian Riots in East Anglia in 1816. London, 1965.
Perman, D., The Shaping of the Czechoslovak State. Leiden, 1962.
Pernot, M., Balkans nouveaux. Paris, 1929.
Perrie, M., "The Russian Peasant Movement of 1905-1907: Its Social Composition and Revolutionary Significance". Past and Present 57 (1972), pp. 123-155.
Pešelj, B.M., "Peasantism: Its Ideology and Achievements", in C.E. Black (ed), Challenge in Eastern Europe. New Brunswick, 1954, pp. 109-131.
Pesonen, P., "Finland: Party Support in a Fragmented System", in R. Rose (ed), Electoral Behavior. New York, 1974, pp. 271-314.
Pesonen, P., "Dimensions of Political Cleavage in Multi-Party Systems". European Journal of Political Research 1 (1973). pp. 109-132.
Pesonen, P., An Election in Finland. New Haven, 1968.
Pfeiffer, R. & Ladrière, J., L'aventure Rexiste. Brussels, 1966.
Pidal, R.M., The Spaniards in their History. New York, 1966.
Pitt-Rivers, J., The People of the Sierra. New York, 1955.
Plowman, D.E.G., Michinton, W.E. & Stacey, M. "Local Social Status in England and Wales". Sociological Review 10 (1962), pp. 161-202.
Poggi, G., Catholic Action in Italy. Stanford, 1969.
Poggi, G., Le preferenze politiche degli Italiani. Bologna, 1968.
Political & Economic Planning, Economic Development in South-Eastern Europe. London, 1945.
Pollock, J.K., "An Areal Study of the German Electorate, 1930-1933". American Political Science Review 38 (1944), pp. 89-95.
Polonsky, A., Politics in Independent Poland. Oxford, 1972.
Pomfret, J.E., The Struggle for the Land in Ireland, 1800-1923. Princeton, 1930.
Porchnev, B., Les Soulèvements populaires en France de 1623 à 1648. Paris, 1963.
Postan, M.M. (ed), The Cambridge Economic History of Europe, I. The Agrarian Life of the Middle Ages. Cambridge, 1966.
Powell, J.D., "Peasant Society and Clientelist Politics". American Political Science Review 64 (1970), pp. 411-425.
Power, E., The Wool Trade in English Medieval History. London, 1941.
Prost, H., Destin de la Roumanie 1918-1954. Paris, 1954.
Puhle, H.R., Agrarische Interessenpolitik und preussischer Konservatismus im Wilhelminischen Reich. Berlin, 1967.
Pullerits, A., Estonia, Population, Cultural and Economic Life. Tallinn, 1937.
Pulzer, P.J., The Rise of Political Anti-Semitism in Germany and Austria. New York, 1964.

Quante, P., Die Abwanderung aus der Landwirtschaft. Kiel, 1958.

Rabushka, A. & Shepsle, K.A., Politics in Plural Societies: A Theory of Democratic Instability. Columbus, 1972.

Radkey, O.H., *The Agrarian Foes of Bolshevism*. New York, 1958.
Radkey, O.H., *The Election to the Russian Constituent Assembly of 1917*. Cambridge, Mass., 1950.
Raeff, M., *Origins of the Russian Intelligentsia*. New York, 1966.
Rama, C.A., *La crise espagnole au XXe siècle*. Paris, 1962.
Ramos Oliviera, A., *Politics, Economics and Men of Modern Spain*. London, 1946.
Rantala, O., "The Political Regions of Finland". *Scandinavian Political Studies* 2 (1967), pp. 117-140.
Rapport de l'Office de Statistique de la République Tchécoslovaque 1925. Prague, 1926.
Raupach, H., "Der interregionale Wohlfahrtsausgleich als Problem der Politik des Deutschen Reiches", in W. Conze & H. Raupach (eds) *Die Staats- und Wirtschaftskrise des Deutschen Reiches 1929-1933*. Stuttgart, 1967, pp. 13-34.
Raymond-Laurent, J., *Le Parti Démocrate Populaire, 1924-44*. Le Mans, 1966.
Redfield, R., *Peasant Society and Culture*. Chicago, 1960.
Rees, A.D., *Life in a Welsh Countryside*. Cardiff, 1950.
Reigrotzki, E., *Soziale Verflechtungen in der Bundesrepublik*. Tübingen, 1956.
Reimann, V., *Zu gross für Österreich. Seipel und Bauer im Kampf um die Erste Republik*. Vienna, 1968.
Rice, S.A., *Farmers and Workers in American Politics*. New York, 1924.
Riggs, F.W., "Bureaucrats and Political Development: a Paradoxical View", in J. LaPalombara (ed), *Bureaucracy and Political Development*. Princeton, 1963, pp. 120-167.
Riggs, F.W., "Agraria vs Industria: Toward a Typology of Comparative Administration", in W.J. Siffin (ed), *Toward a Comparative Study of Public Administration*. Bloomington, 1959, pp. 23-110.
Riksdagsmannavalen åren 1925-1928. Stockholm, 1928.
Roberts, H.L., *Rumania: Political Problems of an Agrarian State*. New Haven, 1951.
Robinson, G.T., *Rural Russia under the Old Regime*. New York, 1949.
Robinson, R.A.H., *The Origins of Franco's Spain*. Newton Abbot, 1970.
Rogger, H. & Weber, E. (eds), *The European Right*. Berkeley/Los Angeles, 1965.
Rokkan, S., "Dimensions of State Formation and Nation Building: A Possible Paradigm for Research and Variations within Europe", in C. Tilly (ed), *The Formation of National States in Western Europe*. Princeton, 1975, pp. 562-600.
Rokkan, S., "Cities, States and Nations: A Dimensional Model for the Study of Contrasts in Development", in S.N. Eisenstadt & S. Rokkan (eds), *Building States and Nations*. London/Beverly Hills, 1973. I, pp. 73-97.
Rokkan, S., *Citizens, Elections, Parties*. New York, 1970.
Rokkan, S., "The Growth and Structuring of Mass Politics in Western Europe: Reflections of Possible Models of Explanation". *Scandinavian Political Studies* 5 (1970), pp. 65-83.
Rokkan, S., "Geography, Religion, and Social Class: Cross-cutting Cleavages in Norwegian Politics", in S.M. Lipset & S. Rokkan (eds), *Party Systems and Voter Alignments*. New York, 1967, pp. 367-444.
Rokkan, S., "Norway: Numerical Democracy and Corporate Pluralism", in R.A. Dahl (ed), *Political Oppositions in Western Democracies*. New Haven, 1966, pp. 70-115.

Rokkan, S., "Electoral Mobilization, Party Competition, and National Integration", in J. LaPalombara & M. Weiner (eds), *Political Parties and Political Development*. Princeton, 1966, pp. 241-265.
Rokkan, S. & Campbell, A., "Factors in the Recruitment of Active Participants in Politics: A Comparative Analysis of Survey Data for Norway and the United States". *International Social Science Bulletin* 12 (1960), pp. 69-99.
Rokkan, S. & Valen, H., "Regional Contrasts in Norwegian Politics", in E. Allardt & Y. Littunen (eds), *Cleavages, Ideologies and Party Systems*. Helsinki, 1964, pp. 162-238.
Rokkan, S. & Valen, H., "The Mobilization of the Periphery", in S. Rokkan (ed), *Approaches to the Study of Political Participation*. Bergen, 1962, pp. 111-159.
Rommen, H., *The State in Catholic Thought*. St. Louis, 1950.
Roos, H., *A History of Modern Poland*. London, 1966.
Rose, R. (ed), *Electoral Behavior*, New York, 1974.
Rose, R. & Urwin, D.W., "Persistence and Change in Western Party Systems Since 1945". *Political Studies* 18 (1970), pp. 287-319.
Rose, R. & Urwin, D.W., "Social Cohesion, Political Parties and Strains in Regimes". *Comparative Political Studies* 2 (1969), pp. 7-67.
Rose, W.J., *The Drama of Upper Silesia*. London, 1936.
Rosenberg, H., *Grosse Depression und Bismarckzeit*. Berlin, 1967.
Rosenberg, H., "Die Pseudodemokratisierung der Rittergutsbesitzerklasse", in H.U. Wehler (ed), *Moderne deutsche Sozialgeschichte*. Cologne, 1966, pp. 287-308.
Rosenberg, H., *Bureaucracy, Aristocracy and Autocracy: The Prussian Experience 1660-1815*. Cambridge, Mass., 1958.
Rosenberg, H., "Political and Social Consequences of the Great Depression of 1873-1896 in Central Europe". *Economic History Review* 13 (1943), pp. 58-73.
Rostow, W.W., *The Stages of Economic Growth*. New York, 1960.
Roth, G., "Personal Leadership, Patrimonialism and Empire-Building in the New States". Paper at the World Congress of the International Sociological Association. Evian, 1966.
Roth, G., *The Social Democrats in Imperial Germany*. Totowa, 1963.
Rothenberg, A., *The Austrian Military Border in Croatia*. Urbana, 1961.
Rothfels, H., "The Baltic Provinces: Some Historical Aspects and Perspectives". *Journal of Central European Affairs* 4 (1944). pp. 117-146.
Rothschild, J., *East Central Europe Between The Two World Wars*. Seattle, 1974.
Rothschild, J., *Pilsudski's Coup d'État*. New York, 1966.
Rothschild, J., *The Communist Party of Bulgaria*. New York, 1959.
Roucek, J.S. (ed), *Slavonic Encyclopaedia*. New York, 1949.
Roucek, J.S., *Balkan Politics*. Stanford, 1948.
Roucek, J.S., "The Czechoslovak Party System", *Journal of Central European Affairs* 1 (1942), pp. 428-445.
Roucek, J.S., *The Politics of the Balkans*. New York, 1939.
Roucek, J.S., "The Working of Czechoslovak Constitutional Democracy", *World Affairs Interpreter* 8 (1937), pp. 159-167.
Roucek, J.S., "Economic Geography of Bulgaria". *Economic Geography* 11 (1935), pp. 307-323.
Roucek, J.S., "Characteristics of Albanian Politics". *Social Science* 10 (1935), pp. 71-79.

Roucek, J.S., Contemporary Roumania and Her Problems. Stanford, 1932.
Rowntree, B.S., Land and Labour: Lessons from Belgium. London, 1910.
Royal Institute of International Affairs (RIIA), The Scandinavian States and Finland: A Political and Economic Survey. London, 1951.
RIIA, Agrarian Problems from the Baltic to the Aegean. London, 1943.
RIIA, Nationalism. London, 1939.
RIIA, The Baltic States. London, 1938.
RIIA, World Agriculture, An International Survey. London, 1932.
Rudé, G., Revolutionary Europe 1783-1815. New York, 1964.
Rudé, G., The Crowd in History. New York, 1964.
Ruin, O., Mellan samlingsregering och tvåpartisystem. Stockholm, 1968.
Rumpf, E., Nationalismus und Sozialismus in Irland. Meisenheim 1959.
Rūsis, A., "Land and Peasant: Latvia", in V. Gsovski & K. Grzybowski (eds), Government, Law and Courts in the Soviet Union and Eastern Europe. New York, 1960.
Russett, B.M., "Inequality and Instability: The Relation of Land Tenure to Politics". World Politics 16 (1964), pp. 442-454.
Russett, B.M., Alker, H.H., Deutsch, K.W. & Lasswell, H.D. (eds), World Handbook of Political and Social Indicators. New Haven, 1964.
Rustow, D.A., The Politics of Compromise. Princeton, 1955.
Rydenfelt, S., Kommunismen i Sverige. Lund, 1954.

Sabean, D., "The Communal Basis of pre-1800 Peasant Uprisings in Western Europe". Comparative Politics 8 (1976), pp. 355-364.
Sabean, D., Landbesitz und Gesellschaft am Vorabend des Bauernkriegs. Stuttgart, 1972.
Sagnac, P., La formation de la société française. Paris, 1945. 2 vols.
Salomon, N., La campagne de nouvelle Castile à la fin du XVIe siecle d'après les Relaciones Topográficas. Paris, 1964.
Salomonsen, P., Den politiske magtkamp 1866-1901. Copenhagen,1968.
Salts, A., Lettlands Wirtschaft und Wirtschaftspolitik. Riga, 1930.
Salts, A., Die politische Parteien Lettland. Riga, 1926.
Sañchez, J.M., The Politico-Religious Background of the Spanish Civil War. Chapel Hill, 1962.
Sanders, I.T., Rainbow in the Rock. Cambridge, Mass., 1962.
Sanders, I.T., Balkan Village. Lexington, 1949.
Särlvik, B., "Sweden: The Social Bases of the Parties in a Developmental Perspective", in R. Rose (ed), Electoral Behavior. New York, 1974, pp. 371-434.
Särlvik, B., "Political Stability and Change in the Swedish Electorate". Scandinavian Political Studies 1 (1966), pp. 188-222.
Sartori, G., "The Sociology of Parties: A Critical Review", in O. Stammer (ed), Party Systems, Party Organization, and the Politics of New Masses. Berlin, 1968, pp. 1-25.
Saville, J., Rural Depopulation in England and Wales, 1851-1951. London, 1957.

Schacter, G., The Italian South: Economic Development in Mediterranean Europe. New York, 1965.
Schafer, B.C., Faces of Nationalism. New York, 1972.
Schattschneider, E.E., The Semi-Sovereign People. New York, 1960.
Schickele, R., Agrarian Revolution and Economic Progress. New York, 1968.
Schiff, W., "Die Agrargesetzgebung der Europäischen Staaten vor und nach dem Kriege". Archiv für Sozialwissenschaft und Sozialpolitik 2 (1925), pp. 465-529.
Schmahl, E., Entwicklung der völkischen Bewegung. Giessen, 1933.
Schmidt, C.T., The Plough and the Sword: Labor, Land and Property in Fascist Italy. New York, 1938.
Schopflin, G., "The Ideology of Croat Nationalism". Survey 19 (1973), pp. 123-146.
Schram, S.R., Protestantism and Politics in France. Alençon, 1954.
Schwabe, A., Histoire agraire de la Lettonie. Riga, 1929.
Schwend, K., Bayern zwischen Monarchie und Diktatur. Munich, 1954.
Schwer, W., Catholic Social Theory. St. Louis, 1940.
Secher, H.P., "Representative Democracy or 'Chamber State'". Western Political Quarterly 13 (1960), pp. 890-909.
Seip, J.A., "Modellens Tyranni. Analyse av Stein Rokkans anvendelse av en sentrum-periferi modell på norsk historie". Paper at Conference on Methodology in History. Röros, 1974.
Semmingen, I., "The Dissolution of Estate Society in Norway". Scandinavian Economic History Review 2 (1954), pp. 166-203.
Senn, A.E., The Great Powers, Lithuania and the Vilna Question 1920-1928. Leiden, 1966.
Seton-Watson, C., Italy from Liberalism to Fascism 1870-1925. London, 1969.
Seton-Watson, H., Eastern Europe Between The Wars. New York, 1964.
Seton-Watson, H., Neither War Nor Peace. New York, 1962.
Seton-Watson, H., The East European Revolution. New York, 1956.
Seton-Watson, R.W. (ed), Slovakia Then and Now. London, 1931.
Shanin, T. (ed), Peasants and Peasant Societies. London, 1971.
Shanin, T., The Awkward Class. Oxford, 1971.
Shanin, T., "The Peasantry as a Political Factor". Sociological Review 14 (1966), pp. 5-27.
Sharp, W.R., The Government of the French Republic. New York, 1938.
Shils, E., "The Intellectuals in the Political Development of the New States", in J.H. Kautsky (ed), Political Change in Underdeveloped Countries. New York, 1962, pp. 195-234.
Siegfried, A., Tableau Politique de la France de l'Ouest sous la Troisième République. Paris, 1913.
Silverman, D.P., Reluctant Union. University Park, Pa., 1972.
Silverman, S.F., "'Exploitation' in Rural Central Italy: Structure and Ideology in Stratification Study". Comparative Studies in Society and History 12 (1970), pp. 327-339.
Silverman, S.F., "Agricultural Organization, Social Structure, and Values in Italy: Amoral Familism Reconsidered". American Anthropologist 70 (1968), pp. 1-20.
Silverman, S.F., "Patronage and Community-Nation Relationships in Central Italy". Ethnology 4 (1965), pp. 172-189.
Simon, C.A., Le parti Catholique Belge, 1830-1945. Brussels, 1958.
Simon, E., Réveil national et culture populaire en Scandinavie. Paris, 1960.
Simon, E.D., The Smaller Democracies. London, 1940.

Simon, H.A. "Theories of Decision-Making in Economics". *American Economic Review* 49 (1959), pp. 253-283.
Simon, W.B., "Politische Ethik und politische Struktur". *Kölner Zeitschrift für Soziologie und Sozialpsychologie* 11 (1959), pp. 445-459.
Sjöblom, G., *Party Strategies in a Multiparty System*. Lund, 1968.
Skendi, S., *The Albanian National Awakening*. Princeton, 1967.
Skrubbeltrang, F. & Hansen, K., *Det danske landbrugeshistorie*. Copenhagen, 1945.
Slicher van Bath, B.H., "The Economic and Social Conditions in the Frisian Districts 900-1500". *Afdeling Agrarische Geschiedenis Bijdragen* 13 (1965), pp. 97-133.
Slicher van Bath, B.H., *The Agrarian History of Western Europe, AD 500-1850*. London, 1963.
Smelser, N.J., *Theory of Collective Behavior*. New York, 1962.
Smith, D.M., *Victor Emanuel, Cavour, and the Risorgimento*. London, 1971.
Smith, D.M., *Italy: A Modern History*. Ann Arbor, 1959.
Smith, R.E.F., *The Enserfment of the Russian Peasantry*. London, 1968.
Snowden, F.M., "On the Social Origins of Agrarian Fascism in Italy". *European Journal of Sociology* 13 (1972), pp. 268-295.
Snyder, L., *The Meaning of Nationalism*. New Brunswick, 1954.
Sorokin, P.A., Zimmerman, C.C. & Galpin, C.J. (eds), *A Systematic Source Book in Rural Sociology*. Minneapolis, 1930-31. 2 vols.
Spekke, A., *History of Latvia: An Outline*. Stockholm, 1957.
Spulber, N., "Changes in the Economic Structure of the Balkans 1860-1960", in C. Jelavich & B. Jelavich (eds), *The Balkans in Transition*. Berkeley/Los Angeles, 1963, pp. 346-375.
Statistique de l'Island. Reykjavik.
Statistique des élections des députés pour l'assemblée nationale ordinaire. (1915-1928). Sofia.
Statistique des élections. (1922-1926). Warsaw.
Statistisches Handbuch für die Republik Österreich. Vienna.
Statistisches Jahrbuch für das Deutsche Reich. Berlin.
Statistisk Årbog for Danmark. Copenhagen.
Statistisk Årbok for Norge. Oslo.
Statistisk Årsbok for Sverige. Stockholm.
Stavenhagen, R. (ed), *Agrarian Problems and Peasant Movements in Latin America*. New York, 1970.
Stavrianos, L., *The Balkans Since 1453*. New York, 1963.
Stavrianos, L., "The Influence of the West upon the Balkans", in C. Jelavich & B. Jelavich (eds), *The Balkans in Transition*. Berkeley/Los Angeles, 1963, pp. 184-226.
Stearns, P., *European Society in Upheaval*. New York, 1967.
Steiner, J., *Die Beziehungen zwischen den Stimmberechtigen und den Gewählten in ländlichem und städtlichem Milieu*. Bern, 1959.
Stiefbold, R. & Koppel, T.P., "The Three 'Lager' in Austrian Electoral History". Paper at the World Congress of the International Political Science Association. Brussels, 1967.
Stiefbold, R., Leupold-Löwenthal, A., Ress, G., Lichem W. & Marvick, D (eds), *Wahlen und Parteien in Österreich*. Vienna, 1966. 4 vols.
Stinchcombe, A.L., "Agricultural Enterprise and Rural Class Relations", *American Journal of Sociology* 67 (1961), pp. 165-176.

Stjernquist, N., "Sweden: Stability or Deadlock?", in R.A. Dahl (ed), Political Oppositions in Western Democracies. New Haven, 1966, pp. 116-146.
Stoetzel, J., "Voting Behaviour in France". British Journal of Sociology 6 (1955), pp. 104-122.
Stoianovich, R., "The Social Foundations of Balkan Politics 1750-1941", in C. Jelavich & B. Jelavich (eds), The Balkans in Transition. Berkeley/Los Angeles, 1963, pp. 297-345.
Stoltenberg, G., Politische Strömungen im schleswig-holsteinischen Landvolk 1918-1933. Düsseldorf, 1962.
Stone, L., "Literacy and Education in England 1640-1900". Past and Present 42 (1969), pp. 69-139.
Strong, D., Austria (October 1918-March 1919): Transition from Empire to Republic. New York, 1939.
Stukas, J., Awakening Lithuania. Madison, NJ, 1966.
Suomen Tilastollinen Vuosikirja. Helsinki.
Svåsand, L., "Stortingsvalget i 1882, en analyse av geografiske og ökonomiske konfliktlinjer". Dissertation, University of Bergen, 1972.
Svensson, J., Jordbruk och depression 1870-1900. Lund, 1965.
Swanson, G., Religion and Regime: A Sociological Account of the Reformation. Ann Arbor, 1967.
Swire, J., Bulgarian Conspiracy. London, 1939.
Swire, J., The Rise of a Kingdom. London, 1929.
Szymanski, A., "Fascism, Industrialism and Socialism: The Case of Italy". Comparative Studies in Society and History 15 (1975), pp. 395-404.

Taborsky, E., Czechoslovak Democracy At Work. London, 1945.
Tarrow, S.G., Peasant Communism in Southern Italy. New Haven, 1967.
Tavernier, Y., La F.N.S.E.A.. Paris, 1965.
Tchitchovsky, T., "Political and Social Aspects of Modern Bulgaria". Slavonic Review 8 (1929-30), pp. 176-187.
Technical and Economic Changes in Danish Farming. 40 Years of Farm Records, 1917-1957. Copenhagen, 1959.
Textor, L.E., Land Reform in Czechoslovakia. London, 1923.
Thermaenius, E., Lantmannapartiet. Dess uppkomst, organisation och tidigare utveckling. Uppsala, 1928.
Thirsk, J. (ed), The Agrarian History of England and Wales, IV. 1500-1640. Cambridge, 1967.
Thomas, A.H., Parliamentary Parties in Denmark, 1945-1972. Strathclyde Survey Research Centre Occasional Paper 13. Glasgow, 1973.
Thompson, F.M.L., "The Second Agricultural Revolution, 1815-1880". Economic History Review, 2 series, 21 (1968), pp. 62-77.
Thompson, F.M.L., "The Social Distribution of Landed Property in England since the Sixteenth Century". Economic History Review, 2 series, 19 (1966), pp. 505-517.
Thompson, F.M.L., English Landed Society in the Nineteenth Century. London, 1963.
Thompson, J.G., Urbanization. New York, 1927.
Thornley, D., Isaac Butt and Home Rule. London, 1964.
Thrupp, S.L., (ed), Millenial Dreams in Action. Hague, 1961.
Tilly, C., "Food Supply and Public Order in Modern Europe", in C. Tilly (ed), The Formation of National States in Western Europe. Princeton, 1975, pp. 380-455.

Tilly, C., *The Vendée*. Cambridge, Mass., 1964.
Tims, R.W., *Germanizing Prussian Poland: The H-K-T Society and the Struggle for the Eastern Marches in the German Empire. 1894-191*. New York, 1941.
Tingsten, H., *Political Behaviour*. London, 1937.
Tirrell, S.R., *German Agrarian Politics After Bismarck's Fall*. New York, 1951.
Todorov, K., *Balkan Firebrand*. New York, 1943.
Tökés, R.L., *Bela Kun and the Hungarian Soviet Republic*. New York, 1967.
Tomasevich, J., *Peasants, Politics, and Economic Change in Yugoslavia*. Stanford, 1955.
Tomasič, D., *Personality and Culture in Eastern European Politics*. New York, 1948.
Torgersen, U., "The Trend Toward Political Consensus: The Case of Norway", in E. Allardt & S. Rokkan (eds), *Mass Politics*. New York, 1970, pp. 93-104.
Torgersen, U., *Norsk politiske institusjoner*. Oslo, 1964.
Tracy, M., *Agriculture in Western Europe: Crisis and Adaptation since 1880*. London, 1964.
Trouton, R., *Peasant Renaissance in Yogoslavia, 1900-1950*. London, 1952.
Tudesq, A., *Les conseilleurs généraux en France au Temps de Guizot 1840-1848*. Paris, 1967.
Tuma, E.H., *Twenty-Six Centuries of Agrarian Reform*. Berkeley/Los Angeles, 1965.

Ulich, R., *The Education of Nations*. Cambridge, Mass., 1961.
Ullman, J.C., *The Tragic Week: A Study of Anticlericalism in Spain 1875-1912*. Cambridge, Mass., 1968.
Urwin D.W., "Germany: Continuity and Change in Electoral Politics", in R. Rose (ed.), *Electoral Behavior*. New York, 1974, pp. 109-170.
Urwin, D.W., "Political Parties, Societies and Regimes in Europe: Some Reflections on the Literature". *European Journal of Political Research* 1 (1973), pp. 179-204.
Urwin, D.W., "The Development of the Conservative Party Organisation in Scotland until 1912". *Scottish Historical Review* 44 (1965), pp. 89-111.

Valen, H. & Katz, D., *Political Parties in Norway*. Oslo, 1964.
Valen, H. & Rokkan, S., "Norway: Conflict Structure and Mass Politics in a European Periphery", in R. Rose (ed), *Electoral Behavior*. New York, 1974, pp. 315-370.
Valen-Sendstad, F., *Norske landbruksredskaper, 1800-1850-årene*. Lillehammer, 1964.
Vallender, T., *I kamp för demokratien. Rösträttsrörelsen i Sverige 1886-1890*. Stockholm, 1962.
van Deenen, C., *Materialen auf Arbeitswirtschaft*. Bonn, 1964.
Varzim, A., *Le Boerenbond Belge*. Paris, 1934.
Venturi, F., *Roots of Revolution: A History of the Populist and Socialist Movements in Nineteenth-Century Russia*. London, 1960.
Verba, S., *Small Groups and Political Behavior*. Princeton, 1961.
Verney, D., *Parliamentary Reform in Sweden 1866-1921*. Oxford, 1957.
Vidich, A.J. & Bensman, J., *Small Town in Mass Society*. New York, 1960.

Vilar, P., La Catalogne dans l'Espagne moderne. Paris, 1962. 3 vols.
Vöchting, F., La Questione Meridionale. Naples, 1955.
Vodopivec, A., Die Balkanisierung Österreichs. Vienna, 1966.
Volkmann, H-E. (ed), Die Krise des Parlamentarismus in Ostmitteleuropa zwischen den beiden Weltkriegen. Marburg, 1967.
von Blanckenberg, P., "Die esteuropäischen Landarbeiter". Berichte über Landwirtschaft 39 (1961), pp. 459-498.
von Hehn, J., Lettland zwischen Demokratie und Diktatur. Munich, 1957.
von Knorring, G., "Krisenjahr in Estland". Baltische Hefte 8 (1962), pp. 86-95.
von Rauch, G., The Baltic States. Berkeley/Los Angeles, 1974.
von Rauch, G., Der Deutsche Orden und die Einheit des baltisches Landes. Hamburg, 1961.
Vucinich, W.S. (ed), Contemporary Yugoslavia. Berkeley/ Los Angeles, 1969.
Vucinich, W.S. (ed), The Peasant in Nineteenth Century Russia. Stanford, 1968.

Wallerstein, I., The Modern World System: Capitalist Agriculture and the Origins of the European World-Economy in the Sixteenth Century. New York, 1974.
Wallin, G., Valrörelser och valresultat. Andrakammarvalen i Sverige 1866-1884. Stockholm, 1961.
Wallner, E.M., Die Reichstags- und Bundestagswahlen im Landkreis Freiburg seit der Jahrhundertwende. Buhl, 1965.
Wandruska, A., "Österreichs politische Struktur. Die Entwicklung der Parteien und der politische Bewegungen", in H. Benedikt (ed), Geschichte der Republik Österreich. Vienna, 1954, pp. 289-485.
Wanklyn, H., Czechoslovakia. New York, 1954.
Warner, C.K., The Winegrowers of France and the Government since 1075. New York, 1960.
Warriner, D., The Economics of Peasant Farming. London, 1964.
Weber, E., Peasants into Frenchmen: The Modernization of Rural France 1870-1914. Stanford, 1976.
Weber, M., The Sociology of Religion. Boston, 1963.
Webster, R.A., The Cross and the Fasces. Stanford, 1960.
Weiner, M., "Political Integration and Political Development", in J.L. Finkle & R.W. Gable (eds), Political Development and Social Change. New York, 1971, pp. 643-654.
Weiner, M., "Political Participation: Crisis of the Political Process", in L. Binder et al, Crises and Sequences in Political Development. Princeton, 1971, pp. 159-204.
West, R., Black Lamb and Grey Falcon. New York, 1940.
Western J.R., The End of European Primacy. London, 1965.
White, L., "Technology and Invention in the Middle Ages". Speculum 15 (1940), pp. 141-159.
Whyte, J.H., "Ireland: Politics without Social Bases", in R.Rose (ed), Electoral Behavior. New York, 1974, pp. 619-651.
Whyte, J.H., Church and State in Modern Ireland, 1923-1970. Dublin, 1971.
Wienzierl, E. (ed), Der Österreichischer und Sein Staat. Vienna, 1965.

Wiles, P., "A Syndrome, Not a Doctrine: Some Elementary Theses on Populism", in G. Ionescu & E. Gellner (eds), Populism: Its National Characteristics. London, 1969, pp. 166-179.
Willemsen, A., Het Vlaamse Nationalisme 1914-1940. Groningen, 1958.
Wiskemann, E., Czechs and Germans. London, 1938.
Wislander, H. (ed), De politiske partiernas program. Stockholm, 1964.
Witt, K., Wirtschaftskräfte und Wirtschaftspolitik der Tschechoslowakei. Leipzig, 1936.
Wittram, R., Baltische Geschichte. Die Ostseelande Livland, Estland, Kurland 1180-1918. Munich, 1954.
Wolf, E.R., Peasant Wars of the Twentieth Century. New York, 1969.
Wolf, E.R., Peasants. Englewood Cliffs, 1966.
Wolf, E.R., "Types of Latin American Peasantry: A Preliminary Discussion". American Anthropologist 57 (1955), pp. 452-471.
Wolf, J.B., France 1814-1919: The Rise of a Liberal Democracy. New York, 1963.
Wolff, R.L., The Balkans in Our Time. Cambridge, Mass., 1956.
Woytinsky, W., Die Welt in Zahlen, 1926.
Wright, G., Rural Revolution in France. Stanford, 1964.
Wright, G., "Agrarian Syndicalism in Postwar France". American Political Science Review 47 (1953), pp. 402-416.
Wright, G., "Catholics and Peasantry in France". Political Science Quarterly 68 (1953), pp. 526-551.
Wright, W.E., Serf, Seigneur and Sovereign. Minneapolis, 1966.
Wunderlich, F., Farm Labor in Germany 1810-1945. Princeton, 1961.
Wylie, L., Village in the Vaucluse. New York, 1964.

Yaresh, L., "The 'Peasant Wars' in Soviet Historiography". American Slavic and East European Review 16 (1957), pp. 241-259.
Youngson, A.J., Overhead Capital. Edinburgh, 1967.

Zagoroff, S.D., Vegh, J. & Bilimovic, A., The Agricultural Economy of the Danubian Countries 1935-1945. Stanford, 1955.
Zariski, R., Italy: The Politics of Uneven Development. Hinsdale, 1972.
Zeman, Z.A.B., The Break-up of the Hapsburg Empire 1914-1918. London, 1961.
Ziegler, D.J., Prelude to Democracy: A Study of Proportional Representation and the Heritage of Weimar Germany 1871-1920. Lincoln, 1958.
Zinner, P.E., Communist Strategy and Tactics in Czechoslovakia, 1918-48. New York, 1963.
Zweig, F., Poland Between Two Wars. London, 1944.

INDEX

Accion Nacional   189
administration, state   25, 34, 52, 63, 66, 85, 97-9, 117, 172, 174, 177, 204
Agrarian Democratic Party; Albania   167
Agrarian International   268
Agrarian Party:
    Austria-Hungary   175
    Estonia   167, 249
    Finland   139, 167, 211, 216, 223-4, 229-30, 237, 240-1
    France   167, 169, 182
    Netherlands   166, 168
    Norway   139, 168, 192, 211, 217, 227, 229, 230, 238-9
    Serbia   168, 213, 268
    Slovenia   168
    Spain   168-9, 188, 212
    Sweden   139-40, 155, 168, 191, 211, 215-7, 219, 229-30, 237-8
Agrarian Union, Bulgaria   167, 175, 179, 204, 214-5, 222, 225-6, 234, 246
agricultural depression   82, 84, 96, 129, 197

agricultural labourers   15-7, 80, 90-2, 96, 128, 138-41, 145-9, 151, 181, 185-7, 258, 264
agrotowns   146, 185
Aizargi, Latvia   183
Alava   196
Albania   65, 73, 75, 83, 166-7, 170, 193-4, 213
Alliance Agricole, Belgium   198
Alpine provinces   32, 38, 45, 49
Alsace-Lorraine   198
America   156, 158
Amsterdam   210
anarchism   89, 93, 186-7, 226
Andalusia   49, 77, 80, 89, 93, 146, 170, 187
animals   43, 51, 71
anticlericalism   141-2, 152, 158, 179, 202, 213, 221
antisemitism   88, 149, 174, 183, 260
Aragon   49
Aargau   210
aristocracy   29-31, 34, 39, 41, 44-8, 55-6, 63, 68, 73, 77-8, 80, 92, 96, 147, 162, 171, 173
Arrow Cross, Hungary   183
Atlantic   58
Austria   32, 38, 43, 49, 53, 63, 65, 68, 73, 76, 83, 88, 94, 98, 103, 119-21, 124, 131-2, 167, 171, 182, 193-4, 199, 211-2

Austria-Hungary 32, 50, 93
autarky, economic 74, 77,
    82, 108
Autonomous Agricultural Union,
        Ruthenia 167
Auvergne 92

Baden 32, 126
Balkans 31, 44, 53, 83, 89,
    103, 170, 172, 224-6
Baltic 25, 42, 47, 49, 54,
    69, 143, 172, 174, 183, 218,
    222, 225, 249
Balts, German 42-3, 68, 70
Banat 219
Basques 187, 196, 208
Bauernbund, Austria 199
Bauernkrieg 36, 38-40, 46
Bauernverband, Switzerland 199
Bavaria 32, 126, 144, 158,
    181
Bavarian Party 211
Bayerischen Bauernbund 144
Belgium 32, 49, 53, 56, 65,
    73, 75-6, 83, 97, 103, 119,
    121, 123, 132, 139, 152,
    157, 163, 166-7, 181, 193-4,
    197, 203, 207
Berlin: 31, 125, 174, 204
        Congress of Berlin 31
Bern 192, 210, 241
Bessarabia 219, 227
Black Death 29
Boerenbond, Belgium 103, 197-8
Boerenpartij, Netherlands 130,
    166, 210
Bohemia 49, 79, 84, 95, 119,
    120, 152, 171, 174, 203, 219
Bolshevism 69, 129, 143, 147

Bosnia 93, 173, 213
bourgeoisie 27, 105, 141, 145,
    174-6, 245, 267, 269
Brandenburg 41-2
bread 44
Britain 11, 24, 49, 53, 59,
    61-2, 65, 73, 78, 83-4, 92,
    98, 103, 113, 121-3, 132,
    155, 162, 166-8, 193-4,
    197-8
Brittany 94, 154, 182
Bucharest 227
Budapest 95, 174, 222
Bulgaria 32, 49, 65, 69-73,
    75-6, 81-3, 89, 95, 97, 105,
    117-8, 121, 153, 167, 175-9,
    193-4, 204, 213-5, 226, 234,
    245-6
Bund der Landwirte:
        Czechoslovakia 167,
        221, 223, 242-3
        Germany 96, 144, 168
Bundschuh 36
bureaucracy 28, 31, 35-7, 50,
    52, 63-4, 82, 97, 102, 107,
    109, 176-7, 183-5, 190, 204,
    212, 215-6, 221, 228, 238,
    242, 269, 271
burghers 62
Burgos 156
Byelorussia 74, 144, 248
Byzantine Empire 28

Calvinism 197, 200
canals 52
candidates, parliamentary 97,
    168, 176, 230, 233

Capitalism 15-6, 23-4, 32,
    36, 39-41, 45-8, 51-4, 57-9,
    64, 67, 71, 79-80, 91-2,
    94-5, 99, 102, 112, 148-9,
    154, 171, 174-6, 178-83,
    185-6, 244, 261, 265, 274
Carinthia 182, 199
Carlism 187, 196
Carol II, Rumania 183, 247
Castile 30, 49, 169, 181, 188
Catalonia 187, 196, 208
Catholic Church 13, 30, 34,
    56, 77, 80, 92, 103-6,
    125-6, 129, 142, 151-2, 158,
    163, 169, 179-81, 185, 189,
    194-207, 213, 221, 223, 248
Catholic Congresses, Italy 198
Catholic Conservative Party,
        Switzerland 139,
        199, 241
Catholic parties 154
Catholic People's Party,
        Netherlands 139
cattle 87, 155, 157
Centre national des jeunes
        agriculteurs 198
Centre Party: Finland 139,
                167, 211,
                223, 230
            Norway 139,
                168, 211, 230
            Sweden 139-40,
                168, 211, 230
                238
cereals: see grain, wheat
Cevennes 169
Chamber of Deputies, France 99
Chiliasm 36, 39, 90, 134,
    180, 260

Christian Democratic Party:
        Estonia 218
        France 152, 211, 212
        Germany 139-40
        Italy 139-40, 145,
            148, 150, 211-2
        Switzerland 139
Christian Farmers Party,
        Lithuania 167, 201,
        218
Christian Historical Union,
        Netherlands 140
Christianity 39, 93
Christian Smallholders Party,
        Hungary 167
Christian Socialist Party:
        Austria 200-1
        Belgium 139, 152,
            197, 201
        Czechoslovakia 242
churches 30, 34, 66, 186,
    189, 255, 257, 269
Cis-Leithania 93, 119, 219
cities 25-6, 36, 47-50, 55,
    60-3, 72, 85, 88, 94, 105,
    109, 117, 129-31, 136, 141,
    149, 161, 163, 170, 173,
    181-3, 186, 190, 196, 206,
    211, 216, 254, 257, 268-9,
    273
citizenship 18, 52, 62
civil wars 129, 143, 144, 155,
    224, 240
Clann na Talmhan 167, 169,
    198, 229
classes 27, 40, 48, 54-6,
    70-2, 75-8, 80, 85, 96, 112,
    127, 131, 144, 176-9, 192,
    215, 251, 273

clergy 34, 196
clientelism 171, 185, 187
climate 77, 157
cloth: see Fextites
coalitions 20, 155-7, 191, 216, 233-52
Codreanu, Corneliu 180
Coldiretti 158
colonies 50, 219
commerce 25-6, 31, 36, 79, 100
commercial farmers 13-17, 26-9, 32, 40, 45-7, 53-5, 58, 71-2, 79-81, 101, 108, 126, 153-4, 173, 177, 251, 263
commodity market 13-5, 47, 62, 191-2, 272
communications 17, 25, 37, 48, 52-3, 60, 62, 89,93-4, 107, 112, 115, 257, 265-7
Communism 18, 74, 84, 109, 126, 143, 153, 157-8, 178, 186, 201, 249
Communist Party: Bulgaria 153, 215
    Czechoslovakia 153, 169, 221, 242
    Finland 142-3,240
    France 139, 141-2, 151, 211
    Germany 145, 147
    Italy 132, 139, 141, 145-6, 148
    Sweden 142

Confédération Générale du Travail 105
Confédération National des Associations Agricoles 105
Confederación Espanola de Derechas Autónomas 169,188
Confederación Nacional Católica Agraria 138
Congress of Berlin 31
Congress Poland 93, 205
conscription 33, 61, 63
Conservatism 62, 135, 138, 145, 147, 150, 154, 157-8, 169, 186, 190, 250
Conservative Party:
    Britain 146, 162, 197
    Denmark 239
    Finland 224, 240
    France 139, 211
    Prussia 96, 146, 197
    Rumania 175, 177, 219
consociationalism 241
Constantinople 170
constitutions 118, 186
cooperatives 46, 53, 71, 79-81, 84, 99-106, 110-2, 141, 149-50, 188, 197, 199, 203, 206, 213-4, 220, 242, 252, 256, 264-5, 267
Copenhagen 115-6, 230
copyholders 27
Cork 155
Corn Laws 61, 92
Corrèze 142
Cortes 183
Cossacks 43
cottagers 60, 69

credit 53, 71, 84, 100-5,
    133-5, 153, 171, 203, 224,
    228, 255
Creuse 142
Croatia 49, 89, 175, 179,
    183, 200, 202-4, 213-6, 227,
    246-7
Crofters' Party 98, 168, 197
Croix de Feu 182
crop rotation 27
Culloden 50
Cumann na n'Gaedheal 155
curia 34, 98, 190
Czechoslovakia 65, 70, 73,
    76, 83, 95, 105, 119-23,
    167, 169, 171-7, 183, 193-5,
    200-2, 208, 219, 222-3,
    237-9, 241-4, 251, 267

dairy farming 79, 100, 103,
    155-7
Danube 68
Denmark 32, 42, 45-6, 49, 65,
    73, 76, 79, 81, 83, 91, 98,
    100, 103, 105, 115-6, 121,
    124, 128, 150, 157, 167,
    171, 189-94, 211, 230, 239
De Valera, Eamonn 119
direct action 35-6, 39, 90,
    111, 135, 160, 198, 257
Dithmarschen 32, 45
Dobrudja 176
Dorgères, Henri 182
drought 36
Dublin 118-9

East Anglia 26
East Elbia 146
Ebro 188

education 46, 61-3, 66, 84,
    95, 112, 127, 173, 176, 189,
    205, 214, 220, 257, 260-3,
    266, 268, 270-1
Elbe 38, 42, 55, 96
elections 90, 97, 112-30,
    137, 143, 151, 166, 176,
    181, 200-1, 205, 210, 214-5,
    219, 228, 237-9, 245-7
electoral systems 96-7, 122,
    215, 228, 247
elites 19, 28, 31, 35-8, 40,
    44-5, 48, 50, 61, 64, 68-9,
    75-7, 82, 98, 107, 111, 173,
    186, 196, 200-1, 228, 253-4,
    259, 261, 265, 269
emancipation 43-4, 54-5
emigration 51, 57, 63, 72
Emilia-Romagna 103, 141, 148
empires 28, 31, 47, 62, 78,
    108, 119, 129, 143, 176, 201,
    205, 250
enclosures 26-7, 32, 35, 41,
    57-8
England 13, 26-7, 31-2, 35-6,
    38, 40, 47, 50, 57-8, 64,
    76, 87, 91, 146, 155, 162,
    191, 197, 254, 256, 272
estates 13-7, 25, 27-30, 32,
    35, 40-4, 49, 54-9, 62, 68,
    70-1, 75, 77, 80, 82, 87,
    91, 93, 144, 146-8, 156, 171,
    174, 190, 206
Estonia 42, 65, 69, 73, 76,
    83, 117-8, 121, 124, 129,
    137, 143, 151, 167, 183, 194,
    218, 245, 249
Estremadura 49, 77, 80
Esztergom 44

ethnicity 106, 125, 135,
  169-70, 172-5, 187-8,
  192-3, 195, 216
Europe: Eastern 18, 24-5,
    30-2, 42-4, 46-50,
    53, 58-9, 63, 67-71,
    75, 77-84, 88-9,
    93-7, 101, 105-9,
    117, 129, 137, 143,
    153, 159, 164,
    169-77, 182-6,
    190-2, 195, 200,
    205-7, 227-8, 244-5,
    250-2, 256, 259,
    261-2, 267
  Northern 29
  Southern 24, 50, 93,
    95, 102-3, 154, 185
  Western 12-4, 28-31,
    39-41, 44-7, 50,
    52-3, 58-9, 63, 72,
    75, 78-81, 84, 94-6,
    100-1, 104-6, 129,
    137, 159-60, 166,
    169, 172-6, 181-2,
    185-9, 192, 200,
    209-10, 227-9,
    250-1, 254, 271

famine 36
Farmers Party: Ireland 167,
    169, 198,
    222, 229
  Lithuania 168
  Netherlands
    168, 211
Farmers, Traders, Citizens
    Party 139, 168-9,
    199, 210-1, 229-30,
    241

Farmers Union, Latvia 143
farmowners 16, 40, 98, 119,
  128, 139, 145, 148-9
farm size 17, 26-7, 29, 31-2,
  46, 69-75, 79, 94, 109, 132,
  136, 150, 155, 171, 217
Fasci Siciliani 89
Federation of Labour,
        Lithuania 218
Federconsorzi 150
feudalism 23-5, 27-33, 35,
  40-2, 44-7, 54-7
Fianna Fail 119, 139, 150, 252
Fine Gael 139, 140, 150, 155
Finland 49, 64-5, 69, 73, 76,
  83-4, 100, 103, 116, 121,
  128-9, 139, 141-4, 151, 167,
  172, 189-90, 193-5, 210-1,
  219, 223-4, 229-30, 237-41
Finnish Party, Finland 190
Finnmark 144, 192
Flanders 26, 47, 152, 197-8
flax 47
Flemish National Front 181
Fleurant Agricola 169
food supply 14, 25, 47, 51,
  58, 61-2, 80, 82, 88, 92,
  130, 135
forestry 57, 120, 142, 191-2,
  221, 223
France 27-9, 32, 35, 40, 49,
  53, 55, 63, 65, 73, 76-7,
  81-3, 87-8, 92, 94, 99, 100,
  103-4, 113, 119-23, 132,
  139-42, 145-53, 156-7, 163,
  167-9, 171, 182, 188-9,
  193-4, 198, 203, 207-9,
  211-2, 252, 256, 272
Franchise 93, 97, 98, 108,
  111, 113, 122, 127

Franconia 158
Frederick IV, Denmark 46
Frederick VI, Denmark 46
Free Conservative Party,
    Germany 204
Free People's (Peasant) Party,
    Denmark 212
French Revolution 34, 62, 79, 92-3
Friends of the People, Norway 66, 189
Friesland 46, 197
Front Paysan 182

Garibaldi 150
Galicia: Austria-Hungary 43, 89, 119-20, 204
    Poland 68, 205, 224, 248
    Spain 187
Gaullists 211
gentry 40, 54, 59, 171, 202
Germany 13, 29, 32, 36-8, 46, 49, 53, 65, 68, 73, 75-6, 79, 83, 88, 93-7, 101-4, 113, 120-1, 124-5, 128-9, 132, 139, 146, 149, 167-8, 180-4, 193-4, 197-9, 204, 207, 211, 224, 248, 254
Government Party, Hungary 202
governments 17-8, 34, 43-4, 52-4, 57-60, 63-4, 72-5, 77-84, 94-98, 106, 130, 136, 153-4, 157, 176-7, 187, 192, 195, 201, 227, 237-52, 255, 257
grain 25, 39, 44, 53, 59, 77, 88, 92, 93, 95, 100, 220

Greece 44, 49, 65, 72-3, 76-7, 83, 167, 170-1, 193-4, 197, 224
Groningen 197
Guizpuzcoa 196
Gutsbesitzer 96-7, 146, 171

Hague 210
Hanseatic League 41, 48
Hapsburgs 43, 64, 103, 108, 119, 203
harvests 35-6, 59, 87, 89, 90, 93, 102, 175, 183
Hats and Caps 34
Heimwehr, Austria 182
Helsinki 216
Hesse 97, 181
Hohenzollern 41, 108
Holstein 45
horticulture 26-7
Hungary 43-4, 49, 54-5, 59, 65, 68-70, 73, 76-7, 80, 83, 89, 95, 167, 173-4, 193-4, 201-2, 221-2, 227-8, 245, 255
Hussite Wars 38, 203

Iberia 30, 75, 254
Iceland 12, 49, 65, 83, 116, 124, 167, 193-4
ideology 19, 89, 160, 165, 175-9, 183, 186-7, 204, 213, 225, 245-6, 250, 259-63
Independent Christian Party, Hungary 167
Independent Smallholders, Hungary 202
index of class voting 131-2

industrialisation 11-2, 16-7,
    23-4, 48, 51-3, 62, 72,
    74-5, 77, 90, 93-4, 100,
    105-8, 112-3, 130, 172-4,
    179, 206-7, 222-3, 242,
    258-61, 267
Industrial Revolution 24,
    27, 50-2, 61, 107-9, 254
industrial workers 78, 82,
    88, 105, 120, 135-8, 142-3,
    175, 179, 186, 212, 215,
    234, 259, 273
institutionalisation 24, 34,
    44-7, 51-2, 82-7, 90, 144-5,
    161, 180-5, 192, 200, 206-8,
    217, 224-5, 231, 246, 250,
    257-62, 269-71
intelligentsia 59, 73, 89,
    175-6, 178, 184, 204, 213,
    215, 226, 228, 267
interest rates 102
Ireland 32, 49, 64-5, 73,
    75-8, 83, 87, 91, 103,
    118-9, 121-2, 139, 150, 155,
    167, 169-70, 193-4, 198,
    207-8, 229, 252
Irish Agricultural
    Organisation 103
Iron Guard 180, 183
Italy 25-7, 29-32, 47-9, 53,
    55-7, 65, 75-7, 80-3, 88,
    93-4, 97, 103-5, 113, 119,
    132-3, 139, 141-2, 145-53,
    156-8, 163, 167, 169, 180-1,
    184-5, 193-4, 198-9, 207,
    211-2, 254, 264

Jeunesse Agricole Catholique
    198

Jews 93, 149, 174, 180, 182,
    194-5, 201, 204, 221
Junkers 96
Jutland 116, 190

Kara-George 44
Klaipeda 316
Königsberg 39
Krestintern 178
Kresy 144, 205
Kun, Bela 69, 74, 201, 245

labourers 15-7, 30-2, 39, 44,
    55-7, 59, 60, 68, 74-5, 80,
    95, 100, 153, 156-8, 183,
    186-7, 222, 264
Labour Party: Estonia 143, 218
            Netherlands 140,
                197
            Norway 139,
                144-5, 238-9
La Mancha 49, 80
Landbouwschap 166
Landbund, Austria 167, 199
Landespartei, Schleswig 157
landlords 17, 24-5, 33-4,
    42-3, 54-7, 66-8, 87, 92-3,
    96, 145-6, 173, 204, 245,
    253, 255, 265
Landlords Party, Estonia 137
landownership 14-7, 23-5, 28,
    30-1, 35, 38, 48, 55, 58, 68,
    87, 128, 132-3, 141-5, 153,
    158-9, 163, 171-2, 255-8,
    264, 272, 274
land redistribution 36, 42-4,
    57, 67-9, 71, 77-8, 92, 94,
    175, 185, 206, 218

land reform 35, 54, 57,
  68-82, 89, 93-5, 108-9,
  128-9, 134, 141-3, 159, 173,
  176, 185-8, 198, 205-6, 219,
  222, 240-5, 252, 256-7
land tenure 13-16, 20, 25-9,
  31, 75-1, 81, 94, 110, 133,
  171, 175-6, 205, 261
language 50, 63-4, 106, 135,
  160, 173, 189, 191, 193,
  195, 199, 204, 227
Lantmannaparti, Sweden 67,
  190
lassit 28
Latgale 167, 201, 218, 227,
  249
latifundia 50, 75, 80, 147,
  185, 187, 254
Latin America 15
Latvia 42, 65, 67, 69, 73,
  80, 83, 117, 121, 129, 143,
  167, 183, 193-4, 200-1, 218,
  245, 249-50
Legions of the Archangel
    St. Michael 183
legislation 43, 54, 62, 70,
  135, 187, 233
Léon 156, 169, 181, 188
Levante 187
Liberalism 62, 67, 141, 147,
  152, 157, 185-6
Liberal Party: Britain 62,
         191, 197
       Denmark 190-1
       Italy 75,
         140-1, 145
       Norway 211
       Rumania 175, 184
       Sweden 151

Liberal Centre Party,
       Denmark 212
Liberal Unionist Party,
       Britain 197
Lithuania 49, 65, 73, 83, 168,
  173, 193-4, 201, 218
livestock 26-7, 42, 47, 54,
  79, 100-1, 156
Livonia 42
local elections 113, 115-6, 119
Loire 63, 212
Low Countries 94, 119
Lutheranism 197, 218, 224
Luxemburg 73, 76, 83, 166,
  168, 193-4

Macedonia 75, 215
Madrid 187
Magyar Agrarian Party,
       Czechoslovakia 167
Magyars 43-4, 174, 195, 200
Maniu, Iuliu 183
manorial estates 30-2, 36, 40,
  46, 49, 54, 102, 109
manorial reaction 41-3, 50, 55
manors 54, 58, 98
market economy 14-7, 23-5, 28,
  31, 33, 39-41, 47-50, 52-4,
  56, 58, 60-3, 71-2, 79-82, 87,
  93, 101, 107-9, 112, 126,
  133-5, 156, 163, 206, 250-4,
  267, 270
Marx, Karl 112
Massif Central 142, 212
meat 79, 156
Mecklenburg 75
Mediterranean 12, 55, 75, 77,
  80, 100, 185
Memel 316

mercantile ownership 28, 53,
    170
merchants 33, 44, 87, 92,
    170, 174
métayeur 27, 29, 35, 142
mezzadro 27, 141
Middle Ages 23, 25-6, 29, 32,
    38, 47, 63
middle classes 45, 48, 54-6,
    59, 72, 77-82, 91-2, 96,
    109, 138, 147, 154, 172,
    176-7, 184-5, 192, 202, 234,
    252, 259, 267, 269
military 31, 33, 36, 38-9,
    42, 44, 55, 63-4, 68, 176,
    190, 266
millenarianism 38-9, 90
mir 30, 46, 101
mobilisation 61, 66-7, 81, 89,
    90, 115-20, 124-6, 129-30,
    134, 144, 147, 153, 159,
    162, 171, 184-6, 190, 197-8,
    205-7, 213, 217, 224, 244,
    263, 270
Moldavia 55, 93, 174-5
Monarchist Party, Italy 145,211
monarchy 24, 27, 34, 45, 78,
    92, 215, 245, 247
monasteries: see churches,
            religion
money 32, 40, 54, 57, 60, 66,
    95, 105, 189, 206, 253, 273
moneylenders 88, 101-2, 174
Moravia 49, 79, 95, 152, 171,
    174, 203, 219-20
Muslims 93, 194
Mussolini 77, 181

Napoleon 56

narodnik 89, 175, 179, 214,
    226, 254, 261
National Coalition, Finland
            224, 240
National Confederation of Direct
        Cultivators, Italy 150
National Democratic Party,
        Poland 204
Nationalism 62-4, 66-9, 74-7,
    89, 91, 108, 155, 173-5,
    178, 180, 183, 187, 203-4,
    207, 240, 261, 270
National Liberal Party,
    Rumania 177, 183, 247
National Party, Transylvania
            168, 183
National Peasants Party,
    Rumania 168, 183-4,
        219, 226-7, 234,
        247, 268
National People's Party,
    Germany 147
National Socialist Party:
    Czechoslovakia 220,243
    Germany 120, 125,
        147-8, 157, 181,
        189, 200
Navarre 196
Netherlands 32, 45, 49, 65,
    73, 76, 81, 83, 97, 101, 104,
    121-3, 130, 132, 139, 166,
    168, 193-4, 197, 211
New Farmers Party, Latvia 167,
            218, 249
New Settlers Party, Estonia
            167, 201,
            218, 249
Niedersachsen 181

nobility 34, 40-5, 54, 62, 68, 91, 190
Noord-Holland 197
Normandy 145, 182
Northern Ireland 76
Norway 29, 32, 49, 54, 60, 65-7, 73, 76, 83, 91, 113-5, 121, 124, 129-32, 139, 144, 150-2, 168, 182, 189-94, 210-1, 218, 227-30, 238-9, 264

Old Czechs 203
Oldenburg 125, 129
Oppeln 126
organisation 17-9, 26, 35, 51, 59, 60, 66-7, 79, 88-91, 95-108, 111-2, 115, 130, 134-6, 141-5, 149-50, 154, 159-61, 164-5, 181, 184, 191, 198, 206-7, 217, 222-5, 231, 234, 256-9, 262-71
Orthodox Church 89, 194, 196-7
Oslo 192
Ostfriesland 125, 129
Ottoman Empire 28, 31, 44, 62, 64, 89, 108, 173
overpopulation 52, 57, 71-2, 87, 93, 95, 100

Paris 63, 142
Parti agraire 169, 182, 216
participation 20, 24, 39, 40, 66-7, 88, 91, 98, 101, 110-30, 152, 162, 172, 188, 217, 235, 238, 243-4, 264-5, 271
Parti paysan 169, 188-9, 212
Pasić Nikola 213, 224

Patrimonialism 28-30, 34-5, 40, 44, 54, 80
Peasant Alliance, Italy 150
Peasant Defence League, France 182
peasant estate 62, 67, 91, 98
Peasantism 82, 174-80, 184, 187, 192, 201, 204-6, 213, 225-6, 244-50, 260-1
Peasant League, Estonia 143, 218
Peasant Party: Croatia 168, 175, 178-9, 183, 200, 203, 213-4, 222, 246-7
    France 167, 169, 188-9
    Italy 167
    Serbia 213, 224, 247
    Ukrainian 168
Peasant Populist Union, Lithuania 168
peasantry 13-7, 25, 28-31, 33-48, 53-6, 59, 60, 66-9, 74, 77, 82-5, 89, 93, 96, 99, 100, 107, 163, 182, 267
Peasant Union: Latvia 167, 201, 218, 249
    Lithuania 168, 201, 218
Peoples' Party: Austria 199, 211
    Rumania 324
    Switzerland 139, 168-9, 210, 230
periphery 42, 47, 50, 58, 91, 162, 187, 195-6, 198, 208, 227

Petka   242-3
Phanariots   174
Piast Party, Poland   168, 204-5, 248-9, 268
Piedmont   29
pietism   38
Pilsudski   245, 248-9
Pius IX   198
Pi y Margall   187
Plunkett, Sir Horace   103
Po   156, 181
Poland   25, 28, 32, 49, 55, 59, 62, 65, 68-74, 77-80, 83-4, 93, 99, 106, 117-21, 168, 173-4, 193-5, 199, 201, 204-8, 222-4, 245-6, 248, 250
political culture   69, 101
political democratisation   12, 17, 24
political mobilisation   11, 17, 19, 23, 35, 43-6, 52, 63-7, 95-101, 108, 111-7, 123, 127, 145-6, 161-5, 171, 188-9, 209, 214, 224, 234, 244, 255, 263, 270
Pomerania   42, 75
Popular Party, Italy   199
Popular Republican Movement, France   152, 211, 212
population   12, 14, 19, 24-5, 35, 42-3, 45-8, 50-2, 55-7, 60-1, 72, 74-5, 82, 94-5, 110, 127, 135-6, 169, 172, 265
Populism   82, 89, 175-82, 214, 251, 260-1

Populist Party: Czechoslovakia   152, 203, 220, 242-3
   Slovakia   200
   Slovenia   106, 213
Portugal   32, 49, 50, 65, 73, 76, 83, 166, 168-70, 193-4
Posen   126
Poujadism   151
Poznan   204-5, 224
Prague   178, 220
prebendal ownership   28
prices   58-9, 62, 66, 83, 87, 93, 133-5, 153-5, 240
priests   34, 89, 106, 170, 197-8, 200, 265
primogeniture   84
profits   26, 28, 41, 54-6, 107, 141
Progressive Farmers Party, Latgale   167, 201
Progressive Party, Iceland   167, 210, 229
prohibition   115, 151
protectionism   79, 81, 84, 93, 96-7, 108, 222
Protestantism   125, 129, 151-2, 182, 194-200, 203
Prussia   28, 30, 32, 34, 39-43, 45, 47, 49-50, 54-5, 75, 81, 96-8, 171, 197, 199, 200

Quisling   182

Radić, Stjepan   178, 246

Radical Party, France 211
              Serbia 213,
                224, 247
              Switzerland
                169, 192,
                199, 211, 241
Radical Venstre, Denmark 191,
          211, 239
railways 52, 147
rebellions 35, 38, 94, 98,
  271
Reconquista 50
recruitment 19, 89, 105
Reformation 38, 62, 125,
  142, 162
Regat 76, 129, 219, 227
religion 33-5, 38, 62-4, 89,
  106, 118, 125-6, 135, 143,
  150-2, 160-2, 170-3, 186-95,
  199, 216, 223-4, 246, 261
representation 13, 34, 62,
  67, 87, 95-9, 166, 206, 208,
  233, 241
republicanism 68, 104, 141,
  154, 187
Republican Party,
       Czechoslovakia 167,
            169, 171, 175,
            177, 200, 203,
            216, 219-22, 225,
            241-4, 268
Restoration, Spain 187
revolution 15, 27, 34, 36-9,
  43-4, 59, 69-70, 74, 77, 82,
  88, 92-3, 100, 111, 144,
  182, 261-2
Rexists 181
Reykjavik 116
Rhine 36, 38

Riga 67, 250
Riksdag, Sweden 190-1, 237
Risorgimento 55
Rittergüter 55, 102, 146
Romanov 108
Rumania 32, 49, 65, 69-73,
  75-6, 83, 89, 93, 106, 121,
  123, 168, 177-80, 183-4,
  193-6, 219, 226-8, 234,
  245-7, 255, 268
Russia 12, 29, 32, 37, 41-4,
  47, 49, 50, 53-5, 68-9, 89,
  93-4, 98, 116, 129, 143,
  147, 174-5, 178-9, 201, 248,
  250, 256
Ruthenia 144, 177, 201

Saeima, Latvia 249
St. Petersburg 204
Sardinia 170
Scandinavia 12-3, 29, 45, 97,
  102-4, 114, 151, 162-6, 171,
  189, 191-2, 206, 208, 210-2,
  216, 226, 230, 237, 251-2, 267
Scania 49, 190
Schleswig-Holstein 45, 147-8,
  157, 181
Scotland 28, 32, 49, 50, 76,
  98, 146, 197
Scythe Cross, Hungary 183
seigneurs 30, 33, 40
Seine 63
Seine-et-Marne 156
Sejm, Poland 248
Serbia 32, 44, 49, 75, 89,
  204, 213, 216, 224, 247
serfdom 28, 37, 41-5, 54-5
sex 114

sharecropper 15, 27-8, 35,
    57, 77, 140-2, 145, 148, 153
Sicily 89, 170
Silesia 42, 171, 203-4, 220
Skupshtina, Yugoslavia 213
Slavs 84
Slovakia 49, 95, 153, 174,
    177, 200, 203, 221-2
Slovenia 89, 106, 200, 213
Smallholders Party: Estonia
                        167
                    Finland
                        130, 167,
                        223
                    Hungary
                        202
Sobranje, Bulgaria 176
Social Democratic Party:
    Czechoslovakia 219,
        242-3
    Denmark 239
    Estonia 137, 143, 218,
        249
    Finland 139, 143, 240
    Germany 140, 144-5,
        147, 158, 211
    Latvia 143, 249-50
    Sweden 139, 155, 237-8
Socialism 89, 135, 141-2,
    152, 157-8, 179, 182-3,
    186-7, 191, 218
Socialist Congresses 157
Socialist International 157
Socialist Party: Czechoslovakia
                    169, 213,
                    242
                Finland 139,
                    143
                France 105, 211

Socialist Party, cont.:
    Italy 181
    Poland 248, 250
Social Movement, Italy 132
Société des Agriculteurs de
                France 104
Sofia 214
Solidarité française 182
Soviet Union 74, 78, 83, 129,
    142-3, 201, 218, 240, 249
Spain 22, 50, 56, 62, 65, 73,
    76-7, 80, 82-3, 105, 113,
    145, 156-7, 168-70, 181,
    187-8, 193-6, 198
Stamboliski, Aleksandŭr 214-5,
    219, 227
Stambolov, Stefan 97
state 12-3, 18, 24-5, 28,
    35-41, 46-7, 51-2, 55, 60-4,
    68, 74-5, 77, 82, 94-6, 106,
    130, 157, 176, 257
Stere 180
Stockholm 216, 230
Storting, Norway 238
strikes 89, 90, 96, 215
Stril War 91
Styria 199
subsistence agriculture 14-6,
    58, 79, 80, 84, 107-9, 126,
    142, 150-4
suffrage 23, 35, 61, 66, 90,
    95, 111, 114-5, 127, 161-5,
    177, 186, 206, 219, 228, 234,
    255, 264-5, 267
Svehla, Antoñin 242
Sweden 29, 32-4, 45, 49, 50,
    53, 62, 65, 67, 73, 76, 83,
    97-8, 114-5, 121, 124,
    128-32, 139, 142, 151, 155,
    168, 189-94, 201, 210-1, 216,
    229-30, 237-9

Swedish Party, Finland 190
Swedish People's Party,
    Finland 190, 211, 223
Switzerland 32, 38, 45, 49,
    65, 73, 76, 79, 83, 119,
    121, 123, 139, 156, 168-71,
    193-4, 199, 208, 211, 237,
    239, 241

Tallinn 129
tariffs 52, 77, 79, 84, 93,
    96-7, 108, 154-5, 224, 242,
    255-6
taxation 31, 34-6, 40, 57,
    61, 66, 74, 84, 87-8, 91,
    93, 166, 176, 188, 190, 212
Tenants Defence Associations,
    Ireland 103
tenure 16, 35, 38-9, 46, 58,
    75, 95, 133, 147, 163, 218,
    269
Teutonic Order 41
textiles 26
Thunder Cross 183
towns 41-3, 47-8, 56, 59,
    62, 81-5, 92, 113-7, 125,
    131, 149, 173, 186, 206,
    266
trade 25-6, 47-8, 59, 81,
    120, 176, 254
transport 17, 25, 37, 52,
    60, 63, 85, 107, 112, 120,
    266
Transylvania 174, 179, 219,
    227
Tsarism 64, 67-8, 143
Tudors 26
Turkey 31, 44
turnout 97, 112-30, 151

Tuscany 141
Tyrol 124

Ukraine 25, 74, 106, 248
Ulster 32
Umbria 141
unemployment 36, 59, 74, 143
Uniate Church 89, 106, 194
unions 89, 96, 103, 105, 149,
    199, 217, 242
uprisings 35-9, 43-4, 63, 88,
    90-5, 130, 257, 262, 265-7
Urals 12
urban elites 40, 44-5, 48, 50,
    68, 93, 97, 163, 171, 189
urbanisation 11-2, 53, 75, 94,
    112-3, 121, 154, 173, 185,
    207
urban-rural 14, 23, 47-8,
    60-2, 78, 85, 97, 106, 109,
    113-9, 123-32, 137-8, 149,
    161-3, 170-92, 196-7, 206,
    212-6, 227, 250-1, 266
Ustasche 183

Vaasa 224
Vatican 141, 201
Vaud 199
Vendée 34, 92
Venstre: Denmark 167, 190-1,
    210-2, 215-6, 225,
    229-30, 239
    Norway 67, 191
Vidzeme 143
Vienna 95, 119-20, 182, 200,
    204
villages 11, 30, 39, 43, 46,
    54, 57, 60, 63-4, 66, 71, 81,
    103, 109, 131, 146, 148, 170,
    185

Vilnius 201
Viscaya 196
Vorarlberg 124

Wales 50, 76, 162-3, 191
Wallachia 55, 174-5
Wallonia 152, 181, 198
war 12, 18, 36, 38, 41-2, 45, 66, 68, 70, 78, 91, 97, 157, 175, 231, 240, 254
Warsaw 174, 224
Weimar 125, 157, 189, 197
Westphalia 38, 97
wheat 77, 156-7, 188
White Mountain, Battle of 203
wine 38, 100
women 114-7, 122-4, 127

wool 26, 80
Württemberg 32, 126
Wyzwolenie Party, Poland 168, 205, 246, 248-9, 268

yeomen 40
Young Czechs 203
Yugoslavia 65, 69-73, 83, 106, 121, 168, 183, 193-4, 208, 213, 216, 224, 245-7
Yugoslav Muslim Organisation 213

Zadruga 46, 101
Zentrum Party, Germany 129, 197, 204
Zürich 210

LIBRARY OF DAVIDSON COLLEGE